The Early Neolithic in Greece
The First Farming Communities in Europe

Farmers made a sudden and dramatic appearance in Greece around 7000 BC, bringing with them domesticated plants and animals, new ceramics and techniques, and establishing settled villages. They were Europe's first farmers, but Catherine Perlès argues that the stimulus for the spread of agriculture to Europe was a maritime colonization movement involving small groups of people. With little competition from local hunter-gatherers, they recreated to an unusual degree a completely man-made environment, neglecting local resources and often relying, despite the cost, on trade with other communities rather than on local raw materials. Drawing evidence from a wide range of archaeological sources, including often neglected 'small finds', and introducing daring new perspectives on funerary rituals and the distribution of figurines, she constructs a complex and subtle picture of early Neolithic societies, overturning the traditional view that these societies were simple and self-sufficient.

CATHERINE PERLES is Professor in the Department of Ethnology at the University of Paris. Her publications include *Préhistoire du feu* (1977) and *Les industries lithiques taillées de Franchthi* (3 vols., 1987, 1990, in press).

CAMBRIDGE WORLD ARCHAEOLOGY

THE EARLY NEOLITHIC IN GREECE

The first farming communities in Europe

CATHERINE PERLES

Institut Universitaire de France
Université Paris X

Illustrations by

GERARD MONTHEL

Centre National de la Recherche Scientifique
'Préhistoire et Technologie'

CAMBRIDGE
UNIVERSITY PRESS

PUBLISHED BY THE PRESS SYNDICATE OF THE UNIVERSITY OF CAMBRIDGE
The Pitt Building, Trumpington Street, Cambridge, United Kingdom

CAMBRIDGE UNIVERSITY PRESS
The Edinburgh Building, Cambridge CB2 2RU, UK
40 West 20th Street, New York, NY 10011–4211, USA
10 Stamford Road, Oakleigh, VIC 3166, Australia
Ruiz de Alarcón 13, 28014 Madrid, Spain
Dock House, The Waterfront, Cape Town 8001, South Africa

http://www.cambridge.org

First published 2001

Printed in the United Kingdom at the University Press, Cambridge

Typeface Trump Medieval 10/13pt   *System* QuarkXPress™ [SE]

A catalogue record for this book is available from the British Library

Library of Congress Cataloguing in Publication data

Perlès, Catherine.
   The Early Neolithic of Greece: the first farming communities in Europe /
Catherine Perlès; illustrations by Gérard Monthel.
   p.   cm. – (Cambridge world archaeology)
Includes bibliographical references and index.
ISBN 0 521 80181 8 – ISBN 0 521 00027 0
   1. Neolithic period–Greece. 2. Agriculture, Prehistoric–Greece. 3.
Greece–Antiquities.   I. Title. II. Series.

GN776.22.G8 P47 2001 338.1'0938–dc21 00–054728

ISBN 0 521 80181 8 hardback
ISBN 0 521 00027 0 paperback

To Eric

CONTENTS

FIGURES

TABLES

ACKNOWLEDGEMENTS

I find it difficult to discuss archaeological data that I have not personally examined. Thus, although this book is not a direct reflection of my specialized field studies, it is based nevertheless on nearly thirty years of familiarity with the Neolithic material from Greece. These studies were made possible thanks to the support of several institutions and many individuals, whose complete list would probably fill the whole page. Let me thank them collectively, but nonetheless wholeheartedly.

Most of the comparative 'fieldwork' (read: museum work) was funded through the 'Commission des Fouilles Archéologiques' of the French Ministère des Affaires Etrangères. The latter showed great open-mindedness in deciding to support an unusual project, based on the examination of collections rather than on new excavations. I am grateful to its members and successive directors. This project also received help and support from the Ecole Française d'Athènes, from the British School at Athens and the American School of Classical Studies, and many archaeological *Ephorias* in Greece who allowed us to examine material from their excavations.

Most of this project was conducted with Jean-Paul Demoule, whose exceptional competence in Balkanic and Western European prehistory is only matched by his in-depth knowledge of Greek '*zacharoplasteia*' (pastry shops). We were joined on several occasions by K. D. Vitelli, who brought us her subtle and critical approach to ceramic technology and to the Greek Neolithic. Several of the following chapters can be viewed as prolongations of the discussions we have had over the years.

I am also happy to recognize my debt to Thomas Jacobsen who entrusted me with the study of the chipped stones from Franchthi and broadened my scientific horizons by including me in a stimulating international team. To Kostas Gallis, who introduced us to the Thessalian Neolithic and generously opened all the collections from the Larissa Museum. To Ernestine Elster, who allowed me to study several unpublished collections entrusted to her. To P. Chrysostomou, A. Dousougli, H. Hauptmann, D. Keller, M. Pappa, R. Rodden, A. Sampson, K. Skourtopoulo, R. Torrence, H. Tzavela-Evjen, S. Weinberg, and K. Zachos, who kindly let us see or study their collections.

My intellectual debts are also too numerous to list in full. I would like to express here, however, my deep admiration for the pioneers of the Greek prehistory: Ch. Tsountas, A. Wace, M. Thompson, W. Heurtley, and more recently, S. Weinberg and D. Theocharis. Their far-reaching interests prefigured an anthropological approach to archaeology, which was not always followed, unfortunately, by their successors. The more I went back, again and again, to their publications, the more I was impressed by the depth of their knowledge, the accuracy and the relevance of their observations. As will be seen, their research still constitutes the basis of much of our present-day knowledge.

Acknowledging the profound and stimulating intellectual influence of several of my (still active) colleagues is equally relevant, even if it may be embarrassing to their modesty. They will easily recognize the numerous ideas that I have avidly borrowed from their own work. In particular, I am happy to recognize my profound debt to Paul Halstead, not only for his unsurpassed knowledge of Greece, past and present, but also for the numerous intellectual venues he opened and which I simply had to follow. I have also greatly benefited from lively discussions with Anticlia Moundrea-Agrafioti, whose friendship survived our numerous scientific disagreements, and with E. Bloedow, J. Cauvin, J. Cherry, A. Coudart, B. Helly, K. Kotsakis, Robin Torrence and J. Wickens.

The realization of this book owes a lot to Magen O'Farrell and Bill Woodcock, who chased the gallicisms in my original manuscript, and to Gérard Monthel, who superbly drafted the illustrations. More indirectly, this book also owes a lot to the constant support, through difficult years, of all my friends and colleagues of the Centre National de la Recherche Scientifique research team, 'Préhistoire et Technologie'. Without them, I may not have found the energy to go on.

My last word is for Eric, for whom this book was undertaken as a contribution to our common fight against his illness. We both lost the fight since he did not live to see it completed, but his critical mind and loving support were the driving forces behind its realization.

INTRODUCTION

Why a book on the Early Neolithic of Greece? The simplest answer is that a book on the subject does not exist. Yet, the Early Neolithic of Greece is the oldest in Europe, probably by several centuries. It is also frequently referred to as the source of all further development in Europe, either through the 'maritime route', along the Mediterranean coasts, or through the inland, Danubian route. Such broad statements reveal how poorly the Early Neolithic of Greece (or, for that matter, the Neolithic of Greece in general) is known outside of a small circle of specialists: the relations between the Greek Early Neolithic and that of the Adriatic coast, on the one hand, and of Bulgaria on the other, are in fact very problematic. Similarly, I have found that specialists of the Near Eastern Neolithic are sometimes incredulous when they discover, through lectures, some achievements of Greek Neolithic societies. In both cases the Neolithic in Greece has been superficially and rapidly considered as a distant yet familiar parallel to better known areas, without further investigation. Providing access to currently available data concerning this period and region, showing that the Greek Neolithic possesses its own originality can, by itself, justify this book.

Other motives can be found within the 'small circle of specialists' itself. Major issues such as the origins of the Neolithic in Greece or the existence of a preceramic phase are still vividly, and sometimes violently debated. More often than not the protagonists are unable to present their arguments fully, and the dialogue resembles a *'dialogue de sourds'*. I hope that a more detailed exposition of the problems, even from a one-sided position (I clearly intend to take sides in the debates), will allow a better understanding of their archaeological bases and lead to more fruitful discussions.

However, the main incentive for writing this book lies elsewhere. I am deeply convinced that the fundamental nature of Neolithic societies has escaped us because we have always, perforce, used inappropriate models of interpretation derived from later and structurally different historical contexts. The latter do not and cannot help us to understand societies that were in the unique position of 'inventing' new solutions to the new problems posed by a life based on a new productive economy. These Neolithic societies explored a whole array of different and transitory socioeconomic systems, whose very diversity cannot but be obscured by later historical processes of homogenization. A 'retour aux sources' is necessary, if we are to avoid following our predecessors in using sim-plistic models that the most obvious data should have contradicted.[1] Thus, I conceived this book primarily for myself, to try and investigate the problems that puzzled me concerning the nature of the Greek Neolithic. It was under-taken out of frustration, so to speak, after a first synthesis in the limited format of a journal article[2] had brought to light, more than solved, the many problems raised by the singularity of the Greek Neolithic. This holds true, in particular, for the Early Neolithic: how did early farmers create the bases for a new social organization when they settled in the vast, unexploited inner basins of Greece? What did they retain of their past? How did they organize their mutual rela-tions and their relations to local hunter-gatherers? How did they conceive their position *vis-à-vis* the new 'natural' world they exploited? Clearly, the Early Neolithic by itself presented enough problems and challenges to justify a volume of its own.

This book is indeed deliberately problem-oriented, and to a large extent, polemic in substance if not, I hope, in tone. I make no pretence of exhaustiv-ity, nor even of a balanced treatment of all aspects of the Neolithic society. Neither was this book conceived as a textbook, providing ready access to neatly ordered categories of data. It is conceived as an interplay between problems and data, one question leading to another, one field of inquiry shedding light on another, with the hope of achieving a better understanding of Early Neolithic societies, their way of life, their economic, social and ideological choices.

As with any anthropological study, this book is laden with theory and theo-ries. However, writing a theoretical book, or building a theory of the Greek Neolithic, was not my purpose. Obviously, my very approach to the data and the interpretative stands defended here *are* based on theory, and *have* theoret-ical implications. They necessarily express personal theoretical positions. But, this is a book intended to be about the Neolithic of Greece, not about myself viewing the Neolithic of Greece. Therefore theoretical discussions will be limited, and the reader will find no statement about my belonging to any of the theoretical 'schools' that are currently fashionable in archaeology. In addition to my French training in technological studies, this is, above all, a deliberate epistemological position: I consider scientific research as a cognitivist process (Giere 1988), which seeks to find, case by case, which amongst the numerous theories available in the literature seems best to fit the data. And I do not believe that, given the complexity of human societies and actions, a single theory can provide answers to all questions.[3]

---

[1] The Neolithic flint mines, known since the nineteenth century, constitute a good example. Their presence did not impend the description, for many decades, of Neolithic economy as autar-kic and non-specialized. A more current example is provided by the absence of villages or habi-tations in Western European megalithic areas. After a century of fieldwork, many authors still argue that the megaliths' builders were necessarily sedentary and that their villages will even-tually be found.   [2] Demoule and Perlès 1993.
[3] As any manual of sociology will clearly exemplify!

Nevertheless, this very notion of 'complex' societies can be viewed as a theoretical leitmotif that runs through the whole book. Early Neolithic societies cannot be deemed as 'simple' just because they happen to be the first agropastoral societies in a given region, or worse, because they happen to be the most ancient societies studied by specialists of the later phases of Prehistory. There exists an unfortunate tendency to consider anything that is 'first' as necessarily 'simple', and thus to consider Neolithic society, the 'first farmers', as less complex than later Prehistoric societies, that is, as composed of a few, small-scale interacting units. But social evolution does not necessarily develop from the simple to the complex, and the Neolithic of Greece provides good counterexamples of shifts from more complex to more 'simple' levels of organization (Perlès 1992). In addition, one cannot obliterate the long Palaeolithic times, during which complex hunter-gatherer societies have been convincingly brought to light (Price and Brown 1985; Price and Feinman 1995). Nor should we forget, finally, that Neolithic societies in Europe are, one way or the other, the outcome of these unique, profoundly original and necessarily complex societies of the Near Eastern Pre-Pottery Neolithic.

A second theoretical perspective that was somehow forced on me by the data, rather than by a personal inclination, is the importance of social and cultural choices even in the most materialistic aspects of society. Though initially tempted to consider that all technical and economic options could be explained in terms of efficiency and rational choices, I finally had to accept that neither the Neolithic of Greece, nor the Neolithic in general, could be understood in those terms without distorting the data. Even the basic choice of raw materials for stone tools, for instance, can ultimately be shown to be the result of social choices, despite all the technical justifications that the respective qualities of the different raw materials can offer.

Finally, my discussions concerning social organization will be strongly oriented by a rather pessimistic view of human (or even, animal) societies, in which competition and conflicts are seen to be inherent to any group, as are tendencies towards the control of power by a few individuals or groups. Thus, despite the postulated simplicity of these earliest farming communities, I shall not consider it as 'normal' to find no evidence of inter-community conflicts, neither will I find it 'normal' to find no sign of institutionalized hierarchy. The question of how an 'egalitarian' organization was maintained throughout centuries or millennia, despite the potential for accumulation and the necessary differentiation of roles and status, constitutes, for me, as pregnant a problem as the emergence of hierarchies.

However, any given social organization is the outcome of historical processes. Thus, before we can address this question, several other problematic issues must be raised. One of the most controversial concerns the very origins of the Neolithic in Greece. The quasi-absence of data on the Mesolithic, in particular in the regions that will be most densely settled during the Early

Neolithic, is a crucial element in the debate. It can always be claimed, indeed, that 'the absence of evidence is no evidence of absence' and that future field-work will eventually reveal a rich Mesolithic that can be deemed a cultural and economic precursor to the Greek Neolithic. However, I shall argue that the scarcity of Mesolithic sites must be taken at face value, that is, as a reflection of a sparse population that mostly exploited dispersed resources of low ener-getic yield. Since recent syntheses of the context of emergence of a productive economy show the latter to be linked with opposite conditions (Gebauer and Price 1992), the Mesolithic in Greece does not appear conducive to an autoch-thonous process of Neolithization. In addition, claims for a local process of Neolithization rely on controversial botanical data and on what I consider to be a misinterpretation of the data from Franchthi and Sidari. Despite a debat-able 'continuity' in occupation at these two sites, best interpreted as a sign of contacts, there is a radical break in technical and economic behaviours all over Greece at the dawn of the Neolithic. The simultaneous appearance of radically new techniques and of domesticated species implies the acquisition of a quasi-encyclopedic knowledge which is thoroughly underestimated. I consider that this knowledge, and the relevant know-how, could only be implemented by groups already familiar with farming and building techniques, with stone pol-ishing, pressure-flaking, spinning, that is, by farming groups coming from the Near East.

However, a recurrent argument against the hypothesis of migrant groups is the impossibility of defining precisely their possible origin. That most domes-ticated species come from the Near East cannot be questioned. But the asso-ciated material, despite punctual and varied analogies, does not resemble that of any specific region of the Near East. Here again, I suggest that we take the data at face value, and instead change our model of interpretation. Rather than postulating strong cultural links and looking for a single origin, as with the Danubian 'wave of advance', I propose that we consider the colonization of Greece according to an 'insular model', that is as a maritime process imple-mented by small pioneer groups, ultimately deriving from different parts of the Levant and Anatolia.

Whether these groups brought pottery with them remains difficult to estab-lish. A long and especially detailed chapter will be devoted to the problem of the 'Initial Neolithic'. Discussions about the presence or absence of pottery in the earliest Neolithic of Greece have been going on for more than thirty years, and a thorough evaluation of the presently available data does not lead to con-clusive answers regarding the so-called 'Preceramic Neolithic'. Nevertheless, it can be shown that these levels do represent a very early phase of the Neolithic in Greece. The sherds they contain may be intrusive or correspond to a phase of limited and 'intermittent' production of pottery, as occurs in the Late Pre-Pottery Neolithic B of the Near East. In both cases, however, these deposits reflect a different attitude towards pottery production and use than during the later phases of the Early Neolithic. Whether or not 'pre-pottery', this phase ought to be distinguished from the Early Neolithic proper.

Marked regional contrasts in the density and nature of settlements characterize the spread of the farming economy over Greece.[4] At the level of resolution given by 14C dates, no regular 'wave of advance' can be brought to light. To the contrary, it can be shown that, already by the Early Neolithic, the very different socioeconomic pathways that characterize the development of Neolithic and Early Bronze Age societies in northern and southern Greece are rooted in opposite social conditions. On a broad level, Early Neolithic settlement is restricted to the dryer part of Greece, whose climate was closer to that of the Near East. However, whereas access to water was clearly not a limiting factor in Thessaly, the foundation of villages in the Peloponnese seems to have been constrained by the availability of well-watered, fertile soils near springs, lakes or marshes. As a result, villages were few and far between, creating social conditions opposite to that of the densely settled Thessaly.

In this respect Thessaly, whose settlement patterns will be studied in more detail, must be seen as the exception rather than the rule. Various environmental factors, such as the possibility of flood-farming or access to various microenvironments, have been invoked to explain the location of settlements over this vast alluvial plain. The results of the present analyses, conducted on eastern Thessaly, contradict these models. Early Neolithic settlement patterns are characterized by an extremely dense and homogeneous network of villages, spreading in all directions, independently of topographic, hydrologic or pedologic factors. They must be seen instead as the result of socioeconomic factors, in an interplay between demography, political regulation, social obligations and agrarian work.

The importance of cereal cultivation and domesticated plants in the diet has, however, been challenged recently. Yet, various calculations show that, even within the very small territories reconstructed in Thessaly, recourse to wild plants or animals as a complement to the diet would not have been necessary. In addition, while taphonomic biases can always cast doubt on the importance of wild plant food, the scarcity of wild animals in the faunal remains demonstrates that wild resources were not only under-exploited, but deliberately neglected. Only strong symbolic oppositions between the wild and the domestic, and the will to assert one's domestication of space, can explain the neglect of wild food resources, but also of local lithic resources and such natural habitats as caves and rock shelters.

It is indeed characteristic of the Early Neolithic that caves, previously favoured and abundantly reoccupied in the Late and Final Neolithic, are almost deserted. The habitat is man-made, clustered, and permanently occupied over

---

[4] Greece will be considered here within its present political borders. With few exceptions, the latter correspond to natural boundaries (mountains or seas).

many generations. If the general pattern of these tell-like villages is very stable, the details of the houses and building techniques are, to the contrary, extremely variable. In contrast to what occurs in the Early Neolithic of Danubian tradition, house style is not used in the definition of a group's identity. I suggest that this may be related to the very permanence of the village itself. By its antiquity and conspicuous visibility, the village materializes the links to the past, the continuity of the community and its ancestral rights over its territory. In this context, individuality and the will to assert one's difference could thus be expressed without endangering the collectivity.

Within these small territories, located in fertile alluvial plains, most villages would not have had direct access to the raw materials needed for the daily used tools and equipment. This simple observation should, by itself, cast doubts on the presumed self-sufficiency of these Neolithic societies. More specific arguments indicate that, in the case of Greece, various forms of specialized production were already occurring by the Early Neolithic. Part-time craft specialization was a basis of socioeconomic organization long before the emergence of centralized political powers. Indirect procurement through exchange from specialized groups can be suggested, for instance, for chipped stone tools, in particular for obsidian and honey-flint blades. However, the differences brought to light between the procurement, production and use of pottery, chipped stone tools and ornament, suggest that craft specialization corresponded to a multicentric economy, where specialization and exchange answered social and possibly ritual functions as well as economic needs. The production of pottery, in particular, goes against familiar assessments and demonstrates the importance of social choices over 'utilitarian' ones: Early Neolithic pottery was, probably consciously, kept out of the domestic functions of cooking and storing food. It was deemed more useful as a means of social display or for rituals, which probably explains, incidently, why hearths and ovens were so elaborately constructed.

The other crafts practised within the villages are less well documented. Understanding the role of bone tools, the function and status of polished stone tools, the ambiguous evidence pertaining to spinning and weaving, and the possible function of several common but enigmatic objects, remains a challenge. The same can be said about the numerous figurines, predominantly feminine. Most plausibly, they served several functions, including mundane ones. Yet, the new social and economic constraints induced by a sedentary, farming life were bound to have consequences on beliefs and rituals. Denying the figurines all ritual function appears, on the whole, a more costly hypothesis than the reverse. One argument that sustains an interpretation of ritual use is the strong correlation between the presence of figurines and the density of settlement. Figurines were needed where interaction was at the highest between neighbouring communities. It is thus probable that they were used in various rituals that ultimately served as a means of integration within a more complex society.

Whatever the case, figurines were related to the world of the living. Perhaps even to the very notion of life itself, but never, during the Early Neolithic, were they related to the realm of the dead. Funerary rituals have been commonly described as especially 'simple': the dead casually buried in pits, in between the houses, without grave goods. I shall argue, to the contrary, that the majority of the burials that we can observe, the intramuros pit burials, are actually the exceptions. That they correspond to individuals who were denied 'normal' funerary rituals (*sensu stricto*), the latter being exemplified by the small cremation burial ground from Soufli Magoula. This reversal of perspective leads to the conclusion that funerary rituals, far from been 'simple', were in fact highly invested and demanding in terms of labour, time and energy.

Nevertheless, one element of the previous interpretations still holds true. Judging from the composition of the cremated population and the grave goods, no sign of 'inequality' can be brought to light. There is indeed no evidence of permanent, transmitted hierarchical status, but various indirect evidence points to an heterarchical organization, with well-differentiated roles and status. The reciprocal interdependence created by such a social organization, together with kinship ties and obligations, would have been instrumental in limiting conflict within the village community. A similar mechanism may have existed between communities. The density of villages in Thessaly was bound to create frequent occasions for potential conflict. Yet, there is no indication of widespread hostility between the various villages. The above-mentioned relation between figurines as well as other objects of special value, and the density of settlement already suggests that rituals participated in mechanisms of social interaction and integration. In addition, given the reliance on trade and exchange even when it was not strictly necessary, I suggest that 'arbitrary specialization' may also have been at play to regulate interactions between the different communities.

The latter hypotheses are, at most, plausible guesses. I do not claim to have solved the many problems that initially motivated this work. Even many factual queries remain unsettled by lack of fieldwork or proper analytical studies. No synthesis can go beyond the present state of the research, and the history of Neolithic research in Greece has not led to a very propitious situation.

Early in the century, the pioneering work of G. Tsountas at Sesklo and Dimini (Tsountas 1908), followed by the syntheses of Wace and Thompson on Thessaly (Wace and Thompson 1912) and Heurtley on Macedonia (Heurtley 1932), had already revealed how rich and often spectacular was the Neolithic in Greece. Despite this early interest and the quality of the work, the organization of archaeological research in Greece, which was geared towards the exploration of the prestigious Classical past, as well as a tendency to consider the Greek Neolithic as a poorer offshoot of the Near Eastern or Balkanic Neolithic, led to a long period of dormancy. Active research programmes were resumed in the 1960s under two distinct influences: in the north, the Germanic 'historicocultural' tradition focused exclusively on chronological frameworks and 'cultures', with very little anthropological perspective; in the south, the Anglo-Saxon school emphasized economic and environmental reconstructions, focusing on individual sites or discrete 'styles', and neglected supraregional frameworks. In all cases, excavations were mostly limited to small parts of the sites. The Greek scholar D. Theocharis stood out as an exception, with his broad interests, in-depth knowledge of the Greek Neolithic as a whole, and extensive excavations at Sesklo. Unfortunately, his premature death still deprives us of a synthesis of his work on this major settlement. Elsewhere, most excavations consisted of small test soundings, often determined and limited by rescue work.

More recently, the Greek Neolithic has again become an active and pioneering field of research. Its strength and interest lie less in the number or scale of the excavations proper, than in the number and variety of innovative methodological studies. Most aspects of the archaeological research have been renewed: systematic field surveys, site definition, regional analysis, faunal analysis, ceramic technology, ethno-archaeological fieldwork, and so forth. These have been admirably reported in a recent publication by E. Alram-Stern (1996) and illustrated by a major exhibit (Papathanassopoulos (ed.) 1996), while several important syntheses, both regional and general, have recently updated the chronocultural frameworks and the remaining problems (Andreou *et al.* 1996; Coleman 1992; Davis 1992; Grammenos 1997).

But even older and more traditional publications can yield important information, when suitably interrogated. Renewed research lies as much in new questions and a new way of looking at the data as in new fieldwork. More fundamentally, I believe it is time we go beyond a simple statement of facts to investigate the deeper structure of these unique, pioneering societies. However important the lacunae, I consider it our duty to try and make sense of what is available at a given moment. Even though all my conclusions must be considered provisional, they should renew the on-going discussions and indicate fruitful perspectives for further research.

CHAPTER I

THE LAND AND ITS RESOURCES: THE GEOGRAPHIC CONTEXT

The natural features of Greece, its climate, topography, water resources and soils, had decisive effects on the Neolithic economy and settlement patterns. They define several distinct provinces, characterized by different historical dynamics throughout the Neolithic and early Bronze Age, whose roots can be traced within the Early Neolithic.

Topography

Paramount amongst those factors is topography, for its impact on the climate and means of communication. The rugged topography of mainland Greece derives from the Alpine orogenic phase and the subsequent epi-orogenic subsidence accidents (Bintliff 1977; Higgins and Higgins 1996; Jacobshagen 1986). The main topographic features are related to a system of ancient sub-marine ridges and furrows of predominant NW/SE orientation. Pelagic and neritic sediments accumulated during the Mesosoic subsidence phase, until the start of the Alpine orogenic phase during the mid-Cretaceous. The latter took place progressively, in a wave-like progression from east to west, uplifting first the continental Hercynian bedrock – the Rhodopes and part of the Pelagonian Zone, with Mounts Ossa and Mavrovouni – then the massive Mesosoic limestones. Important subsidence basins then formed during the epi-orogenic phase, in direct relation with the NW/SE ridge and furrow structure: the West Macedonian Plain (the old Vardar furrow), the Thessalian Plain, the Saronic Gulf and the Kopaïs Basin (Sub-Pelagonian Intermediate Zone), the lowlands of Elis and Messenia. Other subsidence basins have different directions (compare the Gulf of Corinth) and result from still active tectonic movements in this sensitive area at the junction of the African and European plates.

Despite subsidence and active erosion that filled the basins with flysch deposits, the result of this orogenic phase is a largely mountainous country. More than two-thirds of Greece lies above 300 m, and steep mountainous reliefs isolate the subsidence basins, creating constraints on inland communications. The most important barrier to east–west communications corresponds to the youngest uplift, that of the Ionian, Gavrovo–Tripolitsa and Pindus zones, that culminates over 2000 m above sea level. With few passes from the west coast to western Macedonia and Thessaly, the Pindus Range created a climatic and topographic barrier during the Early Neolithic, resulting in profoundly different settlement patterns and traditions on both sides.

The effect of the Mediterranean climate on the mostly massive limestone elevations resulted in particularly steep slopes, which were condusive to important erosion. The sediments washed down by violent seasonal rains accumulated in the many deep depressions of tectonic and karstic origins, which are equally characteristic of the Greek countryside. The contrast between the rugged and steep mountains, overlooking absolutely flat inner basins, remains to this day a powerful experience for anyone who travels on traditional roads and passes. In all probability, the difficulties of inland communications promoted the development of coastal navigation, when important loads, such as obsidian, had to be transported over long distances.

Tectonic activity is also involved in the creation of volcanoes, spreading mainly on both sides of the Pelagonian Ridge. Several recent volcanoes have received archaeological fame: Thera (Santorini) for example, but also, of more concern here, Giali and especially Melos, which provided the bulk of the obsidian used on Neolithic sites. On-going tectonic activity entails troublesome problems for the reconstruction of Neolithic shorelines (Morrison 1968; Stiros and Papageorgiou 1994). The respective roles of eustasy and local tectonic activity remains debated, but there is definite evidence for the submergence of Neolithic coastal sites; detailed work in the Volos Gulf, the Franchthi area and Saliagos area have shown a sea level rise of the order of 5 m during the Neolithic (Cherry 1990; Lambeck 1996; van Andel 1987; van Andel and Lianos 1983, 1984).

Soils

High sea levels during the Tertiary era and the submergence of most of lowland Greece, together with inland lake formations, left an extensive cover of marine and lacustrine marls, sands and conglomerates, which were of great importance for the agricultural potential of the country. Although the lowlands represent no more than 10 per cent of Greece, they constrain most of the country's agricultural lands and offered very favourable conditions to the initial farmers of Greece. The best soils are the water-retentive rendzina soils developed on the Tertiary (Neogene) soft limestone and flysch deposits, on the Pleistocene lacustrine deposits and the colluvial/alluvial sediments of the Late Glacial period. With their good potential for cereal and legume cultivation, these soils constituted the focus of Early Neolithic settlements and agricultural exploitation. The shallow and stony soils of the hill slopes were at that time completely neglected.

However, many of the depressions and inner basins, having little or no outlet to the sea and a poor drainage, were still occupied by large lakes or swamps during the Neolithic. The last ones were only recently drained by modern tech-

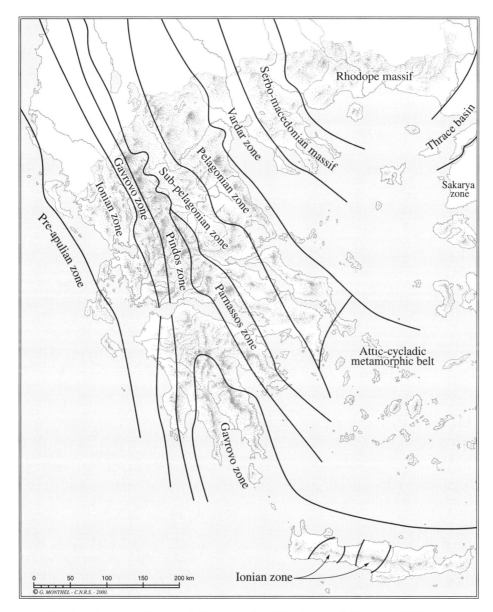

Fig. 1.1 Structural map of Greece (after Higgins and Higgins 1996).

niques, and many lands now under cultivation were unavailable to the Neolithic farmers. Judging from the faunal and carpological data, the latter do not seem to have exploited the specific resources that lakes and swamps could have provided.

The conjunction of mountains, steep slopes, water expanses and sea leads to a highly divided country, with a concentration of agricultural lands in restricted

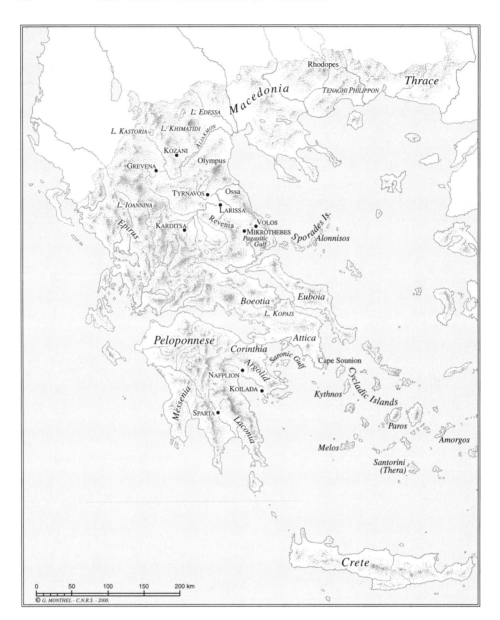

Fig. 1.2 Geographical map of Greece.

areas, isolated one from another by mountainous ranges. Given the lack of navigable rivers, coastal navigation would have thus represented an important means of communication from southern to northern Greece. However, navigation, especially to and from the islands, is rendered difficult by winds, with an unpredictable winter régime and constant northerly Etesian winds in the summer (Heikel 1985). Only experienced seamen could navigate the Aegean sea safely, and even they would have been frequently driven ashore by adverse conditions.

As a consequence, Greece would appear to be a compartmentalized country, with no easy travel from one settled area to the other. Yet those mountains, lakes and seas did not constitute impassable physical barriers. They could be overcome at will, or else maintained for sociological purposes. The Neolithic history of Greece witnesses alternating periods of closed-in regional developments and widespread, interregional interaction. The Early Neolithic is remarkable in this respect: it probably constitutes the period when physical barriers were paramount between the west and the east, but almost completely disregarded within the eastern half of Greece.

Climate

The topography of Greece also has profound consequences on the climate: the high central ridges create an effective barrier against the rain-loaded westerly winds. As a consequence, the western slopes receive a high annual rainfall, but the climate becomes increasingly arid to the east. Neolithic farmers, especially with rain-fed agriculture, were thus faced with almost opposite problems in the western and eastern parts of the country.

Palynological, carpological and faunal evidence, in accordance with general data on the evolution of climate, suggests that the Neolithic climate was broadly comparable with that of today: a Mediterranean climate, with winter rains and dry hot summers. According to Huntley and Prentice (1988), mean summer temperatures around 7000 BC would have been slightly lower than today and rainfall slightly more important. This is reflected in pollen cores by a progressively denser tree cover, with a decrease in deciduous oaks and an increase of ash, hornbeam, lime, hazel, pine and fir (Bottema 1994; Turner 1978; Willis 1992c: table 3). However, regional variations in precipitation and, to a lesser extent, in temperature, induced different vegetational responses: to the east of the Pindus, the change was minimal.

On a broad scale, the climate in Greece varies according to three gradients: a west–east gradient of decreasing rainfall, a north–south gradient of decreasing rainfall and increasing temperatures, and an altitudinal gradient of increasing rainfall and decreasing average temperatures. The north-west is the wettest and coolest region. Annual precipitations can reach 1500 mm and winters are cold and humid. Ioannina (at 470 m above sea level) has an annual mean of twenty-seven days of frost (Vita-Finzi 1978: 149) and is cut from the eastern lowlands by long periods of snow on the mountain passes. The near absence of early Neolithic settlements in this area may well reflect the poor adaptation of early domesticated cereals to these moist and cold winter months (see ch. 6 below).

Behind the Pindus Range, to the east, frost is known but less frequent. The Thessalian climate varies from a modified Mediterranean climate inland to a mild Mediterranean climate in the south-western coastal area (Halstead 1984, 1989a; Sivignon 1975). The mean annual temperature is 11 °C, with sharp contrasts between cool and rainy winter months and very hot and dry summer months. The mean annual precipitation varies regionally from 1000 to 500 mm the further one gets from the Pindus rain barrier (Sivignon 1975).

Further south again, in Boeotia or in the Argolid, days of frost are rare and the mean annual precipitation can drop under 400 mm (Greig and Turner 1974; Forbes 1989; Hansen 1991), which is not much above the minimum requirement for cereal growth (Halstead 1990b). The mean annual temperature reaches 18.5 °C and the driest parts of continental Greece – Argolid and Attica – approach a semi-arid climate. Consequently, periodic droughts must have been a frequent problem, with running years of less than average rainfall: as shown by Ricklefs (quoted in Forbes 1989), inter-annual rainfall variability is all the more important when the annual mean is low.

These climatic variations within Greece, which are often underestimated, played an important, if somewhat paradoxical, role in the regional distribution of Early Neolithic settlements. The better adaptation of early domesticates to drier environments was certainly an important factor. Yet, the variations in the natural vegetation probably played an equally important role.

Vegetation

The sharp climatic contrasts in Greece have a direct impact on the natural vegetation. Following Anastassiades (1949), several zones can be distinguished, of which only the Lowlands, under 700 m altitude, are of relevance here. The Lowlands themselves can be divided according to latitude and longitude into

- the Lowlands Northern belt, moist and cool
- the Lowlands Ionian belt, warm but moist (800 to 1500 mm of rain), which comprises the Western Coast lowlands and Ionian islands
- The Lowlands Aegean belt, dry and warm (300 to 800 mm of rain), which comprises the most important regions for our study: Chalcidiki, Thessaly, Central Greece, north and east Peloponnese and the Aegean Islands

Although most of the Lowlands are today either cultivated or barren, it is considered that the natural climatic vegetation that prevailed during the Neolithic was the oak forest (Bottema 1974, 1979; Greig and Turner 1974; Halstead 1989b; Turner 1978). Cores taken from Lakes Khimatidi, Ioannina, Edessa, Kastoria and Tenagi Phillipon all indicate a progressive reforestation after the Pleistocene, and a climatic woodland of deciduous oaks, elms, ash, lime-tree, hazel, with hazel and pines on the slopes. Early farmers would thus have faced a densely forested land (Halstead 1989b), a claim that has important implications for the reconstruction of past economies.

However, this reconstruction of past environments is debatable. First, the pollen cores on which it is based come from the Northern belt (Macedonia) or the Northern Ionian belt (Epirus), two regions with a substantially higher rainfall than most of Greece. To the contrary, the densest Neolithic settlements are to be found in the Aegean belt, which presents a markedly lower rainfall (Greig and Turner 1974; Hansen 1991: fig. 9). Second, even in northern Greece, the early Holocene deciduous oak forest included sun-loving species such as the *Pistacia terebinthus* or *Sanguisorba minor*, whose presence demonstrates that the forest was still open. In regions located between 400 and 800 m altitude,[1] the forest became denser after the seventh millennium cal. BC, but even in Thessaly this change was not perceptible (Bottema 1994). Third, the pollen diagrams do not record forest clearance, even when it is known to have taken place (Bottema and Woldring 1990), and Mediterranean plants characteristic of naturally open areas are known to be under-represented in pollen cores (Turner and Greig 1975: 203).

Thus early farmers would have faced a dense forest with a good potential for natural rejuvenation mainly in the north and west of Greece (Greig and Turner 1974: 191). It is probably no coincidence that here Early Neolithic sites are extremely rare. In lowland Thessaly, where the densest settlement is observed, the forest would have been naturally more open and less prone to rapid spontaneous rejuvenation. Once cleared, the hot and dry summers and the presence of grazing animals would have prevented the growth of trees in favour of steppe species (Olszewski 1993: 421–2).

From Boeotia southwards, the first Neolithic groups must have encountered an even more open landscape. Hansen (1991: 18) suggests that low-growing shrubs and small trees, such as juniper and terebinth, which are systematically under-represented in pollen cores, would have been the dominant vegetation. According to Rackham (1983), the pollen diagrams from Lake Kopaïs (Allen 1990; Greig and Turner 1974; Turner and Greig 1975; Turner 1978) indicate, for the first half of the Holocene, a deciduous oak woodland on the deeper soils, evergreen oaks on the thinner soils, and a steppe vegetation on the slopes. More generally, Rackham emphasizes the constant presence in pollen diagrams of sun-loving plants that could not flower in the shade, and concludes that 'The pollen record leaves no doubt that, though aboriginal Greece was certainly more tree'd than today, much of it has never been continuously forested in this interglacial' (Rackham 1990: 341). Bottema (1994: 56) recently concurred that the presence of terebinth and juniper indicated a dry open woodland around Kopaïs, at about 8000 BP. The forest may have become denser afterward, but the Lake Kopaïs region would have known a more pronounced Mediterranean climate than northern Greece during the whole Holocene (Bottema 1994: 57; Turner 1978).

---

[1] As remarked by Bottema (1994: 48), there are no pollen cores from 100 to 400 m altitude.

Further south again, the base of a pollen core taken in the ancient Lake Lerna indicates a deciduous oak woodland with a relatively high amount of Mediterranean elements, while Hansen reconstructs the Early Neolithic environment around Franchthi as 'at most' an open woodland with evergreen oaks, pistachio and large areas of herbaceous vegetation (Jahns 1990; Hansen 1991: 144). A pollen core from the Koilada Bay, in front of the Franchthi Cave, confirms an open vegetation in the Late Neolithic period, with low arboreal pollen values dominated by *Quercus cerris* type pollens (Bottema 1990). Contrasting Macedonia, Thrace and southern Greece – Boeotia and the Peloponnese – Greig and Turner (1974: 192) conclude that 'In the south more severe erosion and dryer climate could have prevented forest re-growth and the land, once cleared, only bear evergreen oak shrubs.' Yet, according to Rackham (1982; see also Bintliff 1977: 50), steppe, garrigue and maquis cannot be considered solely as humanly induced degradation stages of the forest. They can also constitute climatic vegetations, depending on soil and precipitation, and the dry climate of the Neolithic period may have been a more effective factor in their development than human activities. Rackham recently concluded that

Southern Greek vegetation in and before the Neolithic period was not a continuous forest, but a mosaic of woodland and steppe, corresponding to the present maquis and steppe. All the pollen diagrams contain pollens of plants such as asphodel which do not flower in shade . . . The pre-Neolithic climate of southern Greece was evidently less arid than it is now, though still not wet enough for continuous forest. (1990: 386–7)

This reassessment of the arboreal cover has important bearings on several aspects of the Neolithic subsistence economy: the nature of the arboreal cover determines the amount of effort that must be put into land clearing, as well as the importance of the problems created by spontaneous forest rejuvenation. In turn, this determines the amount of land that can be cleared and sown for daily consumption, the possibility of creating surplus, and the resources offered for animal grazing. The more open the environment, the less difficult the clearing and maintenance of larger fields and pastures. Above all, the nature of the natural vegetation determines the possible permanence of the fields, and therefore of human habitation.

Natural resources: plants and animals

Regional variations in the vegetation entailed parallel variations in the nature, availability and abundance of natural resources. In theory, the latter might have played a role in the distribution of settlements and their subsistence basis. In practice, however, this factor seems to have been of minor importance: Neolithic farmers apparently made little use of wild resources (see ch. 8 below).

As a consequence, even their nature and abundance are difficult to assess, and the best data, albeit of regional value only, are still provided by the Mesolithic remains from Franchthi.

In the Mesolithic strata of Franchthi, a wide variety of fruit, legumes and cereals, typical of the Mediterranean garrigue, had been exploited: *Pistacia* sp., *Prunus amygdalus*, *Pyrus amygdaliformis*, *Lens* sp., *Hordeum* sp., *Avena* sp., *Capparis* sp., as well as Liliaciae, *Malva*, *Adonis* and *Fumaria*, etc. (Hansen 1991). To this list could probably be added acorns, vines, wild olives, bulbs and roots such as orchids, muscari, *Urginea maritima*, asphodels, carrots and sal-sifis, or leafy plants (*Cichorium*, *Portulaca*, *Crithmum*) that were eaten until recently. Yet few of these species will be found again in Neolithic seed assemblages. The same holds true for wild animals. Of the varied Mesolithic fauna at Franchthi (*Cervus elaphus*, *Sus scrofa*, *Vulpes vulpes*, *Lepus europeanus*, *Meles meles*, *Erinaceus*, and rare remains of large bovids), only red deer and hares, with a few birds and some fish, are still found in any quantity in the Neolithic levels (Payne 1975). In Thessaly and Macedonia, deer, boars, auroch, foxes, *Capra hircus*, hares, beavers, birds and fishes have been found in Neolithic sites, but always in very small quantities (Bökönyi 1986; Halstead 1984; Larje 1987). This indicates which species were present, but provides no detailed information on their distribution and abundance. It is doubtful, at any rate, that wild resources could have answered the needs of large, sedentary populations. According to Halstead (1981a: 315), most wild fruits, tubers and nuts would have grown on barren or high areas, far away from the villages settled in alluvial plains.

The reason why natural resources were seemingly neglected will be further discussed in chapter 8. Meanwhile, it can be noted that, on the mainland, natural plant and animal resources did not influence the location of Early Neolithic settlements, nor their economic organization. On the other hand, the lack of natural resources may have adversely affected the foundation of settlements on the small Aegean islands and may explain the absence of Early Neolithic settlement. The situation there was certainly far more severe. Wild fauna on the islands (still a debated problem), must have been very scarce. On Saliagos, for instance, the only wild species certainly present before human settlement is the fox, although Higgs claims that wild bezoar (*Capra aegragus*) and deer may have been present on some islands (Higgs *et al.* 1968). Wild resources must, at any rate, have been very scarce (Davis 1992). Besides fish and shells, they could not have constituted a relevant complement to the diet. As a consequence, small Aegean islands could not have been profitably settled without the introduction of domestic resources, provided that the problem of water could be solved since many islands have no springs or lakes. This may explain why the smaller Aegean islands were not permanently settled until the Late or Final Neolithic (Cherry 1990).

Mineral resources

The diversified geology of Greece simultaneously entails severe limitations and great potentials in mineral resources. Greece is indeed rich in mineral resources, but their uneven spatial distribution has important economic consequences, promoting specialized production and interregional trade. There is, for instance, an immediate contradiction between the quality of soil resources and the availability of mineral resources: the best soils for cereal cultivation were the light alluvial soils that extend over whole basins. However, these large basins provided no local raw material that could respond to the need for the manufacture of the sickle blades and millstones used to process the cereals.

Broadly speaking, three distributions can be distinguished. To the first group belong clay and several varieties of siliceous rocks that are ubiquitous and of easy access. Clay, in particular, was easily available in all alluvial basins. Every village had access to several sources of clay, and could, if needed, exploit their different qualities. Siliceous rocks – cherts, radiolarites, jaspers, quartz, steatite, serpentine – also abound in all the flysch and limestone series of Greece. But they are frequently of small size and poor quality for flaking: orogenic and tectonic movements created numerous inner flaws that impede flaking. When rolled down by the streams to the plains and basins, they are usually too small and too fractured to allow systematic blade production. Early Neolithic farmers usually neglected these secondary sources, the only ones locally available. They chose, instead, to exploit raw materials coming from good quality primary sources, often located very far from their own settlements.

Other raw materials are indeed found in relative abundance, but only in specific regions: high-quality Tertiary flints in western Greece; high-quality jaspers, embedded in particular limestone formations; and marble, used only occasionally, for figurines, pendants and stone vessels. Their presence in settlements located far from these regions, from the very beginning of the Neolithic, indicates an early knowledge of distant sources, possibly inherited from Mesolithic groups, and widespread systems of exchange. This is confirmed by the exploitation of another regionally restricted resource, marine shells, which were already used and traded inland during the Early Neolithic.

Finally, other sources are virtually unique: the volcanic formations of obsidian (Melos and Giali), andesite (cf. the Saronic Gulf) and emery (Naxos). Interestingly, these unique sources are among the most intensively exploited during the Neolithic (Perlès 1990b, 1992). Even during the Early Neolithic, and despite the difficulties in navigating the Aegean Sea, Melian obsidian is the most widely traded raw material, distributed hundreds of kilometres from its sources.

The distribution of metal ores can also be mentioned, although no metal has yet been found in Early Neolithic sites.[2] Copper is present in many regions of

---

[2] The theoretical possibility cannot be ruled out: metal artefacts dating to the eighth millennium have been found at Çayönü (Muhly 1989).

Greece (McGeehan-Liritzis 1983), but it is unclear that any of the copper objects found in Greek Neolithic sites were actually obtained from local ores. Similarly, the provenance of the very rare gold and silver of Late and Final Neolithic artefacts remains unknown, but gold and silver-rich ores exist in Greece and some may have been exploited by the end of the Neolithic (Gropengiesser 1986).

In summary, Greece presented itself to the first farmers as a land of contrasts and diversity. Mountains and hills, swamps and coastal resources offered the varied – but, arguably, limited – natural resources of this Mediterranean environment. These were the resources exploited by Mesolithic hunter-gatherers, who usually chose to settle in the most varied environments. Yet, for the first farmers, the most attractive features were the totally flat, homogeneous, alluvial basins, circumscribed by steep and rugged mountains. Swamps and lakes occupied parts of these basins, but left enough land of good agricultural value to allow for a dense settlement on their margins. Before cultivating the land, however, the natural forest had to be cleared. Few settlements are found in the regions of highest rainfall, where the forest was densest. Elsewhere, settlements were surrounded by an open Mediterranean forest or mosaic of woodland and garrigue that rapidly gave way to permanent fields and pastures. The rich soils and high water tables of the alluvial basins offered good opportunities for farming, but few resources of quality for the manufacturing of the daily used stone tools and implements. Good sources were often far and widely spaced, and travel to and from the different regions was an arduous task. Generally speaking, Greece offered rich resources, but most of them, whether good agricultural soils, rich pastures, timber wood, marine resources or high quality stones, were concentrated in well-defined and often isolated regions.

Mobility is one obvious answer to the dispersion of basic resources. However, in the context of sedentary farmers, the cost of direct procurement over lands and seas that offered no easy means of travel, becomes very high. In this respect, the topographic and geological diversity of Greece, its natural division into well-defined basins and hinterlands, into seas and islands, can be seen as a fundamental incentive for the precocious development of specialization and trade.

CHAPTER 2

THE MESOLITHIC BACKGROUND

An elusive Mesolithic: absence of evidence or evidence of absence?

Here, I shall use the term Mesolithic in its chronological sense, to designate early Holocene hunter-gatherer assemblages. The period under consideration spans between *c.* 9500 and 8000 BP uncalibrated, or *c.* 8700 to 7000 BC in calendar years. Detailed data-oriented presentations have been offered elsewhere (Perlès 1990a, 1995; Runnels 1995), so I shall focus on issues directly relevant to the problem of the origins of the Neolithic.

The most salient characteristic of the Mesolithic in Greece is how poorly it is known, and how few sites are recorded. Diverging opinions about the significance of this scarcity have led to opposing views on the origins of the Neolithic in Greece. I shall argue that Mesolithic Greece was indeed sparsely populated, and that this low demography rules out the hypothesis of a purely indigenous shift to agriculture.

The few sites known to date concentrate in two main regions: north-east Attica and the Argolid, in eastern Greece, Corfu, the coastal plains of the Acheron and the Preveza region in north-western Greece (fig. 2.1). So far, only four sites have been excavated and published: Sidari in Corfu,[1] Franchthi in the southern Argolid,[2] Zaïmis in Attica and Ulbrich also in the Argolid.[3] The important site of Theopetra, in Thessaly, with a sequence spanning the Palaeolithic, Mesolithic and Neolithic, is currently under excavation by N. Kyparissi-Apostolika. Little has been published so far on the Mesolithic, aside from the exceptional discovery of a human burial (Dianellos 1994; Kyparissi-Apostolika 1999). Finally, J. K. Kozłowski recently undertook excavations in the Klissoura cave (Argolid), but the Mesolithic finds have not yet been published.

Surface sites are equally scarce. Surveys in the northern Argolid led to the discovery of two possible Mesolithic sites, and six others were identified in the coastal area of north-western Greece (Runnels 1995; Runnels *et al.* 1999). All other surveys gave negative results.

Other 'Mesolithic' sites sometimes mentioned in the literature are highly debatable. Theocharis (1967) thought for a while that he had found a

---

[1] Sordinas 1967, 1969, 1970.
[2] Hansen 1991; Jacobsen and Farrand 1987; Payne 1975; Perlès 1990a; Shackleton 1988; van Andel and Sutton 1987.   [3] Markovits 1928, 1932–3; Tellenbach 1983.

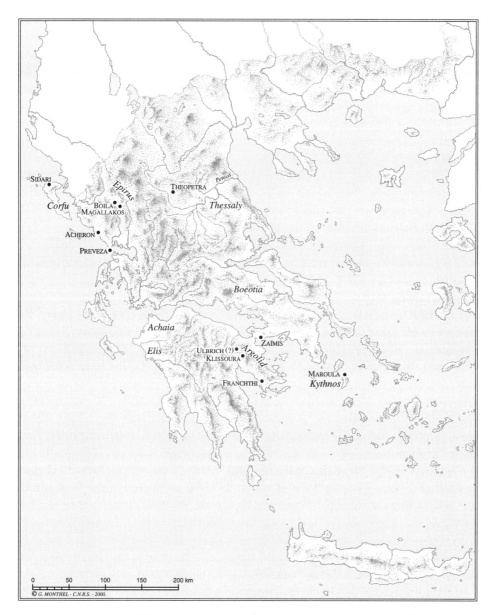

Fig. 2.1 Sites and locations discussed in relation with the Mesolithic.

Mesolithic settlement at Boebe (or Voivi) in Thessaly, an open-air surface site near an ancient lake or marshes. However, the so-called Mesolithic 'microliths' he found there appear to be fragments of broken blades, quite unlike the Mesolithic microliths known in Greece and easily compatible with a Neolithic context. Theocharis himself later recognized that 'it was impossible to isolate a pure Mesolithic level at Boebe' (Theocharis 1973b: 307, n. 17).

Another 'Mesolithic' site frequently mentioned is Maroula, on the Cycladic island of Kythnos. This weathered, open-air surface site yielded four unusual ochre-stained human burials under stone cairns, surrounded by scatters of obsidian and quartz implements. Honea (1975) obtained a surprisingly old 14C date on a bone sample from one of the burials, compatible with a late Mesolithic age.[4] However the nature of the burials rather suggests a Final Neolithic or Early Bronze Age date, a suggestion confirmed by Cherry and Torrence's examination of the site and of the stone tools scattered on the surface (Cherry 1979: 29–30).

The total number of sites currently known thus barely reaches a dozen. Does this scarcity reflect the actual paucity of human settlements in Mesolithic Greece? Alternatively, are most of the Mesolithic sites buried or destroyed? Or is this simply the outcome of insufficient research?

Assessing the meaning of the poverty of sites is crucial to the discussion of the origins of the Neolithic. The demography of the Mesolithic substratum determines in part the potential for local innovations and the role that local groups could have played in the constitution – both cultural and genetic – of the first farming societies (Nandris 1977a: 28). Many authors have considered the paucity of Mesolithic sites, in contrast to the large number of Early Neolithic settlements, as good evidence for a demic diffusion of Neolithic groups into south-eastern Europe[5] (Hansen 1992; Lewthwaite 1986; Perlès 1989a; Runnels and van Andel 1988; van Andel and Runnels 1995). But, if the paucity of sites is simply an artefact of research, as suggested by Chapman (1991: 126) for instance, the distribution and number of Mesolithic sites is irrelevant to the discussion. They cannot stand as an argument against the hypothesis of a local develop-ment, or, minimally, of a substantial contribution of local populations to the development of the Neolithic. More radically, if the Mesolithic sample is biased by geological factors or by lack of research, then no valid comparison can be drawn between the Mesolithic and the Neolithic; no conclusion can be reached regarding the origins of the latter. This is essentially the position advocated by several Greek colleagues in a recent paper (Andreou et al. 1996).

Undoubtedly, several factors could have concurred to result in the destruc-tion or non-visibility of Mesolithic sites in Greece.

(a) First, most sites, with the exception of Theopetra, are located close to the sea, suggesting a preference for coastal locations. Sidari is currently being eroded away by the sea, and the rise of the sea level during the Holocene (van Andel and Shackleton 1982), reinforced by local isostatic movements, could have destroyed many more coastal settlements. Whatever the number of coastal sites destroyed, this factor, however, cannot account for the quasi-absence of sites *inland*.

---

[4] This date (Gx 2837: 7875 ± 500 BP) compares with the 14C Mesolithic date obtained at Sidari, equally late.

[5] i.e., involving a movement of population (Ammerman and Cavalli-Sforza 1984: 6).

(b) Inland sites, on the other hand, could now be buried under several metres of alluvial sediments. They would thus be difficult to spot from surface surveys. Extensive alluviation has been demonstrated in several regions, especially in Thrace and Macedonia. It is thus premature to rule out the possibility that Mesolithic – and for that matter, Early Neolithic – sites are now deeply buried in these regions. However, there are grounds to doubt the importance of this factor in other parts of Greece. The overall stability of the Late Pleistocene and Early Holocene morphology has been repeatedly documented in other basins, where erosional phases are late (Middle to Late Neolithic, Bronze Age or even later), limited in extent, and probably related to agriculture and pastoralism (Allen 1990; Pope and van Andel 1984; van Andel *et al.* 1990; Zangger 1991).

Finally, even deeply buried Mesolithic sites could have been discovered along natural alluvial sections. The latter were systematically explored in several basins during geological or archaeological surveys (see Demitrack 1986; Runnels 1988, 1994 for Thessaly; Chavaillon *et al.* 1967, 1969 for the Elis). Whereas numerous Middle or Early Upper Palaeolithic find-spots have been brought to light, none so far can be attributed to the Mesolithic.

Conversely, the geomorphological stability – many Late Pleistocene terraces and fans are still preserved – makes it doubtful that the majority of Mesolithic sites were eroded away. The abundance of Middle Palaeolithic surface finds demonstrates that ancient sites and finds are well preserved in Greece. In Thessaly, many Early Neolithic settlements are located on Late Pleistocene terraces and alluvial fans; if Mesolithic sites had been present, they too would have been preserved. In the southern Argolid, thorough analyses and evaluations conducted after an intensive survey led to the conclusion that site loss was not really significant (Jameson *et al.* 1994: 228–48).

(c) Given these conditions, one could argue that the paucity of Mesolithic sites in Greece is simply due to a lack of interest and a lack of field research (Dennell 1984: 95). Greece is, on the whole, an unusually well surveyed region (see, for instance, Cherry 1994) but one cannot deny that the Mesolithic was hardly a primary focus. Furthermore, Mesolithic surface finds are undoubtedly more difficult to identify than earlier (especially Middle Palaeolithic) or later material: the stone industry, as it is known from excavated sites, is mostly undiagnostic. The diagnostic elements (the microliths) are precisely those most difficult to spot on the surface.

This could explain why Mesolithic surface sites have been identified only by specialized teams, led in particular by C. Runnels. Yet, teams led by the same scholar failed to spot Mesolithic sites during their surveys of the southern Argolid and Thessaly, although the latter was explicitly designed to search for Upper Palaeolithic and Mesolithic remains (Jameson *et al.* 1994; Runnels *et al.* 1995; Runnels 1988, 1994). Several years earlier, the same had occurred with the specialized surveys along river sections of the Elis, conducted by Chavaillon and his collaborators (Chavaillon *et al.* 1967, 1969).

Systematic surveys in Boeotia,[6] around Nemea in the Argolid,[7] in Euboia[8] or in the Grevena area[9] also produced no evidence of Mesolithic settlements. Results of the long-standing research programmes in Epirus, repeatedly explored by British teams led by E. Higgs, then by G. N. Bailey, support this pattern. No Mesolithic site was ever found during the surveys. Even more significant is that neither the excavations nor the soundings in caves and rock shelters produced conclusive evidence of Mesolithic remains.[10] In all the main Palaeolithic sequences, human occupation stopped before or at the Pleistocene–Holocene boundary.

The Cave Ephoria of Greece has tested or excavated many caves in other parts of Greece during the past few years; except for Theopetra, no Mesolithic has been convincingly reported. Finally, no Mesolithic level was ever discovered in Greece under open-air Neolithic settlements, even when the sterile layers were reached.

In summary, too many surveys and test excavations have now been conducted in Greece to attribute the scarcity of Mesolithic sites primarily to a lack of systematic research (Hansen 1992).[11] Since the natural factors that can lead to site destruction or burial do not account for the lack of sites in natural alluvial sections, in caves and rock shelters, or at the base of Neolithic settlements, I concur with Jacobsen (1993) or Runnels and van Andel (Runnels 1995) to conclude that:

(a) Mesolithic sites were mostly located in coastal or near-coastal areas. That sites remain to be discovered in these areas is beyond doubt, but even the most careful surveys do not suggest a dense settlement pattern.

(b) The quasi-absence of sites inland, in particular within the large and fertile inner basins, must reflect a real archaeological pattern. On the whole, Mesolithic Greece seems to have been sparsely populated, and the population concentrated in specific and especially diversified environments.

In fact, the lack of evidence for human occupation in the large alluvial basins concerns not only the Mesolithic, but the whole period from the end of the Aurignacian to the beginning of the Neolithic (c. twenty-fifth to ninth

---

[6] Bintliff and Snodgrass 1985; Rolland 1980. Surface stone assemblages ascribed to the Final Palaeolithic or the Mesolithic have been mentioned in Boeotia in a preliminary report from Rolland (1980). But these assemblages have not been described and their chronological attribution has not, to my knowledge, been confirmed.

[7] Cherry *et al.* 1988 and unpublished preliminary reports.

[8] Keller and Cullen 1992; Sampson 1980.   [9] Wilkie and Savina 1997.

[10] Bailey, G. 1997a, 1997b; Bailey *et al.* 1983a, 1983b; Dakaris *et al.* 1964; Higgs and Vita-Finzi 1966; Higgs *et al.* 1967. An early Holocene date was obtained in a sounding at Magalakkos, but it does not seem to correspond to the stratigraphy (Hedges *et al.* 1990). Stratum IV of Boila is also considered as possibly early Holocene, but the lithic assemblage is typically Upper Palaeolithic (Kotjabopoulou *et al.* 1999). Absolute dating of this level would be useful.

[11] 'Although it is an argument *ex silentio*, I believe enough area in northern and central Greece has been surveyed to be able to say that if the Mesolithic culture existed in these regions it was sparse to the point of invisibility' (Hansen 1992: 242).

millennium BP inclusive).[12] This contrasts sharply with the ubiquitous distribution of Middle Palaeolithic tools, which can be found almost everywhere on the surface or, *in situ*, in natural sections (Bailey *et al.* 1999; Kourtessi-Philippakis 1986). Even lower Palaeolithic find-spots are more numerous than Mesolithic ones (Runnels and van Andel 1993). The situation during the Mesolithic appears to be the outcome of a long-term trend, witnessing a progressive restriction of the ecological zones exploited by hunter-gatherers in Greece. Remains of human activities dating from the Middle and early Upper Palaeolithic can be found in all kinds of topographic environments: coasts, plains, inner basins as well as hills and low mountains. Hills and mountains seem to be favoured during the Upper Palaeolithic, but alluvial basins and high mountains are seemingly progressively abandoned (Rolland 1985, 1988). This pattern is far from unique: it also obtains in a large part of the southern Balkans, in particular in southern Yugoslavia and in Bulgaria. The large alluvial basins of Anatolia also appear to be uninhabited during the Late Pleistocene/Early Holocene (Balkan-Atli 1994: 59). At the opposite end of the Mediterranean basin, Zilhão (1993: 13) concluded that Late Mesolithic sites were restricted to the estuaries of large rivers and that their absence inland was a 'true reflection of the non-occupation of those parts of Portugal during the Late Mesolithic'. The restriction of environmental zones exploited by Early Holocene hunter-gatherers thus appears to be a pan-Mediterranean phenomenon, not a specific bias of research or preservation in Greece.

However, there is no indication, in Greece at least, that this geographic restriction led to a higher population density. Even areas that were settled appear to have been sparsely populated. Franchthi remains unique in the southern Argolid even after intensive surveys, and the number of find-spots in the Berbati Valley survey or in north-western Greece remains very low. This raises the problem of the subsistence basis and of the abundance of available resources.

Early Holocene Greece: a difficult environment for hunter-gatherers?

Although details of the climatic fluctuations during the end of the Pleistocene and the early Holocene are unnecessary here (see Perlès 1995), a few landmarks are relevant. The Pleniglacial (*c.* 16000 BP) was characterized by a very dry climate that impeded tree growth, except in some altitudinal refuges such as the western slopes of the Pindus Range (Tzedakis 1993; Willis 1992a, b, c). During the Tardiglacial, a slight increase in humidity led to a progressively denser and more widespread arboreal cover in northern Greece (Allen 1990; Bottema 1974, 1979; Greig and Turner 1974; Turner and Greig 1975). The large steppe and prairie herbivores (Bovids and Equids) disappeared from Epirus, and

---

[12] I thank Curtis Runnels for pointing this out to me.

Table 2.1 *14C dates attributed to the Mesolithic*

Sites	Phase	Level	Lab. ref.	Nature of the sample	Date BP uncal.	Calibrated date BC at two sigma	Maximum probabilities	Reference
Franchthi	Lower Meso.	F/AS–195	P–2227	Carbonized matter	9.340±160	8971–8033	8384, 8369, 8356	J. & F. 1987
Franchthi	Lower Meso.	F/AS–195	P–2228	Carbonized matter, NaOH pre-treatment	9.060±110	8343–7924	8058	J. & F. 1987
Franchthi	Lower Meso.	F/AN–218	P–2108	Wood charcoal	9.250±120	8825–8025	8333, 8308, 8258	J. & F. 1987
Franchthi	Lower Meso.	H1–B 139	P–2103	Wood charcoal	9.300±100	8832–8083	8345, 8291, 8275	J. & F. 1987
Franchthi	Lower Meso.	H1–B 126	P–2102	Wood charcoal	9.290±100	8827–8081	8342, 8299, 8272	J. & F. 1987
Franchthi	Lower Meso.	H1–B 139	P–2104	Wood charcoal	9.270±110	8826–8041	8337,8304, 8265	J. & F. 1987
Franchthi	Lower Meso.	F/AN–197	P–2097	Wood charcoal	9.150±100	8409–7991	8093	J. & F. 1987
Franchthi	Upper Meso.	H1–A 117, trench	P–1665	Wood charcoal	9.480±130	9016–8192	8582, 8576, 8526	J. & F. 1987
Franchthi	Upper Meso.	H1–A 101	P–1664	Wood charcoal	8.940±120	8321–7649	8003	J. & F. 1987
Franchthi	Upper Meso.	H1–A 117, residues	P–1666	Wood charcoal	8.740±110	8023–7753	7870, 7816, 7707	J. & F. 1987
Franchthi	Upper Meso.	F/AN–177, residues	P–2106	Wood charcoal	8.730±90	7976–7508	7857, 7820, 7705	J. & F. 1987
Franchthi	Upper Meso.	F/AN–177, trench	P–2096	Wood charcoal	8.710±100	7975–7508	7834, 7828, 7699	J. & F. 1987
Franchthi	Upper Meso.	F/AN–177, residues	P–2107	Wood charcoal	8.530±90	7865–7424	7537	J. & F. 1987
Franchthi	Final Meso.?	G1–22	P–1536	Wood charcoal	8.190±80	7429–6829	7241, 7223, 7201, 7180, 7142, 7119	J. & F. 1987
Franchthi	Final Meso.?	F/F1 43A1	P–1526	Carbonized matter	8.020±80	7242–6610	7005	J. & F. 1987

Site				Material	Date BP	cal range		Reference
Sidari	Mesolithic	Level D	?	?	7.770±340	7493–5893	6548	Sordinas 1967
Theopetra		I10(E): 0.88 m	DEM-142	?	9.722±390	10400–8000	–	Kyparissi 1999
Theopetra		H6/B: 0.70 m	DEM-316	?	9.348±84	8600–8050	–	Kyparissi 1999
Theopetra		H6/B: 0.70 m	DEM-315	?	9.275±75	8490–8080	–	Kyparissi 1999
Theopetra		G9: 1.72 m	DEM-207	?	9.093±550	10100–9700	–	Kyparissi 1999
Theopetra		I10(W): 1.27 m	DEM-125	?	8.674±76	7910–7540	–	Kyparissi 1999
Theopetra		I10(E): 0.75–0.88 m	DEM-120	?	8.525±57	7640–7430	–	Kyparissi 1999
Theopetra		H6/P10/SB: 1.12–1.20 m	DEM-360	?	7.995±73	7050–6610	–	Kyparissi 1999
Theopetra		sq. H6	Simon Frazer University	Human bones		7044–6720	–	

Source: J. & F. 1987: Jacobsen and Farrand 1987.

red deer and ibex became the predominant prey (Bailey *et al.* 1983a, 1983b, 1986; Rolland 1985, 1988). Bailey and his collaborators suggest a very low population density of about fifty individuals for the whole of eastern Epirus (Bailey *et al.* 1986: 35).[13]

Further south, at Franchthi, the Tardiglacial was instead characterized by an early expansion of the Mediterranean garrigue, and a diversified economy based on red deer, wild boar, small fish, marine and terrestrial molluscs, as well as a variety of wild plants (Hansen 1991; Payne 1975; Shackleton 1988). The environment differed greatly from that of Epirus, but it was not necessarily richer. Species diversity cannot by itself be equated with abundance, and the very small size of many of the species exploited at Franchthi – fish, land snails, marine molluscs, lentils, vetches, oats – of low energetic yield, would rather argue for the contrary.

The beginning of the Holocene (tenth millennium BP, from *c.* 8000 to 9500 cal. BC) does not seem to have offered a markedly improved situation. In northern Greece dense mixed oak forests rapidly covered the mountain slopes (Bottema 1974, 1979, 1991; Willis 1992c). The last shelters occupied during the Final Palaeolithic (Klithi, Asprochaliko, Voïdomatis) were abandoned, and the coastal Mesolithic sites of Epirus and Corfu may reflect a withdrawal of the groups into more open and diversified environments. Were the mountainous forests too dense to penetrate or to have supported a large population of red deer, which prefers more open forests (Bridault 1993: 93)?

At Franchthi, in southern Greece, a shrubby garrigue rather than a real forest replaced the earlier and more open garrigue. The economic base in the Early Holocene remained diversified, but with a further decrease in large game hunting[14] and a sharp increase in the exploitation of plant resources (Hansen 1991). Since red deer and wild boar were the most energetically cost-efficient resources that one could exploit around Franchthi, the decrease in large mammals may indicate a scarcity of large faunal resources and the need to rely more intensively on lower-ranked species such as plants, molluscs and small fish.

This economic base changed drastically, however, during the Upper Mesolithic (first half of the ninth millennium BP, *c.* 7900–7500 cal BC), when tuna fishing provided a substantial complement to the diet (Rose, in prep.). The large quantities of fish bones suggest mass fishing and the possibility of storage of large amounts of fish meat. This, or the more specialized activities at the site, may explain the concomitant decrease in the density of seed remains (Hansen 1991).

---

[13] Rolland considers this estimate too low (1988: 49) and argues that plant food could have complemented the meat diet and allowed for a higher population density. But the range of edible plants would have been very limited.

[14] The number of bones recovered during excavation is much lower than in earlier periods (Payne 1975), but the residues from sieving have not been published.

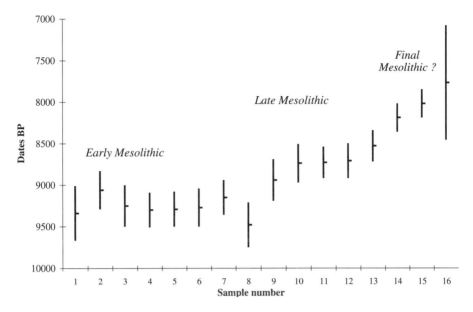

Fig. 2.2 Mesolithic dates (2 s.d.) from Franchthi (nos. 1–15) and Sidari (no. 16). The dates from Theopetra have not been included since they could not be assigned to a particular phase within the Mesolithic.

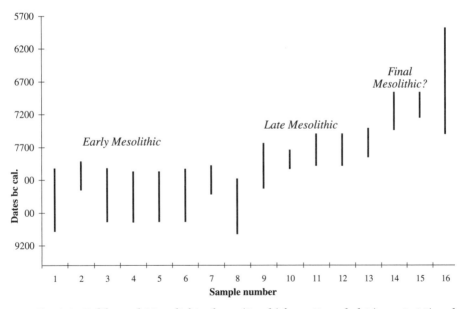

Fig. 2.3 Calibrated Mesolithic dates (2 s.d.) from Franchthi (nos. 1–15) and Sidari (no. 16). The dates from Theopetra have not been included since they could not be assigned to a particular phase within the Mesolithic.

But at Franchthi, at least, the opportunities offered by large-scale fishing lasted only a few centuries – perhaps four centuries, according to calibrated dates – and rapidly came to an end. By the end of the ninth millennium BP (c. 7100–6900 BC) the Final Mesolithic strata yielded only impoverished floral and faunal remains. Hansen (1991: 138, 1992: 241) suggests the cave was then nearly abandoned.

The importance of plant food, terrestrial molluscs and marine resources at Franchthi is not exceptional. Though little has been published on the subsistence remains from the other coastal sites, the presence of snails, seashells, fish and seeds is attested at Zaïmis, Ulbrich and Sidari (Markovits 1928, 1932–3; Sordinas 1969). All these sites indicate the exploitation of diversified and patchy environments, resulting in a large diet breadth, with an apparent emphasis on the exploitation of numerous small-sized species. Land snails and coastal resources could have offset seasonal shortages in plant resources and it is often argued that these r-selected species provide a more stable economic base, less vulnerable to short-term stress, than does large game. But the poor representation of the higher-ranked species, such as red deer and boar, remains to be explained. It is difficult to escape the conclusion that large game was difficult to procure, at least seasonally and/or locally. Seasonal movements from coastal to inland locations might be considered, and the on-going research at Theopetra should prove important in assessing the scope of the Mesolithic economy on a broader ecological scale.

In the meantime, the available data suggest a diversified, but not necessarily rich environment. Even though marine resources were exploited at Franchthi during the whole of the Mesolithic, they provided important nutritional resources only during a relatively short span of time. During most of the Mesolithic, the inhabitants of Franchthi relied on a whole range of small animals and plants, readily available but time-consuming to collect and process.[15] In theory at least, this subsistence base could allow a high degree of sedentism, as was suggested by Cullen (1995). This proposition is based, in particular, on the seasonality indicators of seashells, showing that molluscs had been collected all year round (Deith and Shackleton 1988). However, this pattern could equally well reflect repeated short-term visits to the cave, and I personally consider that none of the Mesolithic sites in Greece, Franchthi included, has produced the heavy equipment, architectural features, artistic production and diversified techniques usually associated with sedentary hunter-gatherers (see the NW Coast Indians, the Natufian or the rich Mesolithic of northern Europe).

[15] Those who equate the diversity of Mesolithic resources with an abundance of resources may not have realized what the exploitation of such small species requires. In the case of wild lentils, for instance, more than 100,000 seeds are needed to make up a kilo! (Ladizinsky 1989: 383, checked by the author.) Considering that wild lentils have only two or three seeds per pod (so that about 10,000 plants would be needed) and that they do not grow in tightly clustered stands, the cost of a lentil soup will be better appreciated!

The cultural originality of the Greek Mesolithic

The light and cursorily made stone and bone implements of the Greek Mesolithic are indeed more suggestive of mobile groups than of sedentary hunter-gatherers. At the same time, they reveal a profound originality that may indicate the relative isolation of Greece during this whole period.

The originality of the Greek Mesolithic, as currently known, is already perceptible by the Pleistocene/Holocene transformations at Franchthi. Mesolithic radiocarbon dates at Franchthi (see table 2.1) range from the mid-ninth millennium cal. BC to the late-eighth millennium (Jacobsen and Farrand 1987; Perlès 1990a). As emphasized by Runnels and van Andel (unpublished manuscript) the calibration of the 14C dates reinforces the importance of the temporal hiatus between the Early Mesolithic and the Final Palaeolithic, the latter being dated to the eleventh millennium cal BC. Yet, the Final Palaeolithic assemblages, that is, lithic phases V and VI, were already fully 'Mesolithic' in typological terms: alongside backed bladelets and double-backed points, including typical 'Sauveterre' points, they yielded numerous geometric microliths such as scalene bladelets, triangles, segments and, more rarely, trapezes, all manufactured with the microburin technique (Perlès 1987).

Comparisons with the rest of Europe would lead us to predict a further increase of microliths at the beginning of the Holocene, but the reverse occurs: virtually all microliths and microburins disappear! During the Early Mesolithic (ninth millenium cal BC , lithic phase VII), the toolkit consists predominantly of crude end-scrapers, notches, denticulates and marginally retouched tools, all made on flakes (Perlès 1990a). Microliths and microburins amount to no more than 10 per cent of the industry, as opposed to 75 per cent in the latest Palaeolithic. Since these are similar to Final Palaeolithic artefacts, it is unclear whether they should be considered *in situ* or as mere contaminants (see Martini 1993, *contra* Perlès 1990a).

Microliths reappear in abundance during the Upper Mesolithic (lithic phase VIII, first half of the eighth millennium cal BC), in close stratigraphical association with tuna vertebrae. The microburin technique is now completely absent, but this is not the only original feature: almost all microliths are made on flakes, not on blades or bladelets as is the case elsewhere in Europe. Few of the 'classic' Mesolithic microliths are present. There are some backed bladelets, trapezes and transverse arrowheads, but triangles or segments are absent and most trapezes have sinuous truncations, instead of concave or straight ones. Yet, the vast majority of the microliths are not typical geometrics but small pieces of various shapes, with multiple backs and/or truncations, often without any cutting edge. The combination of truncations and backed edge occasionally produces various unusual geometric shapes, such as rectangles or squares, but many pieces have asymmetrical, sinuous, unclassifiable shapes.

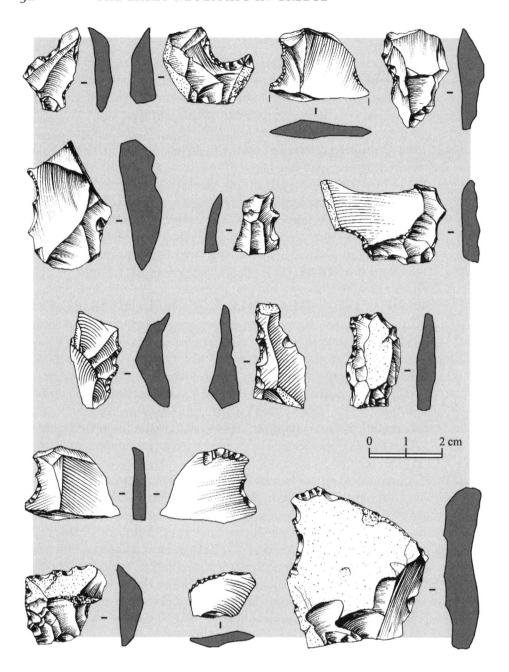

Fig. 2.4 Stone tools from the Upper Mesolithic of Franchthi (after Perlès 1990a).

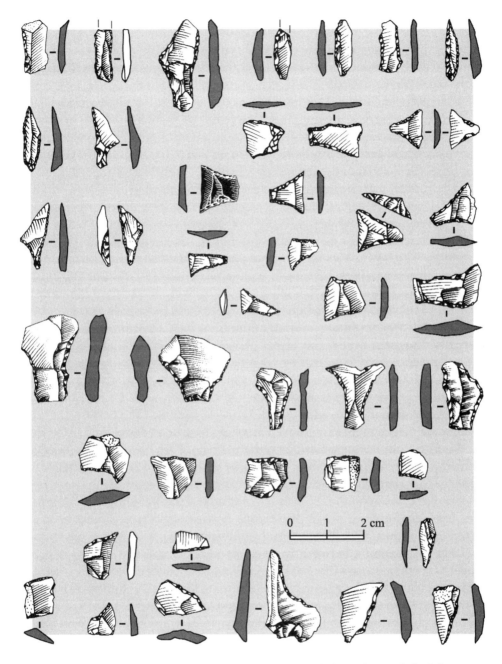

Fig. 2.5 Microlithic tools from the Upper Mesolithic of Franchthi (after Perlès 1990a).

These microliths disappear together with the evidence for tuna fishing during the Final Mesolithic (end of the eighth millennium cal BC, lithic phase IX). The latter again suggests an impoverished hunting and gathering economy, associated with the production of crude flake tools but also of a few fine transverse arrowheads (Perlès 1990a).

Sidari presents a lithic assemblage that compares well, both in technological and typological terms, to the Late Mesolithic of Franchthi. Here again, the assemblage is dominated by small, atypical microliths produced by a combination of backed edges and truncations, with no use of the microburin technique (Sordinas 1969, 1970 and personal observation). Preliminary reports indicate that the surface scatters from the southern Epirus can also be related, in technological and typological terms, to the industries from Franchthi (Runnels 1995, Runnels et al. 1999).

The other categories of artefacts are much rarer, and known only from Franchthi. The Lower Mesolithic produced a typologically restricted bone tool industry that consists exclusively of fragments of points of circular section and of asymmetrical points on flat splinters. By its lack of variety, this industry bears little relation to the elaborate Mesolithic bone industries of western and northern Europe, or of the Natufian in the Near East. Interestingly, bone tools virtually disappear during the Upper Mesolithic, when fishing predominates the subsistence activities. Antler tools are represented only by very rare and dubious 'utilized' antler tips. Grinding implements are similarly rare, in sharp contrast to the spectacular development of grinding tools in the contemporaneous Natufian. Besides a few pebbles used as pounders and pestles, the most interesting pieces include a grooved stone and a fine andesite millstone from the Saronic Gulf (Runnels 1981, Stroulia in prep.). Both have their exact equivalent in the Neolithic and were unfortunately recovered during early excavations, so that their context cannot be considered entirely secure.

Ornaments are represented by a few perforated flat pebbles, natural dentalium beads and pierced shells of Cyclope neritea, especially abundant in the Lower Mesolithic (Shackleton 1988). Unfortunately, no specific association could be documented between personal ornaments and the collective burial recently brought to light by Tracey Cullen (1995), when she reanalyzed the human remains and their stratigraphic context. Although the primary burial of a young man, who apparently died of violent blows to the forehead, was already known and published (Angel 1969), the disturbed – but relatively complete – burials of seven other individuals had gone unrecognized. They lay less than half a metre below the latter, and comprised five inhumations in a flexed position and two cremations. Infants, young adults and adults of both sexes are represented in what may be considered, given the close proximity of all the remains, as a collective or multiple burial (Cullen 1995).[16]

---

[16] It is impossible to state whether all individuals were buried simultaneously or successively.

Individual and collective burials are rather common in Europe and the Near East at comparable periods, and, in spite of Cullen's thorough search, no particular relationship could be established between the Franchthi inhumations or bone scatters and specific funerary rituals in neighbouring areas (Cullen 1995). Consequently, bone and chipped stone artefacts remain the most reliable categories for appreciating the 'cultural' affinities of the Mesolithic in Greece. But this is not an easy task, given their predominantly expedient production! Many characteristics of the Mesolithic stone assemblages can be attributed to functional rather than cultural factors (see discussion in Perlès 1990a). Idiosyncratic traditions, however, are expressed in a series of characteristics unrelated to the formal and functional properties of the tools: quadrangular cores flaked on several surfaces: absence of systematic blade production, even for the trapezes; absence of the microburin technique; very early presence of trapezes and transverse arrowheads (about a millennium earlier than in the rest of Europe); irregular shape of most trapezes. None of these has any known equivalent in the rest of Europe for the same period, nor indeed in the Near East.

Conversely, several elements of continuity can be found between the Final Palaeolithic and the Mesolithic in Greece, in spite of the temporal gap. The exploitation of raw materials is comparable, although the use of obsidian increases slightly during the Late Mesolithic. The flaking methods and conceptions are identical and the domestic tools, such as end-scrapers, notches, denticulates, are similar. A similar degree of continuity occurs in the exploitation of the environment. The species exploited during the Final Palaeolithic and the Mesolithic are the same; the differences are essentially of a quantitative order, with more plants and less large animals. The exploitation of marine resources, often cited as a spectacular feature of Franchthi's Mesolithic, has its roots in the Final Palaeolithic and the presence of obsidian as early as the eleventh millennium confirms the antiquity of seafaring.

Most of the differences between the two periods should probably be attributed to environmental modifications, and to the greater or lesser availability of such primary resources as large game, edible plants and large schools of tuna. These environmental transformations can be due, as noted by Runnels and van Andel (unpublished manuscript), to a longer temporal hiatus than was previously thought. In calibrated years, the hiatus in deposition could have covered more than a millennium, a long enough period for important environmental transformations to have taken place. Although the quasi-disappearance of microliths during the Lower Mesolithic remains puzzling, I consider that a long-term population continuity between the Final Palaeolithic and the Lower Mesolithic remains the most parsimonious hypothesis. The idiosyncratic characteristics of the Mesolithic of Greece would be related to an *in situ* development with fewer external contacts.

Conclusion

Taken together, the data we possess on Mesolithic Greece suggest that

(a) Mesolithic sites were restricted to specific environments, in particular coastal or near-coastal locations, where some settlements may have been destroyed by eustatic rise. Large inland basins, in particular, were almost completely devoid of settlements. Since most systematic surveys were precisely focused on the latter, there is a built-in bias in the present-day representation of Mesolithic sites from surface surveys. However, even in areas were Mesolithic settlements are known, systematic surveys indicate only a low settlement density.

(b) The Mesolithic of Greece reveals distinctive technical traditions, and seems to have been cut off from the widespread Mesolithic trends of the rest of Europe. It differs even more radically from the contemporaneous Natufian of the Near East, but may present some relations with the Mesolithic of southern Anatolia (Perlès 1990a).

(c) The natural environment was either impoverished or more difficult to exploit, leading Mesolithic hunter-gatherers to settle in diversified environments. With the rise in humidity, the development of forests in the north and of shrubby garrigues in the south may have impeded the development of large game. The exploitation of wild plants, molluscs or coastal resources, though time-consuming, would then have been necessary to offset the scarcity of large game.

Mesolithic hunter-gatherers of Greece were also very able seafarers. Many of their crude stone tools were in fact used to work the fibres necessary to make nets, baskets and boats (Vaughan 1990). The latter could have consisted of reed boats, such as the 'papyrella' that was reconstructed a few years ago and used to collect obsidian from Sounion to Melos (Tzalas 1995). The papyrella, based on a Corfiote's model, proved its seaworthiness, but it also confirmed the need for developed nautical skills, which the intensive fishing of tuna, barracudas and groupers had already suggested (Jacobsen 1993).

However, the Mediterranean sea is not very fertile and has a low overall productivity (Powell 1996; van Andel 1987). Van Andel doubts that the fertility was higher during the Early Holocene, and considers that the appearance of intensive fishing was not related to environmental factors (van Andel 1987: 53). Other specialists, on the other hand, attribute the temporary presence of large schools of tuna to rapid and erratic modifications of the temperature and salinity of the water, which were related to the melting of the northern ice-caps (Dennell 1983; Doumenge, *in litt.* 19/8/97). But in neither case is the tuna considered to be a stable and rich staple resource in the long term. Similarly, the Mediterranean garrigues, maquis and forests carry only a limited faunal biomass. This may well account for the rapid adoption of agriculture and animal breeding in the Mediterranean basin, and in Greece in particular, in striking contrast to the long period of coexistence of hunting and farming in the more plentiful regions of central, eastern and northern Europe (see Zvelebil and Dolukhanov 1991 for a synthesis). Whether or not Mesolithic hunter-gatherers of Greece introduced domesticated species themselves (a problem that we shall discuss in the chapter that follows), there can be no doubt that they readily perceived the direct and indirect benefits offered by them. Within a few centuries or less, all traces of the traditional ways of life had disappeared, in favour of a new and complex farming economy.

CHAPTER 3

THE INTRODUCTION OF FARMING: LOCAL PROCESSES, DIFFUSION OR COLONIZATION?

Around 7000 BC,[1] marked changes took place: farmers settled in the previously uninhabited alluvial basins, built permanent villages and introduced domestic plants and animals. Theoretically, several processes could account for this radical shift (Barker 1985: 71): a purely autochthonous process, without external contacts; a local process spurred by the acquisition, through exchanges, of foreign goods and techniques (that is, cultural diffusion); the migration into Greece of foreign groups of farmers and herders, solely responsible for the sedentary Neolithic settlements (that is, demic diffusion); or, finally, a mixed process based on interactions between local hunter-gatherers and incoming farmers.

These various possibilities have each been defended by different – or sometimes the same – scholars. However, few nowadays would support the extreme position of Higgs and Jarman (1969, 1972), who considered possible an entirely indigenous shift to a Neolithic economy, based on the local domestication of animal and plant species. Conversely, none of the advocates of a demic diffusion, such as Childe (1957, 1958) or Ammerman and Cavalli-Sforza (1984), denied that some degree of interaction could have taken place between indigenous groups and immigrant farmers. Yet even without calling for extreme models, there remains ample space for widely differing perspectives, depending on the respective roles attributed to local hunter-gatherers or to foreign migrant groups.

Indigenist models and the claims for the local domestication of plants and animals

Autochthonous, or 'indigenist' models have progressively gained importance in Greece as in the rest of Europe, in opposition to the purely migrationist views advanced until the end of the 1960s (Weinberg 1970: 570–1). Whilst acknowledging the exogenous origins of some at least of the domestic plants and animals, these models consider that no movements of populations need to have occurred.[2] Exchanges, or the natural spread of plants and animals, could alone account for the introduction and adoption of domesticated species.

---

[1] Around 8000 BP uncal., or 7000 cal BC. See discussion of the 14C dates below, pp. 84ff.
[2] e.g., Barker 1985: 71; Bogucki 1988: 50; Dennell 1983: 163–8; Gimbutas 1974: 279; Milojčić 1973; Theocharis 1967: 171, 178; Wijnen 1981: 101–2.

This position was first defended in Greece by the great scholar Theocharis, who stated that 'the earliest phase of the new stage, the Preceramic, has not so far yielded any evidence for direct diffusion from any particular direction' (1973b: 34–5). His stand was echoed shortly afterwards by Gimbutas (1974: 279), following their joint excavations at Achilleion: 'It is apparent then that in Southeastern Europe an autonomous, full-fledged Neolithic culture developed synchronically with that of the Near East.' Dennell, in the same years, dismissed the potential migrants as 'invisible colonists' (Dennell 1983: 165), and invisible they have remained, up to now, in the eyes most Greek scholars (e.g., Kotsakis 1992; Kyparissi-Apostolika 1999; Protonotariou-Deïlaki 1992).

To make a local process possible, these 'indigenist' models must rely, implicitly or explicitly,[3] on a long phase of 'pre-adaptation' to herding and cultivation through the control of local plant and animal species.[4] The transition to the Neolithic could then be viewed as a long process, rather than as the sudden event implied by migrationist models. This perspective received support from repeated claims of local domestications of various plants and animals in Greece itself or in other Mediterranean countries. However, detailed examinations of these various instances cast doubts on their validity.

A long-lasting misinterpretation: the local domestication of plants at Franchthi

E. S. Higgs and M. R. Jarman, themselves specialists of prehistoric Greece, were amongst the most extreme advocates of a European locus of domestication. They considered that the domestication of sheep, goats and pigs in the Near East was 'not warranted', that cattle were probably domesticated earlier in Europe than in the Near East, and that the domestication of cereals in the Near East was 'not certain' (Higgs and Jarman 1969: 36–8).

There was little basis at the time for such statements. However, the subsequent discovery at Franchthi of wild lentils and cereals in the Palaeolithic and Mesolithic strata came as an apparent confirmation: it established the existence of the postulated 'pre-adaptation phase', during which a familiarity was progressively acquired with the newly exploited legumes and cereals. Even more decisive was the possibility, mentioned in preliminary reports, of progressive morphometrical changes in the lentils (*Lens* sp.) from the Mesolithic to the Neolithic. This suggested that a gradual transformation from wild to domestic could have occurred locally (Hansen 1978, 1980; Hansen and Renfrew 1978). Barley also occurred both wild, in the Late Palaeolithic and Mesolithic deposits, and domesticated in the Neolithic strata. Although in this case no progressive morphological transformation was documented, it too has been

---

[3] Stated differently, these arguments are comparable to the three necessary conditions in continuity models advanced by Ammerman (1989: 164).

[4] Dennell 1983: 165; Guilaine 1976; Higgs and Jarman 1969; Zvelebil 1986, 1994.

considered as potentially locally domesticated (Dennell 1983: 160–1; Hansen and Renfrew 1978). As a consequence, Franchthi became one of the most frequently quoted examples in support of a European domestication of both legumes and cereals.

Two decades later, however, Hansen firmly rejected these hypotheses (Hansen 1991, 1992). After a thorough examination of the seed remains, she demonstrated that the major increase in lentil size coincided exactly with the introduction of domesticated emmer wheat and two-row barley, therefore with the beginning of the Neolithic. In the meantime, genetic studies had demonstrated that the wild progenitor of the cultivated lentil is *Lens orientalis* (= *Lens culinaris* subsp. *orientalis*), whereas the wild species at Franchthi were probably *Lens nigricans* or *Lens ervoïdes*. *Lens orientalis* is probably present in southern Greece (Polunin 1987; Hansen 1991: 52; *contra* Ladizinsky 1989; Zohary 1989), but according to Hansen (1992: 235) it would not have grown in the immediate vicinity of the site. Finally, she noted that a full metre of deposits separated the last occurrence of wild barley and the first remains of domesticated barley (*Hordeum* cf. *distichum*) (Hansen 1991, 1992: 235–8). She thus denied an 'indigenous development' (Hansen 1991: 163) and concluded that 'the data available from Franchthi Cave and the southern Argolid most strongly suggest an immigration of new people with an agricultural economy based on a Near Eastern complex of emmer wheat, lentils and ovicaprids' (Hansen 1992: 241).[5]

The same argument holds true for Greece as a whole, since in all early Neolithic settlements known so far domesticated plants appear all together, never gradually. In addition, distribution maps and genetic studies show that the wild progenitors of einkorn and emmer wheats (*Triticum dicoccum* and *T. monococcum*), chickpeas (*Cicez arietinum*), broad beans (*Vicia faba*), bitter vetch (*Vicia ervilia*) and probably peas (*Pisum sativum*) are found only in the Near East (Ladizinsky 1989; van Zeist 1980; Zohary 1989; Zohary and Hopf 1993). Although flax and chickpeas are rare in Early Neolithic Greece, the 'eight founder crops' as defined by Zohary for the Near East (Zohary 1989: 359; Zohary and Hopf 1993) are all present: emmer, einkorn, barley, pea, lentil, chickpea, bitter vetch and flax. This original set of cultivated plants remained stable for a long time: early farmers of Greece had little inclination to experiment with new species. In this respect, negative evidence is also revealing: *Papaver somniferum*, one of the few European domesticates unknown in the Near East, has never been identified in Neolithic seed assemblages from Greece. Yet, its presumed wild progenitor (*P. setigerum*) is well represented in the European Mediterranean basin (van Zeist 1980: 133–4), which suggests that these first farmers, coming from a region where the plant was unknown, were

---

[5] As will be discussed later (pp. 46ff), I agree that new groups probably settled at Franchthi. However, I believe that the first domesticates were initially introduced by the local inhabitants of Franchthi and that the changes of population took place later.

not aware of the potential of this local species. Similarly, oats were seemingly not cultivated in the Near East nor in Greece during the Neolithic (Zohary and Hopf 1993: 77), although it was collected in the wild during the Mesolithic at Franchthi (Hansen 1991).

One cannot, therefore, but agree with Hansen's firm conclusion: 'Thus, the model of indigenous development of agriculture in Greece cannot be supported by the existing evidence from central and northern Greece and is not at all supported by the evidence from Franchthi Cave' (Hansen 1992: 243; see also Hansen 1991: 174–1; Renfrew J. 1973: 203; van Zeist 1980; Zohary and Hopf 1993).

The claims for animal domestication in Europe

Investigations concerning the origins of the domesticated animals have been less thorough and the topic remains more controversial. The debates have revolved around two distinct aspects of the problem: first, the presence in Europe of potential wild progenitors for the domesticated species, and second, their effective domestication. In this respect, the situation differs for ovicaprines, bovids and suids.

Ovicaprines had always been considered as Near Eastern species until remains of sheep were claimed in several European Mesolithic sites. The presence of sheep before the Neolithic would thus prove that it had a local progenitor and was locally domesticated.[6] However, most of the cases in support of the latter claim have since been refuted: the domestic sheep from the Mesolithic levels of Chateauneuf-les-Martigues are now considered intrusive (Poplin *et al.* 1986: 42) and the same possibility has been raised for the ovicaprines from Dourgnes and Gazel (Rowley-Conwy 1995; Zilhão 1993: 48–9). The sheep from Gramari have been reidentified as *Ibex* (Poplin *et al.* 1986), and possible confusion with *Rupicapra* or *Capra pyrenaica* is suggested in other instances (Helmer 1992: 105; Zilhão 1993: 49). There is thus currently no strong case for a European domestication of sheep or goat (Rowley-Conwy 1995; Vigne 1994).

On the contrary, wild *Bos* and *Sus* are definitely present in Mesolithic Europe. Furthermore, the bones of domestic *Bos* from Argissa, dated from about 8800 BC, remained for a long while the earliest evidence of domestic cattle. It was thus logical to conclude that *Bos* had been domesticated in south-eastern Europe, not in the Near East (Boessneck 1962; Bökönyi 1974). However, early domesticated bovids and suids have since been discovered in the Pre-Pottery Neolithic B of the Levant (Helmer 1992) and on Cyprus (Briois *et al.* 1997), so

---

[6] Barker 1985: 71; Dennell 1983: 162; Guilaine 1976: 212. None of the sites they discuss is located in Greece, but if ovicaprines were present in Mesolithic Europe, they could obviously have been indigenous in Greece also, or introduced from Europe rather than from the Near East. A brief discussion of these instances is therefore relevant for Greece also.

that the chronological argument *per se* is no longer tenable. In addition, no transitional forms between wild and domesticated *Bos* and *Sus* have been recognized in Europe (Helmer 1992; Rowley-Conwy 1995; Tresset 1996; Vigne 1993). As a consequence, most specialists now consider that most if not all domestic animals, dog excepted, were introduced from the Near East (Boessneck 1985; Gautier 1990; Helmer 1992; Driesch 1987).[7] This position has received apparent confirmation by recent genetic data on the domestic *Bos* (Wuetrich 1994).

At any rate, the discussion should not revolve only around individual species: one must also take into account the *simultaneous* appearance of the main domesticated plants and animals. If *Bos* and pig had been domesticated in Greece or in Europe, why would they appear at exactly the same time as the Near Eastern plants and animals, never earlier or later? This simultaneity strongly argues for a common origin; since most other species are demonstratedly of Near Eastern origins, the probability is high that all were initially domesticated there and subsequently introduced to Greece and Europe.

However, the introduction of exogenous plants and animals does not necessarily imply important movements of *human* populations. As stated earlier, several authors recognize the Near Eastern origins of the domesticates but consider that they were introduced into Greece by simple exchanges with Near Eastern groups.

Can the Neolithic spread by 'cultural diffusion'?

According to the models of 'cultural diffusion', goods would have been passively exchanged between farming and non-farming groups, and the real 'actors' of the economic transformation would have been the local hunter-gatherers. This presupposes: first, that the local hunter-gatherers were in a position to acquire these goods; and second, that the Mesolithic population was dense enough to account, by itself, for the demographic expansion observed during the Early Neolithic. It also implies that one should observe a continuity in traditions, at least in the domains least affected by the economic transformations.

The exchange of livestock, seeds and techniques: an encyclopedic knowledge

In this context, too little thought has been given to the very notion of 'exchanges' and to their practicability. 'Exchanging' live domesticates is not like exchanging a pot, a joint of meat or an ornament. Acquiring live animals and plants implies at first a transformation of everyday life's organization. As emphasized by Zilhão (1993: 54), 'it might be difficult for hunter-gatherers to reconcile the possession of domestic animals with their traditional economy,

---

[7] Yet Bökönyi, for instance, always remained a strong advocate of a local domestication of *Bos* (Bökönyi 1989: 318).

given the incompatibilities in terms of mobility and timing of resource acquisition that such a possession might imply.'

From a longer term perspective, knowledge of the habitats, specific requirements, breeding, cultivation and storage techniques of the approximately
fifteen new domesticated species would have been needed if they were to
survive and develop, which they did! The current lack of evidence for a 'pre-
adaptative' stage means that such knowledge and skills would have had to be
acquired together with the plants and animals themselves. Knowledge, in
theory, can be transmitted and learned by words. However, the communication
of abstract knowledge requires far more common linguistic background than
the mere exchange of artefacts. Such bilingualism could only have been
acquired through repeated contacts, of which Mesolithic Greece offers no indications. The problem is different but even more acute for the empiric know-
how, the practical skills, which no discourse can teach and which must be learnt
through individual practice. In these conditions, I find it more than doubtful
that so many different plants and animals could have been introduced *simultaneously* in Greece without the active participation of the original farmers.

This becomes all the more evident if one considers that these new concepts
and techniques concern not only plants and animals, but every single domain
of activity, whether technical, social or ideological. Contrary to what would be
expected in the case of mere exchanges by local groups, archaeological evidence
for a continuity in traditions is even more invisible than the old 'invisible
colonists' of R. Dennell. In fact, almost every aspect of the earliest Greek
Neolithic points to a complete break in traditions.[8]

The production of chipped stone artefacts is now entirely oriented towards
the production of blades and bladelets.[9] Pressure flaking, unknown during the
Mesolithic, is now predominant. There is little, if any, typological similarity
between the Mesolithic and the early Neolithic assemblages. The 'microlithic
component', claimed as evidence for continuity (Milojčić 1962), is mostly an
artefact of analyses: the Neolithic 'microliths' are, more often than not, fragments of highly regular obsidian blades that were bound to break into trapezoidal fragments through trampling or use. The Early Neolithic trapezes
sharply differ from the Mesolithic ones: they are made on pressure-made blades
instead of flakes, the width to length ratio is reversed, and they bear rectilinear
truncations instead of sinuous ones.

The Neolithic polished axes, chisels or adzes have no local antecedents.
The bone industry of the early Neolithic requires an elaborate knowledge of
bone and antler working which cannot be traced to the scarce Mesolithic artefacts. Early Neolithic ornaments or decorated pieces differ sharply from the

---

[8] Since the Initial Neolithic, or 'Preceramic Neolithic', which will be discussed below (ch. 5), is
similar to the Early Neolithic (aside for the scarcity of sherds), the arguments presented here
remain valid whether or not an aceramic phase is considered to be present in Greece.

[9] The flakes being only by-products of this blade production.

scarce pierced pebbles and shell beads of the Mesolithic. The clay, polished shell and stone pendants, the 'earstuds', 'sling bullets' and stone seals with geometric patterns, have no local roots, but strongly recall Anatolian artefacts (Mellaart 1965: 115). All in all, as recognized by Dennell himself (Dennell 1984: 95), 'there are virtually no indications of any local antecedents' in the artefactual assemblage and no argument for continuity can be found at this level.[10]

On a more general level, the use and conception of space, as well as the nature of the settlements, are also in complete opposition. To the caves and short-term settlements of the Mesolithic can be opposed the permanent villages of the Neolithic. With the exception of Franchthi, Sidari and Theopetra, which will be discussed below, Neolithic sites are all founded on virgin soils in the large alluvial basins devoid of Mesolithic occupation.[11] Conversely, several regions with Mesolithic occupation, such as Attica, Argolid and Epirus, are especially poor in early Neolithic settlements. Even at Franchthi, the main focus of the settlement shifted during the Early Neolithic from the cave to the outside terraces, and probably also to a settlement that is now submerged in the bay (Gifford 1990).

Local processes: the demographic problems

Considering these sharp contrasts, the mere presence of a few sites occupied during both the Mesolithic and the Neolithic cannot by itself constitute an argument in favour of an indigenous process, nor of a local origin for the farming groups that settled in the alluvial basins. In this respect, the rarity of Mesolithic sites – less than a dozen, compared with the approximately 250 to 300 Early Neolithic sites recorded in Greece – casts further doubts on the possibility of an entirely indigenous process: 'Where the Mesolithic population appears to have been particularly sparse, as in Greece and the Aegean Sea, it is difficult to envisage a non-diffusionist model of the introduction of food production' (Lewthwaite 1986: 64; see also Nandris 1977a: 28).

Going beyond an impressionistic statement of population growth is difficult, however. The relative effects of the different biases affecting Mesolithic and Neolithic sites are difficult to evaluate. Neolithic sites are undoubtedly much easier to spot than Mesolithic ones, and should therefore be better represented. On the other hand, the duration of the Mesolithic was twice that of the Early Neolithic *sensu lato*, and the higher degree of mobility should have led to the

---

[10] As will have been noticed, Dennell radically altered his views on the origins of the Neolithic in the Balkans in his 1983 and 1984 publications.

[11] Tringham's early statement that the earliest agricultural communities of temperate Europe settled in areas where hunting/fishing populations were virtually absent (Tringham 1968: 67–68) may be partly challenged in temperate Europe (Nandris 1971b: 68), but so far holds true for Greece.

formation of many more sites per group than in the Neolithic. These difficulties could be offset by concentrating on regions that have been systematically surveyed but the differences in settlement patterns impede any valid estimation. There are several Mesolithic sites in the Argolid and Epirus, for instance, but the Early Neolithic is singularly rare in these areas. Conversely, the 116 EN1 and EN2 sites from eastern Thessaly (Gallis 1989) can be considered as a fair estimate of the minimum number of sites, but Thessaly is characteristically devoid of Mesolithic sites![12] Consequently, neither the general figures for Greece nor more precise regional ones allow a determination of population growth from the Mesolithic to the Neolithic.[13] Nevertheless, the order of magnitude of the differences in site numbers, as well as the increase in site surface, implying larger groups, is such that an influx of population clearly appears to be required.

An inescapable hypothesis: the presence of foreign colonists

In conclusion, a re-examination of the currently available data supports none of the basic assumptions underlying a purely local model of development. The sudden rise in the number and superficies of the settlements almost certainly required immigration of new populations. Domesticated plants and animals were introduced simultaneously, which required a diversified and complex farming knowledge that could not be casually transferred in the course of traditional exchanges. Finally, no element relating to ancient local traditions, either technical or symbolic, can be observed in these first farming settlements.[14] That farming was introduced by immigrant groups now seems an inescapable conclusion (Demoule 1993; Zvelebil 1995), even for earlier supporters of an indigenist model (Dennell 1992). In the case of Crete, where no pre-Neolithic occupation is known,[15] the case for external colonization is even stronger. It also demonstrates purposeful and planned displacements of populations (see below, p. 59). However, there is no need to evoke 'a massive influx of agricultural colonists', to borrow Dennell's terms. Several pioneer groups, of no more than a few hundred persons altogether, would have been sufficient to sustain the demographic expansion of the Early Neolithic, especially if they interacted and married with indigenous groups. Hunter-gatherers were indeed present in Greece at the time these first farmers arrived. Even though their respective territories do not seem to have overlapped at the start, the local Mesolithic groups could have undoubtedly come in contact with sedentary villagers and become instrumental in the spread of the Neolithic.

[12] Except for Theopetra on its northern margin and already out of the basin proper.
[13] Not even to mention the problem of estimating the population in each settlement!
[14] One exception, the arrowheads, will be discussed below.
[15] Broodbank and Strasser 1991; Cherry 1981, 1990.

Interactions between farmers and local hunter-gatherers

The significance and nature of interactions between farming communities and hunter-gatherer groups have been a recent focus of interest in Europe.[16] In Greece, such studies, when not mere a priori statements, can rely only on evidence from Franchthi and Sidari.[17] The available data from these two sites suggest that interactions between early farmers and local Mesolithic groups did occur, but through slightly different modalities. They also suggest that this phase of interaction was of a brief duration, and that major cultural breaks occurred in both sites *after* the initial introduction of domesticated species.

Continuity and discontinuity of occupation at Franchthi

Three successive phases must be considered at Franchthi: the Final Mesolithic (end of the eighth millennium cal BC), the Initial Neolithic,[18] which dates from the very beginning of the seventh millennium, and the Early Neolithic (Franchthi Ceramic Phase 1), which covers part of the seventh millennium.

The Final Mesolithic has already been described as a phase of sparse occupation, relying on the exploitation of wild resources and on the production of a crude, flake-based, lithic industry (see above, p. 30). The Initial Neolithic which follows is poorly represented: it is located in a restricted area of the cave, but marked by very clear changes in the sediments. Unfortunately, this 'Grey clay' stratum was severely disturbed by more recent occupations (Jacobsen and Farrand 1987; Perlès 1990a; Vitelli 1993). The scarce archaeological remains present an ambiguous and challenging set of characteristics, some clearly demonstrating continuity, others equally clearly alien to local traditions. Significantly, elements of both continuity and change cross-cut the various behavioural domains.

Continuity in the use of space is evidenced by the restriction of the occupation to the cave itself. It is also exemplified in the subsistence domain by a few seeds of the traditionally collected wild plant species (Hansen 1991), and even more strongly by the exploitation of marine molluscs, still dominated by *Cerithium vulgatum* (Shackleton 1988). Amongst the artefacts, the bulk of the chipped stone tools, a crude flake-based industry dominated by notches, endscrapers and denticulates, also points to strong continuities in tool production and use.

At the same time, however, radically new elements make their first appear-

---

[16] Chapman 1991; Dennell 1984, 1985, 1992; Lewthwaite 1986; Runnels and van Andel 1988; Sherratt 1990, 1995; Zvelebil 1986; Zvelebil and Dolukhanov 1991.

[17] The Mesolithic/Neolithic transition was probably represented also at Zaïmis, but the original publication (Markovits 1928, 1932/1933) and Tellenbach's (1983) subsequent study indicate, in my opinion, severe mixing of the strata. It is also represented at Theopetra, but not yet published.

[18] Also referred to as 'Preceramic Neolithic' or 'Franchthi Ceramic Interphase 0/1'.

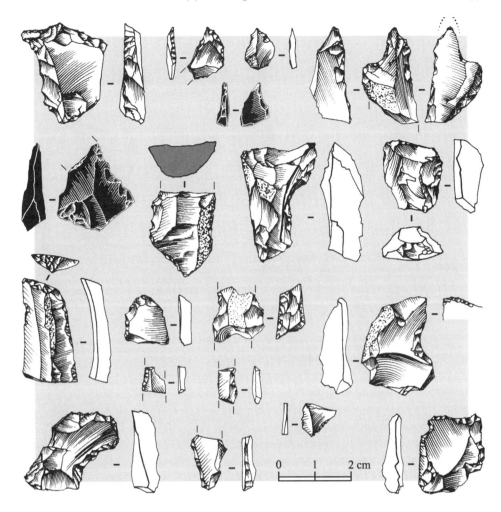

Fig. 3.1 Lithic tools of Mesolithic tradition, from the Initial Neolithic at Franchthi (after Perlès 1990a).

ance. The chipped stone tools now include a few pressure-flaked blades and elongated trapezes, manufactured on good quality raw materials, for which there is no evidence of a local production. A few sherds, which will be discussed below (see below, ch. 5), were found in the Initial Neolithic stratum. More significantly, domesticated ovicaprids suddenly become heavily predominant in the faunal assemblage (Payne 1975). *Sus* is scarce, and only a few bones could be attributed to either *Bos* or *Cervus*; given the small size of the sample and the fragmentary state of the bones, the status of *Bos* (?) and *Sus* could not be specified (Payne 1975). A few seeds of emmer wheat (*Triticum turgidum*, ssp. *dicoccum*) and two-row barley (*Hordeum vulgare*, ssp. *distichum*) indicate, in parallel, either that agriculture was practised or that grains were exchanged

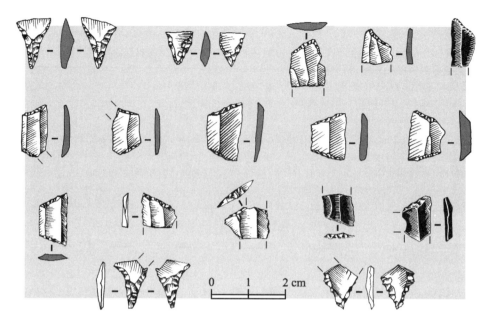

Fig. 3.2 Final Mesolithic transverse arrow-heads and Initial Neolithic trapezes from Franchthi.

(Hansen 1991).[19] *Triticum monococcum*, *Hordeum vulgare vulgare* and *Pisum*, usually associated with two-row barley and emmer wheat in Early Neolithic sites of Greece,[20] are absent. Although this might indicate the acquisition of only a subset of the cultivated plants already available, it could also be due to the very small size of the seed sample for this phase (see below, table 5.1). However, considering both the faunal and botanical data, there remains the possibility that the full set of domesticated species had not yet been acquired during this initial phase of contact.

The quantitative paucity of the data limits the possibility of interpretation. However, taken at face value, the mixture of traditional and innovative elements suggests the selective adoption through exchanges, by the local groups from Franchthi, of some aspects of the Neolithic economy and technology. At the same time, traditional activities and techniques were not completely abandoned, nor was the traditional, mobile, conception of space and life.

Despite this transitional phase, Franchthi cannot be taken as a case for a genuine process of local development from the Mesolithic to the fully established Early Neolithic (*contra* Chapman 1991). A more drastic change occurred later, between the Initial Neolithic and the Early Neolithic. At this time the densest occupation shifted from the cave to the Paralia (the seaside), different

---

[19] Since this Initial Neolithic at Franchthi is contemporaneous with fully farming sites elsewhere in Greece (see following chapter), the possibility that the cereals and pulses were obtained by exchange cannot be eliminated.   [20] See chapter 8 below.

species of seashells were collected, new domesticates were exploited[21] (Hansen 1991; Payne 1975; Shackleton 1988), the chipped stone production became oriented towards fine bladelets of obsidian and new ornaments and bone tools appeared. Even the few sherds from the Initial Neolithic, if not considered intrusive,[22] do not support an argument for continuity between the Initial Neolithic (or INT 0/1 in ceramic phasing) and the Early Neolithic (Franchthi Ceramic Phase 1, or FCP 1):

Whether or not pots were used when the 'gray clay' deposit in the cave and the Paralia deposits on basal red were being formed, the abrupt increase in quantity and variety of pottery in FCP 1 points to an abrupt change in cultural practices, and possibly to a hiatus in site use between INT 0/1 and FCP 1. (Vitelli 1993: 39)[23]

The evidence from Sidari

The available data from Franchthi thus suggests an initial phase of contacts between local hunter-gatherers and farming groups, followed – possibly after a short temporal hiatus – by a fully developed Early Neolithic, which no longer bears any evidence of local traditions. At Sidari, contacts and interaction appear to have taken place under slightly different conditions. Here again, three phases must be distinguished: a Mesolithic phase (level D), where the exploitation of sea resources was well represented; a first Neolithic phase (level C base), with evidence of incised pottery as well as of exploitation of sheep or goat; and finally, an 'Early Neolithic' stratum, characterized by a classic Adriatic 'Impressa' ware (Sordinas 1969, 1970). The two pottery-bearing strata were separated by a thick sterile layer (level C top). Contrary to what obtained at Franchthi, the earliest Neolithic at Sidari is in stratigraphic and sedimentological continuity with the Mesolithic. In addition, the presence of pottery is indisputable: it is abundant,[24] different from that of the upper level, and the sterile layer between the 'Incised pottery' stratum (C base) and the 'Impressa pottery' stratum (level C top) precludes any effect of trampling or contamination. On the other hand, the chipped stone industries of the Mesolithic and earliest Neolithic, re-examined by the author,[25] show a great stability in flint-knapping conceptions and techniques, even though the typology of the tools has been modified. No mention is made of bovid remains, polished celts, grinding implements or ornaments. It would seem that, as at Franchthi, the full set

---

[21] For instance *Triticum monococcum* and *Bos* (if it is confirmed that domestic *Bos* does appear, as suggested by preliminary studies in Early Neolithic levels only (Payne 1975)).

[22] See discussion see below, pp. 80ff.

[23] A hiatus is further confirmed by the marked sedimentological change between the two phases (see Jacobsen and Farrand 1987).

[24] A single small sounding yielded 374 sherds in this earliest pottery-bearing horizon (Sordinas 1969: 406), as opposed to 19 sherds for the 'gray clay stratum', in the cave of Franchthi (Vitelli 1993: 37–8).

[25] Jean-Paul Demoule and I are grateful to Professor Sordinas for granting permission to examine the material from Sidari.

of Neolithic artefacts and domesticates is not yet present in the earliest Neolithic phase.

The pottery from this level is original both from a technological and stylistic point of view (Sordinas 1969).[26] It is poorly fired or fired to a very low temperature, dissolves in water, and bears an unusual pattern of incised decoration. This could indicate that the groups inhabiting Sidari adopted the idea of ceramic-making but not the specific techniques found in contemporaneous productions. In this case, the adoption of some domesticates and a new technology by a local group with only minimal outside contacts seems plausible. Here again, however, there is no clear indication of a cultural continuity between the earliest Neolithic and the 'Early Neolithic' stratum. These levels are separated by a thick sterile layer, they are dated to several hundred years apart and contain quite different ceramics.

The most striking contrast between Franchthi and Sidari is seen in their sherd density: the Initial Neolithic at Franchthi corresponds, at most, to a period with very little use of pottery (see discussion below, ch. 5), while at Sidari, pottery is immediately well represented. This difference coincides with the differences in 14C dates between the two sites: whereas the Initial Neolithic at Franchthi is dated to the very beginning of the seventh millennium, the Mesolithic and earliest Neolithic of Sidari are dated to the mid-seventh millennium (respectively 7770 ± 340 BP[27] and 7670 ± 120 BP) (Sordinas 1969). Consequently, both the Mesolithic and the earliest Neolithic of Sidari could be contemporaneous with 'Early Neolithic' occupations of Thessaly, Macedonia and Argolid, where pottery was in regular use. Conversely, the dates of the Initial Neolithic from Franchthi correspond to the earlier, so-called 'Preceramic Neolithic' (ch. 5). It would seem, therefore, that the inhabitants of Sidari, cut off from the main early Neolithic settlements of eastern Greece by the Pindus Range, had maintained their traditional foraging for longer than those of Franchthi.

The role of Mesolithic groups in the development of farming

At both sites, however, idiosyncratic traits are rapidly lost after the initial phase of contacts. Here, as elsewhere, the influence of local hunter-gatherers on the development of farming communities would seem, on first reading, to be almost nil. The only possible exception relates, and this is certainly significant, to the cynegetic domain. Like their Mesolithic counterparts, the rare Early Neolithic presumed projectile heads are all transverse, rather than

---

[26] The unique character of the ceramic from this level recalls similar phenomena in Western Europe, where stylistically and technologically distinct wares have been attributed to hunter-gatherer groups, contemporaneous with the early Linearbandkeramik (Modderman 1982; van Berg 1990).

[27] Admittedly not a very informative date, given the standard deviation.

pointed. Despite technical and stylistic differences, this may indicate the influence of local Mesolithic hunting traditions, or Mesolithic hunters themselves,
on early Neolithic groups.[28]

Yet, this limited signature of the local Mesolithic traditions does not preclude Mesolithic groups playing a more fundamental and more subtle role in
the development of the Neolithic. Contacts did take place, and, as pointed out
by Dennell (1984: 102), nothing in the data from Greece suggests that they were
agonistic in nature: there are no obvious defensive structures in Early Neolithic
settlements (see below, ch. 9) and weapons are conspicuously rare. Instead,
Dennell underlines the advantages of peaceful relations between initial agricul-
turalists and their aboriginal neighbours, and notes that 'indigenous groups possessed considerable and potentially useful knowledge of the resources and
terrain' (1984: 109). Yet, he stresses that those groups would have been even
more important as a source of mates and labour, especially when new settlements were founded: 'agrarian communities would have gained through
tapping the breeding potential of their aboriginal neighbors' (Dennell 1984: 110;
see also Chapman 1991). Obviously, given the apparent low density of the
Mesolithic population, this second aspect is difficult to substantiate in Greece.
On the other hand, the exploitation of lithic raw materials probably provides a
good illustration of the value of local knowledge: Melian obsidian is present in
large proportions in the earliest Neolithic settlements as far north as Thessaly.
The new settlers may well have desired a regular supply of this unusually good
raw material, which is especially suited to pressure-flaking (Demoule 1993: 3).
It is uncertain, however, whether they knew the location of the Melian sources,
and doubtful that they would have taken the trouble to go to Melos themselves
to procure the obsidian (Perlès 1990b). On the other hand, some Mesolithic
groups were already exploiting the Melian sources and were quite accustomed
to the long voyages it required (Perlès 1990a). Exploitation of the obsidian and
possibly also of honey-flint sources could have given the local groups a valuable exchange good. Following Helms (1988), one may suggest that knowledge
of these exotic sources would have imbued the local Mesolithic groups with a
special prestige.

In a symmetrical way, local groups could have been attracted by many
aspects of the newcomers' way of life, which may have represented a 'perceived
change in status' (Dennell 1984: 110). More pragmatically, the Neolithic way
of life, particularly well adapted to this new environmental context, certainly
provided for a greatly improved subsistence basis (see below, ch. 8).

---

[28] This is not the only instance where local hunter-gatherers seem to have transmitted their
weapons and techniques of hunting to early farming groups: it has also been observed in western
Europe (Augereau 1993; Gronenborn 1990; van Berg 1990: 114, 119).

CHAPTER 4

FOREIGN COLONISTS: WHERE FROM?

Paradoxically, even if the Near Eastern origin of several domesticated species is now well established, the precise origin of the farmers themselves remains as elusive as ever. No satisfactory link has been established with any specific region of the Near or Middle East, and the most obvious candidate, western Turkey, has not yet provided evidence of Neolithic settlements as early as those of Greece.

The 'random' parallels between Greece and the Near East

Depending on whether one envisions a rapid or a slow movement of expansion, the reference sites for comparisons differ. According to the model of Ammerman and Cavalli-Sforza, western Anatolia and Greece belong to the same isochron. This would imply a roughly simultaneous expansion of farming groups in the two areas (Ammerman and Cavalli-Sforza 1984). Given the dates of the earliest Neolithic sites in Greece,[1] the best comparenda should thus belong to the Final Pre-Pottery Neolithic B (PPNB) and the Early Pottery Neolithic of the Near East, that is, to phase 5 (6900–6400 cal BC) in the general chronological scheme of Aurenche *et al.* (1987; see also Cauvin 1985).[2]

Yet, if the spread of farming groups were a slow movement, it would be more appropriate to turn to earlier sites, of the late phase 4 (late PPNB, *c.* 7600–6900 BC).[3] The Late PPNB was indeed qualified by Cauvin (1989: 19; 1994: 107ff.) as the period of the 'great exodus', when Initial Neolithic farming groups started to migrate out of the 'nuclear zone' and to colonize the Taurus, central Anatolia, the deserts and the temperate Mediterranean zone. This expansion corresponds chronologically with the development of second generation cereals (hexaploid wheats), the domestication of several pulses, the generalization of herding and the domestication of bovids.[4] Cauvin thus suggests that an

---

[1] See discussion of the radiocarbon dates in chapters 5 and 6 below.

[2] Reference sites for this period are, for instance: Byblos (EN), Ras Shamra VB, Çatal Hüyük VIII–II, Amuq A, Ali Kosh (Mohammad Jaffar phase) (Aurenche *et al.* 1987).

[3] With sites such as Abu Hureyra, Bouqras, Ramad, Ras Shamra VC, Abu Gosh, Çatal Hüyük XII–IX, Suberde, Jarmo (PPN), etc.

[4] However, the recent discovery of cattle bones at Shillourokambos on Cyprus, dated to the beginning of the eighth millennium, would put the domestication of cattle further back in time (Guilaine *et al.* 1997/8).

Fig. 4.1 Near Eastern sites mentioned in the text.

enlarged economic base allowed the exploitation of more diverse environments (Cauvin 1989: 20–1, 1994). Although demographic pressure has often been invoked to account for such territorial expansions, Cauvin convincingly shows that there is no evidence for a rise in population density. Instead, he attributes this expansion to the social and symbolic mutations defining the rise of the Neolithic, and to the 'conquering spirit' that characterized the Late PPNB. Consequently, the absence of a demographic surplus in the Near East can no longer be considered an argument against demic diffusion in Greece (see

Dennell 1983: 156, 1984: 101), and the colonization of Greece could be viewed as the ultimate episode of this general dynamic.[5] Aside from the Near Eastern domesticates, is there, however, sufficient artefactual evidence to support this hypothesis?

A long list of analogies between Near Eastern and Early Neolithic artefacts from Greece can be easily drawn. It includes schematized and figurative human figurines, 'sling bullets' or sling-stones, bone 'belt hooks', 'stamp-seals' with geometric patterns, stone 'earstuds', stone vessels, greenstone axes, sherd spindle whorls, and so forth. Amongst the many shared techniques is the use of mudbricks, plastered floors, buttresses, complex composite hearths, bone tool manufacture, pressure-flaking,[6] and so forth.

However, what is the significance of such lists?

First, some similarities pertain to categories of artefacts of widespread distribution, such as the sherd spindle whorls, the sherd-discs, the sling bullets, the axes and adzes. These artefacts show little stylistic, and sometimes technical investment, and it could be argued that their presence in both regions is the outcome of simple functional parallels. Even if a shared technical background is recognized, they can be of no use in defining precise cultural affinities.

Second, other analogies relate to techniques that imply a particular knowledge, or to stylistically distinctive artefacts such as the figurines, the 'bone hooks', the earstuds and the stamp-seals. The similarities are strong, and often very striking, but their interpretation in terms of direct filiation raises severe problems. The most striking formal analogies point alternately to the Levant, the Jordan valley or Anatolia, while similar artefacts from the Near East and Greece are sometimes dated from several centuries or even millennia apart. Even when the dating is fairly compatible, most artefactual analogies remain contextually isolated. For instance, the bone hooks, stamps-seals and earstuds from Thessaly undoubtedly strongly resemble those of Çatal Hüyük. On the other hand, the clustered houses, painted floors and walls, the plastic representations and human skulls within the houses, have no equivalent in Greece. The typology and, in large part, the technology of the chipped stone assemblages are conspicuously different, and some characteristic bone tools of Çatal Hüyük are absent from Greece (see Nandris 1971a and Sidéra 1998 about bone spoons, for instance).

Can we thus legitimately isolate one or two categories of artefacts or techniques, while ignoring others? Why do formal analogies cover such a wide time-span? Why do they alternately point to Anatolia, the Levant, the valley of the Euphrates or the Taurus? Why are they never 'complete'? Why, if the first

---

[5] 'Puisqu'il semble bien que nous soyons au point de départ d'un mouvement de diffusion appelé à outrepasser largement, dans tous les sens, les limites du Levan' (Cauvin 1989: 21).

[6] Which is rare or absent in the Levant proper, but well attested in eastern Anatolia (Cauvin M.-C. and Balkan-Atli 1996): it was recognized in particular at the base of the PPNB sequence of Çafer Höyük (Calley 1985), at Çayönü (Redman 1982) and is probably present at Çatal Hüyük (see Bialor 1962, fig. 4). It is also well represented in western Anatolia (personal observation).

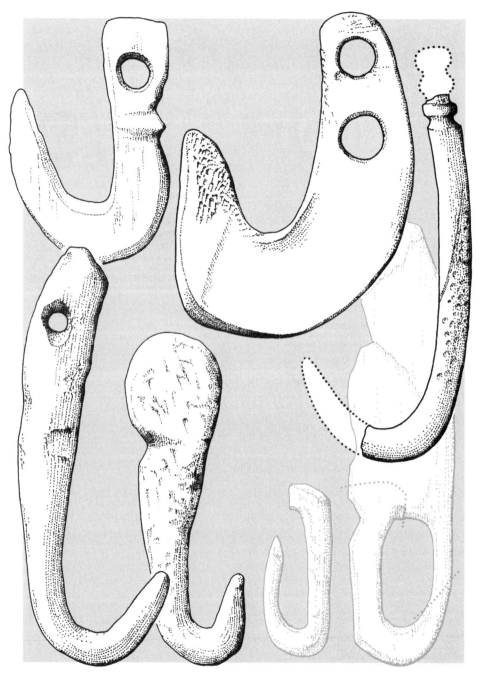

Fig. 4.2 Bone hooks from Çatal Hüyük (top left, bottom left and centre, after Mellaart 1965 and 1971) and Soufli Magoula (top row, centre and right, after Theocharis 1967). Preform of a bone hook from Nea Nikomedeia (bottom right, after Rodden 1965).

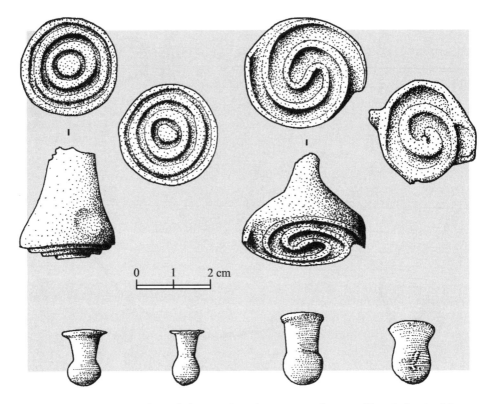

Fig. 4.3 Top row, from left to right: clay stamps from Tell Halula, Sesklo, Çatal Hüyük and Nea Nikomedeia (after Makkay 1984, Mellaart 1964, Molist Montaña 1996, Theocharis 1973). Bottom row, from left to right: stone earstuds from Hacilar, Soufli Magoula, Sesklo (after Mellaart 1965 and Theocharis 1967).

farmers did come from the Near East, are we unable to pinpoint a precise geographic origin (Cauvin 1994: 186)? Two different observations might be relevant at this point.

Farming expansion and the loss of cultural identity

First, the impact of the local Mesolithic groups, which appear to have been rapidly assimilated, would obviously have promoted original technical and stylistic characteristics in Greece itself. Yet, this alone cannot explain why the artefactual analogies with the Near East offer no coherent picture as regards the origin of these artefacts and their users.

Secondly, the search for strong and coherent cultural affinities may be misleading. The European 'Danubian' model of farming groups spreading over vast areas, while retaining a marked cultural and stylistic homogeneity, might be

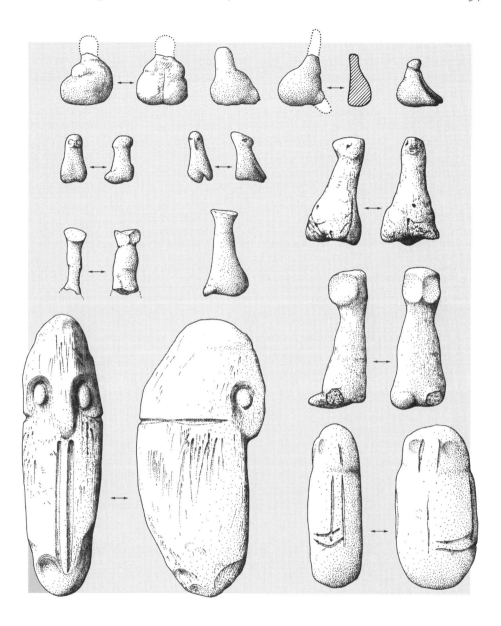

Fig. 4.4 Schematic figurines. Top row, from left to right: clay figurines from Beidha, Çayönü, Sesklo, shell figurine from Magoula Karamourlar. Second row, from left to right: clay figurines from Mureybet, Magoula Karaïkia, Soufli Magoula. Third row, from left to right: Mureybet, Nevalı Çori, Soufli Magoula. Bottom row: stone figurines from a Yarmoukian context to the left and from Sesklo to the right (after Balkan-Atli 1994, Cauvin 1978, Gallis and Orphanidis 1996, Stekelis 1972, Theocharis 1973, Theocharis 1976 (1977), Wijnen 1981).

the exception rather than the rule. As remarked by Cauvin, the vast movements of colonization of the PPNB are frequently accompanied by radical transformations in material culture, even when no local influences can be invoked.

Plus généralement, on constate que même sur des distances relativement faibles, les marqueurs culturels d'une diffusion par ailleurs bien établie paraissent rapidement contrebalancés par d'autres traits, qui ne sont pas seulement des rémanences des groupes indigènes acculturés . . . mais aussi le résultat d'une créativité autonome des nouvelles communautés installées . . . Ce renouvellement rapide des techniques et des données stylistiques au fur et à mesure que l'on s'éloigne de l'origine du courant de diffusion peut finir par poser de sérieux problèmes pour déterminer cette origine. (Cauvin 1989: 23–4)[7]

The Taurus and central Anatolia, where no Mesolithic is known, provide clear examples of such transformations in both material culture and symbolic representations. Closer to Greece, the Neolithic of Crete – an indisputable case of colonization – illustrates the same phenomenon: as soon as some agro-pastoral groups settled in Knossos, they developed a thoroughly original culture (Evans 1964, 1968, 1971), as though the colonization of new regions by small groups led to a 'founding effect' and a complete break and reorganization of traditions. This very process has recently been brought to light in Cyprus, where the earliest Preceramic level of Shillourokambos still retains strong Levantine affinities, rapidly lost in the following centuries (Guilaine *et al.* 1993, 1994, 1995, 1997/8). Greece might then be another example of a more general phenomenon whose causes remain obscure,[8] but which can inform us concerning the processes underlying these colonizations.

The colonization of Greece: an insular model

As noted earlier, artefactual analogies between Greece and the Near East display two main characteristics: they are *selective* on the one hand and *heterogeneous* on the other. The parallels that can be established with the Near East come from different regions and even different periods. This obviously makes no sense if one envisions the spread of the Neolithic as the regular advance of small communities, which founded new villages not far away from their previous settlements.

Runnels and van Andel have recently criticized, rightly in my opinion, this concept of a gradual 'wave of advance' of Neolithic groups, suggested some years ago by Ammerman and Cavalli-Sforza (1984). The data from the Near East

---

[7] Generally speaking, one can observe that even over relatively short distances idiosyncratic cultural features in an otherwise well-established diffusion are rapidly counterbalanced by other features. The latter are not only reminiscences of acculturated indigenous groups, but also the outcome of an autonomous creativity within the newly settled communities . . . This rapid renewal of techniques and styles, the further one gets from the origin of the diffusion, may end up creating severe problems for determining that origin. (Translation by the present author.)

[8] Cauvin suggests that a temporary pastoralist way of life would have led to the rapid loss of most sedentary techniques (Cauvin 1994: 219).

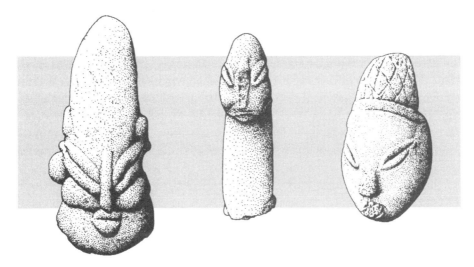

Fig. 4.5 'Coffee-bean' eyed figurines. Left: Sha'ar ha Golan (after Stekelis 1972). Centre: Magoula Karamourlar (after Theocharis 1973). Right: Achilleion (after Theocharis 1973).

undoubtedly support their thesis: that of rapid displacements of small groups over long distances, ultimately settling in favoured environments, far from their original homes. Here, again, the colonization of the Taurus and central Anatolia are good examples of long distance colonizations through inland routes. That of Crete, through a maritime route, is equally striking and probably more familiar. Let us recall that the islands of Karpathos and Rhodes, located between Turkey and Crete, have been well surveyed and that no Early Neolithic has ever been found.

Long-distance colonizations in early phases of the Neolithic[9] are thus exemplified by both inland and maritime routes, and both can be considered for the Greek mainland. No Early Neolithic site has yet been found in Greek Thrace or eastern Macedonia, the logical passage for an inland penetration from the Near East to Greece. This absence has often been discussed and most frequently attributed to the effects of deep alluviation. Indeed, Özdoğan recently found early Neolithic levels with monochrome and painted wares, strongly reminiscent of Thessalian 'proto-Sesklo' wares at Hoca Çesme, in Turkish Thrace (Demoule 1993; Özdoğan 1993). This settlement could theoretically constitute a good 'missing link' between Anatolia and Thessaly. However, the 14C date corresponds to a late phase of the Early Neolithic, requiring further evidence to support an early route of penetration through Turkish Thrace. In addition, the absence of sites further west, in Greek Thrace and Macedonia,[10]

[9] See also the foundation of Neolithic settlements in Mesopotamia (Huot 1994).
[10] Fotiadis 1985; French 1964, 1970; Grammenos 1991; Heurtley 1939; Renfrew 1986: 480.

remains a major problem. It is possible that substantial alluviation has obscured early Neolithic sites in northern Greece, especially if these were short-term occupations. Even Late Neolithic occupations can lie under 3 m of alluvial deposits, as demonstrated by the on-going excavation at Makri, in Thrace (Efstratiou 1993). A recently undertaken coring project in Greek Thrace may thus lead to substantial revisions in site distributions, although the easternmost part of Macedonia and Thrace would have been much less affected by alluviation (*idem*). Indeed, Palaeolithic tools have been recently found in eastern Macedonia (Efstratiou 1992; Kourtessi-Phillipakis 1992), showing that some at least of the most ancient prehistoric sites were not so deeply buried that they escaped recognition. As noted by Andreou and his collaborators (1996: 585):

The absence of sites (in Central Macedonia) cannot be accounted for by geomorphological factors alone, unless early sites were ephemeral and were located exclusively on the alluviated or eroded areas – an interesting possibility but one that clearly needs additional firmly dated regional geomorphic and archaeological support.

On the contrary, 'Early Neolithic' settlements are known in western Macedonia. However, in my opinion, the sites located north of the Aliakhmon display strong Balkanic affinities. I consider that they were probably settled from the north rather than from the south or the east, at a later date than Thessaly. As for Nea Nikomedeia, which is located north of the Aliakhmon and displays many similarities with Thessalian assemblages, its revised (later) dates do not support the possibility of a stopping point along an east–west axis of penetration.

Given this current absence of early settlements in north-eastern Greece, an island-hopping route, from the Anatolian or Levantine coasts to mainland Greece, can be considered as equally plausible (Davis 1992; Jacobsen 1993; Renfrew 1986: 480; Wijnen 1993: 326). Navigation has been known in Greece since the Late Pleistocene, as indicated by the presence of Melian obsidian in the Final Pleistocene and Early Holocene levels from Franchthi (Perlès 1979, 1987; Renfrew and Aspinall 1990). The colonization of islands such as Cyprus, Corsica and Sardinia, even before the Neolithic (Cherry 1981, 1990), confirms a widespread experience of navigation all over the Mediterranean and deliberate movements of colonization by sea routes (Broodbank and Strasser 1991; Jacobsen 1993).

In this respect, wide-ranging trade networks, which could have included obsidian, have been considered to be an important incentive to the development and spread of agriculture (Runnels and van Andel 1988). Although no artefacts are known to have been exchanged between Greece and the Near East during the early Holocene, it is probable that regular navigation in the Aegean, whether for fishing or procuring raw materials, led to a widespread knowledge of the landmasses that existed far away.

Unfortunately, there is no definite early Neolithic settlement on the islands between Anatolia and Greece that supports the model of maritime colonization either (Phelps 1981–2: 365). The only possible exception is the Cyclop's Cave on the islet of Youra near Alonyssos in the Sporades, but it has still to be fully investigated before any definite assessment can be made (Sampson 1996a, 1996b). Regardless of this, the absence of settlements on small islands is a general feature of the period, and may simply reflect the reluctance to settle in restricted environments with few potential resources. As emphasized by Davis (1992: 702):

> The recognition that the Aegean was being navigated long before the introduction of agriculture to Greece has obvious and important repercussions for how the process by which agriculture was spread from the Near East to Greece is viewed: clearly an absence of evidence for settlement in the earlier phase of the Neolithic in the Greek islands no longer requires us to postulate the existence of a more northern route of migration for Neolithic immigrants, for which there has been precious little evidence. The Aegean sea of the later Palaeolithic was navigable and navigated.

This scenario is reinforced by the newly developed hypothesis of intentional movements of colonization (Broodbank and Strasser 1991, Davis 1992). If the settling of groups in new regions was not the effect of more or less random dispersal movements but was the result of planned and organized operations, then long distances may have been crossed with no more than temporary halts between the points of departure and arrival. Brief stops on the islands, which would leave few archaeological remains, are therefore one possible explanation for the lack of Early Neolithic sites on the Aegean islands. This hypothesis is supported by the colonization of Crete, where, as pointed out by Broodbank and Strasser (1991: 237), 'the first domesticates at Knossos represent the full Anatolian-Balkan Neolithic faunal and floral "package" without any indication of filtering'. In their opinion, this indicates that:

> The maritime transfer of a nucleus of humans and domesticates suitably balanced to establish a farming community would demand sufficient planning to indicate a deliberate intent to colonize *somewhere* (whether the point eventually reached or not). Models of passive, accidental dispersion through stochastic or natural processes, that have been successfully applied to the colonization of islands by certain animal and plant species, may explain some early hunter-gatherer maritime dispersions . . . but present an implausible scenario for the movement of agriculturalists together with their attendant fauna and flora. (Broodbank and Strasser 1991: 237)

Since the current evidence for continental Greece also supports the simultaneous introduction of all domesticated species, the same argument could be applied there. There are no grounds to believe that the settlement of mainland Greece, either by land or by sea, can be compared with the slow movements of populations characteristic of the Cardial or Danubian 'waves of advance'. On the contrary, it seems to relate to these long-distance expeditions, well exemplified in the Mediterranean by the colonization of Crete, Corsica and the Balearic islands, for instance. Such a pattern of expansion may in fact explain why no precise geographical origin can be found.

Of multicultural pioneer groups

These long-distance expeditions were undoubtedly difficult and fraught with risk. Not everyone would have been willing to embark on such expeditions, and it is difficult to imagine that a whole Anatolian or Levantine community, for instance, would have suddenly decided to move to Thessaly. More plausibly, these pioneers were small groups of adventurous individuals, who did not carry, possess or choose to retain the whole technical and cultural heritage of their original communities.[11] This would account for the selective character of the analogies that can be brought to light.

They also may well have been of different geographical and cultural origins, which would account for the heterogeneity in the parallels that can be drawn between Greece and the Near East. There are many different sea routes linking the Levant and Turkey to Greece, and no reason to postulate a single origin once the progressive 'wave of advance' model has been dismissed. The Near and Middle East themselves provide ample evidence for numerous and repeated displacements of early farming groups in all directions during the Pre-Pottery Neolithic and the Pottery Neolithic (see Cauvin 1994; Huot 1994). Most historically documented cases of colonization also involve populations of various origins, and the fact that the Cretan Neolithic wheat is *Triticum aestivum*,[12] as opposed to *T. dicoccum* and *T. monococcum* on the mainland,[13] adds support to the hypothesis of different original homes.

Consequently, I suggest that the first pioneer groups in Greece would have been constituted of (adventurous) individuals, continuing the PPNB 'great exodus', and having followed different pathways from their original ancestral 'homes' up to Greece. Each would have retained some, but only some, of their most valuable symbols and techniques. This in turn would explain the selectivity and heterogeneity of the parallels that can be drawn between Greece and the Near East. There is, at any rate, no indication that the contribution of Anatolia would have been more important than that of the Levant, a fact that can easily be accounted for if the hypothesis of maritime displacements is retained.

[11] K. D. Vitelli suggested (*in litt.*, Nov. 1993) that if pioneer groups left because of social unrest, linked to early sedentism, they may well have deliberately altered all stylistic features in their material culture.
[12] Which is found in central Anatolia at Can Hasan III and Çatal Hüyük (Mellaart 1975: 97–8; Renfrew J. 1973: 202).
[13] *T. aestivum* has also recently been identified at Giannitsa, in western Macedonia. I take this to confirm that western Macedonia was not colonized from the south, but from the north, through the Rhodopes.

However, the list of 'random analogies' between Greece and the Near East is not so random! First, both regions are linked by strong structural analogies in terms of their subsistence base, settlement patterns and exploitation of space (Demoule 1993). Second, many technical analogies relate to architecture, a domain that has revealed itself as a strong expression of cultural identity (Coudart 1990, 1991, 1993). Finally, the most striking artefactual analogies concern objects that required special care in manufacture, such as the carved and polished stone seals, earstuds and stone vessels that were probably related to symbolic functions or to status. As though in a process of general reorganization and innovation in the domain of material culture, symbolic artefacts or symbol-ically loaded techniques remained more strongly linked to earlier traditions.

Once settled in mainland Greece, these various groups would have found natural conditions very similar to those of the Near East and that would have posed no problem of adaptation for the domesticated species. If only for demo-graphic reasons, the different groups would have merged together rapidly and progressively absorbed local Mesolithic populations. Then, new, idiosyncratic traditions would have emerged rapidly, a process that would have further obscured our search for origins.

However, an ambiguity remains concerning the precise period during which this colonization took place. Most parallels were drawn with Pre-Pottery Near Eastern settlements: does this imply that farming was introduced before pottery was in general use, and that the first Neolithic settlements in Greece were founded during a 'preceramic' period?

CHAPTER 5

THE EARLIEST NEOLITHIC DEPOSITS: 'ACERAMIC', 'PRE-POTTERY' OR 'CERAMIC'?

A biased debate

The status of the earliest Neolithic in Greece is still a matter of debate. Is it, as first suggested by Milojčić, an 'Aceramic', or 'Preceramic' Neolithic?[1] Is it, as claimed by many, a fully ceramic Early Neolithic? Or could it represent a discrete 'ceramic' phase that this simple dichotomy has thus far obscured?

Milojčić was the first to suggest that a 'Preceramic' Neolithic may have existed in Europe, as it did in the Near East (Milojčić 1952). His subsequent excavations at Argissa in Thessaly seemingly brought the confirmation he sought: the basal levels were conspicuously poorer in sherds than the overlying ceramic Neolithic levels (Milojčić 1955, 1956, 1959b, 1960; Milojčić *et al.* 1962). Soon after, Evans published the preliminary results of his excavations at Knossos, where he too recognized 'aceramic' levels at the base of a long Neolithic sequence (Evans 1964). Meanwhile, Theocharis had undertaken trial excavations at several other Thessalian sites, where he also uncovered levels that he considered 'Preceramic' (Sesklo from 1956 on, Soufli in 1958, Achilleion in 1961 and Gediki in 1962). He then published the first synthesis of the 'Preceramic' in Greece in his doctoral dissertation 'The dawn of Thessalian Prehistory'[2] (Theocharis 1967).

However, as early as 1970, Nandris reviewed the published evidence and firmly concluded, 'It is now clear that the Greek "PPN" is by no means aceramic' (Nandris 1970: 193). Gimbutas thus decided to resume excavations at Achilleion, one of the sites where Theocharis had identified 'preceramic' deposits. After two seasons, she reached a definite conclusion: 'One of the primary objectives of our investigations at Achilleion was to find the posited aceramic or "Pre-Pottery" period of the Neolithic of southeastern Europe. We have negatively succeeded: it does not exist at this site' (Gimbutas 1974: 282). Unshaken, Theocharis continued to publish brief reports of his 'preceramic'

---

[1] The three terms: 'aceramic', 'preceramic' and 'pre-pottery', have been used alternately. Milojčić chose 'Preceramic' in the title of the Argissa monograph and Theocharis (1967: 171) preferred it to others because the levels it referred to were stratigraphically older than the ceramic Early Neolithic levels. On the other hand, Evans, more cautious about the status of this phase, chose the more neutral 'aceramic' that does not bear chronological implications. I shall here use the term 'pre-pottery' to refer to levels that contain small baked-clay artefacts, such as figurines, but no pots.　　[2] Published in Greek as *I Avgi tis Thessalikis Proïstorias*.

excavations at Sesklo, whereas most authors followed Nandris' and Gimbutas' conclusions (Dennell 1984; Lichardus and Lichardus-Itten 1985; Payne 1975). This scepticism was most recently expressed by Bloedow (1991, 1992/3) after a thorough critical evaluation of the stratigraphy and associated finds from Sesklo, Argissa and other supposedly 'aceramic' sites: 'A re-examination of the evidence has shown that the thesis of an aceramic cultural phase in Greece involves serious problems . . . When all the above factors are combined, the case for an aceramic cultural phase in Greece appears to have little to support it' (Bloedow 1991: 43). At the same time, however, Greek scholars were again taking up the defence of the 'preceramic' phase in Greece (Kotsakis 1992; Protonotariou-Deïlaki 1992) and the most recent synthesis on the prehistory of northern Greece has left the problem open (Andreou *et al.* 1996).

If this debate has gone on unabated for twenty-five years, it is clearly because it raises, implicitly or explicitly, questions more fundamental than the mere presence of pottery. To some extent, the status of the sherds can indeed be considered secondary: for most of its partisans, what a 'preceramic' phase demonstrated was an *in situ* development of a productive economy in Greece (Theocharis 1973b: 31). Denying its existence was denying that such a process had occurred in Greece:

Ces éléments [faune et plantes domestiques], en contradiction complète avec les sites pré- ou protonéolithiques du Proche-Orient prouvent qu'une économie productrice déjà purement néolithique existait bien à Argissa . . . Malgré tout, l'appelation d'un 'Néolithique précéramique' continue d'être employée. Or, cette appelation implique l'idée d'une évolution à partir d'un Néolithique sans céramique, dont on tire parfois argument pour prouver l'existence d'une genèse locale de la civilisation néolithique grecque (Theocharis 1973) (Lichardus, in Lichardus and Lichardus-Itten 1985: 231).[3]

The debate was thus largely semantical and ideological. Semantical because everyone plays with the ambiguity between 'pre-ceramic', that is, devoid of baked-clay artefacts, whatever their nature, and 'pre-pottery', that is, devoid of baked clay pots, and used the presence of figurines for instance to deny the absence of pottery. But more important, certainly, are the ideological implications. Lichardus, for instance, rejected the term 'pre-ceramic' in Greece not because he specifically denied the absence of pottery, but because he denied the local origin of the Neolithic in Greece.

However, there is no logical necessity to relate a 'preceramic' phase with a local process of Neolithization: a 'preceramic phase', *sensu stricto*, may have also existed in Greece if the latter was settled by farmers before pottery was in use. Even though we have already argued that the Neolithization process was not

---

[3] 'These elements [domesticated plants and animals], in complete contradiction with the pre- or protoneolithic settlements of the Near East, demonstrate that there was a characteristic Neolithic production economy at Argissa . . . Nevertheless, the term "Aceramic Neolithic" continues to be used. This term conveys the notion of an evolution starting from a Neolithic phase devoid of pottery, and sometimes serves to prove the local genesis of the Greek Neolithic civilization.'

entirely indigenous, the question remains: when were the first farming settlements founded in Greece? Did the first farmers bring with them a knowledge of pottery-making, or was pottery-making an independent development in Greece?

The data on which we can rely come mostly from old excavations, some of which were not even fully published. Pending new and specifically oriented excavations, the problem will clearly not be solved (Andreou *et al.* 1996). Yet, I believe it can be clarified by considering three distinct questions:[4]

(a) Are these 'aceramic' deposits homogeneous in terms of content and features?
(b) What is the status of the sherds they contain?
(c) Do they constitute a *chronological phase*, earlier than the Early Neolithic? If so, what relation does it bear to the 'Pre-Pottery Neolithic' of the Near East?

The sites and excavations

The existence of an 'aceramic' or 'preceramic' phase was established on the basis of deposits conspicuously poor in pottery sherds found at the bottom of a few Neolithic sequences. Such deposits are not common, even when the sterile has been reached.[5] So far, they have been claimed at Argissa, Gediki, Soufli Magoula and Sesklo in Thessaly, at Dendra and Franchthi in the Argolid, and in level X at Knossos in Crete.[6]

A brief presentation of each site will be given first. Their homogeneity, in terms of content, will be examined through the economic remains, architectural features and artefactual remains. I shall then consider the problem of the pottery and the status of the sherds, before discussing the dates and the chronological relations with the 'Pre-Pottery Neolithic' of the Near East.

---

[4] Bloedow (1991, 1992/3) has recently addressed the last two questions but his conclusions differ from mine; readers are advised to read both sets of publications. On the other hand, I will not refer much to Tellenbach's synthesis on the Balkan Preceramic (Tellenbach 1983), which I do not find reliable.

[5] But this does not constitute an argument against the existence of a preceramic phase: settlements were founded progressively during the Early Neolithic, and not all sites can be expected to yield a complete sequence.

[6] Milojčić (1960) and Theocharis (1958, 1961/2) mentioned other possible 'preceramic' sites based on surface recovery. 'Preceramic' levels have also been suggested in some Cretan caves (see Cherry 1990) and in the cave of Sarakinos, in Boeotia, underlying Late Neolithic levels (Touchais 1978: 696; Spyropoulos 1973: 263–4). Without any detailed report or conclusive evidence, we shall not discuss these sites. A preceramic phase has also been recognized by Tellenbach at Zaïmis, in Attica. This was based on the identification by Boessneck of domesticated species in the faunal remains of the (sherdless) stratum VII (Tellenbach 1983: 38). I consider, however, that the lithic industries demonstrate major contaminations and mixing throughout the sequence and Tellenbach himself recognizes that the lithics from stratum VII may in fact derive from stratum VIII. It is thus possible that the bones also are intrusive. Finally, E. Protonotariou-Deïlaki (1992) has added Lerna to the list; she probably refers to the bottom of the 'large cavities going down to 0.60 m' mentioned by Caskey in his report of the 1956 excavations (Caskey 1957: 160), or to the bottom of pit DB and BE (Caskey 1958: 138, 139) that yielded only 'a few bits of pottery' (Caskey 1957: 160) or 'almost no sherds' (Caskey 1958: 139). Caskey himself interprets them as clay extraction pits, later reused as rubbish pits.

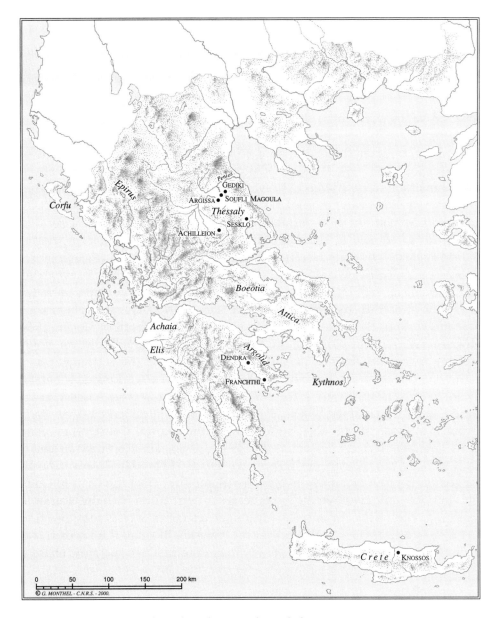

Fig. 5.1 Sites attributed to the Initial Neolithic.

Knossos

Though the Neolithic of Knossos may ultimately have a different origin than that of mainland Greece (see above, ch. 3), its 'preceramic' levels pose similar problems. In addition, if Crete was indeed settled during a preceramic phase, as was Cyprus, then there is no reason to reject a priori that the same could have occurred on the mainland.

During his 1957–60 excavations in the Central Court of Knossos, Evans recognized a 10 to 30 cm thick 'aceramic' stratum (stratum X) that lay directly on the bedrock (Evans 1964, 1968). He claimed to have found it again in 1969–70, in two small soundings (ZE and X) where the 'aceramic' deposits were supposed to have reached almost 2 m thick (Evans 1971). Sounding X was located at the southernmost point of the Central Court, and ZE not far away, to the south.

The excavated area in the Central Court was about 55 square metres; it yielded evidence of a fully Neolithic economy, with hexaploid wheat, emmer, barley, domesticated ovicaprids, pigs and cattle. The skeletons of seven children were uncovered during the excavation. Apart from pits and post-holes, there were no architectural remains. Stone axes, chert, obsidian and bone tools were present, but Evans noted the 'complete absence of pottery' (Evans 1964: 140), at least in the lower half of the deposit. He was cautious, however, not to overemphasize the absence of sherds and interpreted the settlement as a 'camp', suggesting that the excavated area represented a 'working area' outside the main settlement (Evans 1968: 267). The situation is more obscure in the small X and ZE soundings, where several stratified mudbricks and stone walls, identical to those of the 'EN1' stratum IX of the Central Court, were recognized. Some sherds were present at the top of the 'aceramic' stratum in sounding X, which Evans considered as intrusive (Evans 1971: 102). However, he did not completely rule out an equivalence with stratum IX of the Central Court (EN1), although he favoured the hypothesis of a correlation with the 'aceramic' stratum X. One of the reasons was the unique character of one of the two fired clay figurines discovered in these deposits. However Bloedow, for his part, considers them as one more reason to doubt the existence of an aceramic phase at Knossos (Bloedow 1991: 39–40).

Gediki

A trial trench was dug by Theocharis in 1962 at Gediki (also transliterated Gendiki or Ghediki), 10 km east of Soufli in eastern Thessaly (Theocharis 1962b: 73–6). At the bottom of the trench, a small level of circa 0.20 cm, devoid of pottery, was separated from the first EN (Early Neolithic) pottery-bearing level by a sterile layer of yellow river sand, 6 cm thick. Gediki is the only site where a sterile layer separates the so-called 'preceramic' level from the EN levels, though a hiatus can also be invoked at Franchthi (see *supra*, p. 49). No sherds were found in the 'preceramic' level, as opposed to 150 sherds in the overlying 'Frühkeramikum level'. Carbonized seeds of domesticated wheat, barley and lentils were present (Renfrew J. 1966). Although the exact dimensions of the trench are not recorded, it must have been very small (see section in Theocharis 1962b: 74). Sampling effects cannot be ruled out, and larger excavations may have revealed the presence of pottery in the basal stratum.

Soufli Magoula

In 1958, Theocharis opened two small trial trenches at Soufli Magoula, on the bank of the Penios river (Theocharis 1958: 78–6, 1962b: 82–3; Wijnen 1981: 61–2). Under the ceramic EN, he identified a fairly thick stratum (*c.* 1 m), overlying the bedrock and bearing no pottery, which he divided into three sublevels (see section in Wijnen 1981: 61). Beaten clay floors separated the different building phases of this 'Pre-pottery' Neolithic stratum. No sherds were found, as opposed to *c.* 250 in the EN1/EN2 levels (levels 7–10). The latter included 95 tiny body fragments (Wijnen 1981: 61–2), which indicates careful excavation techniques. A wild olive stone was recovered in the lowest non-pottery level, together with domestic wheat and pulses (Renfrew J. 1966). Considering the small size of the excavations, the 'aceramic' stratum at Soufli poses the same problem as at Gediki. Indeed, Gallis undertook rescue excavations several years later at Soufli, about 60 m away from Theocharis' soundings, and did not find comparable deposits: a late Early Neolithic directly overlaid the sterile basal sediments (Gallis 1975, 1982). However, due to the distance between the two excavated areas, the possibility of horizontal variations in the occupation of the settlement should not be ruled out.

Sesklo

Theocharis investigated the 'aceramic' levels of Sesklo between 1956 and 1968.[7] He identified 'aceramic' strata at the base of several trenches on the Acropolis as well as in his 'sector C' (or *Gamma*), located opposite the streambed to the west of the Acropolis and at a similar absolute altitude. Unfortunately, due to the premature death of D. Theocharis, the final publication of those findings has not yet appeared.

According to preliminary publications,[8] 'aceramic' levels were reached in seven different trial trenches mostly on the north-eastern side of the Acropolis. All were of unspecified, but small size, due to the preservation of overlying

[7] Tsountas, in his earlier excavations at Sesklo, had not recognized an 'aceramic phase' but Theocharis claimed that it was present at the bottom of Tsountas' 'Old section', in levels not reached at the time (Theocharis 1957).

[8] Theocharis 1957, 1962a, 1962b, 1962c, 1963a, 1963b, 1965, 1966a, 1966b, 1967, 1968a, 1968b, 1971, 1972a, 1972b, 1973a, 1973b, 1973c, 1976a, 1976b, 1977; Wijnen 1981. See Bloedow 1991 for a good synthesis.

Neolithic buildings. Where indicated, the thickness of the stratum varied from 0.3 m to more than a metre. A similar deposit was excavated in trench 2 of sector C; it did not yield a single sherd, although the sediment was sieved, unlike that from the Acropolis trenches. An oval pit of approximately 4 m × 3 m, dug into virgin soil, was uncovered there and yielded bone and stone implements together with faunal remains (Wijnen 1981: 27).

The total area represented by the 'Aceramic' excavations is difficult to estimate, but by combining the indications given by Wijnen (1981) and Theocharis (see above, note 18), it appears that it was over 60 square metres. This is little compared to the total excavated area and, in several other trenches, especially below the Acropolis (sectors A, B, D and E), a ceramic-rich Early Neolithic directly overlaid the sterile soil. As pointed out by Bloedow (1991), this 'aceramic stratum' poses two major problems:

> (a) Does it constitute, at least on the NE side of the Acropolis, a real *stratum*, that is, a continuous deposit with homogeneous geological and archaeological characteristics? Or does it represent only localized deposits, in between trenches where the pottery EN directly overlaid the sterile soil?
>
> (b) Can it be considered as 'aceramic', since sherds are present, at least on the Acropolis, in the 'uppermost' part of the stratum from most trenches. Or are the sherds intrusive?

Argissa

The lowest levels at Argissa, on the bank of the Penios near Larissa, were excavated by Milojčić on a surface of 60 square metres. Under ceramic EN deposits, he uncovered a 30 cm thick layer that was conspicuously poorer in sherds but not in lithic, bone and faunal remains. It overlaid a series of pits and post-holes dug into virgin soil and equally poor in potsherds (Milojčić *et al.* 1962; see also Bloedow 1991). The faunal and seed remains, studied respectively by Boessneck (1962) and Hopf (1962), indicate a fully Neolithic economy based on the exploitation of domesticated species. Besides rather abundant stone and bone tools – which, contrary to Milojčić's claims, do not differ significantly from EN assemblages – a sling bullet, an earstud (or ear-plug) and a 'fish hook', all apparently of fired clay, were found in two of the pits. Even more problematic is the presence of sherds in the 'preceramic stratum', one of the major arguments against the existence of such a phase. Milojčić himself considered them as intrusive (see below, pp. 81–82).

Achilleion

Achilleion requires brief mention since it played a crucial role, first in the affirmation, then in the refutation of an 'aceramic' phase in Greece. Gimbutas resumed excavations at Achilleion in 1973 and 1974, after Theocharis had claimed to find, during trial excavations in 1961, 'aceramic' deposits at the base of the stratigraphy (Theocharis 1962b: 71–3, 1967: 74–5). Gimbutas herself did not find comparable deposits and concluded that no 'preceramic' existed at the site (Gimbutas 1974: 282). However one may remark that: (a) no later excavation was conducted where Theocharis had located his trial trenches (southwest of square E); (b) the trenches nearest to Theocharis' excavations (E, F1, F2, F3 and Test Pit South) did not reach the sterile deposits; and (c) the sterile deposits were only reached in a limited part of squares A and B, about 30 metres away from Theocharis' trenches (Gimbutas *et al.* 1989, chs. 1 and 2). The demonstration would have been stronger had a complete stratigraphy been excavated, down to the sterile layers, where Theocharis thought he found 'aceramic' deposits. There is indeed no reason to assume that the surface occupied by the earliest settlement was comparable in size to that of later periods. It may well have been, on the contrary, substantially smaller.

Franchthi

The 'Initial Neolithic' at Franchthi, already discussed for its associated Mesolithic and Neolithic features, had been tentatively qualified as 'Preceramic' in very early reports (Jacobsen 1969: 376). This 'gray clay' stratum constitutes a clearly identified geological and archaeological deposit in the cave, interstratified between Mesolithic and ceramic-rich Neolithic strata (Jacobsen and Farrand 1987). On the contrary, the 'basal red' stratum of the Paralia that yielded rare sherds and lithic artefacts will not be discussed here (*contra* Vitelli 1993, ch. 5) since it is dated from the Late Pleistocene (Wilkinson and Duhon 1990). The cultural artefacts cannot be contemporaneous with the deposition of the sediment and must have been introduced by trampling or other contamination sources (Brochier J.-E. 1994; Nielsen 1991; Villa and Courtin 1980).

The 'gray clay' stratum was uncovered in four adjacent trenches of the FF1/FA sector within the cave (FF1, FAN, FAS and A). It constitutes a continuous deposit over an extent of about 16 square metres, though locally disturbed (Jacobsen and Farrand 1987). It was also present in the HH1 sector (trenches H2A, H, H pedestal, H1A and H1B) but was there heavily contaminated by later disturbances (Jacobsen and Farrand 1987; Vitelli 1993). Consequently, this area will not be considered here. As mentioned previously (see ch. 2), domesticated animal bones and a few cultivated cereal seeds appear for the first time in this deposit. It also contained a few sherds, which will be discussed below.

Dendra

Dendra is located in the village of the same name in the Argolid, and was excavated in 1976 and 1977 by E. Protonotariou-Deïlaki. A preliminary report was published in 1992 (Protonotariou-Deïlaki 1992). Dendra is a very peculiar site, which consists of fifteen large pits. Two shallow pits, interpreted as 'violations', contained EN1 material, including pottery. All the others were deep pits dug into the soft local limestone,[9] with convex walls, irregular delineations, lateral 'niches' and irregularly shaped floors; the pits touched each other, and two of them communicated by an underground opening. They contained clay 'hearths' and 'sills', fragments of large unbaked bricks and stone slabs that are claimed to have been used for inner walls. The excavator interpreted these pits as semi-subterranean dwellings that recalled caves or rock shelters by their irregular shapes. They would have been covered by domed roofs of small branches and clay, supported by posts. According to the report, only one of the large pits yielded some EN1 pottery; the others contained only stone tools of flint and obsidian,[10] bone tools, a few celts, and stone sling bullets. Amongst the rarer items were a fragment of a stone vessel, a clay figurine, earstuds and a possible fragment of a clay hook. Seed remains and animal bones demonstrate a fully Neolithic economy, with ovicaprids predominant in the fauna.

The interpretation of Dendra is difficult without a detailed report of the site and the finds. Contrary to all other 'preceramic' sites, the Dendra pits were not overlaid by a well-defined Early Neolithic stratum that would demonstrate their relative anteriority. Furthermore, these deep cavities have no close equivalent in Greece. By their shape and dimensions, they recall extraction pits. The scarcity or absence of pottery could be related to the nature of the activities carried out on the site, rather than to a chronological phase.[11] Yet, the few ornaments and the figurine are difficult to explain in this context, unless the extraction pits were associated with a settlement. There is, however, no way this hypothesis can be confirmed with the presently available data: it is impossible to tell whether any exploitable resource was present at the site and the hypothesis of subterranean dwellings cannot be ruled out, despite the exceptional depth of the pits. Radiocarbon dates may help clarify the age and hence the nature of the site. Meanwhile, the few indications given by the archaeological remains suggest an early – if not necessarily 'preceramic' – date: the published 'figurine' (pl. 17, g) and the presence of earstuds (not illustrated) would suggest a date within the first half of the Early Neolithic.

Pending a fuller report and radiocarbon dates to determine the exact date and nature of the site, we shall refrain from referring to the Dendra data in the following discussions.

---

[9] The depth is not specified in the report. My recollection, based on a visit to the site after the excavations, is that they reached 1.5 m or more.

[10] According to the author, the chipped stones recall those of the Palaeolithic and the Mesolithic; this observation is not supported by the material I saw on display in the Museum of Nafplion. All pieces were typical Neolithic obsidian and honey-flint blades of high quality, including several sickle blades.

[11] The extreme scarcity of sherds in the vast Middle Neolithic mining field of Jablines, which was very carefully excavated, is a good example of this situation (Bostyn and Lanchon 1992).

Characterization and homogeneity of the 'pre-pottery' deposits

The economic basis

The economic basis in all these deposits is clear: it is a fully Neolithic economy based on agriculture and herding, and is broadly comparable in all sites.

Cultivated cereals and pulses predominate in the seed assemblages (see table 5.1). An intriguing aspect of the distribution of cereals is the overwhelming predominance of bread-wheat (*T. aestivum s. l.*) at Knossos, where it amounts to more than 90 per cent of the seeds. Due to a lack of comparative data in Crete, it is impossible to say whether this reflects a specialized agricultural system on Crete, or the chance discovery of an unusually large, pure cache. The presence of bread-wheat, unknown in the small assemblages from the mainland sites, is not the unique feature at Knossos: the lithic and ceramic assemblages from Knossos also bear little relation to those of the mainland (Evans 1964, 1968, 1971). This reinforces the hypothesis that the Knossos settlers were of a different origin than those of Thessaly or southern Greece.

Except at Franchthi, which was already discussed (in ch. 2), almost all the domesticates exploited during the Neolithic are present at each site: sheep, cattle, pigs and dogs for the animals, einkorn, emmer, six-row barley and lentils for the plants (Hansen 1991; Hopf 1962; Kroll 1981, 1983, 1991; Renfrew J. 1966). The only species that has not been identified with certainty in the faunal assemblages is goat (table 5.2). At Argissa at least, von den Driesch (1987: 2) considers this could be due to the high number of small unidentified mammal bones and to the lack of sophisticated methods for distinguishing sheep and goat at the time of the study.

In all cases, however, faunal and floral remains are indistinguishable from Early Neolithic ones. They indicate a fully Neolithic subsistence basis: no 'transitional stage' can be identified, at least in the newly founded Neolithic settlements. This, as discussed in the preceding chapter, demonstrates the introduction in Greece of a fully formed farming economy, and this might support an 'Early Neolithic' date for these deposits. However, a fully developed Neolithic economy also characterizes the late PPNB of the Near East (Cauvin 1997); the subsistence basis does not allow any specific conclusion regarding the 'aceramic' status of these deposits.

Architectural remains

Most of the 'aceramic' levels are characterized by the presence of pits or depressions and by the absence of any clear elevated architectural remain. In this respect they present a striking homogeneity.

It will be recalled that Dendra was remarkable due to its large pits, interpreted by the excavator as semi-subterranean dwellings. At Sesklo also, Theocharis

Table 5.1 *Seed remains from the Initial Neolithic levels*

	Gediki (Renfrew 1966)	Sesklo, samples 1 and 2 (Renfrew 1966)	Sesklo (Kroll 1983)	Argissa (Kroll 1983)	Argissa (Hopf 1962)*	Soufli (Renfrew J. 1966)	Franchthi (Hansen 1991)	Knossos, stratum X (Evans 1968)
Triticum dicoccum (= *T. turgidum* ssp. *dicoccum*)	44 (62%)	6	A	A	present	present	14	10 (c. 0.3%)
Triticum monococcum	2 (3%)		B	B	present			10 (c. 0.3%)
Triticum aestivum s.l.								2900 (c. 91%)
Hordeum vulgare vulgare			B	D	present**			11 (c. 0.3%)
Hordeum vulgare ssp. *distichum* (= *Hordeum distichum*)	9 (12.5%)	1	(present according to Kroll 1991)				3	
Hordeum vulgare ssp. *distichum* var. *nudum*	1 (1.5%)							15 (c. 0.4%)
Pisum sp.	5 (7%)	5	(present according to Kroll 1991)					
Vicia/Lathyrus sp.								
Vicia sp.	4 (5.5%)					present	2	
Vicia ervilia			D	A				
Lens sp.			D	A			6	210 (c. 6.5%)
Lens culinaris (= *Lens esculenta*)	4 (5.5%)		(B according to Kroll 1981, for combined samples from Sesklo and Argissa)					
Malva sp.			(D according to Kroll 1981 for combined samples from Sesklo and Argissa)					52 (c. 1.5%)

Taxon						
Ficus carica				B		B
Rubus fruticosus				D		
Prunus amygdalus					1	
Pistacia atlantica	2 (3%)		74	A		
Quercus sp.	1		(present according to Kroll 1991)		1	
Olea					probably present	
Celtis cf. *tournefortii*					1	
Sambucus ebulus				D		D
Lithospermum arvense					1	
Cruciferae sp.					3	
Avena sp.				D		
Lolium temulentum				D		D
Alkanna sp.					4	
Portucala oleracea				D		
Graminae				B		D
Chenopodiaceae				B		A
Polygonaceae				D		D
Fabaceae				D		D
Capparidaceae				B		
Cyperaceae				B		
TOTAL	71	10	209	65	35	>3200

Notes:

Sesklo and *Argissa*: A: present in all samples. B: present in ⅔ of the samples. C: present in half of the samples. D: present in less than half of the samples. Botanical remains from Franchthi (Hansen 1991), and probably from Sesklo and Argissa (Kroll 1983), were recovered through flotation, though precise archaeological context is unavailable. The other samples were hand-picked.

* Plant remains from level XXIX (the 'Hut') have not been included since the level is Early Neolithic. ** Identified in the original publication as *Hordeum vulgare* L. *polystichum* var. *tetrastichum*.

Table 5.2 *Faunal remains from Initial Neolithic strata, in number of rests*

	Knossos Stratum X	Franchthi	Argissa	Sesklo C	Dendra
Sheep/goat	332 75%	predominant	1820 84%	58 66%	predominant
Sus	82 18.5%	present in small quantity	221 (includes 5 wild?) 10%	10 11%	
Bos	29 6.5%	?	114 (includes 11 wild?) 5%	21 23%	
Canis	1 0.2%	?	4		
Red deer		?	4		
Roe deer			3		
Lepus	1 0.1%		8		
Vulpes		present in small quantity	1		
Birds		present in small quantity	5		
% Domestic	c. 100%		99%	100%	
% Wild	<0.1%		1%	0%	
Total identified	445		2195	89	
Total number of fragments	510		3507	?	

Source: After Higgs and Jarman 1968 (Knossos), Payne 1975 (Franchthi, partial sample), Boessneck 1962 (Argissa), Schwartz 1981 (Sesklo).

found numerous 'pits' and 'post-holes' and he refers to five 'pit-dwellings' on the Acropolis. In addition, he mentions 'foundation trenches' around two of the dwellings, in trenches 2 and T (Wijnen 1981: 11). In sector C, another 'pit-dwelling' *c.* 3 m × 4 m was also uncovered. The archaeological remains were concentrated within this large pit; next to it was a mass of 'amorphous sterile clay', which had apparently been dug out from the pit (Wijnen 1981: 17). Theocharis (1973b: 35) interprets these structures as the remains of small huts built with posts and mud walls. The plans published by Wijnen (1981: figs. 6, 7 and 10) confirm the presence of shallow trenches and depressions, but the limited excavations, lack of data on the spatial distribution of the material and absence of any clear patterning, make the interpretation rather hazardous. Wijnen actually vigourously denies the existence of pit-dwellings in a later publication:

It is highly questionable that the pits, which have been discovered in both section C (fig. 3) and on the Akropolis are pit-dwellings, as has been suggested before. In the first place there are no indications of wall or roof supports. In the second place a pit would have been a very uncomfortable dwelling place: even a summer torrential rainfall will fill a pit for at least 10 cm with water which dries only slowly. These pits, which in all cases were dug in the yellow virgin soil, served quite probably to other purposes – like winning clay for e.g. building activities or for storage. (Wijnen 1992: 57)

The remains from Argissa are of a similar nature: large oval pits of 2 to 4 m in diameter and less than a metre deep, dug into the sterile soil and sometimes cutting each other, 'post-holes' outside the pits of circa 0.12 to 0.25 cm in diameter, and in one instance, a hearth (Milojčić *et al.* 1962). The pits are irregular in shape and, apparently, in profile; it is doubtful that they all had the same function. Numerous fragments of baked clay 'daub' or 'clay lining' mixed with vegetal fragments were uncovered in the pits. They were especially numerous in pit *alpha,* and Milojčić suggests it was lined with clay and used for cereal storage. This pit does have more vertical walls than most others, but its dimensions at the opening (2 m×2.60 m) precludes this use: the storage of cereals requires a tightly closed atmosphere.

No pits are mentioned from the small excavation at Soufli Magoula, where the basal 'preceramic' level (PK I) rested on a layer of river pebbles. According to Theocharis, these pebbles were brought in as a floor pavement. The second level (PK II) was subdivided by a series of 'clay soils' and contained one hearth surrounded by stones (Theocharis 1958: 83–4). Theocharis apparently did not consider the possibility of fluvial deposits and there remain doubts regarding the anthropic nature of the pebble and clay features, especially in such small trial excavations.

The pits and so-called post-holes found in the other sites are not easy to interpret. The pits readily evoke clay extraction pits associated with daub constructions, and daub is indeed attested at Argissa. Considering the large size of the pits, extraction would have been on a scale large enough for huts or houses, but the absence of a clear patterning of the 'post-holes' in between the pits does not support the hypothesis of large regular buildings in the excavated areas. Alternatively, the large and shallow pits *beta* and *delta* at Argissa could represent the floors of dug-in houses with walls of reed or daub, whereas the smaller and deeper pits would have served other functions. Given the state of the available data, there is no way to test these or other alternatives, and the very presence of 'architecture' in these levels remains to be demonstrated.

Interestingly, Cauvin notes that in the Near East many long-lasting tell settlements also begin with a level devoid of architectural remains, generally attributed to the settlement of nomadic groups (Cauvin 1994: 262). However, I would rather consider the association 'pits + daub' as an indication that built structures already existed, if only as light structures. If most of the pits were extraction pits, the near-absence of pottery could then be related to their early filling, before much pottery was used and discarded at the site.

Bone and stone artefacts

Assemblages from the 'aceramic Neolithic' levels, especially in Thessaly, appear to be homogeneous and strikingly similar to the overlying Early Neolithic assemblages. Sesklo and Argissa, for instance, have yielded a well-made typically Neolithic bone industry comprised of awls, spatula and chisels (Milojčić *et al.* 1962; Wijnen 1981). At Soufli Magoula, Theocharis (1958) uncovered two bone hooks, one at the limit of the 'preceramic' and the Early Neolithic, the other well into the 'aceramic' stratum; both evoke similar items from Çatal Hüyük (Mellaart 1967: pl.100).[12] In the same site, a seashell with a carefully polished lip could have been used as a vessel (Theocharis 1958: 82). Ground stone implements include grinding stones, pestles, flat sandstone and schist 'palettes', sometimes pierced (Theocharis 1967, pls. XI and XIIa). A few possible fragments of ground or polished celts were found at Argissa, but the latter appear to have been rare. The only indication of the production of stone vessels is a fragment of a marble vessel uncovered at Argissa in stratum XXXIb (Milojčić *et al.* 1962: 21, pl. 20, no. 3).

The characteristic pressure-flaked blade industry is already based on the exploitation of several distant raw material sources: obsidian from Melos (Renfrew *et al.* 1965), honey-flint blades of probable western origin, and grey-green flint from the Pindus. At Argissa the used/retouched pieces are heavily dominated by marginally retouched blades followed by light, unretouched 'sickle-blades' with a well-marked gloss. All other types – notches, end-scrapers, truncations, etc. – are represented only by a few specimens each. The latter include trapezes manufactured on regular, pressure-flaked blades, but in very limited number.

A high frequency of pendants and earstuds is also characteristic of these levels. The restricted excavation of the 'pit-dwelling' in sector C (level D) of Sesklo yielded 4 steatite beads, together with 8 polished stone earstuds (Wijnen 1981: 46–7). Several others came from the Acropolis (trench 2 and 1965 excavations), 4 greenstone specimens were uncovered at Soufli Magoula (Theocharis 1958: fig. 16), and 2, including one of clay, in stratum XXXIb at Argissa (Milojčić *et al.* 1962: pl. 20, no. 4 and 5).[13] A flat bead of schist was found at Argissa (Milojčić *et al.* 1962: pl. 8, no. 7) and a shell pendant at Soufli (Theocharis 1958: 82).

---

[12] A third one, from Sesklo, is illustrated in Theocharis 1973b (fig. 100c), but its exact provenance is not specified.
[13] Clay earstuds were also found at Sesklo (Wijnen 1981: 46–7), but it is unclear whether any belongs to the 'preceramic'.

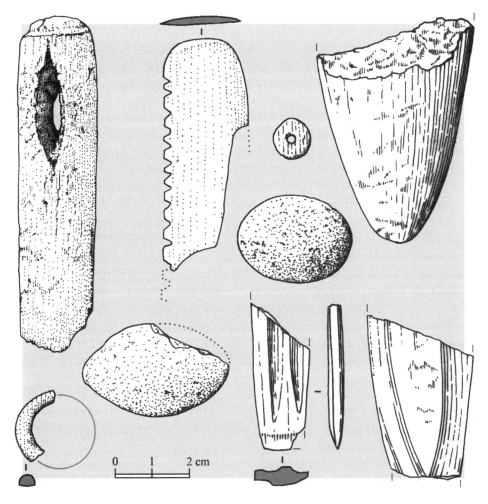

Fig. 5.2 Miscellaneous bone, clay and stone (to the right) artefacts from
Thessalian Initial Neolithic contexts (after Milojčić-v. Zumbusch
and Milojčić 1962 and Theocharis 1967).

A 'Ceramic' Neolithic: baked clay figurines and artefacts

The clay earstud from Argissa is not, by far, the only baked clay object found
in the 'preceramic' deposits from Greece; in fact, the latter are quite varied.
Several clay 'figurine' fragments were uncovered at Sesklo, including one from
the 'pit-dwelling' in stratum D, sector C (Wijnen 1981: 45). The specimen illustrated by Theocharis (Theocharis 1973b: 36 and pl. XXII, 4d) is very schematic,
and identified as such only by comparison with Palaeolithic examples. A clay
object from Soufli, described by Theocharis as a 'clay figurine ear-plug'
(Theocharis 1973b: pl. XXII, g), confirms the ambiguity of these representations.

A cylindrical clay fragment from stratum XXXIb at Argissa, interpreted as a possible figurine fragment, seems even more problematical (see Milojčić *et al.* 1962: pl. 8, no. 8).[14] Other clay objects include a fragmentary 'hook' (or 'anchor') from pit *gamma* at Argissa (Milojčić *et al.* 1962: pl. 6, no. 45), a small spherical clay bead from Soufli (Theocharis 1958: fig. 16), and two bi-conical 'sling bullets', again at Argissa and Soufli. The baked clay sling bullet from Argissa came from the second level of pit *alpha* and was associated with some sherds, while that from Soufli Magoula was found in the uppermost 'preceramic' level (Milojčić *et al.* 1962: 15; Theocharis 1958: 82). As noted by Weinberg (1970: 568–9), both pieces might come from the overlying EN assemblages, but the other baked clay artefacts render the presence of sling bullets quite plausible in this context.

Could these baked clay artefacts be attributed to contaminations, as will be suggested for the sherds? I believe not, at least for the most part. Several came from levels entirely devoid of sherds, and these artefacts are much rarer than sherds in the overlying EN deposits. If (or when) contaminations occurred, the chance that they contained fragments of figurines, beads or earstuds is much lower than for sherds. The presence of baked clay artefacts in the 'aceramic' levels is almost certain, but this is not by itself an argument against a Pre-pottery Neolithic, *sensu stricto* (*contra* Bloedow 1991: 34–5). Fired clay artefacts are already present in the Near Eastern PPNB, when no pottery was manufactured (Cauvin 1978: 101, 122–6). On the other hand, they demonstrate that these deposits are not 'pre-ceramic': the firing of clay was undoubtedly known. What remains uncertain is the status of the pottery sherds: are we dealing with a 'Pre-pottery' Neolithic, when fired-clay vessels were not yet in use, if not with a 'preceramic' Neolithic?

The uncertain status of the 'pre-pottery' sherds

Two unbaked but painted sherds were discovered in the middle 'aceramic stratum' at Soufli (Weinberg 1970: 569). More significantly, each of the 'Pre-pottery' strata from reasonably large excavations – Argissa, Sesklo, Franchthi and Knossos – contained sherds of baked pottery, albeit in small quantity. Their stratigraphic distribution within the claimed 'Pre-pottery' deposits goes from almost none at the base to several dozen at the top. However, the stratigraphic conditions differ from site to site and must be discussed individually.

All we know about the presence of sherds in the Central Court of Knossos is that a small amount of pottery was found in the first 15 cm of the 'aceramic stratum', after which it stops. No details are given. The X and ZE soundings also yielded some sherds, which were considered intrusive (Evans 1971: 102 and note 2).

---

[14] Anthropomorphic figurines were also discovered at Knossos, but in the problematic sounding X (Evans 1971: 102). None was found in the main excavation (see discussion above).

At Sesklo, Theocharis described an 'Oldest Pottery horizon' under the EN1 stratum, which contained few and 'primitive' sherds from about 8 to 10 different pots, in the deep levels of trench 2 on the Acropolis (Theocharis 1963a: 42). Two of the sherds were unfired, others badly fired, and all were crudely made. Theocharis thus defined a phase of incipient experiments in pottery-making, but Wijnen doubts its reality:

The identity of the so called Early Neolithic Ia pottery (the very coarse clumsily made ware) is very uncertain: except for the pottery exhumed from the lowest level of trench 2A in section B (excavated during the 1976 season), it has never been discovered in an unmixed level. Theocharis himself has never been very conclusive as to whether the pottery he had discovered in a stratum directly overlying the non-pottery bearing stratum had been exhumated from an unmixed level or not. (Wijnen 1981: 34)

Further down, 'sporadic sherds' were found in the uppermost part of the 'Pre-pottery' deposit that underlay this 'Oldest Pottery horizon'; unfortunately no quantitative or stratigraphic details are given (see Bloedow 1991). Wijnen herself, who had ample opportunity to study the finds and discuss them with Theocharis, does not mention sherds from any of the 'Pre-pottery' deposits, even when the latter were sieved (Wijnen 1981).

With the presently available data, it is impossible to state how many sherds came from the 'pre-pottery stratum' at Sesklo. They appear to have been rare at most and mainly located at the contact with ceramic-bearing strata. Pure deposits lacking pottery and directly overlying the virgin soil were found at least in sector C. Consequently, the problem is not so much whether there existed deposits without pottery at Sesklo, but whether there existed a 'pre-pottery *phase*', earlier than the ceramic Early Neolithic I. Insisting on the virtual importance of Early Neolithic deposits that would have directly overlain the virgin soil – that is, with no 'aceramic stratum' at the base – Bloedow aptly remarks that

It is unfortunate, therefore, that in no instance is their location correlated with those where an 'Aceramic Stratum' was identified. And yet this is of the greatest importance, for if an area where pottery appears directly on virgin soil were situated either next to or near an aceramic stratum, one might indeed question whether, despite the existence of such a stratum, there was in fact an aceramic cultural phase . . . It seems quite possible that the site was ceramic from the beginning, and that the places where pottery was not found lay outside the points where it was being used or discarded. Of course, the opposite could also be true – that the non-pottery places are earlier than those where pottery was found immediately above virgin soil. (Bloedow 1991: 31)[15]

Argissa is the 'preceramic' stratum that yielded the highest absolute number of sherds: 122 altogether in the pits and in stratum XXXI.[16] The sherds are

---

[15] A sound argument, provided that one can exclude trampling to account for the sherds in or on the virgin soil. See Franchthi, Paralia, for an instance of trampling.

[16] Plus 179 from stratum XXIXa, which was alternatively considered as pure EN or 'transitional'. The relative number of sherds in the 'aceramic' stratum proper is probably comparable to that of Franchthi, given the larger excavated area.

identical to EN sherds and their number diminishes from the top of the stratum to the bottom: 56 in level XXXIa, 49 in XXXIb, 7 in XXXIc and 10 in the basal pits. Milojčić thus considered them as intrusive and emphasizes the post-holes, pits and animal burrows that may have been responsible for contaminations (Milojčić *et al.* 1962: 8, 14). The relatively high number of sherds at Argissa, coming from 60 square metres, is not incompatible with this hypothesis: the *c.* 100 sherds from the 'talus' and 'Pleistocene basal red' on the Paralia at Franchthi, which cannot but be intrusive, came from a much smaller area (see Vitelli 1993; map 4). But the pits may also represent, as suggested above, early clay extraction pits that were filled before many sherds were discarded, or may correspond to a phase of low pottery production and use, as concluded by Bloedow (1991).

The situation differs at Franchthi, where the earliest Neolithic corresponds to a discrete stratigraphic unit and where possible contaminations ought to be more easily spotted. The 'gray clay stratum' yielded a very small quantity of sherds,[17] which Vitelli thoroughly analyzed in her chapter devoted to 'Ceramic Interphase 0/1'. She recorded a total of at least nineteen sherds, usually of small size, over an area of several square metres from the FF1 and FA trenches (Vitelli 1993: 37–8). These sherds, when they could be weighed,[18] amounted to *c.* 4 to 25 grams in each excavation unit.[19] In contrast, the overlying units, dating from the Early or Middle Neolithic, usually contained between 200 and 4000 grams of sherds.

The 'gray clay stratum' had been cross-cut by numerous pits of FCP2 date,[20] including three children's burials (Vitelli 1993: 38 and note 4, p. 40). After a thorough contextual examination of the stratigraphic distribution of the sherds, Vitelli concluded:

With the exception of that pit [East section of FF1, Quad. A], if it did penetrate the area of FAN, and a few units in FAS above the Fr 48 burial (units 137S, 138S, 138S, 140S), all the disturbances were recognized and isolated during excavation of the 'gray clay' stratum. Nevertheless, ample opportunity existed for slight contamination in the units in the 'gray clay' by later material. (Vitelli 1993: 38)

Indeed, most of the sherds that Vitelli was able to examine 'are in no way distinguishable from FCP1 Lime MB sherds.[21] They may well all be intrusive FCP 1 sherds' (Vitelli 1993: 39). Several observations confirm that at least some of the units in the 'gray clay' stratum were contaminated. First, three of the sherds

---

[17] Leaving aside the heavily contaminated sector of the HH1 trenches. Looking at it from 'the other side' (i.e., from the Neolithic downward), Vitelli notes that 'In the southwestern cluster of trenches (Trenches A, FAS, FAN, FF1: see plan 5), however, the abrupt decrease in sherds from overlying units (see Document 1) takes place within a clearly defined stratum' (Vitelli 1993: 38).

[18] Some sherds, which were considered by the excavators as clearly intrusive, were discarded at the time of excavation.

[19] With a total of approximately 150 g (Vitelli 1993: 38). The highest figure (25 grams) corresponds to one large sherd.

[20] FCP2 = Franchthi ceramic phase 2. It is equivalent to the Middle Neolithic in other chronological schemes.   [21] Franchthi ceramic phase 1, Lime Monochrome Burnished.

come from the above-mentioned units in FAS,[22] which overlaid an FCP2 child burial. Contaminations are also demonstrated by the presence of a few sherds in the underlying Mesolithic levels, including Monochrome Urf sherds belonging to the FCP2 phase (see Vitelli 1993, document 1, tables 8 and 12). Some of these came from units excavated immediately after cleaning passes and may be related to the effects of the 'cleaning', but this is not the case, for example, with the 'Monochrome Urf' sherds found in FA 151S, which are clearly intrusive. Therefore, contamination of the deposits in the 'gray clay' stratum and underlying deposits has to be acknowledged,[23] and Vitelli did note an apparent spatial relation in FA between the distribution of sherds and the presence of pits (Vitelli 1993: 38–9).

Altogether, one third of the sherds found in the 'gray clay stratum' from FF1 and FA were recovered either on the surface of the stratum or in the first excavated unit.[24] Cross-cutting with the overlying stratum during excavation is highly plausible. Conversely, the majority of the excavation units that removed the 'gray clay stratum' were actually devoid of sherds, especially at the bottom of the stratum (see Vitelli 1993, document 1, tables 3–13). In FA, out of the 21 units assigned to this phase, 13 did not contain sherds and these units were concentrated in the bottom half of the trench. Nevertheless, as cautioned by Vitelli, there is also a risk in considering, a priori, *all* sherds as intrusive:

Suppose that the first pots used at Franchthi, whether produced locally or brought there from elsewhere, were very few in number. Their scarcity, novelty, and perhaps function might well have made them precious. If handled carefully, perhaps infrequently, they would break infrequently, and probably be mended when they did break. Few sherds would be generated and discarded. With that scenario, we should expect contemporary deposits to include very few sherds, and they would often be the fragments too small to mend . . . Until more conclusive evidence is produced that the units with sherds in the 'gray clay' stratum are reworked and the sherds are accompanied by other certainly intrusive materials, we cannot claim an 'Aceramic neolithic' deposit at Franchthi. It is worth considering the possibility that pottery use began with few vessels, rarely broken. (Vitelli 1993: 39)[25]

The possibility that pottery use began with few vessels, rarely broken, is indeed plausible and the two possibilities are not mutually exclusive. To complicate the matter, one cannot rule out entirely functional hypotheses: Nandris' hypothesis of Greek 'aceramic' settlements being related to sheep-herding could be especially relevant in the case of Franchthi (Nandris 1984: 20).

---

[22] Units FA 137S and 139S, overlying the burial in FA 141S.

[23] It will be recalled that *c.* fifty sherds were trampled down the 'Red Pleistocene deposits' on the Paralia.

[24] This is the case in FAS, where three of the six sherds were found in the first excavated unit of the gray stratum (135S). Since the remaining three sherds from this trench came from the units overlying the FCP2 burial, no sherd in FAS can seriously be considered as potentially *in situ*.

[25] Vitelli suggests here that additional proof of reworking should come from other categories of material. This of course would reinforce the case, but, considering the quantitative disproportion between sherds and other kinds of remains in the ceramic Neolithic deposits, the probability that sherds would be the most frequent contaminants is very high.

According to this hypothesis, the absence of sherds would be due to the function of the settlement rather than to the ignorance of pottery manufacture. However, in later Neolithic sites definitely identified as Neolithic sheep pens (see for instance Maggi *et al.* 1991, 1992), pottery is normally present.

At this stage of the discussion, no definite conclusion can be reached, either about Franchthi or about any of the other sites. Only by underestimating the amount of disturbances in *any* stratified Neolithic deposit could the few 'pre-pottery' sherds be considered as definite evidence that pottery was in use at these sites. Yet, this should not lead us to ignore the alternative possibility that few pots were used and discarded, as suggested by Vitelli for Franchthi and Bloedow for Sesklo and Argissa.[26]

In both cases, however, these deposits would result from different behaviours, in terms of ceramic use, than the classically defined Early Neolithic: either pottery was not produced at all, or it was produced in much lower quantity. The problem, then, is whether such behaviours should be related to the initial phases of a settlement's occupation, or to the initial phases of ceramic-making. In the first alternative, clay extraction pits, for instance, would have been filled with rubbish before much ceramic had been broken and discarded; similar sherd-poor pits would then be expected in settlements founded at a later date.[27] In the second alternative, little or no pottery would have been made, used and discarded; this would be characteristic of a very early chronological phase, before pottery became of more common usage. The few 14C dates available must, in consequence, be considered and compared with the dates of the ceramic Early Neolithic: do these deposits represent a discrete chronological phase? Or do they belong, chronologically speaking, to the Early Neolithic?

14C dates: arguments for a discrete phase

Although he published the first complete list of dates for the 'pre-pottery' levels, Coleman still considered that

The relationship between the inhabitants of Greece in the Early ceramic Neolithic and those in the Mesolithic and putative Aceramic Neolithic is still somewhat uncertain (Weinberg 1970: 571–2; Milojčić-von Zumbusch and Milojčić 1971: 139–41), and the possibility of some chronological overlap between levels at sites where pottery was in use and Aceramic Neolithic levels has already been mentioned. (Coleman 1992: 252)

Only fourteen dates have been assigned to 'pre-pottery' Neolithic levels (see table 5.3). I believe, however, that their number is enough to warrant discussion and clarify the chronological position of the deposits.[28] The dates come

---

[26] This would hold true also for Soufli, Gediki and Knossos: Halstead 1984: 4.1.2, Theocharis 1967: 173.   [27] As was suggested by Caskey at Lerna (Caskey 1957, 1958).

[28] This renewed discussion of the 'preceramic dates' was rendered possible by the publication in Coleman 1992 of several unpublished dates from Argissa, communicated by H. Hauptmann and not available when Bloedow addressed the same problem (Bloedow 1992/3).

from four different sites (Knossos, Franchthi, Argissa and Sesklo) and four different laboratories: British Museum (BM), Pennsylvania (P), Heidelberg (H) and
Los Angeles (UCLA). The datings were performed over two decades or more, so
that systematic bias due to early radiocarbon datings cannot have affected the
whole set of dates.

The modal values of the dates range from 8130 to 7250 BP uncalibrated (see
fig. 5.4 and table 5.3) or 7480 to 5960 cal BC[29] (fig. 5.5), but eleven of them fall
between 7500 and 6500 BC. Apart from the three most recent dates, which fall
into the second half of the seventh millennium, they can be considered as very
early for a European Neolithic: many would say suspiciously early. A close
scrutiny of these dates is therefore needed and we shall successively consider
the archaeological context and consistency of the dates within each site, the
consistency of the results between the different laboratories and the internal
consistency of all the dates.

Archaeological contexts and internal consistency within each site

None of the sets of dates obtained from each site is devoid of problems. The
three samples from Knossos come from a small location in the Central Court,
yet their modal values span almost 300 years (see table 5.3). The earliest,
BM–124 (8050 ± 180 BP) was in fact part of the same wood stake as BM–278
(7910 ± 140 BP), but was processed by acetylene, whereas BM–278 was processed by scintillation counting (Evans 1971: 117). According to Bloedow
(1992–3: 6), the latter should thus be retained. Yet it also differs substantially
from BM–436 (7740 ± 140), which came from a carbonized grain found nearby
(*Radiocarbon* 11: 280). Theoretically, seeds are short-lived samples and should
date the archaeological occupation more accurately than wood (Waterbolk
1983). On the other hand, seeds have often been observed to give younger dates
than associated samples, and problems of carbon fixation are possibly involved
(Binder, personal communication).[30] However, the three dates remain internally compatible at two standard deviations. All actual ages between 8000 and
7700 BP (or 7000–6700 cal BC) would be compatible with the three samples;
there are no *archaeological* reasons to reject them all, though it must be kept
in mind that the wood stake may be earlier than the site occupation itself.

The three dates from Franchthi cluster more tightly (around 7800/7900 BP)
although the samples come from three different trenches, but all within the
'gray clay' stratum. P–1392 (7790 ± 90 BP) comes from a unit contaminated
with Middle Neolithic and later material (Vitelli 1993: 37), but the date itself
can hardly correspond to these late intrusions. P–2094 (7930 ± 100 BP) comes

---

[29] All dates were calibrated with the programme Calib 3 (Struiver and Reimer 1993) and are given
at two standard deviations, unless stated otherwise.
[30] Which may be why Manning retains a date earlier than 8000 BP for Knossos (Bloedow 1992/3:
6, n. 52).

Table 5.3 *14C dates for the Initial Neolithic levels*

Site	Level	Lab. ref.	Nature of the sample	Date BP uncal.	Calibrated date BC at 2 sigma	Maximum probabilities	References
Knossos	X, Pit F, area AC, level 27, central court	BM–124	Carbonized wood stake	8050±180	7483–6465	7030	RC 5: 104
	X, Pit F, area AC, level 27, central court	BM–278	Carbonized wood stake	7910±140	7244–6427	6700	RC 11: 280
	X, Pit F, area AC, level 27, central court	BM–436	Carbonized seed near the wood stake	7740±140	7006–6230	6535 6522 6487	RC 11: 280
Franchthi	FAS–143	P–2094	Charcoal + sediment	7930±100	7044–6479	6756 6743 6713	RC 17: 201
	FF1–44B5	P–1527	Charcoal + sediment	7900±90	7036–6473	6694 6680 6661	J. & F. 1987. RC 13:366
	A–63	P–1392	Wood charcoal	7790±140	7034–6367	6591 6585 6561	RC 13: 365
Argissa		UCLA–1657A	Bone	8130±100	7422–6708	7044 6999 6915 6903	Milojčić 1973: 250
		UCLA–1657D	Bone	7990±95	7240–6562		Milojčić 1973: 250
		H–889–3080	?	7760±100	6994–6337	6544	Coleman 1993
		H–896–3082	?	7740±100	6991–AD 1955	6635 6622 6487	Coleman 1993
		H–894–3081	?	7520±100	6477–6070	6372	Coleman 1993

Site	Context	Lab no.	Material	Date BP	Calibrated range		Reference
Seklo	63.124B, sq. 1 to XXX, 'end of preceramic'	P-1681	Charcoal + soil	7755 ± 97	6992–6387	6542 6511 6507	RC 15: 370
	sq. B, depth 4.32 m, 'end of preceramic'	P-1682	Charcoal + soil	7483 ± 72	6451–6171	6357 6317 6304 6275 6246	RC 15: 370
	sq. B1, depth 4.10/4.20 m 'first sherds'	P-1680	Charcoal + soil	7300 ± 93	6352–5959	6122 6087 6063	RC 15: 370

from a good 'Initial Neolithic' or FCP INT 0/1 context, devoid of any sherds (Perlès 1987: doc. V.1, Vitelli 1993: 37). It is, archaeologically speaking, the most reliable of the three. The third date (P-1527, 7900 ± 90 BP) comes from a series of units in the 'gray clay' stratum devoid of sherds or diagnostic lithics and attributed to the Neolithic on stratigraphic and faunal bases.

All three dates are internally coherent and come from a well-defined geological stratum. The contextual data do not contradict the attribution to the Initial Neolithic of Franchthi. However, these dates could, theoretically, pose a problem not found at the other sites, that of contamination by earlier, Mesolithic, material. The similarity of Final Mesolithic and Initial Neolithic lithic assemblages would not have permitted the recognition of contaminations, but the preliminary faunal data do not suggest important mixtures. Furthermore, the two strata are very distinct in texture and colour, and mixed units were kept separate during the excavations. There is no reason to reject these very early Neolithic dates due to suspicions of Mesolithic contaminations.

Contextual information is much less precise for the two other sites. Milojčić himself published only two dates from Argissa: UCLA–1657A: 8130 ± 100 BP and UCLA–1657D: 7990 ± 95 BP (Milojčić 1973: 250; Protsch and Berger 1973). These very early dates were obtained from bone samples and seem to have represented early attempts at dating the bone collagen itself. The problems related with early datings on bone are thoroughly discussed by Bloedow (1992–3), and may explain why these UCLA dates are earlier than three Heidelberg dates, published about twenty years later (Coleman 1992). The latter range from 7760 ± 100 to 7520 ± 100 BP (figs. 5.3 and 5.4, nos. 8, 11 and 12) and only the first two – H–889–3080: 7760 ± 100 and H–896–3082: 7740 ± 95 BP – compare well with other 'pre-pottery' dates. Unfortunately, no stratigraphic information has been published for any of these samples, and whether this discrepancy can be explained in archaeological terms is impossible to say.

The contextual data from Sesklo, thoroughly discussed by Bloedow (1991: 40–2), are imprecise and sometimes contradictory. This is all the more unfortunate since two of the three dates appear to be too recent for the 'pre-pottery' phase claimed by Theocharis, when compared with Early Neolithic dates from the same site. The earliest date (P–1681: 7755 ± 97 BP) is said to correspond to the 'end of the aceramic', but with no depth indication. The other two samples were taken respectively at 4.10/4.20 m and 4.32 m in square B. According to Bloedow's reconstruction of the stratigraphy, which had to deal with the contradictions among the various preliminary reports, P–1680 (7300 ± 93), the sample at 4.10 m, would correspond to the appearance of the first sherds; this may explain why it is so late (Bloedow 1991: 41). P–1682 (7483 ± 72), supposedly coming from the 'preceramic' level down below, is more than two standard deviations away from most other 'pre-pottery' dates and no explanation can be provided. Both dates were rejected by Theocharis (1973b: 119) as 'irrational'.

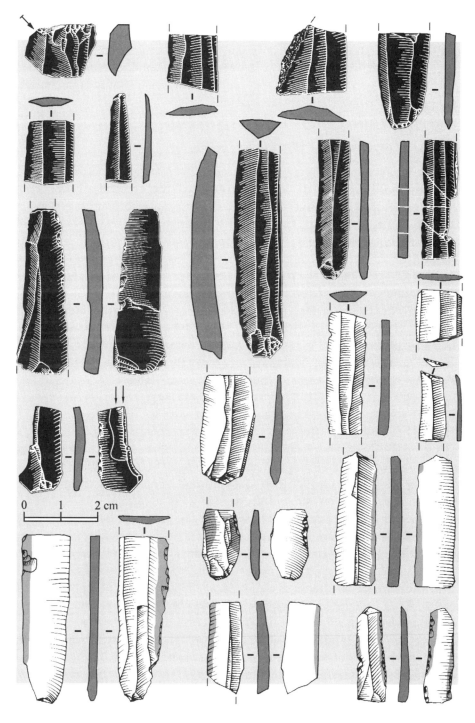

Fig. 5.3 Obsidian and flint tools from the Initial Neolithic ('preceramic') deposits at Argissa.

Obviously, none of these sets of dates is devoid of archaeological problems. However, most dates could be considered too high rather than too low. Franchthi, nevertheless, is the only site where potential contaminations by earlier material could theoretically have taken place, and there is no indication that this is the case. If the dates are indeed too old, one should consider laboratory problems rather than contaminations.

Consistency among the different laboratories.

To check for systematic discrepancies among the different laboratories (Baxter 1983; Waterbolk 1983, 1987), I used the forty-two dates from Early and Middle Neolithic Achilleion as a test, since they allow comparisons among four different laboratories: Groningen, La Jolla, Pennsylvania and UCLA. Especially relevant are samples from the same level or successive levels dated by different laboratories. The comparisons indicate that Groningen might give younger dates than Pennsylvania for comparable samples, and that UCLA might give dates older by an order of 200 years than La Jolla or Pennsylvania.

The British Museum had not dated any sample from Achilleion, but Waterbolk (1987: 41) notes that in the Near East early BM dates appear to be systematically too old. It is therefore important to bear in mind that both BM and UCLA dates might be systematically older than the P and H dates. Figures 5.3 and 5.4 confirm this trend on our specific set of dates.

Internal consistency of the 'pre-pottery' dates

Apart from the three most recent ones, which will be discussed below, the dates align regularly along a chronological axis, from c. 8100 to 7800 BP in modal values or 7400–6500 cal BC (figs. 5.3 and 5.4). The two earliest – Argissa UCLA–1657A: 8130 ± 100 BP and Knossos BM-124: 8050 ± 180 BP – have often been quoted as evidence that the Neolithic began in Greece before 8000 BP. But BM and UCLA dates were precisely suspected of being too old, and both datings were problematic. As a consequence, these dates might be slightly too old and the earliest Neolithic in Greece might date to c. 8000 BP, or 6900 BC.

The following dates cluster between *circa* 8000 and 7800 BP in modal values (fig. 5.4). When calibrated, they spread regularly between 7200 and 6500 BC (fig. 5.5)[31] and constitute a coherent, if not very tight, cluster of dates.

Finally, two dates from Sesklo – already referred to as 'irrational' – and one from Argissa clearly stand out as more recent (figs. 5.4 and 5.5, nos. 12, 13, 14) and the probability that they belong to the same series is low.[32] They fully coincide with Early Neolithic dates, which implies either that the samples have been wrongly

---

[31] They divide into two subgroups when calibrated at one standard deviation, but the two subgroups do not correspond to different sites or different strata, and should be attributed to random effects on small samples.

[32] They do not overlap with any other when calibrated at one standard deviation.

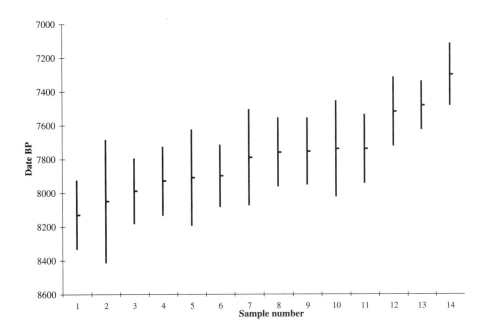

Fig. 5.4 Radiocarbon dates assigned to Initial Neolithic levels (BP).

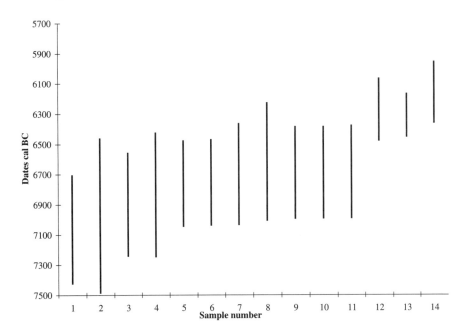

Fig. 5.5 Calibrated radiocarbon dates assigned to Initial Neolithic levels.
1: Argissa, UCLA–1657A. 2: Knossos, BM-124. 3: Argissa,
UCLA–1657D. 4: Franchthi, P–2094. 5: Knossos, BM–278.
6: Franchthi, P–1527. 7: Franchthi, P–1392. 8: Argissa, H 889–3080.
10: Sesklo, P–1681. 11: Argissa, H–896–3082. 12: Argissa,
H–894–3081. 13: Sesklo, P–1682. 14: Sesklo, P–1680.

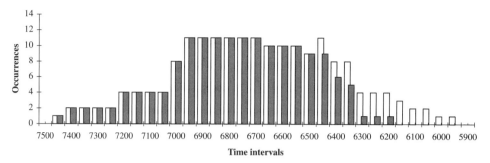

Fig. 5.6 Projection of the calibrated Initial Neolithic 14C dates according to fifty-year time intervals. In white: all dates assigned to Initial Neolithic levels. In grey: projection without the dates considered aberrant.

assigned to 'pre-pottery' deposits, or that the deposits were contaminated by Early Neolithic material. In either case, these three dates should be rejected.

Leaving aside these outlying dates, the projections as histograms of intervals (fig. 5.6) cluster between 7050 and 6450 cal BC (8150–7500 BP),[33] where all ten dates are represented. This time range can thus be retained with the highest probability for dating the 'pre-pottery' deposits, though any shorter period of time within this range is compatible with all the dates.[34]

Given this coherent distribution and the absence of specific archaeological grounds to reject the samples, these 'pre-pottery' deposits can be dated to the first half of the seventh millennium cal BC. How does this compare with Mesolithic dates on the one hand, and with Early Neolithic dates on the other hand? Do these levels represent a discrete chronological phase, distinct from either or both?

Comparisons with the Mesolithic dates

The chronological relations between the Late Mesolithic and the 'Pre-pottery' Neolithic are difficult to establish since the Late Mesolithic has not been securely dated. No contextual information has yet been provided for the Theopetra Mesolithic dates and they cannot be used in the present discussion, whereas the majority of the Mesolithic dates from Franchthi derive from Early and Late Mesolithic contexts, rather than Final Mesolithic. The latter do not overlap with the Neolithic dates (fig. 5.7): Early Mesolithic dates cluster between 9500 and 9000 BP, or 8800–8000 BC, and Late Mesolithic dates cluster between 9000 and 8500 BP, or 8300–7500 BC.

Only two samples from Franchthi (P–1536 and P–1576) have been tentatively

---

[33] The dates have not been weighted, so that dates with large standard deviations tend to take too much importance in these histograms. At one standard deviation they spread between 7050 and 6450 cal. BC (c. 8100–7700 BP).

[34] The best represented interval at one standard deviation is between 6600 and 6650 BC, but the distribution is then far from normal.

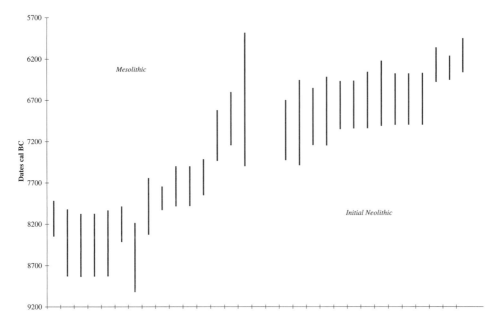

Fig. 5.7 Calibrated radiocarbon dates assigned to Mesolithic and Initial Neolithic levels.

attributed to the Final Mesolithic, but without direct contextual evidence. P-1536 (8190 ± 80 BP), from G1–22, was assigned to the Final Mesolithic according to P. Mellars' preliminary observations of the lithics,[35] and should be the more reliable of the two. P–1575 (8020 ± 80 BP) was taken in an excavation unit almost devoid of lithics (FF1 43A1) and the phase attribution could not be confirmed. The date from G1 overlaps only slightly with the Initial Neolithic dates from Franchthi. It is compatible with the hypothesis of two distinct, successive phases. On the contrary, the date from FF1 overlaps completely the Initial Neolithic dates of the site; since a sherd was found in this unit (Vitelli 1993: table 3, p. 224), a wrong attribution or contaminations by later material might be invoked. Both dates, on the other hand, overlap with Initial Neolithic dates from other sites, and so does the rather poor dating from Sidari, level D. This might indicate a contemporaneity between the last phases of the Mesolithic and the Initial Neolithic, but the contextual information – or, in the case of Sidari the dating itself – is too unsatisfactory to be taken as definite evidence.

Comparison with the Early Neolithic dates

The Early Neolithic dates will be discussed later in more detail. For the moment, in order to avoid any involuntary biases, all dates attributed to the

---

[35] Which could not be restudied later, all the labels having fallen from the pieces.

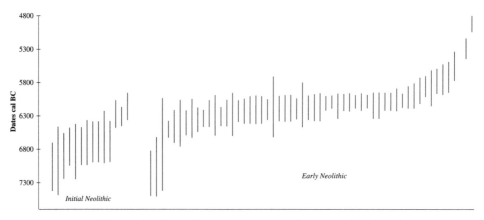

Fig. 5.8 Calibrated radiocarbon dates assigned to Initial and Early Neolithic levels.

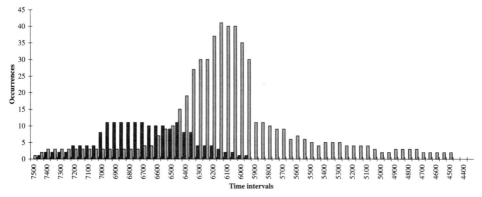

Fig. 5.9 Projection of the Initial Neolithic calibrated 14C dates according to fifty-year time intervals. In black: Initial Neolithic dates. In grey: Early Neolithic dates.

'Pre-pottery' and the Early Neolithic have been considered here. This 'raw sample' clearly shows aberrant dates, especially the three latest dates from the 'Pre-pottery' phase and the three earliest dates from the Early Neolithic.[36] Apart from these dates, the graph shows a clear and very gradual alignment (fig. 5.8), with the EN dates starting just after the latest 'pre-pottery' dates, after 6400 cal BC (or about 7650 BP). The projection as time intervals (fig. 5.9) confirms the relative antiquity of the 'pre-pottery' dates, even when aberrant dates are retained. It clearly suggests the presence of two distinct sets of dates with a point of inflexion at *circa* 6500–6400 cal BC.[37] Despite the small number of

---

[36] Which there are very good reasons to reject (see below, ch. 6).

[37] This is also clearly shown by means of the two series: 7785 BP (standard deviation: 221) for the Initial Neolithic, and 7317 BP (standard deviation: 408) for the Early Neolithic. When the dates that depart from more than two standard deviations from the mean are eliminated in both samples, the figures become respectively 7823 BP (s.d.: 182) and 7313 (s.d.: 354).

'pre-pottery dates', the radiocarbon chronology thus supports the stratigraphic data and confirms the chronological anteriority of the 'pre-pottery' levels in most sites.

This 'Initial Neolithic' differs from the Early Neolithic by its stratigraphical position, relative antiquity and absence or scarcity of pottery. In all other domains, it appears indistinguishable from the earliest Early Neolithic. One could argue, consequently, that it represents only the earliest phase of the Early Neolithic (Bloedow 1992/3), and in many respects, this is true. However, the successive Neolithic phases in Greece have been precisely defined on the basis of transformations in pottery style and production. Whether the Initial Neolithic corresponds to a period when pottery was not in use, or whether it corresponds to a period when it was still extremely scarce, it is distinct, in terms of ceramic production, from the Early Neolithic. On the basis of the presently available data, it should be recognized as a discrete phase, even if only to promote further research and discussion.

From chronology back to pot production: Greece and the Near East

If the existence of an early chronological phase characterized by, at most, a very limited use of pottery is accepted, we are then faced with an unsuspected analogy with the Near East. In the Near East also, the full pottery stage is preceded by a period of sporadic production of clay pots, well into the 'Pre-Pottery' Neolithic! The earliest clay pots come from Mureibet in Syria and are dated to 9500 BC, but these rare and very small pots were not followed by a continued production of pottery (Cauvin 1978: 101). Accidental firing when the house burned down is now considered a possibility (Le Mière and Picon 1998). Fired clay pots, associated with other elements of a 'fire technology' – lime and plastered floors, white wares, baked figurines, sling bullets, 'tokens', etc. – reappear only between 7500 and 6900 BC, in a few settlements of the Levant, the Middle Euphrates and in the plain of Konya in Anatolia (Cauvin 1985: 169–70; 1989: 19). During this early phase, the pots are alternately described as fired, poorly fired or unfired. These early pottery productions, distributed 'erratically' in various sites, were first discussed by Hours and Copeland (1982) who coined the term 'intermittent potteries'. The burnished pottery of Tell Assouad[38] and the painted pottery of Bouqras are amongst the better known, but isolated sherds in good stratigraphic contexts were also found at Suberde (Bordaz (1968) talks about 'une expérience sans lendemain') and in the lower levels of Çatal Hüyük. There, eight sherds were recovered from one 'shrine' in the lowest level (X), two or three in each of the 'shrines' from level IX, one from level VIII and none from levels VII and VIB (Mellaart 1964: 81).

---

[38] The dates of Tell Assouad have recently been questioned on typological grounds (Cauvin 1994: 200).

The generalization of ceramic production occurred only later. It is well dated to *circa* 6900 BC, and marks the beginning of the Pottery Neolithic, or PNA (Cauvin 1985: 173, 1989). Yet, even during the first half of the seventh millennium, large areas, for which the term PPNC (Pre-pottery Neolithic C) has recently been coined, remain devoid of pottery (Rollefson and Simmons 1986; Gopher and Gophna 1993). Interestingly, the presence of fired clay pots in the PPNB of the Near East does not seem to have led to a rejection of the term 'Pre-Pottery"!

The existence of a phase with sporadic production and use of pottery in the Near East, dated between 7500 and 7000 BC, is important to the discussion of the origins of pottery in Greece. According to the available 14C dates, the first farmers who came to Greece may have belonged to a late phase of the PPNB,[39] when pottery production was still rare and sporadic. Other fired clay artefacts arc noticcably more frequent in the PPNB of the Near East, and this also accords well with the data from Greece. The initial stages of the Neolithic in Greece could, consequently, have presented a similar pattern, with a sporadic pottery production limited to some sites only.[40]

Conclusion

This parallel changes the terms of the debate over a 'pre-pottery' phase in Greece: viewed in this broader perspective, the dichotomy between 'sherds' and 'no sherds' appears of secondary importance. If it is admitted that Greece was settled by late PPNB groups coming from the Near East, then some at least of these groups must have known about pottery-making. A basic knowledge of pottery-making must have been present, whether or nor it was regularly implemented. And it is, I believe, this old-rooted knowledge that allowed the later development of local traditions in pottery manufacture, which were technologically and stylistically independent from the Near East (Chapman 1994b: 138; Wijnen 1993).

As suggested by Vitelli, these earliest pots may well have had, just as the clay figurines, a special role and value. In this respect, a parallel may be established with another newly introduced technique, stone polishing, that was mostly applied to the production of probable ornaments, the 'earstuds'. Cauvin's insights on the significance of the fired clay pots and polished stones in the Near East may well be relevant for Greece also:

---

[39] An hypothesis already put forward by Gordon Childe, although based on an absolute chronology that cannot be fully accepted today: 'They [the immigrants] may well have been in the pre-pottery stage' (Childe 1958: 43; see also p. 39).

[40] I consider, indeed, that the arguments in favour of contaminations by Early Neolithic deposits remain strong, especially at Franchthi.

Ainsi, ni la pierre polie, ni la céramique, lorsqu'on parvient à observer réellement les premiers temps de leur surgissement, ne paraissent alors des inventions 'adaptatives', puisqu'on les perçoit plutôt dans un contexte ornemental ou religieux qu'utilitaire. Tout se passe comme si toute découverte vraiment importante, parce qu'elle résulte de la maîtrise d'un matériau nouveau ou d'une façon radicalement nouvelle de manipuler un matériau usuel, imprégnait ses premiers produits d'un tel prestige qu'elle les réservait à des domaines plus 'valorisants' que la satisfaction des besoins biologiques. C'est ce qui nous fait dire que toute invention de ce niveau passe d'abord par un moment 'symbolique', et que cette phase y paraît d'autant plus nécessaire que la dite invention est, à terme, plus riche en applications révolutionnaires. (Cauvin, 1978: 103)[41]

As will be shown by later discussions, however, Neolithic pots in Greece seem to have retained at least part of this symbolic value, even when pot production became more common. In this respect, as in many others, the Early Neolithic appears to be a direct outcome and continuation of the Initial Neolithic.

Yet, the suggested filiation between the Near Eastern PPNB and the Initial Neolithic from Greece does not mean that they can be equated. Even if there exists an early productive phase in Greece with little or no use of fired clay pots, it does not parallel the Near Eastern PPN. The Initial Neolithic in Greece is not the outcome of a local and progressive differentiation. Its subsistence basis was introduced from elsewhere, fully formed: the domesticates may all be of Near Eastern origin, and the presence of hexaploid barley, for instance, shows that domestication had been under way for a long time.[42] Its short duration and comparatively late dates cannot be compared with the long and gradual transition observed in the Near East. If continuity is to be sought, it is clearly with what follows, not with what precedes (Nandris 1970: 196, 199). As expressed by Dennell (1984: 96): 'To some extent the problem of whether or not the Greek aceramic is real is a trivial one . . . even if the pre-pottery Neolithic of Greece exists, it does not seem to have been the equivalent of that of Syria, Jordan, Israel, or the Zagros.'

[41] 'Thus, when one is able to observe their very first manifestations, neither polished stone nor ceramics appear to be "adaptive" inventions, since they are related to ornamental or religious rather than utilitarian contexts. It seems as though any really important discovery, because it results from the mastery of a new raw material or from a completely new way of manipulating a familiar one, imparted such prestige on its first products that they were confined to more valued domains than the satisfaction of mere biological needs. This leads us to suggest that any invention of that level passes first through a "symbolic" phase, and that this phase appears to be all the more necessary that this invention carries, in the long run, revolutionary applications.'

[42] Conversely, the fact that Greece was not an area of primary development of a Neolithic economy cannot, by itself, preclude the possibility of an early pre-pottery phase: all the domesticated species were introduced to Cyprus from the continent, and yet a long pre-pottery Neolithic is well exemplified there (Le Brun 1981, 1984; Le Brun (ed.) 1989, 1994; Stanley Price 1979).

CHAPTER 6

THE SPREAD OF THE EARLY NEOLITHIC IN GREECE: CHRONOLOGICAL AND GEOGRAPHICAL ASPECTS

The definitions of the Early Neolithic in Greece

The Early Neolithic[1] is a phase of long duration, witnessing the expansion of farming over Greece and the multiplication of large sedentary villages. Besides the first widespread presence of pottery, it is characterized by well-built houses, elaborate house equipment, long-distance circulation of goods and abundant evidence of symbolic expression. With the possible exception of its earliest stage, the Early Neolithic is not a 'transitional' or 'formative' phase. On the contrary, it sets the stage for what will prove to be, in its fundamental structures, a remarkably stable socioeconomic organization throughout the Neolithic.

The Early Neolithic is classically defined on the basis of its pottery, with the predominance of small and medium-sized open bowls, often monochrome and well burnished, more rarely decorated with simple painted patterns or with impressions. Low ring feet are a common feature. The Early Neolithic starts with the first relatively abundant ceramic production (Monochrome phase) and ends with the appearance of characteristic Middle Neolithic (MN) ware, the Urfirnis in the Peloponnese or the Sesklo ware in Thessaly for instance.

Despite marked differences in the ceramic productions, the Early Neolithic was not immediately distinguished from the Middle Neolithic. Tsountas (1908), followed by Wace and Thompson (1912), divided the Thessalian Neolithic into two periods only, corresponding to the present-day Sesklo (MN) and Dimini or Late Neolithic (LN) cultures. Tsountas had, however, already recognized the specificity of the earliest monochrome wares at Sesklo (Tsountas 1908: 159–60).

The term 'Early Neolithic' was first used in 1937 by Weinberg at Corinth (Weinberg 1937). Ten years later, he established it as the first of a tripartite division of the Greek Neolithic, and correlated the Early Neolithic of the Peloponnese and Corinthia – with a variety of monochrome, variegated and

---

[1] Or 'Phase 1' according to Demoule and Perlès 1993. Had an earlier chronological phase been established when we wrote our article, the Initial Neolithic could have been labelled 'phase 1' and the Early Neolithic 'phase 2'. I am not going, however, to introduce more confusion with yet another chronological scheme.

simply painted pottery – to the earliest monochrome wares from Sesklo (Weinberg 1947: 174–6). In parallel, Milojčić (1950/1) introduced the 'Vor-Sesklo Kultur' of Thessaly, which was to become, shortly afterwards, the latest sub-phase of his Thessalian 'Early Neolithic' (Milojčić 1959b). Tsountas' 'Period A' (Sesklo period) became the Middle Neolithic, while his 'Period B' (Dimini) became the Late Neolithic. This tripartite scheme rapidly gained acceptance and is now used all over central and southern Greece. In Central and eastern Macedonia, to the contrary, the Balkanic phasing is more usually followed. As a result, the 'Early, Middle or Late' Neolithic of the two regions are not contemporaneous.[2]

In both Thessaly and southern Greece, important stylistic and technical changes in ceramic production give firm groundings to the distinction between an Early and a Middle Neolithic. But these changes are progressive, as are the changes in most other aspects of life: the taxonomic distinction should not mask a fundamental continuity between the two periods. However, the suggestion that the two periods should again be reunited under the term 'Early Neolithic', in order to fit a 'pan-European chronology' (Lichardus *et al.* 1985) would result in considering a millennium as a single phase, masking both the chronological and cultural specificity of the Early Neolithic in Greece. Indeed, one of its most original features is its antecedence, in absolute chronology, in comparison to any other 'Early Neolithic' in Europe.

Chronology and duration of the Early Neolithic

Fifty-six radiocarbon dates, from ten different sites, have been assigned to Early Neolithic levels (table 6.1).[3] Fifty of them make up a remarkably coherent set, six others stand out as clearly problematic.

As shown in figs. 6.1 and 6.2, nine-tenths of the dates align, by their modal values, in a regular progression from 7700 BP to 7000 BP, or *c.* 6500–5700 cal BC, with a large majority comprised between 6400 and 6400 BC. Conversely, even a casual visual examination of the graph shows several completely offset dates, which do not overlap with the bulk of the other dates. Some are apparently too old, some apparently too young.

---

[2] The Early Neolithic, as defined is this chapter, is basically not represented in central and eastern Macedonia. The Thessalian Middle Neolithic, or Sesklo period (phase 2), corresponds roughly to the Early Neolithic of Macedonia. The early Late Neolithic of Thessaly (Tsangli-Larissa and Arapi, phase 3) corresponds to the Middle Neolithic of Macedonia. The later Late Neolithic (Dimini period, *stricto sensu*, or phase 4) corresponds to the Late Neolithic in Macedonia.

[3] This list of dates has been compiled from various sources and checked, whenever possible, in *Radiocarbon*. Coleman's list (Coleman 1992) is by far the most accurate and complete. My own list includes, in addition, the new dates from Nea Nikomedeia and the revised dates from Servia and Ayios Petros. The dates from Knossos have not been taken into account except for the sample from stratum IX, since correlation between the Cretan and the Continental 'Early Neolithic' are far from clear.

Table 6.1 14C dates assigned to Early Neolithic levels. Dates are classified by chronological order. Their number corresponds to that of the graphs.

Sample number	Site	Level	Lab. ref.	Nature of the sample	Date BP uncal.	Calibrated date at 2 sigma	Maximum probabilities	References	Observations
1	Elateia	Tr.1, floor at 2.30 m	GrN–3039	Charcoal	8240±110	7497–6825	7270	Weinberg 1962 RC 5: 183	Same provenience as GrN–3502. Considered too old by excavator
2	Nea Nikomedeia	Near original level	Q–655	Charcoal	8180±150	7503–6625	7230, 7200, 7180, 7140, 7120, 7090	RC 4:69 Jadin 1983–4 Pyke and Yiouni 1996	Given as 8190± BP in Theocharis 1973 and Efstratiou 1985
3	Nea Nikomedeia	EN1	GX–679	?	7780±270	7418–6040	6650	Jadin 1983–4 Pyke and Yiouni 1996	
4	Franchthi	FF1 42 B1	P–1525	Charcoal + earth	7700±80	6624–6378	6470	Jacobsen and Farrand 1987 – RC 13: 365	
5	Sidari	Level C base	GXO–771		7670±120	6703–6216	6450	Sordinas 1969: 401	
6	Achilleion	Level Ib, B-1-31	UCLA–1882B		7260±155	6758–6065	6420	Gimbutas et al. 1989	
7	Sesklo	EN, depth 3.88 m, 63.122	P–1679	Charcoal + soil	7611±83	6591–6222	6420	RC 15:370	'Earliest pottery Neolithic'
8	Knossos	Area AC, strat. IX, area 1C, level 24	BM–272	Charcoal	7570±150	6627–6049	6410	Evans 1968 RC 11:279	'Immediately above stratum X'

9	Nea Nikomedeia	EN 1– A4/3, feature A	P-1202	Organic fraction	7557±91	6537–6180	6390	RC 9: 335, Pyke and Yiouni 1996	NaOH pre-treatment. Very probably first building period. Should be approximately contemporary with P-1203A and Q-655.
10	Achilleion	IIB-D-2-22, prof. 315 cm	LJ-3180	Charcoal	7550±60	6461–6215	6380	Gimbutas et al. 1989–RC 19: 25	Given as 7510±50 BP in Gimbutas 1974. Given as phase IIa in RC
11	Argissa	Burnt post of EN house	GrN-4145	Charcoal	7500±90	6463–6069	6369, 6270	Milojčić 1973 RC 9: 129	Given as 7560±90 BP by Milojčić
12	Achilleion	'Ia'–Test Pit East	LJ-4449	Charcoal	7490±15	6593–5995	6360, 6310, 6280, 6260	Gimbutas et al. 1989; RC 22: 1040	Given as level A–1–32 in RC and as 7540±140 in Gimbutas 1974. More probably Ib, according to the context
13	Elateia	NE quadrant of trench 1, basis, 3.10 m	Grn-2973	Charcoal	7480±70	6450–6171	6360, 6320, 6300, 6280, 6250	Weinberg 1962 RC 5: 182	
14	Achilleion	Ia–B–2–26	P-2118		7470±80	6452–6062	6350, 6330, 6300, 6280, 6250	Gimbutas et al. 1989; RC 17: 201	Given as 7471±77 BP in Gimbutas 1974. More probably phase Ib according to context – Wijnen (in litt.)

Table 6.1 (cont.)

Sample number	Site	Level	Lab. ref.	Nature of the sample	Date BP uncal.	Calibrated date at 2 sigma	Maximum probabilities	References	Observations
15	Achilleion	Ia–Test Pit East	UCLA–1896A		7460±175	6599–5959	6290, 6230	Gimbutas et al. 1989; RC 19: 26	More probably phase 1b according to context – Wijnen (in litt.)
16	Achilleion	Ib – A–2–27	GrN–7437		7440±55	6386–6071	6220	Gimbutas et al. 1989	
17	Sesklo	EN, trench 63, W, 68.98	P–1678		7427±78	6414–6048	6220	RC 15: 370	'Earliest pottery Neo'. Provenience questioned by Bloedow 1991
18	Nea Nikomedeia	H6/1a+H7/A	OXA–1605	Seed of *Hordeum vulgare*	7400±90	6413–6010	6190	Pyke and Yiouni 1996	'Reduced carbon'
19	Nea Nikomedeia	K6/1FG	OXA–1606	Seed of *Lens culinaris*	7400±100	6419–6000	6190	Pyke and Yiouni 1996	'Reduced carbon'
20	Nea Nikomedeia	H6/1a+H7/A	OXA–4282	Seed of *Hordeum vulgare*	7400±90	6413–6010	6190	Pyke and Yiouni 1996	'Humic acids'
21	Achilleion	Ib–B–1–30	GrN–7438		7390±45	6358–6055	6185	Gimbutas et al. 1989	
22	Asfaka	without	I–1959		7380±240	6619–5716	6180	Higgs 1968	
23	Nea Nikomedeia	NN B 5/1, 644	OXA–3874	*Capra* bone	7370±80	6377–6005	6180	Pyke and Yiouni 1996	'Ion-exchanged gelatin'
24	Nea Nikomedeia	NN C 9/1, L644	OXA–3876	*Bos* bone	7370±90	6385–5995	6180	Pyke and Yiouni 1996	'Ion-exchanged gelatin'

No.	Site	Context	Lab code	Material	BP	Cal range	Cal BC	Reference	Notes
25	Elateia	Floor of bothros in Tr.2, at 2.70 m	Grn-3037	Charcoal	7360±90	6381–5989	6180	Weinberg 1962 RC 5: 182	Given as trench 3 in RC
26	Achilleion	Ib – B–1–26– 354/363 cm	LJ-3329	Charcoal	7360±50	6349–6042	6177	Gimbutas et al. 1989; RC 19: 26	Given as 7370±50 BP in Gimbutas 1974
27	Sidari	Level C top, 'impresso'	GXO-772		7340±180	6467–5805	6170	Sordinas 1969: 401	
28	Achilleion	IIb–A–1–18 (dump)	P-2120	Charcoal	7340±70	6357–5999	6170	Gimbutas et al. 1989; RC 17: 201	
29	Nea Nikomedeia	C1 Spit 3 A	OXA–1604	Seed of Triticum dicoccum	7340±90	6373–5979	6170	Pyke and Yiouni 1996	'Reduced carbon'
30	Achilleion	IIb–D–2–18	UCLA– 1896C		7330±100	6377–5966	6170	Gimbutas et al. 1989	Given as 7330±95 BP in Gimbutas 1974 and Coleman 1992
31	Achilleion	Ib	LJ-3184	Charcoal	7320±50	6217–6008	6162, 6136, 6128, 6082, 6076	Gimbutas et al. 1989; RC 19: 26	Given as B–2–27 in RC and as 7280± 50 BP in Gimbutas 1974
32	Achilleion	IIa– B–1–19– 295/315 cm	LJ-3328	Charcoal	7300±50	6188–5999	6122, 6087, 6063	Gimbutas et al. 1989; RC 19: 25	Given as 7310±50 in Gimbutas et al. 1989
33	Nea Nikomedeia	NN D 8/2, J358	OXA-3873	Ovis bone	7300±80	6340–5970	6120, 6090, 6060	Pyke and Yiouni 1996	'Ion-exchanged gelatin'
34	Achilleion	IIa–A–1–21	GrN-7436		7295±70	6222–5977	6120, 6090, 6060	Gimbutas et al. 1989	
35	Achilleion	IIa-A–2–22– 280/292 cm.	LJ-3326	Charcoal	7290±80	6229–5966	6120, 6090, 6060	Gimbutas et al. 1989; RC 19: 25	Given as level IIb in RC

Table 6.1 (*cont.*)

Sample number	Site	Level	Lab. ref.	Nature of the sample	Date BP uncal.	Calibrated date at 2 sigma	Maximum probabilities	References	Observations
36	Achilleion	IIa–B–5–24– 340/345 cm	LJ–3186	Charcoal	7290±50	6186–5994	6118, 6089, 6058	Gimbutas et al. 1989; RC 19: 26	Given as 7250±50 BPin Gimbutas 1974 and 7300±50 in Gimbutas et al. 1989
37	Nea Nikomedeia	EN 2, B4/1, ash pit	P–1203A	Organic fraction	7281±74	6220–5967	6120, 6090, 6060	RC 9: 335	NaOH pre-treatment
38	Achilleion	II a – B–5– 20/21, prof. 315/325 cm	LJ–3325	Charcoal	7280±50	6183–5989	6115, 6092, 6055	Gimbutas et al. 1989; RC 19: 25	Given as 7290±50 BP in Gimbutas 1974
39	Franchthi	H 37 Y	P–1667	Charcoal + earth	7280±90	6338–5955	6120, 6090, 6060	Jacobsen and Farrand 1987; RC 13: 365	NaOH pre-treatment
40	Nea Nikomedeia	NN F6/1 FC PD, 0470	OXA–3875	Sus bone	7280±90	6338–5955	6120, 6090, 6060	Pyke and Yiouni 1996	'Ion-exchanged gelatin'
41	Achilleion	II a – A–1–26	P–2117	Charcoal	7270±80	6220–5958	6110, 6090, 6050	Gimbutas et al. 1989; RC 17: 201	Given as 7273±76 in Gimbutas et al. 1989
42	Achilleion	sq. A, D2–4, lev. 8 et D3 lev. 8	P–2128	Charcoal	7270±80	6220–5958	6110, 6090, 6050	RC 17: 200	Not published in Gimbutas et al. 1989
43	Nea Nikomedeia	K6/1FG	OXA–4283	Seed of *Lens culinaris*	7260±90	6224–5893	6110, 6100, 6050	Pyke and Yiouni 1996	'Humic acids'

No.	Site	Context	Lab no.	Material	BP date	Calibrated range	Date	Reference	Notes
44	Achilleion	IIb D-2-22	LJ-3181	Charcoal	7240±50	6174–5970	6042	Gimbutas et al. 1989; RC 19: 25	Same sample as LJ-3180 (no. 10). Given as 7200 ±50 BP in Gimbutas 1974 and 7250 ±50 in Gimbutas et al. 1989
45	Achilleion	IIb D-2-18	LJ-3201	Charcoal	7210±90	6185–5860	6010	Gimbutas et al. 1989; RC 19: 25	Given as D-2-19 in RC and as 7210 ±80 BP in Gimbutas 1974
46	Elateia	Tr. 2, floor at 2.55 m	GrN-3041	Charcoal	7190±100	6185–5816	6000	Weinberg 1962 RC 5: 183	
47	Nea Nikomedeia	C1 Spit 3 A	OXA-4281	Seed of *Triticum dicoccum*	7100±90	6116–5731	5960	Pyke and Yiouni 1996	'Humic acids'
48	Nea Nikomedeia	C1 Spit 2 A	OXA-1603	Seed of *Triticum dicoccum*	7050±80	6014–5709	5940, 5910, 5880	Pyke and Yiouni 1996	'Reduced carbon'
49	Elateia	Tr.1, floor at 2.30 m	GrN-3502	Charcoal	7040±130	6151–5620	5930, 5910, 5870	Weinberg 1962 RC 5: 183	Given as trench 2 in RC. 'Beginning of painted wares'. Same provenience as GrN – 3039 (no. 1)
50	Franchthi	FAS 129	P-2093	Charcoal + soil	6940±90	5964–5600	5750	Jacobsen and Farrand 1987 RC 17: 201	
51	Nea Nikomedeia	C1 Spit 2 A	OXA-4280	Seed of *Triticum monococcum*	6920±120	5981–5529	5730	Pyke and Yiouni 1996	'Humic acids'

Table 6.1 (cont.)

Sample number	Site	Level	Lab. ref.	Nature of the sample	Date BP uncal.	Calibrated date at 2 sigma	Maximum probabilities	References	Observations
52	Servia (Varythimides)	From fill of pit sealed by late EN courtyard	BM–1157	Charcoal	6905±87	5950–5593	5720	Radiocarbon 21:349, Coleman 1992	Considered too recent
53	Argissa	?	UCLA–1657E	Bone	6700±130	5772–5340	5580	Milojčić 1973	
54	Servia	UN 3644	BM–1885R	Collagen	6590±210	5848–5072		Bowman et al., RC 32(1): 72	The previous date of 6360±190 has been revised by BM
55	Knossos	EN1, West Court, sounding AA/BB, level 279, 286	BM–1372	Charcoal (combined samples)	6482±160	5634–5068	5430	Evans 1968 Radiocarbon 24: 159	
56	Elateia	Tr.1, floor at 2.30 m	GrN–2454	Humic fraction	6370±80	5440–5141	5280	Weinberg 1962 RC 5: 183	Same sample as GrN–3502 (no. 49). Considered too recent. Published as a date from Argissa by Theocharis 1973 and Efstratiou 1985

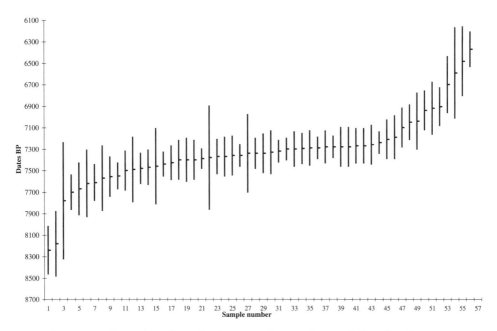

Fig. 6.1 Radiocarbon dates (BP) assigned to Early Neolithic levels.

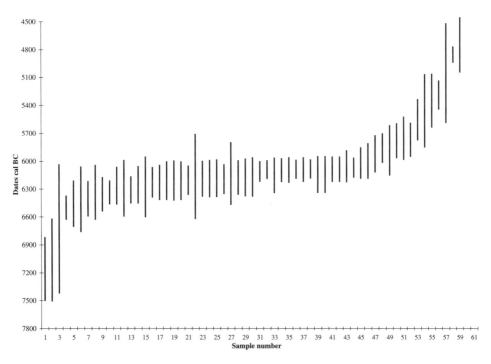

Fig. 6.2 Radiocarbon dates (BC calibrated) assigned to Early Neolithic levels.

Dates seemingly too old

The oldest dates assigned to Early Neolithic contexts are so obviously aberrant that one may wonder why they should be discussed at all. The reason is that these dates are amongst the most widely quoted for the introduction of the Neolithic in Greece. Yet, they come from series of datings in the early sixties, and showed, even then, obvious discrepancies *vis-à-vis* other dates from the same contexts.

 Weinberg wisely judged the 8240 ± 110 BP date from Elateia (GrN–3039, no. 1) as too high, since it came from the same context as GrN–3502, dated to 7040 ± 130 BP. He rejected it as doubtful (*Radiocarbon* 5: 183). To the contrary, the 8180 BP $\pm$ 150 BP date from Nea Nikomedeia (Q–655, no. 2) was widely publicized, despite a difference of 600 to 900 years from other dates from the same occupational level (P–1202, no. 9 and 1203A, no. 37). It was to become the most widely cited date for the 'introduction' of the Neolithic in Greece, despite early rejections by Weinberg (1970, n. 3) and Bintliff (1976a: 241). Twelve new dates from Nea Nikomedeia, recently obtained on the Oxford accelerator confirm, with no age earlier than 7400 BP, that it is aberrant and should be rejected. The same holds true for another date from this site (GX–679, no. 3): its provenience is problematic and its very large standard deviation (7780 ± 270 BP) gives it little significance. All three dates will thus be omitted from further discussions.

Dates seemingly too young

As would be expected considering the risk of contaminations by later material, dates that appear to be too young are slightly more numerous. The last four dates, which do not overlap with the others at one standard deviation, immediately stand out as anomalous. One is from Elateia again (GrN–2454, 6370 ± 80 BP, no. 56) and was done on the humic fraction of the same charcoal as GrN–3502. It too was rejected by Weinberg, this time as too young, and was not included in the site's monograph.

 The three other latest dates come from Servia (BM–1885R, no. 54), Argissa (UCLA–1657E no. 53) and a so-called EN1 level from Knossos (BM–1372, no. 55). No contextual information is given for any of these dates and the nature of the sample is unknown at Argissa, but contaminations by later material or wrong attributions are plausible. In the case of Knossos, it would tend to confirm the lack of correlation between the continental phasing and that of Knossos.

 The mean value of EN dates is 7313 ± 354 BP. All but one of the samples that we have here discussed differ from the mean by more than two standard deviations. The statistical probability they belong to the original group of EN dates is less than 5 per cent, leading to their rejection.

A last group that ought to be discussed consists of the remaining six latest dates (nos. 47–52), slightly offset from the rest of the distribution (Nea Nikomedeia, nos. 47, 48 and 51; Franchthi, no. 50; Servia no. 52; and Elateia, no. 49).[4] These dates barely overlap with the others at one standard deviation, but remain compatible at two standard deviations. All are later than 6000 BC, so that they correspond to the first period of time also well represented among Middle Neolithic dates. Dating problems may be involved in some cases,[5] but regional differences in the transition from the Early to the Middle Neolithic are equally plausible. Nearly all the oldest dates for the Middle Neolithic come from a single site (Achilleion), which deprives us of a valid chronological and geographical overview of this transition. As a consequence, these late dates should not be rejected based on the presently available evidence.

The central dates

The remaining dates, by far the more numerous, present a neat alignment between 7700 BP and 7200 BP in modal values (see fig. 6.1), but tend to cluster, when calibrated, between 6400 and 6000 BC (see fig. 6.2). This tight clustering masks, however, numerous internal discrepancies when each site is considered individually. Achilleion, for instance, provides several cases of reversed datings in relation to the stratigraphy. Since I do not intend to discuss the dating of the Early Neolithic at the more refined level of subphases for instance, these cases will not be detailed here. I consider them as inevitable in complex stratigraphic contexts where detailed taphonomic analyses have not been conducted.[6] However, since these biases can be considered as randomly distributed and since all the samples were associated with clearly identified Early Neolithic material, the series of dates as a whole can be considered as representative for the period.

When aberrant dates are excluded, the time range best represented is between *c.* 6400 and 6050 BC (see fig. 6.3), and this interval should thus be considered as a fair estimate of the actual age and duration of the Early Neolithic. However, because almost half of the dates ($n = 20$) derive from a single site, Achilleion, there was a risk of distorting the distribution by giving the latter too much weight. As a test, I calculated the mean of the Early Neolithic dates with and

[4] There are also four dates, indicated on a section, from the base of the sequence of Plateia Magoula Zarkou (Gallis 1996b). They range from 5750 to 5800 cal. BC, and seem to correspond also to this late phase of the EN. To my knowledge, they have not been published with full references.

[5] Such as Elateia (where we have already met problems) and Nea Nikomedeia, where the new accelerator datings on the humic acids of seeds gave on average younger dates than on the reduced carbon. Two out of the three dates under discussion were done on humic acid; the third however was done on the reduced carbon of one of the same seeds.

[6] If a reliable internal chrono-stratigraphy was to be established, the taphonomic context, whether an actual house-floor, a later pit, debris of a collapsed wall, a dumping area, etc., would obviously have required thorough evaluations. But this would have been feasible only in a minimum number of cases.

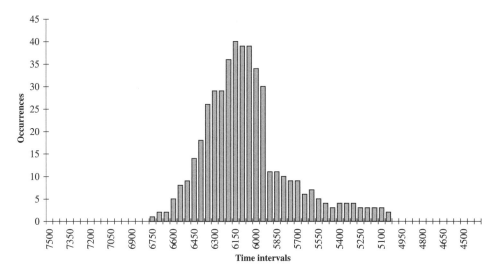

Fig. 6.3 Projection of the Early Neolithic 14C dates (BC calibrated)
according to fifty-year time intervals. Dates considered aberrant
have not been taken into account.

without Achilleion.[7] The results are in fact remarkably stable: 7336±204 BP
with the Achilleion dates, 7315±233 BP without.[8] The large proportion of
dates from Achilleion does not distort the general representation. The duration
of the Early Neolithic can thus be estimated at about 500 years, and dated to *c.*
7600 BP to 7100 BP, or *c.* 6540 to 5950 cal BC.

Five hundred years undoubtedly constitutes a long period of time. But this
long duration is confirmed by the almost perfect continuity between Early
Neolithic dates on the one hand, and Initial Neolithic and Middle Neolithic
dates on the other. It also fits well with the importance of Early Neolithic
deposits in many sites, which often reach a depth of more than four, and sometimes as much as ten metres. Retaining the taxonomic division of an 'Early
Neolithic' chronologically distinct from the Middle Neolithic has at least the
advantage of bringing to light this long phase, which would be obscured if a
general Balkanic phasing were followed. In turn, it raises the problem of chronological differentiation and regional diversification along the course of these five
centuries.

Early Neolithic subphases and facies

The Early Neolithic has been tentatively subdivided into different subphases
according to the region, but the classical confusion between ceramic facies and

---

[7] The distributions are fairly normal, so that the means can be considered meaningful.
[8] These means were calculated after the few dates discussed above were eliminated.

chronological phases has hindered any clear understanding of its chronological structure. Since the present study does not focus on chronology, only minimum indications will be given here, insofar as they are necessary for the subsequent analyses. In addition, these chronological problems already reveal some of the most significant contrasts between northern and southern Greece.

The detailed definitions of the regional subphases and the problems involved have been exposed recently by Gallis for Thessaly and by Coleman for the whole of Greece (Coleman 1992; Gallis 1992). In Thessaly, Milojčić's tripartite division of the Early Neolithic has been the most widely used, in spite of the serious difficulties it involved. After excavating at Otzaki and Argissa, Milojčić divided the Thessalian Early Neolithic into three successive subphases (following the Präkeramikum): the Frühkeramikum or 'Early Monochrome'; the Proto-Sesklo or 'Early Painted', which includes 'polished' wares; and the Vor-Sesklo phase, also called 'Developed Monochrome' or 'Pre-Sesklo', with Monochrome and Impressed/Incised wares (Milojčić 1956, 1959a and b). Theocharis also retained a tripartite division of the Early Neolithic, but emphasized intraregional variations (Theocharis 1962b, 1967, 1973b: 47). In south-eastern Thessaly, at Sesklo, the first two subphases were defined according to Milojčić's scheme, but the latest subphase (EN3) was characterized by Monochrome wares, without Impressed or Incised wares. In western Thessaly, on the contrary, Impressed/Incised wares were supposed to be introduced earlier than in north-eastern Thessaly, and to be wholly contemporaneous with the earliest painted wares (see also Hourmouziadis 1971a, 1971b).

In spite of the early recognition of its limited regional value, Milojčić's Thessalian sequence has been endowed with unwarranted general validity. The three subphases of north-eastern Thessaly are too often taken, especially outside Greece, to characterize the whole of the Greek Early Neolithic. In fact the validity of Milojčić's sequence outside individual sites can be questioned, as pointed out as early as 1970 by Nandris (Halstead 1984: ch. 4; Nandris 1970: 193ff.). The Otzaki ceramic sequence itself does not follow the scheme closely, so Milojčić-von Zumbusch and Milojčić (1971: 146–7) had to introduce further subdivisions of the EN in their monograph. More generally, the existence of a Monochrome phase has been debated (Nandris 1970: 193, 199), a pure 'Pre-Sesklo' has not been found outside eastern Thessaly, Painted and Incised/Impressed ceramics are most often found all together,[9] and Incised wares are not found at Sesklo. Accordingly, Gallis (1994: 58) considers that, for the time being, there is no acceptable chronological framework for the Early Neolithic of Thessaly. Wijnen, on the other hand, retains a tripartite chronology for the Thessalian Early Neolithic, but considers that the three subphases can only be distinguished by the relative proportions of the different wares (Wijnen 1993).

[9] cf. Achilleion (Gimbutas *et al.* 1989), Magoulitsa 1 (Papadopoulou 1958) and Prodromos in western Thessaly (Hourmouziadis 1971b), Nea Nikomedeia in western Macedonia (Rodden 1964b: 115).

Further south, in Boeotia, Weinberg (1962) recognized only two sub-phases at Elateia: the Monochrome phase ('First phase'), followed by the introduction of the first painted, white-slipped and black-burnished wares ('Second phase'). Coleman also suggests a bipartite rather than a tripartite subdivision in the Peloponnese: an early phase characterized by the pre-dominance of Monochrome wares, including the 'Variegated' or 'Rainbow' ware, and a later phase characterized by the addition of various Red Patterned wares and a distinct Black Burnished ware (Coleman 1992: 259). Yet, despite detailed ceramic studies, Vitelli (1993) was unable to find any chronological differentiation within the Early Neolithic at Franchthi. The same may also hold true at Nea Makri, in Attica, where quite distinctive white-filled wares are present right from the beginning of the sequence (Theocharis 1954, 1956).

As is clearly apparent, the internal phasing of the EN is still impinged by severe methodological problems, which will have direct bearings upon our sub-sequent studies. Limited excavations, important regional variations, disconti-nuities in site occupations, contaminations, etc., all concur to blur chronological schemes. The consequence is paradoxical: in Thessaly everyone acknowledges that the tripartite scheme reflects, to a large extent, regional or even local facies rather than successive phases (Gallis 1992), but it remains the only possible way to classify and characterize sites. If the 'monochrome' EN1, characterized by a very limited use of painting, and the beginnings of EN2, marked by the development of simple painted wares, seem to reflect actual chronological developments, they are then followed by a marked regionaliza-tion of the ceramic production that is not yet accurately defined or taken into account in 'chronological' schemes.

The interesting point, however, is that chronological schemes are no better defined elsewhere, but for opposite reasons. At least three phases have been identified in Thessaly, only two in Boeotia, and none in the latest studies from the Peloponnese and Attica. These contrasts follow contrasts in settlement density: the denser the settlements, the more diversified the ceramics – the scarcer the settlement, the more homogeneous and stable the ceramics. The two phenomena may obviously be related: the denser the settlement, the more numerous the excavations and the better our grasp of regional and chrono-logical diversity. Yet, a contrast of a similar order can be observed during the Middle Neolithic, in situations where the number of excavations is not at stake. One should not reject, therefore, the possibility of a *sociological* relation between the two phenomena. The drastically different sociological conditions that obtained in the different parts of Greece, as indicated by the study of set-tlement patterns, may have led to a multiplication of ceramic styles in the densely settled areas, and an emphasis on uniformity in the regions of sparse settlement.

Human implantation and settlement patterns: a contrasted distribution

The first striking element of the Early Neolithic in Greece, to which we have already alluded, is the sheer number of sites. Nearly 250 sites are attributed to the Early Neolithic,[10] and a further 50 are considered as potentially EN.[11] This is in sharp contrast to the scarcity of Mesolithic sites. On the other hand, the Early Neolithic has been shown to last several centuries: a progressive spread of EN farming settlements all over Greece during several centuries could easily have led to an even greater number of sites. But a simple examination of the distribution of sites, as well as more detailed analyses of settlement patterns, reveal that the model of progressive and regular expansion does not hold true in Greece. Not all regions were settled, the density of settlement varied widely, and the founding of new villages did not take place regularly during the course of the centuries (see also following chapter). The Early Neolithic is well represented, from Thessaly on, in the eastern part of Greece. It has not, so far, been documented in central and eastern Macedonia, in Thrace, in the Sporades and Cycladic islands.[12] The importance and thoroughness of the field surveys vary from region to region and account, to a certain degree, for the contrasts in settlement density. But the fact remains that Early Neolithic farmers had well defined criteria in the choice of regions in which they chose to settle.

Hills and sedimentary basins

Not surprisingly, the first contrast opposes the hills and mountains, almost devoid of sites, and the sedimentary basins that attracted a dense settlement – a pattern opposite to that observed during the Mesolithic.

By comparison with other Mediterranean regions, where Neolithic hill-sites or mountain sites seem to complement plain sites as short-term animal pens, hunting camps or ritual sites (see Beeching *et al.* 1991; Maggi *et al.* 1990, 1991), the scarcity of hill sites appears anomalous. Caves, for instance, are almost completely neglected during the Early Neolithic. Of the *c.* 300 EN or potentially EN sites recorded in Greece, only 9 are caves.[13] Amongst these, only 3 are definitely occupied during the EN: Franchthi, Theopetra, Archondaria and

---

[10] This figure comes from a compilation of Greek Neolithic sites derived from many different sources. I do not claim that my files are exhaustive and some attributions are questionable. However, it gives an order of magnitude.

[11] These figures must be well under the reality, since the different regions of Greece have been very unevenly surveyed.

[12] Despite repeated claims to the contrary (see for instance Marangou L. 1985), there is no stratigraphic or radiochronological evidence for Early (or Middle) Neolithic *settlement* on these islands.

[13] Franchthi, the Cave of Nestor, Choirospilia, Theopetra, Arcondaria, Portes, Kokora Troupa. Tsoungiza also was occupied then, but was not really a 'cave' (Cherry *et al.* 1988).

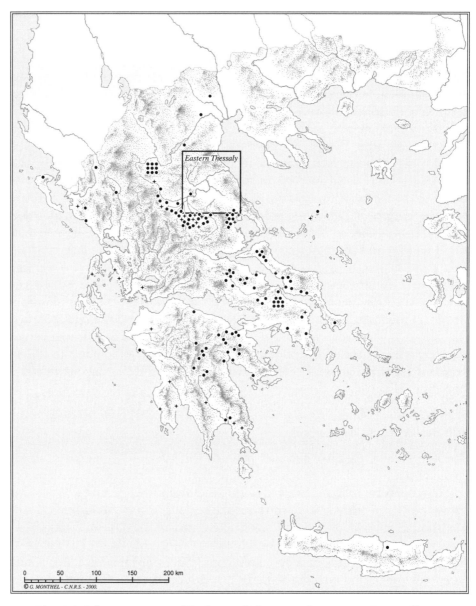

Fig. 6.4 Schematic map of Early Neolithic sites known in Greece (for eastern Thessaly, see fig. 7.3). Dots: EN sites or groups of sites. Crosses: sites of uncertain EN attribution.

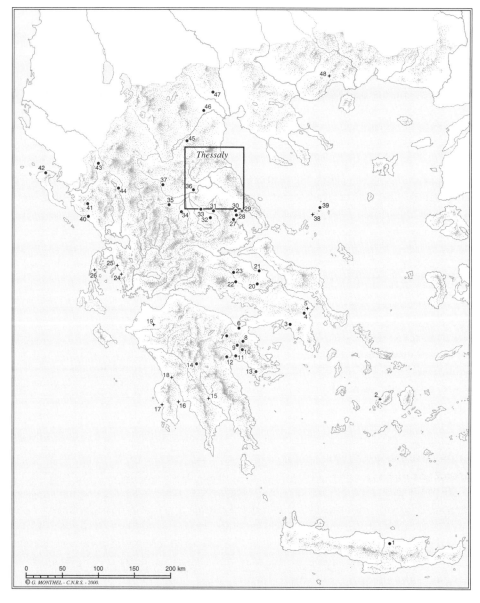

Fig. 6.5 Map of Neolithic sites from Greece mentioned in text (for eastern Thessaly, see fig. 7.3). Dots: Early Neolithic sites. Stars: later Neolithic sites or uncertain Early Neolithic sites. 1: Knossos. 2: Saliagos. 3: Athens (*Agora, Acropolis*). 4: Nea Makri. 5: Marathon (*Cave of Pan*). 6: Corinth. 7: Nemea (*Tsoungiza*). 8: Berbati. 9: Prosymna (*Argive Heraion*). 10: Dendra. 11: Koutsoura. 12: Lerna. 13: Franchthi. 14: Asea. 15: Kouphovouno. 16: Kokora Troupa. 17: Cave of Nestor. 18: Malthi Dorion. 19: Portes. 20: Sarakinos. 21: Halaï. 22: Chaeronea. 23: Elateia. 24: Ayios Nikolaos (*Astakos*). 25: Arcondaria. 26: Choirospilia. 27: Daudza. 28: Pyrassos. 29: Dimini. 30: Sesklo. 31: Tsangli. 32: Achilleion. 33: Myrini. 34: Prodromos. 35: Magoulitsa. 36: Plateia Magoula Zarkou. 37: Theopetra. 38: Ayios Petros. 39: Cyclop's Cave (*Youra*). 40: Ephyra. 41: Paramythia. 42: Sidari. 43: Asfaka. 44: Kastritsa. 45: Servia. 46: Nea Nikomedeia. 47: Giannitsa B. 48: Dikili Tash.

possibly Choirospilia. Even Franchthi is but a partial exception, since the main occupation was outside the cave, on the 'Paralia'.

The definite focus of most surveys on alluvial plains and basins may partly account for this situation. Yet several surveys have systematically included, or even focused on hill caves and rock shelters, without finding evidence of Early Neolithic occupations (Wickens 1986 for Attica, who emphasizes the absence of EN occupation; Runnels and van Andel 1993 for Thessaly; Rolland 1980 for Boeotia). Although more work should be devoted to this problem, it would appear that the subsistence economy of the Greek Early Neolithic, contrary to what occurred in other Mediterranean areas, was not based on a complex terri-torial exploitation system comprising both the fertile plains and surrounding hills. It appears to have relied, for the most part, on the exploitation of the sedi-mentary plains and basins proper, from a permanent village base with no con-spicuous satellite sites. This will have important bearings on the analysis of husbandry practices and procurement of raw materials.

The east/west contrasts

Not every alluvial basin, however, presents the same density of permanent set-tlements. This is a second conspicuous contrast, which opposes eastern and western Greece. Apart from a few sites in Epirus and on the west coast[14] and three (questionable) sites in Messenia,[15] Early Neolithic sites all concentrate in the eastern half of Greece (see fig. 6.4).

Neogene and Quaternary formations, the favoured *loci* of Early Neolithic implantations, are in effect more largely distributed in eastern than in western Greece (Kraft *et al.* 1985). However, even large areas of Quaternary alluvium in western Greece appear to be devoid of Early Neolithic sites. In some instances, deep alluviation, enhanced by the higher rainfall in the west, might have buried early settlements. But examination of the sections published by Chavaillon *et al.* (1967, 1969) for Elis, for example, shows that recent alluviation is very shallow and could not have buried any but the most short-lived settlements. Similarly, the recent alluvium in the Sparta plain and in Messenia is of limited expansion, yet no settlements were found, even on the older formations (Bintliff 1977, map. 3, p. 446; map 1, p. 513).

On the whole, the pattern seems to be too systematic to be explained solely by geological factors. Even if a number of sites have been recently buried or eroded away, they could not have compared, in density and importance, with those of north-eastern Greece. At the minimum, this implies a real contrast in the density of long-lasting settlements between eastern and western Greece.

---

[14] Sidari on Corfu, Asfaka, Kastritsa, Ephyra, Paramythia, Choirospilia and Ayios Nikolaos.
[15] Malthi Dorion, the Cave of Nestor and Kokora Troupa. The presence of a distinct EN stratum has not been confirmed in any of the three sites.

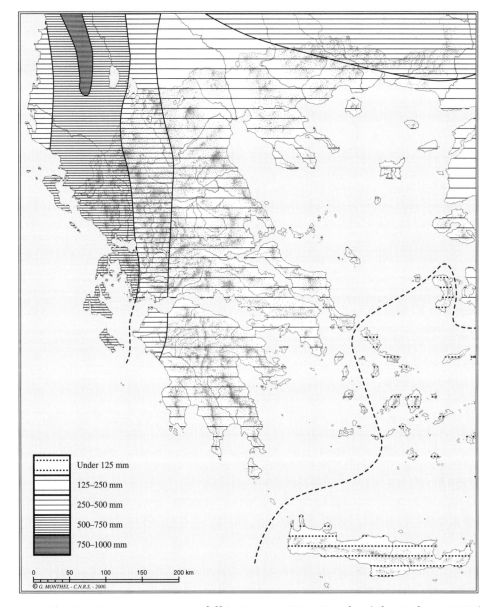

Fig. 6.6 Mean summer rainfall in Greece, May–October (after Polunin 1987).

According to Weinberg (1970: 575), this distribution suggests 'an eastward and seaward orientation'. However, Psychoyos (1988) recorded only twelve EN sites on the coast, and the impressive number of sites with no immediate access to the sea renders the latter explanation implausible.[16] On the other hand, the east–west distribution of Early Neolithic sites closely follows hydrometric curves (Polunin 1987: 16–17). The vast majority of known EN sites are located in the *driest* part of Greece, with a mean present-day annual precipitation of about 600 mm or less.[17]

How can this apparent paradox be explained? Two facts are worth considering: first, the regions exploited present the natural conditions closest to those of the Near East, which minimizes the problems of species adaptation to new environmental conditions and in particular to higher precipitations, a major problem for cereals (Hillman and Davies 1990: 184–6); second, by definition, the drier regions were also those where natural forest rejuvenation after clearance would have been the most limited, and the most easily checked down by fieldwork and animal pasture. In spite of the higher risk of drought that this choice entailed, Early Neolithic farmers may thus have preferred natural environments to which their Near Eastern domesticates were already well adapted, and which did not entail shifting cultivation.

North–south contrasts
Even within eastern Greece the density of sites shows important regional variations. The highest number and density are found in Thessaly, where a very old survey tradition, initiated early in the nineteenth century, has now brought to light several hundred settlements. However, although substantial work has been done in the past twenty years in Epirus, Macedonia, Magnesia, central Greece, Laconia, Argolid and Euboia, for instance, the density of known Early Neolithic sites remains substantially lower.

The complete absence of Early Neolithic sites in central and eastern Macedonia has already been discussed (above, ch. 4). In western Macedonia and central Greece, long-term settlements are definitely present, but their density appears to be much lower than in Thessaly. Further south, in the Peloponnese, the overall density of sites is still lower, even in well-surveyed alluvial basins such as the Berbati–Limnes basins, Nemea basin, southern Argolid or Laconia (Cavanagh *et al.* 1996; Cherry *et al.* 1988; Jameson *et al.* 1994; McDonald and Rapp 1972; Wells 1996). Peloponnesian sites are few, often separated one from the other by 5 to 20 km, and located in small alluvial basins (see fig. 6.4). Asea, Lerna, Franchthi, FS 400 in the Berbati basin and Corinth constitute good examples of these widely spread and demonstably isolated settlements. Further south again, in the

---

[16] Even taking into account the submersion of coastal sites. See Bintliff 1976a, 1977; Psychoyos 1988; van Andel and Shackleton 1982.
[17] According to Nandris (1977a: 42, 45) this holds true not only for Greece but also for the Macedonian–Bulgarian region.

Cyclades, no settlement from the Early or Middle Neolithic has been identified, despite systematic surveys and the demonstrated use of resources from the islands – especially obsidian from Melos (Cherry 1981, 1990; Davis 1992).

Even within the Peloponnese, there seems to be a decrease in the density of sites from the north-east to the south and south-west (Cherry *et al.* 1988). Again, several factors may be at stake: alluviation is one of them, as demonstrated by the discovery through coring of a Middle Neolithic site in the Argive plain under 5.5 m of Holocene sedimentation (van Andel and Zangger 1990). Yet Holocene sediments are of localized extent and many settlements are located on still-preserved Neogene or Pleistocene surfaces (Bintliff 1976b). Cherry *et al.* (1988) note that early sites in the Peloponnese tend to be smaller than in northern Greece,[18] and suggest that many sites may have been short-lived settlements, difficult to spot unless systematically surveyed. It is also noteworthy that several southern sites are 'flat-sites' rather than tells. One may wonder if the EN settlement at Corinth, for instance, would have been spotted if it had not been located right under the Classical city. In this respect, the overall north–south contrast might reflect important differences in the nature and density of settlements.

This decreasing gradient in the density of long-duration settlements from north to south, Macedonia excepted, approximately parallels gradients of increasing mean temperatures, decreasing annual rainfall and, consequently, increasing inter-annual fluctuations. Mean annual rainfall is not only higher, but also more stable in the large basins of the north than in the south (Halstead 1981b). Except in the most favourable areas, these conditions would have prevented the development of long-duration settlements until complex systems of crop rotation, crop complementarity and drought-resistant species were developed. According to van Andel and Runnels (1987: 70–1), early agricultural settlements in southern Greece were constrained by the necessary presence of permanent springs, allowing for cultivation in spring-fed meadows. This hypothesis was confirmed by a detailed study of settlement patterns in the Argolid and Corinthia, which led Johnson to the following conclusion:

The EN–MN village farming sites were located in areas with abundant groundwater, near spring-watered meadows, perennial streams and lakes, reflecting the choice of an homogeneous type of landscape with well-watered alluvial soils of high potential for arable agriculture. Such locations have a strictly limited distribution in southern Greece. (Johnson M. 1996b: 282–3)

The complete absence of fresh water on several Cycladic islands would thus explain the absence of early settlements, although the small superficies, the

---

[18] Johnson does not share this opinion and notes that several EN settlements in Argolid and Corinthia are over 1 ha. (Johnson M. 1996b). The answer actually depends on the figures retained for Thessalian *magoules*. If French's estimates are used, then the Peloponesian sites compare well with those of Thessaly (French, n.d.). If Gallis' estimates are preferred, then Peloponnesian sites are indeed smaller (Gallis 1992).

lack of resources and the difficulties of early navigation would also have limited the possibilities of permanent settlement (see discussion in Cherry 1990). As stated by Davis (1992: 704), the technical and sociological possibilities of widespread exchange may have been a prerequisite for permanent settlement of the small, impoverished islands.

This last observation underlines the fact that the density of settlements may have been determined not only by environmental factors, but also sociological factors. An important aspect of settlement patterns all over eastern Greece is the apparent relation between the spatial extent of the alluvial basins and the *density* – not only the number – of sites: the larger the basin, the more numerous and closely spaced the settlements. The rationale behind such a relation is not altogether clear, since, in theory, the smaller basins could have accommodated many more sites if the territory of the settlements was similar to that reconstructed for Thessaly (*c.* 2.3 km in diameter: see ch. 7 below). Environmental factors are partly responsible, since the larger basins are also the best watered. As pointed out by Johnson, the more restricted distribution of favourable locations in southern Greece may have prevented the fission of the community (Johnson M. 1996a). Yet, I suspect that sociological and demographic factors are also at stake. A higher demographic base in the larger basins would have facilitated the exchange of mates, labour and subsistence goods, therefore sustaining economic and demographic growth (Halstead 1989a, 1992).

Whatever the case, the obvious implication of such contrasting densities is that the resulting socioeconomic context was quite different in the densely populated plains of Thessaly and the more sparsely populated hills of the Peloponnese. In the first case, maintaining a dense network of social relations between different communities was easy, although some mechanisms must have been at work to limit potential conflicts resulting from close contact between neighbouring communities. In the second case, exemplified by the Peloponnese, *maintaining* contact with other communities must have been the major structuring factor in social organization. In both cases, strong integrative mechanisms are implied, but for different purposes and presumably of a different order.

Yet, the singularity of Thessaly, with its unusually high settlement density, must again be emphasized: Thessalian settlement patterns, which will be studied in more detail in the next chapter, are *not* representative of Early Neolithic Greece. On the contrary, they constitute a unique phenomenon, which requires specific explanations.

CHAPTER 7

A CASE STUDY IN EARLY NEOLITHIC SETTLEMENT PATTERNS: EASTERN THESSALY

The exceptional density of long-term Neolithic settlements in Thessaly was recognized from the beginning of the century. In the decades that followed, successive surveys gradually increased the number of sites identified, bringing the total to more than 300. In 1984, Halstead exploited an already impressive corpus and offered the first thorough analysis of settlement patterns in Thessaly (Halstead 1984). Although the details of his analyses have remained unpublished, the main diachronic and synchronic conclusions can be found in several papers (e.g., Halstead 1977, 1981a, 1989a, 1989b, 1994, 1995). Not much can presently be added to his analyses of western Thessaly, the Karditsa plain. In the meantime, however, Gallis had resumed surveys in eastern Thessaly with his collaborators, leading to the publication of a systematic 'Atlas of prehistoric settlements in eastern Thessaly' (the ATAE). This included several newly discovered sites and refined chronological attributions, as well as various statistics on the chronological distribution of sites, the duration of their occupation, their size, etc. (Gallis 1992).

Relying on Gallis' Atlas and recent geomorphological fieldwork (van Andel *et al.* 1995), van Andel and Runnels published another study that concentrated on the palaeo flood-plains of the Larissa basin. Though more restricted in scope than the previous analyses, its conclusions differed and were the basis of important theoretical developments on the causes and dynamics of the Neolithic expansion (van Andel and Runnels 1995).

Both Halstead on the one hand, and van Andel and Runnels on the other, concluded that the distribution of sites was uneven, that sites were clustered rather than dispersed, and that the clustering of sites in specific environments revealed deliberate choices. They parted, however, on the nature of these choices. Halstead had characterized the micro-environments, in a radius of 1 and 2 km around each site, according to four different categories: primary and secondary arable land, wetlands and rough grazing (Halstead 1984: table 6.7). He found that preference was given to locations providing access to the most varied micro-environments, whereas homogeneous tracks of primary arable land were avoided[1] (Halstead 1984: 6.4.3; see also Barker 1985: 63). However, van Andel and Runnels reached different conclusions by counting the number

---

[1] The use of diversified micro-environments would have constituted a good risk-buffeting strategy (see Halstead 1981b, 1990b; Halstead and Jones 1989).

of sites located on terraces or alluvial fans on the one hand, on flood-plains and wet bottom-lands on the other: the main focus of settlement would have been the flood-plains and wet bottom-lands that permitted spring flood-water farming.

The present study was undertaken parallel to Runnels and van Andel's, after the publication of Gallis' Atlas.[2] It is based on a larger sample of sites than the two other studies and includes all reported sites: Halstead had left out the Revenia, whereas van Andel and Runnels had concentrated on the Penios valley, the Tyrnavos and Nessonis areas. The conclusions I reached differ quite fundamentally from the previous ones: I found no clustering of sites in specific environments, that is, I found no evidence that the location of sites could be explained by environmental factors, whether soils, topography or hydrography. To the contrary, I came to the conclusion that if environmental factors played a role, it was a repulsive, rather than an attractive one.

The geology of the Larissa plain

The quality of the database is in large part related to the recent geological history of the region. The Quaternary geology, geomorphology and hydrogeology of Thessaly have been studied in particular by H. Schneider (1968) and by Demitrack (1986); several subsequent papers summarized and discussed their results (Gallis 1992; van Andel *et al.* 1990; van Andel and Zangger 1990). More recently, Helly and his collaborators challenged several interpretations after a detailed study of the tectonic and hydrological history of eastern Thessaly (Caputo *et al.* 1994; Helly *et al.* 1994, 1996).

Thessaly, the largest lowlands of Greece, is a well-defined subsidence basin of late Tertiary origins. It is limited on all sides, along a system of major NW/SE faults, by steep and elevated mountains (the Pindus, the Olympus, the Ossa, the Mavrovouni and the Othrys, which reach 2,000 m). The only two accesses to the sea are through the narrow Tempe gorge to the north-east, and between the Othrys and Mavrovouni mountains to the Pagasitic Gulf, or Gulf of Volos. The primary Thessalian Basin was created during the Pliocene and subsided into two grabens, the Karditsa Plain to the west and the Larissa Plain to the east. The two plains are separated by a low central ridge, constituted of Neogene lacustrine sediments that had accumulated in the original depression. This ridge, called the Revenia or Mid-Thessalian Hills, now culminates at about 700 m.

A new and still active tectonic episode started during the Middle/Late Pleistocene. Through a series of WNW/ESE faults, it broke the Larissa basin into a series of successive depressions of decreasing altitude (see fig. 7.1). To the north, the Tyrnavos Basin became an independent and strongly subsident basin that drained the Penios and the Titarisios, coinciding with their alluvial plains.

---

[2] Part of this chapter was published in Halstead 1999.

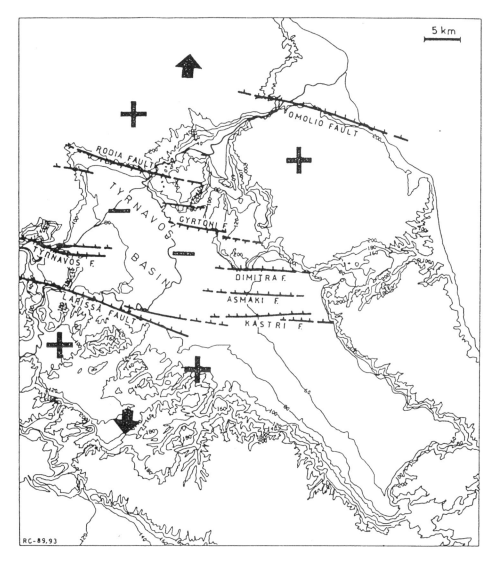

Fig. 7.1 Structural map of eastern Thessaly showing the major normal faults activated during the Middle Pleistocene–Holocene extensional regime (after Caputo *et al.* 1994).

Until recently the flood-plain extended up to the Nessonis lake, which had formed along the Gyrtoni fault. The Penios flood-plain deposits can be divided into a higher group, of Late Pleistocene and Middle Holocene age, and a lower group, of historical age (Demitrack 1986; Halstead 1984; Schneider H. 1968). Importantly, the most extensive deposits are constituted by the Ayia Sofia alluvium (see fig. 7.2), the earliest of the higher flood-plain deposits (or *Niederterrasse*, Schneider 1968). This alluvium was deposited between

LEGEND

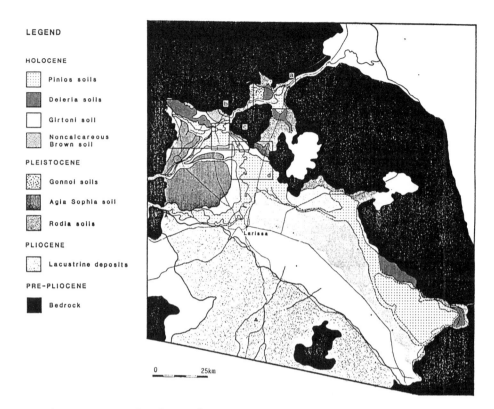

Fig. 7.2 Regional soil map for eastern Thessaly (after Demitrack 1986).

c. 40,000 and 27,000 BP, and is topped by a mature palaeosol, the Ayia Sofia soil. According to van Andel and Zangger (1990: 149), the latter corresponds to the onset of the last dry glacial maximum. Alluviation resumed on a smaller scale with the Mikrolithos alluvium, deposited on the edge of the Ayia Sofia alluvium between *c.* 14,000 and 10,000 BP. It was followed by another interruption in deposition and the development of the Noncalcareous Brown soil. Finally, the Gyrtoni alluvium, which buried the Mikrolithos alluvium, was deposited between *c.* 5000 and 4000 BP and marked the end of the construction of the higher flood-plain (Demitrack 1986; van Andel and Zangger 1990). The present flood-plain, more limited, is constituted by two alluvial episodes of historical date, 5 to 15 m below the *Niederterrasse* (Demitrack 1986; Schneider H. 1968; van Andel and Zangger 1990). As a result, only the Gyrtoni and the two historical episodes of alluviation could have buried Neolithic settlements. All three, however, are of limited extent.

The Tyrnavos Basin is separated from the lower-lying Eleftheri basin to the south-east and from the southern Larissa plain to the south by the low Chasambali Bulge, which culminates at 63–66 m above sea level, only a few metres higher than the Nessonis (Caputo *et al.* 1994). The intermittent Asmaki river cuts through the Chasambali Bulge. It could thus periodically drain the high waters of the Nessonis into the Eleftheri Basin. The very low Niamata bulge, which again corresponds to a fault, separates the Eleftheri Basin from the east of the southern Larissa Plain.

The southern Larissa Plain itself remained mostly unmodified when the whole basin was faulted (Caputo *et al.* 1994). It is not directly drained by the Penios but constitutes an endoreic basin, fed by the streams coming down the Mid-Thessalian Hills from the west and the Mavrovouni from the east. A west–east section reveals a complex palaeogeographic zonation. To the west, the unstable soils of the Mid-Thessalian Hills provided abundant sediments that were transferred, through a 'bypass zone' where many EN settlements are established, down to an altitude of 60–50 m. There they accumulated and formed large, flat, inconspicuous alluvial fans (Caputo 1990; Helly *et al.* 1996). Further east, lacustrine deposits accumulated in the past Karla lake or marshes, between 48 and 46 m above sea level. On the eastern limit of the depression, small steep alluvial fans were created by the sediments eroded down from the Mavrovouni. Unfortunately, the dates and depth of the alluvial fans, especially those created by the erosion of the Mid-Thessalian Hills, are not yet ascertained. This creates severe problems for estimating how representative the distribution of known sites is in this area.

The representativeness of the distribution of sites

A rapid look at the distribution map (fig. 7.3) immediately reveals two zones that present opposite patterns and must be discussed separately. The largest one, which comprises the Tyrnavos Basin, the Revenia and the western side of the Larissa Basin, shows a high density of settlements. On the other hand, the lowest-lying areas are almost devoid of sites.

The settlement-rich zone

More than half of all EN sites are located on the Late Pleistocene Ayia Sofia surface or on the Neogene sediments of the Revenia (Mid-Thessalian Hills). The preservation of these old land surfaces up to the present ascertains that few if any Neolithic settlements are either buried under sediments or have been destroyed by erosion. Theoretically, only sites marginally located on the Mikrolithos alluvium and later buried under the Gyrtoni formation (of *c.* 2.5/3 m deep) could be presently invisible. None, however, has so far been recorded through coring, excavation or examination of natural sections.

On the other hand, the course of the Penios, especially north of Larissa, has been notoriously unstable (Caputo *et al.* 1994; Demitrack 1986; Helly *et al.* 1994). Some settlements, such as Argissa, were partially eroded by the vagaries

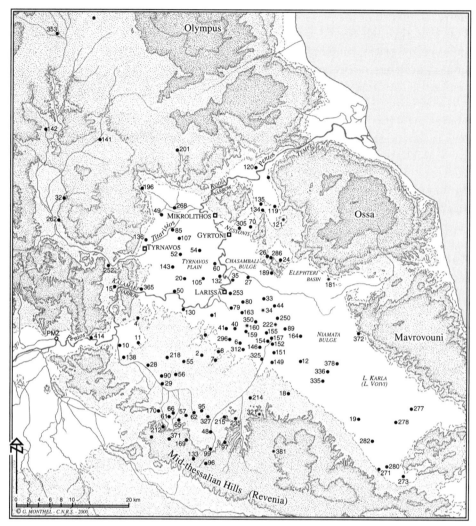

Fig. 7.3 Early Neolithic 2 sites (dots) and unspecified Early Neolithic sites (stars) from eastern Thessaly. Numbers and first name according to the ATAE (Gallis 1992); traditional appelation in brackets. 1: Larisa 2. 2: Mesorrachi 1 (*Magoula Vrastires*). 3: Larisa (*Magoula Vrastero*). 4: Mandra 1 (*Lithotopos*). 6: Nikaia 13 (*Magoula Karatsoli 1*). 7: Nikaia 11 (*Magoula Pigadoulia*). 8: Nikaia 12 (*Magoula Boukoum*). 10: Mandra 2 (*Magoula Gueka*). 11: Rachoula 1. 12: Melia 2 (*Magoula St'Ambelia*). 15: Damasi 4 (*Magoula Tourcoyefira*). 18: Moschochori 1 (*Magoula Bisler*). 19: Armenio 2 (*Trani magoula*). 20: Dendra 2 (*Otzaki*). 24: Kalochori 3 (*Nessonis 7*). 26: Nesson 2 (*Nessonis 2*). 27:Omorphochori 1 (*Magoula Nechali*). 28: Koilada 1 (*Magoula Asprogi*). 29: Krannon 1 (*Magoula Chalkiades*). 32: Domeniko 1. 33: Melissochori 4 (*Magoula Alki Tepe*). 34: Melissochori 1 (*Meteseli magoula*). 35: Larisa 9 (*Soufli magoula*). 40: Larisa 7 (*Magoulitsa*). 41: Larisa 6 (*Karagatz magoula*).

of the Penios. Here again, however, the relatively small spatial extent of the recent flood-plain makes it unlikely that many long-term settlements could have been completely eradicated.

On the whole, the geological conditions in the higher-lying areas of the Larissa Basin are thus unusually favourable for the preservation and visibility

Caption to Fig. 7.3 (*cont.*)

44: Galini 1 (*Megali magoula Karagatz*). 46: Giannouli 1 (*Arapi*). 48: Zappeio 2 (*Magoula Koutsouro*). 49: Tyrnavos 3 (*Megali Vrysi Tyrnavo*). 50: Dendra 1 (*Argissa*). 52: Ambelonas 3 (*Magoula Karagiozi*). 54: Phalanni 1 (*Magoula Tatar*). 55: Mesorrachi 2 (*Magoula Vrastira*). 56: Krannon 5 (*Mavros lofos*). 57: Ayios Georgios Larisas 5 (*Magoula Bei*). 60: Dasochori 2 (*Orman magoula*). 61: Ayios Georgios Larisas 2 (*Magoula Vrasteri*). 62: Ayios Georgios Larisas 7 (*Magoula Gamina*). 65: Ayios Georgios Larisas 3 (*Magoula Dragasti*). 66: Ayios Georgios Larisas 4. 70: Makrychori 4 (*Rachmani*). 79: Larisa 5 (*Magoula Arapadiki*). 80: Melissochori 2 (*Mesiani Magoula*). 85: Ambelonas 6 (*Magoula Goltsou*). 89: Glavki 2 (*Magoula Kavaki*). 90: Krannon 3 (*Orenia*). 95: Kyparissos 3. 96: Chalkiades 2 (*Mezini Magoula*). 97: Zappeio 5 (*Magoula Roïdies*). 99: Chara 2 (*Magoula Paliambela*). 105: Giannouli 4 (*Magoula Marmara*). 107: Ambelonas 5 (*Magoula Eske Bler*). 119: Elateia 1 (*Magoula Elatia*). 120: Gonoi 1 (*Besik tepe*). 121: Pournari 1 (*Bounarbasi*). 130: Terpsithea 1 (*Magoula KEMP*). 132: Dasochori 1 (*Magoula Prochoma*). 133: Chara 1 (*Magoula Panagiou*). 134: Makrychori 3 (*Magoula Sygourotopi*). 136: Tyrnavos 1 (*Magoula Marmara*). 138: Loutro 1 (*Magoula Anemomylos B*). 141: Elasson 2. 142: Kephalovrysso 1 (*Kephalovrysso*). 143: Dendra 3. 146: Nikaia 3 (*Magoula Kardara*). 149: Chalki 9. 152: Chalki 6. 154: Platykambos 5. 155: Galini 3. 157: Platykambos 2 (*Magoula Panagias*). 159: Melissochori 6 (*Magoula Karaïkia 1*). 160: Melissochori 5 (*Magoula Karaïkia 3*). 163: Melissochori 3. 164: Prodromos 2. 169: Kyparissos 2. 170: Doxaras 1. 189: Omorphochori 3 (*Gediki*). 196: Lygaria 2. 201: Ano Argyropouli 1. 212: Ayios Georgios Larisas 6. 214: Nees Karyes 3. 215: Zappeio 1. 218: Eleftherai 1. 222: Platykambos 4 (*Magoula Nekrotapheiou Platykambou*). 235: Zappeio 3. 250: Platykambos 1. 252: Damasi 3. 253: Larisa 3. 262: Mesochori 1. 268: Deleria 1 (*Magoula Ayios Athanasios*). 271: Velestino 3 (*Magoula Mati*). 273: Ayios Georgios Pheron 1 (*Magoula Tambouri*). 277: Stefanovikeio 5 (*Magoula Hadzimissiotiki*). 278: Stefanovikeio 2 (*Magoula Karamourlar*). 280: Velestino 2 (*Magoula Agropikiou*). 282: Ryzomylos 2 (*Platomagoules Ryzomylou*). 286: Nesson 1 (*Nessonis 1*). 296: Nikaia 5 (*Magoula Karatsoli*). 305: Gyrtoni 5 (*Magoula Stimeni Petra*). 312: Nikaia 9 (*Magoula Ambelia*). 325: Nikaia 19. 321: Sofo 1. 327: Zappeio 4 (*Petromagoula*). 335: Kypseli 3 (*Magoula Tsanaka 1*). 336: Melissa 1 (*Magoula Asprochoma*). 350: Galini 5. 353: Tharandaporon 1. 365: Platanoulia 2 (*Magoula Platanoulia*). 371: Kyparissos 4 (*Magoula Tsouka*). 372: Amygdali 1. 378: Lofiskos 1. 381: Kalo Nero 4. 414: Piniada 1.

of archaeological sites. The long-term mound settlements characteristic of Thessaly, the *magoules*, are normally clearly visible on the flat Thessalian Plain. In addition, the near absence of forests and extensive modern ploughing facilitate the recovery of artefacts during field-walking. Finally, as the total depth of archaeological deposits normally supersedes that of Holocene alluvium (Gallis 1992: 224, 233), only shallow short-term settlements could now be completely buried in areas affected by recent alluviation. However, this potential risk concerns only a minor fraction of the region under study, which is for the most part located above the level reached by Holocene sedimentation. It can thus be concluded that, at least in the higher-lying areas, geological factors did not significantly affect the distribution of sites.

On the other hand, none of the surveys conducted in eastern Thessaly was 'intensive' as defined by modern standards,[3] and it appears inevitable that some sites have escaped recognition.[4] In addition, the surveys and oral inquiries have been heavily oriented towards tell sites, or *magoules*, that is, towards long-duration settlements. All the potential biases in site recovery, whether of geological or archaeological origins, would predominantly concern short-term sites with shallow stratigraphies. In this respect, the analysis of settlement patterns must be considered as an analysis of *long-duration settlements*.

The settlement-void zone

A spectacular void in the distribution of sites, whose limit aligns along the N/W–S/E axis of the basin, was recognized long ago. Since this void area includes the historical Nessonis and Karla lakes or marshes, it was presumed that an older and larger lake covered most of the area. The maximum level reached by this lake was estimated by Grundmann at *c*. 63/64 m (as opposed to 44 m in historical times), because of the conspicuous alignment of Neolithic sites at this approximate altitude (see fig. 7.4). The few sites that were known at the time below this limit (nos. 277, 256, 257, 330) were all located on small emerging rocks, and considered to have been islands (Grundmann 1937). According to this model, the absence of settlements under the 63/64 m line would thus reflect an actual archaeological feature.

But this high shoreline was questioned after the discovery by Theocharis of Magoula Karamourlar (ATAE, 278), at about 50 m, emerging as a low mound in the southern Larissa Plain. Hence the humorous remark by Halstead: 'In L1 [the

---

[3] They were, however, thorough enough for several early scholars to ponder over the absence of sites in areas they had surveyed: see Wace and Thompson 1912: 6–7; Grundmann 1937; Kirsten 1950.

[4] Bintliff (1994a: 9) notes that even during intensive surveys in Boeotia only a small fraction of prehistoric sites were recognized. But the situation is more favourable in Thessaly, where the artefacts from prehistoric sites are seldom obscured by the abundance of Classical remains.

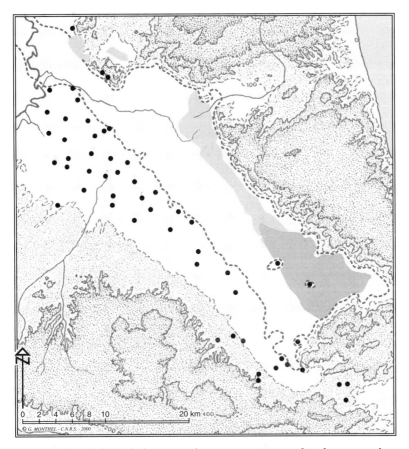

Fig. 7.4 Map of Neolithic sites known in 1937 and indication of 'Grundmann's line' (after Grundmann 1937).

lake Karla area] the high (63 m) Neolithic and Bronze Age shoreline proposed by Grundmann (1937) for L. Karla has evaporated with the discovery of Petromagoula,[5] Yefira Asmakiou[6] and Karamourlar. The burial of sites by sediment deposited during high lake levels of historical date now seems a more likely explanation for the paucity of sites here' (Halstead 1984: 6.4.1, see also 2.4). The newly discovered EN site of Lofiskos 1 (ATAE, 378), also located slightly below the 63/64 m, can now be added to the list.

There are, in fact, several other reasons for dismissing the hypothesis of a large paleo-lake extending over the whole of the Larissa Basin. First, Grundmann's line at 63–64 m represents only a crude approximation: the

---

[5] This must be a mistake, since the Petromagoula listed by Halstead (1984, 628) is on the edge of the Volos plain. There is another Petromagoula (Gallis 1992, 327), but this site is well within the Mid-Thessalian Hills.   [6] A Late Bronze Age site at the north end of the lake.

altitude of the hypsometrical curve immediately under the relevant settlements actually varies from 60 to 70 m. Secondly, recent work by Helly and his collaborators has shown that the low-lying basins of eastern Thessaly functioned as a series of largely independent depressions, alternately filling with water and drying up under the influence of tectonic and climatic factors. The old Karla lake itself probably never expanded above an altitude of *c*. 50 m, as demonstrated by the preservation at 51/54 m above sea level of a palaeo-shore line dated to 30,000 BP (Caputo *et al.* 1994; Helly *et al.* 1996).

Why, in those conditions, would sites nevertheless align on a line roughly parallel to (if well above) the ancient lake shore? According to Caputo, this rough alignment might correspond to the limit of the alluviation zone of the streams coming down the Revenia. Permanent settlement would have been impeded by periodic destructive floods (Helly *et al.* 1996: 12). Only sites locally protected from such alluviation could have been established – or have remained visible – at a lower altitude. This would have been the case for Karamourlar, located well to the south of the plain where the amount of sediments carried by the local streams is much less important.

However, since little is known of the depth and date of these alluvial fans, the possibility that sites have been buried under the sediments, as initially suggested by Halstead, cannot be ruled out either. These settlements would have filled the 'gap' between the lowest-lying settlements presently known (Grundmann's line) and the permanent lake or marshes, at *c*. 50 m of altitude. The available data suggest that the depth of the Holocene deposits in the southern Larissa plain is limited: 3 to 4 m for the last seven millennia (Bottema 1982; Caputo *et al.* 1994; Demitrack 1986). This is just under the average height of Neolithic *magoules* – 4 m according to Gallis 1992 – or even occasionally of Early Neolithic deposits that can reach 4 to 10 m. Here again, *if* sites are buried under Holocene sediments, these would be mostly 'atypical', with shallow stratigraphies.[7] Their presence along water expanses would constitute an unexplained anomaly.

Our analysis of settlement patterns suggests yet another explanation: the void area between *circa* 50 and 60 m of elevation can more simply correspond to the agricultural territory exploited by the settlements nearest to the lake margin. These would have left insufficient space for the foundation of other settlements, with a territory of normal dimensions.

It is thus unnecessary to postulate invisible sites near the Karla or the Nessonis lakes. Even if such sites existed, they would have been of a different nature than the long-term settlements of the higher-lying areas. Conversely,

---

[7] Since Halstead has shown a strong correlation between depth of sedimentation and number of archaeological phases, this would mean that all sites located nearest to the lake shores were either of short duration, or 'flat' extensive sites rather than mound-sites. This would contradict what is known in the rest of eastern Thessaly, where, according to Gallis' Atlas, less than 3.5 per cent EN sites show no later prehistoric occupation. As for 'flat sites', they are only known through the settlement below the Acropolis at Sesklo.

given their unusually good conditions of preservation and visibility, the representativeness of long-term settlements can be considered optimal. However, the multiplicity of phases represented at each site raises, in turn, dating problems. Since most sites are known only from surface finds, how reliable is their chronological or cultural attribution?

The problems of chronological attributions

EN strata are usually covered by thick deposits corresponding to later Neolithic or Bronze Age occupations. As experience shows, however, Early Neolithic occupations can still be identified, at least on the side of the mounds (Halstead 1984: 6.2.3). But if EN deposits can normally be recognized, the archaeological visibility of their different subphases or facies varies drastically.

Initial Neolithic occupations cannot be identified through surveys alone, since no artefact is exclusively characteristic of this phase. The situation is not altogether different for the earliest ceramic subphase, the EN1 Monochrome: Monochrome pottery is present in all the more recent subphases of the Early Neolithic and other diagnostic artefacts are rare. The EN3 poses similar problems: the characteristic Impressed/Incised wares of N/E Thessaly are absent from S/E Thessaly, where EN3 assemblages contain a high proportion of Monochrome wares.[8]

The rarity of characteristic artefacts implies that the sample of Initial Neolithic, EN1 and EN3 settlements cannot be considered as quantitatively representative. Conversely, the characteristic Proto-Sesklo painted ware of the EN2 allows a more secure and systematic identification. I have, therefore, focused the spatial analyses on the EN2, limiting the discussion about EN1 and EN3 to qualitative aspects. Yet, even for EN2, real contemporaneity between sites cannot be proven. Potential shifts of settlements within the EN2 period cannot be ruled out. The following study must therefore be considered as a working model. In addition, no control through fieldwork was possible after the study was undertaken; consequently, many questions remain unanswered.

EN1 settlements

Eastern Thessaly is characterized by a very high number of Early Neolithic sites: 117 altogether, for an estimated surface of *c.* 1150 km². However, the Early

---

[8] These problems may explain some discrepancies between the different specialists. In several instances, the phasing or subphasing given by Halstead (1984; the latter derives from French, s.d.), Wijnen (1981) or Gallis (1992) do not coincide. When later works have added precision to the chronological or cultural attribution, I have used the most recent attributions. In cases of real discrepancies (a phase, subphase or facies indicated as present by French, Wijnen or Theocharis, but as absent by Gallis), the site has been mapped with special symbols and left out of statistical computations.

Neolithic was of long duration and the large number of sites does not necessarily reflect a massive and sudden population influx at the beginning of the Neolithic. With a steady growth rate of 1 per cent over the long term, a rate considered average by Ammerman and Cavalli-Sforza in an early farming context (Ammerman and Cavalli-Sforza 1984: 80), the population would have doubled every sixty-nine years (Caralli-Slorza 1984: 71). Theoretically, a founding population of 200 in the Initial Neolithic could have increased to more than 30,000 after the *c.* 500 years of the Early Neolithic. Supposing a constant population in each village, as will be argued below, and an average of 200 inhabitants, the large number of EN settlements is easily accounted for. Unfortunately, the chronological resolution is insufficient to test the model of a steady increase in the number of settlements. The great difference in the number of recorded EN1 and EN2 settlements, as well as the apparent decrease in the number of EN3 settlements, might actually suggest the contrary. However, too many biases affect the comparisons to make any quantitative discussion meaningful. In the meantime, EN1 data are best approached from a purely qualitative point of view.

   Gallis (1992) recorded a total of fourteen EN1 sites (see fig. 7.5), a figure necessarily below the actual number. Despite this bias, the distribution of EN1 settlements is already informative. EN1 sites show a wide distribution over eastern Thessaly. Settlements are found in the Tyrnavos Basin, the southern Larissa Plain (under 100 m), the low Mid-Thessalian Hills (between 100 and 200 m) and in the high valleys of the Titarisios (no. 32, Domeniko 1). According to Gallis' Atlas, the north-eastern part of the basin, around Nessonis and Makrychori, and the southernmost plain, around Stefanovikeio, appear to be devoid of settlements. However, Theocharis (1967) and Wijnen (1981) had identified EN1 pottery on nine other sites, mostly located on the fringes of the already observed distribution: in particular, Magoula Karamourlar (no. 278) in the southernmost Larissa Plain, Nessonis 1 (no. 286) and Gonnoi (no. 120) in the north-eastern part.

   Whether or not one includes these additional sites, EN1 sites clearly do not cluster into a 'core area' or over specific pedological units (see fig. 7.5); nor do they align along preferred axes such as the Penios valley or its tributaries. Although a few sites are located along the present-day course of the Penios (Magoula Tourkoyefira (no. 15), Argissa (no. 50), Magoula KEMP (no. 130), Soufli (no. 35)), they are neither more numerous nor denser than the sites located away from the main river axes. On the contrary, they exemplify the independence of Early Neolithic settlements *vis-à-vis* hydrographic, topographic or pedological features and show that a dynamic of expansion in all directions had already taken place, probably during the Initial Neolithic.

EN2 settlement patterns

Besides seven unspecified 'Early Neolithic' sites that may also have been occupied during this period, Gallis' Atlas lists 106 EN2 sites, a figure that will not

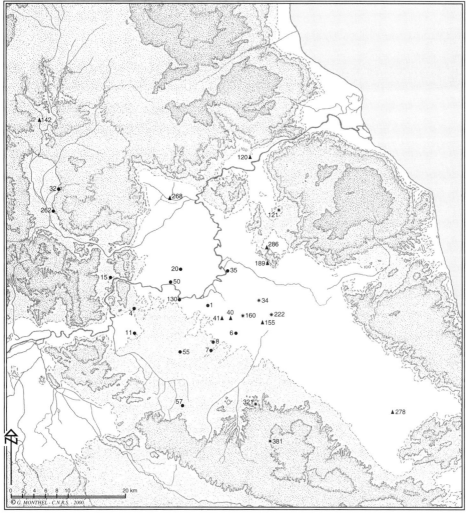

Fig. 7.5 Early Neolithic 1 and unspecified Early Neolithic sites from eastern
Thessaly. Numbers and first name according to the ATAE (Gallis
1992). Traditional appelation in brackets. Dots: EN1 settlements
according to Gallis 1992. Triangles: EN1 settlements according to
Wijnen 1981. Stars: unspecified Early Neolithic settlements. 1: Larisa 2.
4: Mandra 1 (*Lithotopos*). 6: Nikaia 13 (*Magoula Karatsoli 1*).
7: Nikaia 11 (*Magoula Pidagoulia*). 8: Nikaia 12 (*Magoula Boukoum*).
11: Rachula 1. 15: Damasi 4 (*Magoula Tourcoyefira*). 20: Dendra 2
(*Otzaki*). 32: Domeniko 1. 34: Melissochori 1 (*Meteseli magoula*).
35: Larisa 9 (*Soufli magoula*). 40: Larisa 7 (*Magoulitsa*). 41: Larisa 6
(*Karagatz magoula*). 50: Dendra 1 (*Argissa*). 55: Mesorrachi 2 (*Magoula
Vrastira*). 57: Ayios Georgios Larisas 5 (*Magoula Bei*). 120: Gonnoi 1
(*Besik Tepe*). 121: Pournari 1 (*Bounarbasi*). 130: Terpsithea 1 (*Magoula
KEMP*). 155: Galini 1. 160: Melissochori 5 (*Magoula Karaïkia 3*).
189: Omorphochori 3 (*Gediki*). 222: Platykambos 4 (*Magoula
Nekrotapheiou Platykambou*). 278: Stefanovikeio 2 (*Magoula
Karamourlar*). 268: Deleria 1 (*Magoula Ayios Athanasios*).
286: Nesson 1 (*Nessonis 1*). 321: Sofo 1. 381: Kalo Nero 4.

be reached again for a single ceramic facies until the Late Neolithic (see fig.7.3). This total comprises a few sites located in the high valleys of the tributaries of the Titarisios, or otherwise off-centred. If one restricts the sample to sites located in the inner basins and Revenia Hills, the number is reduced to 92, still a very high figure.[9] This drastic increase compared with the number of EN1 sites undoubtedly reflects both a higher number of settlements and the better visibility and long duration of the EN2 facies. To analyze the spatial distribution of the settlements, I followed the procedures implemented by J. Cl. Decourt, B. Helly and Y. Auda in their study of Thessaly from the seventh to the second century BC, which I found best fitted for homogeneous environments (Auda *et al.* 1990). When necessary, Gallis' data were complemented by observations from other scholars, in particular from Theocharis.

Regional distribution of the sites

The general distribution of the sites follows and amplifies the pattern already observed for the EN1, that is, a wide distribution over the plains, the lower hills and the adjacent valleys (see fig. 7.3). One of the most important contributions of Gallis' recent work is the demonstration of a dense settlement in the Mid-Thessalian Hills (between 100 and 200 m), which includes several sites located between 200 and 400 m.

More precisely, visual examination of the distribution of EN2 *magoules* over eastern Thessaly reveals a fairly even and dense distribution around and between three void zones. The largest void, oriented NW/SW, corresponds to the already mentioned depressions of the Karla and Nessonis lakes, below Grundmann's line. In the southern part, only one site is located east of these depressions (no. 372): quite precisely where the Niamata sill divides these low-lying areas into two separate basins, the 'Karla lake' and 'Eleftheri depression'.[10]

More surprising are two void areas in the Mid-Thessalian Hills, which, to my knowledge, had not been previously reported. They are surrounded by a large number of settlements, and no geological or topographical map gives any clue as to why they should have been avoided. I doubt that *magoules* have been completely eroded away, and suspect some adverse environmental factor: both areas correspond to areas of low-density settlement in Classical and Modern times (see Auda *et al.* 1990; Sivignon 1975). According to Helly (*in litt.* 8/94), water availability may be at stake, but the problem will not be solved without renewed fieldwork. Meanwhile, these areas have been retained in all statistical calculations, so that the density of settlements in the Mid-Thessalian Hills should not be artificially inflated.

[9] This figure would appear to contradict, locally at least, the affirmation that 'the density of settlement in Early Neolithic Europe appears to have been low' (Dennell 1984: 101).

[10] A concentration of settlements is also visible further north, just in the alignment of the Chasambali Bulge.

This raises the more general the problem of access to water sources. The absence of concentrations near water sources is a striking feature in an area where the present mean annual rainfall is between only 500 and 600 mm (Sivignon 1975). Since the Holocene climate supposedly approximates to that of today, water availability must have been a problem, especially during the long summer drought. Water was available in the perennial rivers, the Penios and the Titarisios, the seasonal streams, the lakes and marshes, and in a few perennial karstic springs such as the Iberia spring near Velestino (Sivignon 1975: 64–5). Many sites, however, are located 8 to 10 km away from any of these sources and both humans and cattle would have had to cross the territories of several other villages to reach them. It is possible that wells,[11] cisterns or intentionally equipped ponds are yet to be identified.

Distance of each site to its nearest neighbour

The distance between each site and its nearest neighbour,[12] based on the map published by Gallis (1992), was computed for all EN2 sites. The very small distance between settlements, in Thessaly as a whole, had already been emphasized by Halstead in his initial study (Halstead 1984: 6.4.5). The restriction of the analysis to eastern Thessaly and the addition of new sites further reduce the figures. The mean distance of each site to its first-order nearest neighbour is 2.7 km ($s\,n-1 = 2.08$) for 105 sites,[13] with 60 per cent of the sites actually located at less than 2.5 km from their nearest neighbour (see fig. 7.6). If one excludes the outlying settlements in the mountains, the mean distance between the 92 sites of the central area, the plains and Revenia, is reduced to 2.25 km ($s\,n-1 = 1.1$).

This figure is strikingly low for such an early phase of the Neolithic, when the rest of Europe had not yet turned to farming. In addition, the small distances between sites do not correspond to the familiar alignments along major axes such as rivers, lakesides or communication routes. What is most characteristic is that often not one but *several* sites are located at roughly the same distance from each other, in a reticulated, multidirectional pattern (see fig. 7.7).

A non-random distribution

The small distances between sites indicate a dense settlement, but do not inform us directly about the pattern itself. Statistical tests are thus required to

---

[11] Neolithic water-wells, sometimes very carefully built up, are known in several cultures of Europe, the Near East and northern Africa (see Close and Wendorf 1992; Galili *et al.* 1993; Huot 1994; Vaquer 1990).
[12] Because the computation considered the distance of *each* site to its nearest neighbour, the symmetrical distances, when two sites are each nearest to the other one, were counted twice (*contra* Auda *et al.* 1990). Counting the 'symmetrical' distances only once, as suggested by Upton and Fingleton (1985), modifies the results only very slightly: the mean distance for all sites is 2.7 km (standard deviation: 2.1). For sites located in the Larissa basin and Mid-Thessalian Hills only, it becomes 2.41 (standard deviation: 1.1).   [13] One site was missed in the computations.

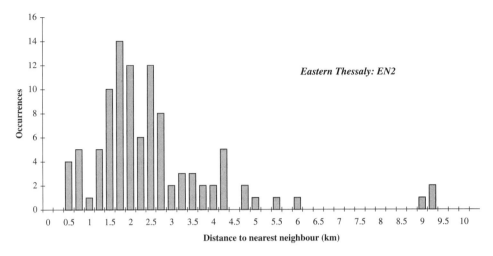

Fig. 7.6 Distribution of the distances between first-order nearest
neighbours.

estimate whether the distribution of sites can be considered random, or
whether, on the contrary, it is more clustered or more regular than would be
expected following a random hypothesis.

I have used three different formulas to test the hypothesis of a random distribution: two from Clark and Evans (1954) and one from Donnely (in Upton
and Fingleton 1985).[14] All showed that the hypothesis of a random distribution
could be firmly rejected.[15] However, these statistics did not support, either, the
hypothesis of site clusters. Compared to a random distribution, the distribution

[14] I thank Y. Auda for his help and precision concerning the use of these formulas.
[15] Clark and Evans' formula reads as follows:

$$E(W) = \frac{1}{2\sqrt{1}}$$

and

$$var(W) = \frac{4-\Pi}{4N I \Pi}$$

where N = number of sites, 1 = density of sites. The surface under study has been estimated at
1150 km^2 and the number of sites is 99. Thus:

$$\frac{W-E(W)}{\sqrt{var(W)}} = 6.51$$

a figure far above the null hypothesis (n = 1.96).

Donnely's formula takes into account the effects of the periphery and interdependence of distances.
His formula reads as follows:

$$E(W) = \frac{1}{2\sqrt{1}} + \frac{0.0514P}{N} + \frac{0.041P}{\sqrt{N^3}}$$ where P = perimeter, estimated at 150 km

$$\frac{W-E(W)}{\sqrt{var(W)}} = 5.1$$

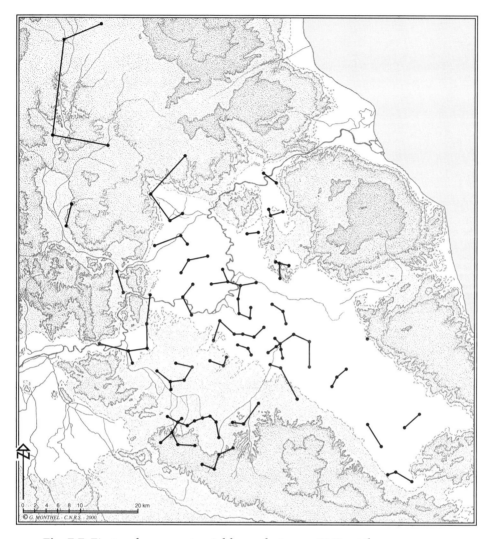

Fig. 7.7 First-order nearest neighbours between EN2 settlements.

of sites in eastern Thessaly appears statistically more *regular*, not more *clustered* than would be expected under the null hypothesis.

Theoretical 'areal' territory.

The regular spatial distribution of settlements is best visualized when the theoretical 'areal' territory for each site, based on the mean distance from nearest neighbour, is represented graphically (Auda *et al.* 1990)[16] (see fig. 7.8). A circular

---

[16] As indicated by Auda *et al.* (1990) this model presupposes that each territory extends uniformly around its centre, the settlement proper, and that the surface of each territory is identical.

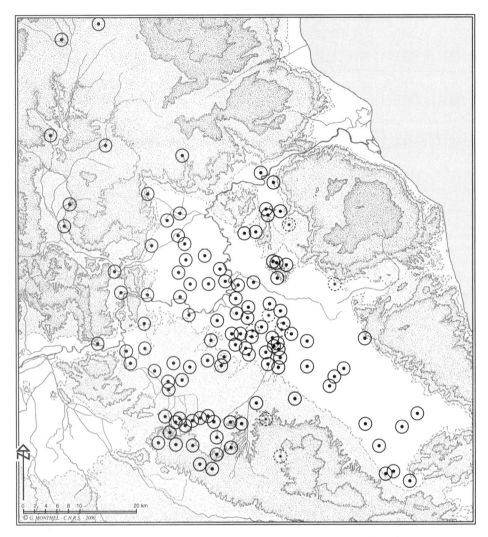

Fig. 7.8 Theoretical areal territories of EN2 settlements, based on mean distance between nearest neighbours.

territory, of a diameter equal to the mean distance between the sites, is represented by a circle centered on the settlement.[17] Each village territory would thus approximate to 430 to 450 hectares. In many subregions, theoretical areal territories are neatly adjacent and fill most of the available space. This would confirm that the model does, in a large part, reflect the actual prehistoric terri-

[17] In order to reconstruct theoretical areal territories, Auda *et al.* (1990) used the mean distance plus two standard deviations. When I tried this (or even the mean distance plus one standard deviation) there was so much overlapping between individual territories that I had to revert to the actual mean.

torial organization, with a regular distribution of sites at about 2.3 km from each other in all directions.

However, different degrees of fit *vis-à-vis* this model can be observed, according to the various subregions: in the Tyrnavos Basin and the southernmost part of the Larissa Plain, for instance, the distance between sites is almost double that theoretically expected. The Thiessen polygons, which, contrary to areal territories, emphasize *differences* in theoretical territories, reflect these slight regional nuances very clearly.

Thiessen polygons

The Thiessen polygons reveal two clusters of very small territories, south of Larissa on the 60–100 m plain and in the adjacent lower Mid-Thessalian Hills (the Revenia), between 100 and 200 m of altitude (fig. 7.9). Many polygons are closed and fairly regular in shape, confirming a dense and regular spatial distribution. However, the further one gets from these two centres, the larger the territories become, with a mean distance between sites reaching 3 km in the Tyrnavos Basin. Although this trend is probably partly real, the Thiessen polygons automatically take into account any bias in the database: the misidentification of a single site (or subphase in a site) will automatically enlarge the theoretical territories of all surrounding sites. This may be the case in the southern Larissa Plain, for instance, where the polygons appear to be very irregular in shape. Elsewhere, to the contrary, the regularity of the distribution suggests actual regional variations.

Regional variations

I have divided eastern Thessaly into six subregions according to Halstead's scheme, with the addition of the Mid-Thessalian Hills: the NW plain (Tyrnavos Basin, region L2), the NE plain (region L3), the central plain (south of Larissa, region L4.1), the southern plain (region L4.2), the low Mid-Thessalian Hills (100–200 m) and the higher Mid-Thessalian Hills (above 200 m). Table 7.1 synthesizes the data.

The density of sites provides a first, but rough, estimate of regional differences. It is lowest in the NE plain (Nessonis–Makrychori), the Mid-Thessalian Hills (or Revenia) and the Tyrnavos Basin, highest in the central Larissa Plain. But equally 'low' densities mask different situations: the mean distance between neighbouring sites in the NE region – Halstead's region 'L3' – and the Mid-Thessalian Hills is very small (respectively 1.6 and 2.1 km) and the low overall density simply reflects large unoccupied areas, such as the Nessonis marshes. On the contrary, a more distant spacing of sites of *c.* 3 km matches the lower overall density in the Tyrnavos basin. These sites are located on the

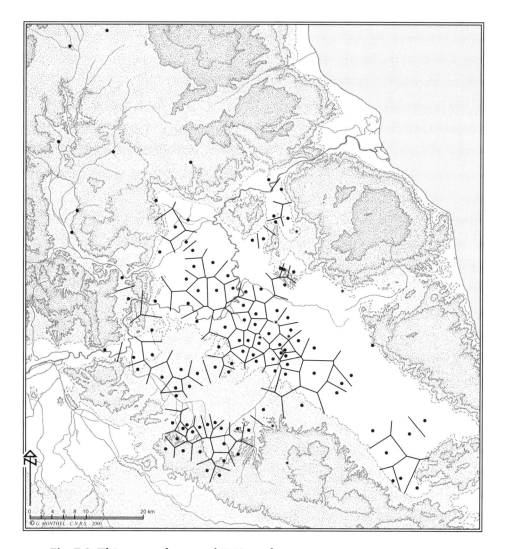

Fig. 7.9 Thiessen polygons of EN2 settlements.

Ayia Sofia soil, and, unless the latter was in effect less favourable for early Neolithic agriculture than those of the Mid-Thessalian Hills and southern plain,[18] there is no obvious explanation.

The closest spacing of sites and highest density are reached in the southern Larissa Plain, with 12.4 sites per 100 km^2 (or 13.4 if one includes the sites of uncertain EN2 attribution). But the southern Larissa Plain – Halstead's region L4 – must itself be divided into two units: the southernmost part, which is also

---

[18] Bintliff (1976b: 271–2) does consider the rendzina soils developed on the Neogen marls and flysch in the Peloponnese better suited for agriculture than the Pleistocene 'Older Fill', so this could hold true in Thessaly also.

Table 7.1 *Main parameters of the distribution of EN2 sites in eastern Thessaly*

Region	Code of the region	Approx. surface in square km	Number of EN2 sites	Density of sites per square km	Mean distance to nearest neighbour
Mountains, valleys of the Peneios tributaries, Penios valley above the Kalamakiou narrows	V	not meaningful	12	not meaningful	x: 5.83 $\sigma n-1$: 4.15
Eastern edge of Karla depression			1		
NE sector: Nessonis/Gonnoi	L3	150	8 certain 2 uncertain	0.053 to 0.066	x: 1.6 $\sigma n-1$: 0.71
NW sector: Tyrnavos	L2	210	15	0.071	x: 3 $\sigma n-1$: 1,05
Southern Larissa	L4	290	39 certain, 3 uncertain	0.124 to 0.134	Northern part (n=28) x: 1.91 $\sigma n-1$: 0.75 Southern part (n=11) x: 2.75 $\sigma n-1$: 1.4
Mid-Thessalian Hills (Revenia)	MTH	500	30 certain 2 possible	0.066 to 0.07	100–200 m of alt. (n=23) x: 2.1 $\sigma n-1$: 1.24 200–400 m of alt. (n=7) x: 2.25 $\sigma n-1$: 0.4
Total plains	L2+L3+L4	650	62 certain 5 possible	0.09 to 0.098	x: 2.5 $\sigma n-1$: 1.09

Table 7.1 (*cont.*)

Region	Code of the region	Approx. surface in square km	Number of EN2 sites	Density of sites per square km	Mean distance to nearest-neighbour
Total plains and Mid-Thessalian Hills	L2 + L3 + L4 + MTH	1150	92 certain 7 possible	0.08 to 0.086	x: 2.25 σn−1: 1.1
All sites	All		105 certain* 7 possible		x: 2.7 σn−1: 2.08

Notes:

Surface estimations are derived from Halstead (1984); the number of 'certain' sites corresponds to the number of sites where EN2 is specifically mentioned in Gallis' Atlas (1992).

'Possible' sites are EN sites with no facies indication, or EN2 sites mentioned by other scholars.

'Possible' sites were not taken into account in the computations, except in the highest figure for the density.

* The actual number of sites listed in Gallis as EN2 is 106.

the driest, contains few sites (n=11) and the latter are irregularly distributed (mean distance to nearest neighbour = 2.75 km with a standard deviation of 1.3). In the northern half, on the contrary, sites are more numerous (n=28) and much more closely and regularly spaced (m = 1.85 km; s = 0.74).

Therefore, the highest density of sites and closest spacing are reached in the lower-lying plains of Nessonis and Larissa, with the Mid-Thessalian Hills under 200 m of altitude following closely. In the Tyrnavos region the density is lower, with sites more distantly spaced. This unusually large spacing and – comparatively – low density of sites in the Tyrnavos basin[19] explains why van Andel and Runnels (1995), who concentrated on the Penios flood-plain, the Tyrnavos and the Nessonis basins, concluded that the density of settlements was higher in the flood-plain and wet basins than on the terraces, here represented only by the Tyrnavos region. When the elevated areas located above 64 m south of the Penios are also taken into account, the relation is reversed.

Synthesis

This analysis leads to several important conclusions.

1   On a general level, sites are widespread all over eastern Thessaly, with no particular clustering near the valleys and flood-plains or in areas of diversified micro-environments. The absence of clustering, in particular along water sources, is especially striking as this region characterized by hot and dry summers.
2   When environmental factors play a role, it is a repulsive one: some areas are avoided, either because they were seasonally flooded or marshy, or because they may have been too dry.
3   Detailed regional analysis shows that the highest density of sites is reached in areas that (a) were never flooded – the Revenia and Larissa Plain; (b) correspond to the most homogeneous environments; and (c) do not correspond to specific soils: one group is found on the Revenia Pliocene marls, the other on the colluvial sediments of the Larissa Plain.
4   Thus, no positive relation can be established between settlement choice or settlement density and natural features such as water proximity, floods, soils, and varied topography.
5   On the contrary, the most striking result of these analyses is the regularity of the distribution pattern in the settled areas, even allowing for minor regional variations.[20] The distribution of settlements appears to be independent of variations in topography, soils, proximity of water sources, etc. Fundamentally, Early Neolithic 2 settlements avoided some areas, for reasons still unexplained, but spread according to a regular grid of *c.* 2.3 km in all directions around and between these areas.

[19] I would not dismiss the possibility that settlements have been missed in the Tyrnavos Basin.
[20] They are clearly minor when set in the perspective of the Early Neolithic in general.

The contemporaneity of the sites

However, before this is taken as a true reflection of Thessalian EN2 settlement patterns, the problem of contemporaneity must again be raised: are all the settlements strictly contemporaneous – in which case the reconstruction of the territories cannot be far from the truth – or are we observing palimpsests of successive lateral shifts? In the latter case, neither the reconstructed distances between villages nor the theoretical territories would have much significance.

Most EN settlements of Thessaly meet the criteria used by Kaiser and Voytek (1983) to differentiate permanent settlements from shifting settlements. Shifting settlement patterns seem difficult to reconcile with the stratigraphical depth, evidence for successive floors, and rebuilding of houses on the same foundations (see ch. 9 below). Although a demonstration of strict contemporaneity is impossible, the hypothesis of a *systematic* shift of settlement, as known elsewhere in Europe, does not adequately fit the architectural and chronostratigraphic data. This does not preclude episodic relocations due to various hazards. Such relocations are suggested by anomalies *vis-à-vis* the theoretical model, such as the overlaps between two reconstructed territories. In some cases, such as Karagatz Magoula (no. 44) or Prodromos in western Thessaly, the sites are so close to each other that a 'double settlement' can be considered. A short lateral displacement is possible in cases like Nessonis I and II, which may have been successively occupied:[21] the village would have been rebuilt just nearby, thus retaining the same territory.

On the whole, however, the depth of sediments for the Early Neolithic strata, which ranges from about 2 to 4 metres on average, is compatible with a continuous occupation for two to four centuries.[22] But whether or not sites are strictly contemporaneous, the fact remains that villages *have* been established on a regular grid of 2.3 km or less. The spatial pattern brought to light remains true even if some sites had been temporarily abandoned.

From environmental to socioeconomic factors

How can this pattern be explained? First, the settled area comprises alluvial fans, flood plains, Pliocene hills, alluvial plains and so on. This suggests that the network is basically independent from environmental features and that the main factor in the implantation of settlements was socioeconomic.

Second, this pattern corresponds closely to what Haggett presents as a model of progressive colonization in a homogeneous plain, from dispersed initial

---

[21] Unfortunately, the different subphases and facies indicated by Theocharis (as quoted in Wijnen 1981) and Gallis (1992) are contradictory.
[22] The rate of build-up in Balkanic tell settlements as a whole is approximately one metre per century (Demoule, oral communication).

centres (Haggett 1973: 60). In our case, the initial centres would have been EN1 settlements belonging to the 'Monochrome phase'. EN1 sites are much more difficult to identify through surface surveys than EN2 sites, and the quality of the sample is certainly lower than for EN2 sites. However, in the present state of our data, the 14 to 23 EN1 sites[23] are spread widely over the whole territory considered. So far, Haggett's model fits the eastern Thessalian data.

Third, the distribution identified also corresponds very closely to what Bintliff described for central Greece in the Classical times: a progressive infilling of villages 2.5 km apart, starting from more dispersed centres (Bintliff 1994b). After having tested his model on other regions of Greece, Bintliff even considers this regular network of villages, 2.5 km apart, as 'characteristic of rural Greece in classical times'. If this is the case, this characteristic pattern originates several millennia earlier, not long after the first farmers settled in Greece. Yet, can the same mechanisms account for it in both periods? I believe the answer is yes.

Drawing on the work of C. Gamble (1982), J. Davis (1991), P. Halstead (Halstead 1981a; Halstead and Jones 1989), T. Whitelaw (1991) and A. Sherratt (1981) for instance, a fairly straightforward interpretation can be suggested. The EN2, judging by the number and density of sites, must have been a phase of demographic expansion. An increase of population over a threshold of *circa* 200/300 individuals in each village would have created sociological problems, unless some political control was installed. Alternately, the village could split and a fraction of the population could found a new settlement.

In parallel, any increase in village population would have progressively entailed an increase of cultivated surfaces and pastures. This can be met either by cultivating fields further and further away from the village, or by the foundation of new villages with their own independent territory. Enlarging the areas under cultivation or pasture increases labour costs, travelling to and from the fields, manuring the fields, and risk during periods of time-stress, in particular during the harvests (Halstead and Jones 1989). In contrast, a regular scission of the village, with the foundation of new ones close to the parent one, presents the advantage of limiting the population within each village, limiting the distances to fields and pastures and reducing labour costs, while retaining easy relations with one's kin. Needless to say, such a pattern presupposes cooperation rather than conflict, but it could apply both to Neolithic rural communities and to historical communities. It could also be tentatively argued that mean distances between Neolithic Thessalian villages are generally lower than in Classical times precisely because no pack or draft animal was available.

The specificity of the EN2 settlement patterns of Thessaly can thus be related to a higher initial level of population, relative to the size of the basin, a

---

[23] Gallis lists only fourteen EN1 sites, but Theocharis (1967) and Wijnen (1981) had identified nine other EN1 sites.

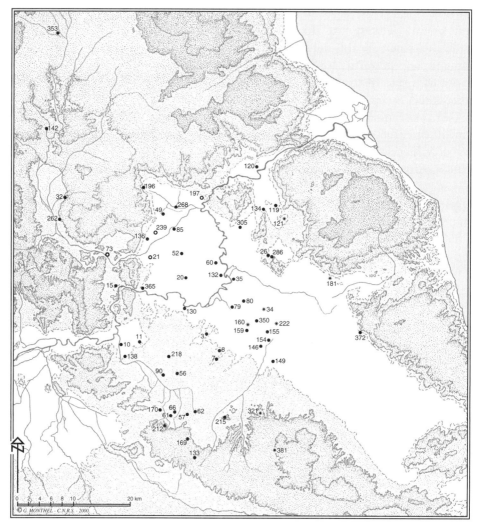

Fig. 7.10 Early Neolithic 3 sites (dots) and unspecified Early Neolithic sites (stars) from eastern Thessaly. Numbers and first name according to the ATAE (Gallis 1992). Traditional appelation in brackets.
3: Larisa 8 (*Magoula Vrastero*). 7: Nikaia 11 (*Magoula Pidagoulia*). 8: Nikaia 12 (*Magoula Boukoum*). 10: Mandra 2 (*Magoula Gueka*). 11: Rachoula 1. 15: Damasi 4 (*Magoula Tourcoyefira*). 20: Dendra 2 (*Otzaki*). 21: Tyrnavos 5 (*Magoula Tsalma*). 26: Nesson 2 (*Nessonis 2*). 32: Domeniko 1. 34: Melissochori 1 (*Meteseli magoula*). 35: Larissa 9 (*Soufli*). 44: Galini 1 (*Megali magoula Karagatz*). 49: Tyrnavos 3 (*Megali Vrysi Tyravou*). 52: Ambelonas 3 (*Magoula Karagiozi*). 56: Krannon 5 (*Mavros lofos*). 57: Ayios Georgios Larisas 5 (*Magoula Bei*). 60: Dasochori 2 (*Orman magoula*). 61: Ayios Georgios Larisas 2 (*Magoula Vrasteri*). 62: Ayios Georgios Larisas 7 (*Magoula Gamila*). 66: Ayios Georgios Larisas 4. 73: Damasi 1. 79: Larisa 5 (*Magoula Arapadiki*).

sustained demographic growth and the unique opportunity to spread in all directions within a homogeneous natural environment. The regular spacing of settlements suggests units of comparable size and importance; the reconstructed territories, based on the mean distance between sites, can be estimated at about 430 to 450 ha each. According to the presently available evidence, all settlements appear to be autonomous: there is no indication of economic complementarity between plain sites and hill sites, for instance. As a consequence, the territory of each settlement would have had to include all the fields, pastures and forests required for human and animal alimentation and for water and wood provisioning. As we shall see in the following chapter, the number of people and animals that such territories could have supported cannot have been very high.

The tight clusters of EN2 sites left little or no space for the foundation of new settlements in between existing ones. The process of regular scission would have fairly rapidly met its limits. Sometime during the EN2, the number of villages reached a maximum that was maintained throughout the Middle Neolithic. Although the EN3 facies is restricted to the northern half of eastern Thessaly, it is certainly significant that only five new foundations have been recorded.

The EN3 facies

Fifty-three sites only, or about half the number of EN2 sites, have yielded the characteristic EN3 Impressed/Incised wares (see fig. 7.10). All sites are concentrated in the northern half of eastern Thessaly, where they remain evenly distributed over the countryside, but more widely spaced than EN2 sites. On the contrary, no site attributed to the EN3 has been found in the southern half of

Caption for Fig. 7.10 (*cont.*)
80: Melissochori 2 (*Mesiani magoula*). 85: Ambelonas 6 (*Magoula Goltsou*). 90: Krannon 3 (*Orenia*). 119: Elateia 1 (*Magoula Elatia*). 120: Gonnoi 1 (*Besik tepe*). 121: Pournari 1 (*Bounarbasi*). 130: Terpsithea 1 (*Magoula KEMP*). 132: Dasochori 1 (*Magoula Prochoma*). 133: Chara 1 (*Magoula Panayou*). 134: Makrychori 3 (*Magoula Sygourotopi*). 138: Loutro 1 (*Magoula Anemomylos B*). 142: Kephalovrysso 1. 146: Nikaia 3 (*Magoula Kardara 2*). 149: Chalki 9. 154: Platykambos 5. 159: Melissochori 6 (*Magoula Karaïkia 1*). 160: Melissochori 5 (*Magoula Karaïkia 3*). 168: Kyparissos 1. 169: Kyparissos 2. 170: Doxaras 1. 196: Lygaria 2. 197: Rodia 2 (*Magoula Pera Machaia Rodias*). 212: Ayios Georgios Larisas 6. 215: Zappeio 1. 218: Eleftherai 1. 222: Platykambos 4 (*Magoula Nekrotapheiou Platykambou*). 239: Tyrnavos (*Magoula Karagatz*). 262: Mesochori 1. 268: Deleria 1 (*Magoula Ayios Athanasios*). 286: Nesson 1 (*Nessonis 1*). 305: Gyrtoni 5 (*Magoula Stimeni Petra*). 321: Sofo 1. 350: Galini 1. 353: Tharandaporon 1. 365: Platanoulia 2 (*Magoula Platanoulia*). 381: Kalo Nero 4.

the region, the limit cross-cutting the Larissa Plain and the Mid-Thessalian Hills. This distribution confirms Theocharis' observation concerning the absence of Incised/Impressed wares in southern Thessaly, where the last EN subphase, as recognized at Sesklo, is characterized by the predominance of Monochrome wares (Theocharis 1967). Yet the restricted distribution of the Impressed/Incised wares may not be the only reason why EN3 settlements are few: a number of sites, from all regions, are abandoned for some time during or at the end of the EN2/EN3 period.

The abandonment of EN2/EN3 settlements

Altogether, twenty-seven EN2 and EN3 settlements, that is, one site in four, are abandoned for the entire Middle Neolithic, sometimes even longer. Their distribution is not uniform: more than two-thirds (17 or 18) are located in present-day river beds, near marshes, or along Grundmann's line, parallel to Lake Karla.

This apparent correlation with water expanses can be fortuitous: other settlements in the same or similar environments remain occupied during the MN (Middle Neolithic). Still, the high proportion of sites seemingly abandoned between the EN2 and the MN3 or LN (Late Neolithic) along Grundmann's line, for instance, is rather puzzling (see table 7.2). According to the chronological status given to these facies, two very different alternatives can be put forward.

(a) These ceramic facies have no chronological value, and simply happened not to be represented in these sites.[24] The so-called MN3 would directly succeed the EN2 or the EN3. The absence of MN1 along the lake is not surprising, since this facies concentrates in the Revenia Hills. The absence MN2 is more surprising, since it is well represented in neighbouring sites of the Larissa Plain. According to this hypothesis, only sites that yielded no Middle Neolithic at all can be considered as abandoned at the end of the Early Neolithic, but their spatial distribution appears difficult to relate to specific environmental factors.

This is the view held by Gallis (1992), who insisted on the presence of all diagnostic MN wares in each 'subphase', and did not differentiate the various MN facies in his own analyses. However, the absence of sites with EN3 and (MN1) MN2 wares along the 'lakes' margins remains unexplained. Consequently, it is worth considering the possibility of a real hiatus in occupation.

(b) The absence of several facies might alternatively indicate temporary abandonment of the site. In this case, the retreat from the lake and river margins cannot be fortuitous, and could be related to renewed flooding, erosion or alluviation.

---

[24] Or not recognized.

Table 7.2 *EN2 sites located nearest to 'Grundmann's line' and facies represented*

Grundmann's no.	ATAE no.	Altitude of underlying hypsometric curve	EN1	EN2	EN3	MN1	MN2	MN3	LN	FN
		Southern Karla lake, 'Lake' centre								
125	277	50–1 m		X			X		X	
–	278	50 m	?	X	X				X	
		SW Karla, Phere								
A	273	80–100 m		X			X	X		
A	282	70 m		X				X	X	X
		SE Larissa								
–	19	70–5 m		X			Unsp.	MN		
–	378	55 m		X					X	
–	164	62 m		X				X	X	
22	89	67 m		X				X	X	
–	250	67 m		X				X	X	
21	44	64 m		X	X		X	X	X	
132	33	64 m		X					X	
29	27	64–5 m		X						
		Tyrnavos basin								
133	60	68–70 m		X	X		X	X	X	X
36	54	65 m		X			X		X	X
		Nessonis								
A	189	80 m	?	X					X	
		Eastern Karla								
–	372	50 m		X			X	X	X	

Note:
The altitudes are given according to Helly (*in litt.*), from detailed topographic maps.

'Short-term' modifications over two to three centuries of the course of the Penios and the extent of the Nessonis and Karla lakes are well exemplified in Historic periods (Helly *et al.* 1994); the same probably held true during the Neolithic. In the present case, indications of environmental transformations are provided by the renewed phase of aggradation that led to the deposition of the Gyrtoni alluvium. This episode was dated to about 5000 BC (uncalibrated), because no EN or MN site was found to be contemporaneous with it (Demitrack 1986: 39; van Andel and Zangger 1990: 150). However, the sample of sites augered is small, and its formation could possibly have started one or two hundred years before, at the end of the Early Neolithic.[25] According to Demitrack, van Andel and Zangger, the erosion would have been triggered by one millennium of deforestation and agriculture (Demitrack 1986; van Andel et al. 1990; van Andel and Zangger 1990). Yet, they do not rule out climatic modifications. In addition, Helly and his collaborators note that the frequent variations in the water level and its spatial distribution are not systematically related to climatic fluctuations or density of population (Helly et al. 1994, 1996). Similarly, Bintliff underlines that 'It should be noted that the last century has witnessed truly massive deforestation and human interference in Greece, perhaps more than ever before, but no aggradation has ensued' (Bintliff 1976b: 273). In fact, minor tectonic events in the still active faults[26] would have been sufficient to induce important transformations in the distribution of water expanses (Helly et al. 1994, 1996). Such a regional cause, with limited regional effects, could account for the permanence of settlement in the south-ernmost part of the depression. Alternately, if Caputo and Bravard's hypothesis is right (see above, p. 130), the gradual infilling of the lower-lying depressions by sediments flowing down the Mid-Thessalian Hills may have led to a progressive backward shift of settlements in areas most strongly affected by alluviation. Several natural factors, not mutually exclusive, could thus account for a temporary retreat from the lakes' margins and river beds.

Conclusion

Whatever the cause, a minimum number of twenty-seven sites was temporarily abandoned after the EN2, while at least eighteen were founded during the MN. Assuming, for the reasons detailed above, that the number of inhabitants in each village did not substantially increase, this supports the hypothesis of an approximately stable population, with episodic relocations of settlements. The presently available data do not accommodate simple models of demographic expansion, paralleled by a continuous and regular increase in the number of sites through time. Judging by the number of settlements, one would rather witness a rapid initial growth followed by a long period of stability.

The highest number of settlements attributed to a single facies is attained with the EN2. These settlements are remarkably evenly distributed over eastern Thessaly; no preference for specific soils, topographies or resources can be shown. The commonly held idea that the earliest sites were restricted to the alluvial plains is contradicted by more recent studies: nearly half of all known

---

[25] This is all the more possible since the dating of the Gyrtoni alluviation was mainly based on an auger coring at the site of Gyrtoni 2, then thought to have been first occupied during the Late Neolithic (Demitrack 1986: 38). But Gallis' Atlas now cites some Middle Neolithic at the site (Gallis 1992).

[26] Such as a slight uplift of the Rodia Fault, which would impede the outflow of the Penios through the Rodia pass and provoke widespread flooding, first in the Nessonis Basin, then, through the Asmaki, in the Eleftheri Basin.

sites are located in the Revenia Hills, and 5 per cent are even located above 400 m of altitude. This independence *vis-à-vis* natural features seems to indicate a pattern of expansion determined more by socioeconomic factors than by environmental ones. New settlements would have been created to cope with increased population, a strategy that would have been beneficial in terms of labour costs and political organization. The new settlements would then have regularly filled the space, at small distances from their parent settlements. In this respect, Thessaly was unique in offering the rare opportunity to spread along a 'two-dimensional network' over a wide area (van Andel and Runnels 1995: 494).[27] This in turn created unique conditions: each village was within sight of several others. Exchange (Halstead 1992, 1994; Halstead and O'Shea 1982), but also direct co-operation between members of different villages, would have been greatly facilitated when large taskforces were required. This would have ensured the prosperity that allowed for a steady demographic expansion. If, as suggested by Shennan (1992: 537), the density of sites is a measure of prosperity, EN Thessaly does appear to have been especially prosperous.

Thessaly, however, is only a small part of Greece; a sustained demographic expansion in Thessaly could have led to the foundation of new settlements further away, in the smaller alluvial basins (van Andel and Runnels 1995; see critics in Wilkie and Savina 1997). In spite of the problems involved with more limited systematic surveys, there can be little doubt that the density of sites in other regions of Greece is below that known in Thessaly. Early radiocarbon dates for sites outside Thessaly, such as Franchthi, Sidari and Nea Nikomedeia, show that this is not due to a later colonization process, with less time for the multiplication of settlements. In other words, the settlements in the smaller basins of eastern Greece do not appear to be related to outflows of Thessalian populations, a point of view reinforced by the stylistic and technical differences in pottery (see ch. 6 above). Although the data are admittedly limited, there is no indication, at least for the time being, of a regular, 'gradual expansion' of agricultural communities all over Greece, according to Ammerman and Cavalli-Sforza's model.

No 'core area' can be identified, and the earliest farming communities appear to have settled in dispersed and varied environments. The dynamic of expansion seems to have followed very different rates according to the region, and even where agriculture was practised very early, such as in the Argolid, the density of sites remained markedly lower than in Thessaly.[28] Whether on a regional or global scale, the spread of the Neolithic in Greece appears to be a complex, non-linear phenomenon, regulated by sociological factors as much as environmental ones.

---

[27] As pointed out by Halstead (1984: 6.4.2), EN foundations proved extremely successful in the long term: even if some were temporarily abandoned, almost all EN settlements were reoccupied at one time or another during prehistoric times.

[28] This is supported by the systematic surveys conducted over several years in the southern Argolid (Jameson *et al.* 1994) and by Wells and Runnels in the northern Argolid (Wells 1996).

CHAPTER 8

EARLY NEOLITHIC SUBSISTENCE
ECONOMY: THE DOMESTIC AND THE WILD

For several decades, the exploitation of domesticated species as potential food resources has been considered a prime – or rather, the prime – factor in the process of Neolithization.[1] This view was recently challenged in the light of archaeological data from the Near East, America and Japan, which suggest that domesticated species werc initially too limited in number and scope to have had much dietary importance.[2] In parallel, the relative importance of domesticates in fully developed Neolithic economies has been re-evaluated – and downplayed – in large areas of eastern, central and western Neolithic Europe.[3] Does this mean that the quasi-exclusive reliance on domesticated plants and animals, considered a characteristic of Greek Neolithic communities, should also be re-evaluated?

In Greece as elsewhere, taphonomic biases and unequal recovery techniques can lead to widely differing interpretations of the subsistence economy. A debate over the importance of domestic resources in the Early Neolithic of Greece, which were traditionally viewed as predominant, has recently been opened by Björk (1995). Halstead himself, who had defined the economy as typically agro-pastoral in several influential papers which will be largely followed here (Halstead 1977, 1981a, 1984, 1989a), recently argued that the importance of wild resources may have been underestimated due to poor preservation and recovery (Halstead 1989b: 29).

Yet, even if wild resources were locally available, it does not necessarily follow that they were exploited on a large scale. Subsistence economy is culturally based, and must be studied as the expression of social choices within the possibilities offered by the environment and the level of technical development. Which species are exploited, and how, depends as much on traditions and ideology as on economic considerations. I shall argue here that wild resources were not only little used, but deliberately left out of the staple diet. This 'cultural' conception of the subsistence basis and economic system echoes the recent work of Cauvin (1997) on the very origins of agriculture and herding; it is certainly significant that several of the earliest economic choices brought to light by Cauvin are maintained throughout the Early Neolithic of Greece, a few hundred years later, under roughly similar natural conditions.

[1] Childe 1934, 1951a; Braidwood 1960; Binford 1968.
[2] Cauvin 1997; Gebauer and Price 1992; Hayden 1992; Runnels and van Andel 1988.
[3] Dennell 1992; Thomas 1991; Zvelebil and Dolukhanov 1991.

This issue will constitute the major focus of the present study. However, a thorough understanding of early Neolithic economy would also require a good grasp of several other parameters: the degree of sedentism, the existence of transhumance practices, the relative contribution of plants and meat to the diet, the cultivation practices, and so forth. These will be only briefly alluded to, due to the lack of relevant data and analyses.

Permanent settlements do not necessarily imply full sedentism. Year-round sedentism needs to be established independently, in particular through archaeo-zoological and archaeo-botanical studies. Unfortunately, very little work has been done on this problem in Greece. Prodromos, where Halstead suggested year-round occupation, constitutes a unique exception (Halstead and Jones 1980: 106; Halstead 1984: 7.1). Since Prodromos appears to be fairly typical of EN permanent settlements, it can be hoped that the result can be generalized.

However, year-round occupation of the main settlement does not, in theory, preclude seasonal movements by a subgroup. Flocks can be led away during the dry summers to graze on richer pastures, in particular in the hills and mountains. Many authors, however, especially in Greece, consider pastoralism or even seasonal transhumance to be related to controlled market economies and, consequently, of a necessarily late date (Cherry 1988; Halstead 1990a). Yet transhumance and pastoralism have been suggested for Early Neolithic sites both in the Near East and in Mediterranean Europe, that is, precisely in the countries nearest to Greece from an ecological point of view. Besides archaeo-zoological data, the evidence derives mainly from the nature of the settlements (Cauvin 1994: ch. 17) or from specific micromorphological signatures in cave sediments, characteristic of animal pens (Cocchi Genick 1990; Courty *et al.* 1991).

Such evidence, however, cannot be brought forward for Early Neolithic Greece. Contrary to what occurs elsewhere in the Mediterranean basin, where a complex system of territorial exploitation prevails,[4] there is no indication that caves or rock shelters were regularly used as temporary animal pens or hunting camps. Layers of compact white sediments in the Franchthi cave do look similar to typical sediments from animal pens, but this alone does not imply seasonal occupation. The sample of shells analyzed for seasonality is too small to be conclusive,[5] and the cave could have been used as an annex to the main settlement, located on the Paralia or in the bay.[6] Cave occupation has been shown to be extremely limited during the Early Neolithic, and no open-air temporary settlement has yet been recognized in the Early Neolithic. Both increase drastically during the Late and Final Neolithic, a fact taken by several

[4] See Binder 1991; Brochier J. E. 1991; Courty *et al.* 1991, for 'Early Neolithic' examples.
[5] They do spread, however, over the winter, spring and autumn (Deith and Shackleton 1988).
[6] See Wilkinson and Duhon 1990 on the discovery through coring of an EN/MN settlement in the bay.

authors to indicate precisely the emergence of a more mobile pastoralism
(Demoule and Perlès 1993; Johnson M. 1996a, 1996b; Wickens 1986). Though
more data are clearly required, full sedentism and year-round occupation of the
villages in the plains so far appear to be the norm in the Early Neolithic.

This hypothesis has important implications for the problem of the relative
importance of meat and plant food in the diet. The relative contribution of
animals and plants to the diet is impossible to assess directly from the recoverable data. Yet, in environments such as Greece, 'plant foods usually provide
the staple diet, with meat and milk products as an important but essentially
secondary resource' (Payne 1985: 234). Indeed, given the lack of evidence for a
transhumant pastoral system, meat could not have been the main source of
calories: this would have required flocks too large to sustain year-round in the
lowlands (Halstead 1981a: 313). Consequently, 'in most parts of lowland
Greece, cultivated plants will have been far more productive per unit area as a
staple resource than animal products' (Halstead 1987a: 77). One can thus conclude that agriculture, rather than herding, was the main source of daily food.
But in such a system, shortage of labour and climatic hazards could easily lead
to temporary failures and crises. Livestock would then play an important role
in coping with food shortage, both because it could be eaten (or milked?) and
exchanged for grain. According to Halstead, 'in the absence of a market, livestock was probably more important as a *store* than a regular *source* of wealth'
(Halstead 1993: 65).[7] Nevertheless, the importance of animals in most traditional societies is usually not directly economic or dietary. Animals are a main
constituent of bride-wealth, gifts and offerings, and meat is mostly consumed
during festive and ritual occasions. Keeping herds of animals in the Neolithic
may have been even more a social than an economic necessity.

The cultivated plants

There is a long tradition of seed collection and identification in prehistoric
Greece (Hansen 1985). The earliest determinations for the Neolithic go back to
Tsountas' work in Thessaly: seeds of *Triticum, Vicia, Quercus, Panicum miliaceum* identified by Wittmack were published (Tsountas 1908: 359). Seed determinations became more frequent after the 1960s, with the work of Jane
Renfrew in Thessaly (1966, 1973, 1979) and of van Zeist and Bottema (1971) at
Nea Nikomedeia, but systematic flotation was not introduced until the seven-
ties, during the excavations at Franchthi (Hansen 1991).[8] Contextual information is usually lacking and the most detailed lists of seeds, published by Kroll
(1981, 1983, 1991), come from scarp cleanings only. Seed samples are thus

---

[7] Italicized by the author.
[8] Unfortunately, despite flotation of the sediments, the levels that can be securely attributed to
the Early Neolithic within the cave at Franchthi have produced almost no seeds. They will not
be considered here. There are also no data for Knossos 'Early Neolithic I'.

heterogeneous, both qualitatively and quantitatively. That strong patterns should nonetheless come to light is all the more remarkable.

Seed assemblages are heavily dominated by cultivated cereals and pulses (see table 8.1 below). Among the cereals, by far the most common are the glume wheats, *Triticum dicoccum* (emmer) and, to a lesser extent, *T. monococcum* (einkorn). Bread wheat (*T. aestivum*), a free-threshing wheat, is very rare in mainland Greece.[9] According to Halstead (1989a) the rarity of bread wheat in mainland Greece may be related to its greater vulnerability in storage, but Hansen also alludes to its more demanding soil and edaphic requirements (Hansen 1988). Six-row barley (*Hordeum vulgare*) is also present in all sites. Several varieties have been identified, including the naked one, especially abundant at Nea Nikomedeia.

Legumes are also well represented, both in terms of frequency of occurrence and percentage of seeds. The most abundant are lentils (*Lens culinaris*), peas (*Pisum sativum*) and bitter vetch (*Vicia ervilia*). A large and so far unique deposit of Grass pea (*Lathyrus sativus*), a common fodder crop in present-day Greece, was uncovered at Prodromos 2 (Halstead and Jones 1980; Jones and Halstead 1995). Chickpea (*Cicer arietinum*), on the other hand, is represented by a single seed in an EN context at Otzaki and might be intrusive (Kroll 1981).

Though it is impossible to say whether it was eaten or used for technical purposes, the presence of flax (*Linum usitatissimum*) at Otzaki should also be noted, since flax has long been considered as completely absent from these regions (van Zeist 1980: 132).

Modern observations indicate that the combination of cereals with the more labour-intensive pulses would have been a good risk-buffeting strategy, since pulses seem to withstand periodic droughts better than cereals (Forbes 1989). But the relative importance of the different crops is notoriously difficult to assess, as the preservation of the seeds in archaeological contexts depends in large part on processing and storage procedures.[10] It is even more problematic with samples that have not been collected by flotation[11] and lack contextual information. Nonetheless, the overall distribution of species does not appear to be random and systematic patterns can be observed: *Triticum dicoccum* is always the predominant cereal in number of seeds, and often the predominant species (up to 50 per cent of the total assemblage at Prodromos 2). It is followed by *T. monococcum*, or by *Hordeum vulgare*. Altogether, cultivated cereals amount to two-thirds of the total seed assemblage at Achilleion, Soufli and

---

[9] It should be recalled that it was overwhelmingly predominant at Knossos, in the 'aceramic' stratum X. It was also recently found in an Early Neolithic context at Giannitsa B, in western Macedonia (Valamoti 1992). In both cases, its presence could indicate that the settlers were of a different origin than in the rest of Greece.

[10] Dennell 1974, 1984; Hillman 1981; Hubbard 1975, 1976; Jones G. 1987, 1992.

[11] Only the new samples collected by Kroll at Otzaki, Argissa and Sesklo (Kroll 1981, 1983) and the recently excavated samples from Giannitsa B were floated. As indicated above, at Franchthi the sediments from the cave itself were also floated, but yielded extremely few EN seeds.

Table 8.1 *Seed remains from Early Neolithic contexts*

	Seeds counts					Synthetic list		
	Argissa (Hopf 1962)	Achilleion phases I and II (Renfrew 1989)	Prodromos 2 (Halstead and Jones 1980)	Soufli (Renfrew 1966)	Nea Nikomedeia (Van Zeist and Bottema 1971)	Sesklo (Kroll 1991)	Otzaki (Kroll 1991)	Argiss (Kroll 1991)
Triticum monococcum	Present	19 11%	285 17%	4	276 2.5%	present	present	preser
Triticum dicoccum (= *T. turgidum* ssp. *dicoccum*)		65 38%	826 49%	20	2859 26%	present	present	preser
Triticum aestivum s.l.						present	present	
Hordeum vulgare								
Hordeum vulgare vulgare (= *H. hexastichum*)	present					present	present	preser
Hordeum vulgare ssp. *distichum* (= *Hordeum distichum*)			17 1%	10	present*			
Hordeum vulgare ssp. *distichum* var. *nudum*					2168 20%			
Hordeum sp.		33** 19%	12 0.7%					
cf. *Panicum miliaceum*	1							
Cerealia indet.								
Pisum sp.			281 16.5%	8				
Pisum sativum s.l.					48 0.5%	present	present	preser
Vicia ervilia					37 0.3%	present	present	preser
Lens sp.	present	16 9%	13 0.8%					
Lens culinaris (= *Lens esculenta*)				3	5431 50%	present	present	preser
Cicer arietinum							present	
Lathyrus sativus			200 12%					

by site					Frequency of taxa amongst the different samples				
Giannitsa B Valamoti 1995)	Servia V (Ridley and Wardle 1979)	Sesklo, EN1 (Kroll 1983)	Sesklo, EN2 (Kroll 1983)	Argissa, EN2 (Kroll 1983)	Otzaki EN2 (Kroll 1983)	Otzaki, EN2 or EN3 (Kroll 1983)	Sesklo EN3 (Kroll 1983)	Prodromos 2 (after Halstead and Jones 1980)	Nea Nikomedeia (after van Zeist and Bottema 1971)
present		A	A	A	A	A	x	C	D
present		A	A	A	A	A	x	C	A
present					C	D	x		
		D	C		D				
				A	B	A	x		
	present		?					D	
					?				B
								C	
		B	A	A	A	B			
				D		C		D	
									B
		C		D		C			
present		A		A	A	C		D	
									B
						D			
								D	

Table 8.1 (cont.)

	Seeds counts					Synthetic lists		
	Argissa (Hopf 1962)	Achilleion phases I and II (Renfrew 1989)	Prodromos 2 (Halstead and Jones 1980)	Soufli (Renfrew 1966)	Nea Nikomedeia (Van Zeist and Bottema 1971)	Sesklo (Kroll 1991)	Otzaki (Kroll 1991)	Argissa (Kroll 1991)
leguminosae sat. indet.					3 0.02%			
Linum usitatissimum							present	
Vitis vinifera subsp. sylvestris sp. (=Vitis vinifera)		1 0.6%				present		
Ficus carica						present	present	
Prunus cf. spinosa					Frgt.			
Pistacia sp.		7 4%				present*		
Pistacia terebinthus/ atlantica								
Pistacia atlantica						present		
Quercus sp.		13 7.5%	47 3%		10 0.1%	present*		
Cornus mas			14 0.8%		3+frgt. 0.02%			
cf. Crataegus	present							
Sambucus ebulus, Sambucus sp.								
Buglossoides arvensis (= Lithospermum arvense)								
Fumaria sp.								
Avena sp.		14				present	present	present
Galium sp.		1 0.6%						
Galium spurium								
Galium sp. / Asperula sp.								
Lolium temulen-tum, L. temulen-tum/remotum								

by site	Frequency of taxa amongst the different samples								
Giannitsa B Valamoti (1995)	Servia V (Ridley and Wardle 1979)	Sesklo, EN1 (Kroll 1983)	Sesklo, EN2 (Kroll 1983)	Argissa, EN2 (Kroll 1983)	Otzaki EN2 (Kroll 1983)	Otzaki, EN2 or EN3 (Kroll 1983)	Sesklo EN3 (Kroll 1983)	Prodromos 2 (after Halstead and Jones 1980)	Nea Nikomedeia (after van Zeist and Bottema 1971)
		D		D	D	B	x		
	present					C			
present		D							
		A	A	D	A	A	x		
	present								
present									
		A	A						
								D	D
present	present							C	D
present				D					
		B	A	D		D	x		
					D	D			
		B	C	D	D	C	x		
		B	A	B	D				
present									
present					D	D			

Table 8.1 *(cont.)*

	Seeds counts					Synthetic lists		
	Argissa (Hopf 1962)	Achilleion phases I and II (Renfrew 1989)	Prodromos 2 (Halstead and Jones 1980)	Soufli (Renfrew 1966)	Nea Nikomedeia (Van Zeist and Bottema 1971)	Sesklo (Kroll 1991)	Otzaki (Kroll 1991)	Argissa (Kroll 1991)
Bromus sp., cf.	1							
Bromus sp.	0.6%							
Portucala oleracea								
Scleranthus sp.								
Agrostemma githago								
Neslia sp.								
Stellaria sp.	1 0.6%							
Polygonum sp.								
Rumex sp.								
Rumex sp.								
Graminae								
Chenopodiaceae								
Polygonaceae								
Plantaginaceae								
Fabaceae								
Leguminosae								
Caryophyllaceae								
Capparidaceae								
Cyperaceae								
Euphorbiaceae								
Number of samples								
Total	170	1695	45	>10,835	957	677	124	

Notes:
Frequency of taxa in the different samples: A: present in all samples. B: present in two-thirds of the samples. C: present in half of the samples. D: present in less than half of the samples, x: one sample only. In Prodromos and Nea Nikomedeia, only samples of more than thirty seeds have been taken into consideration. No quantitative data are available for Sesklo, Argissa and Otzaki. The synthetic lists provided by Kroll (1991) are given alongside the detailed distributions because of important precisions in seed identification.

by site		Frequency of taxa amongst the different samples								
Giannitsa B (Valamoti 1995)	Servia V (Ridley and Wardle 1979)	Sesklo, EN1 (Kroll 1983)	Sesklo, EN2 (Kroll 1983)	Argissa, EN2 (Kroll 1983)	Otzaki EN2 (Kroll 1983)	Otzaki, EN2 or EN3 (Kroll 1983)	Sesklo EN3 (Kroll 1983)	Prodromos 2 (after Halstead and Jones 1980)	Nea Nikomedeia (after van Zeist and Bottema 1971)
present		?					x		
					D		x		
					D				
		C		D			x		
						D			
present									
present									
present		B	C	B	C	C	x		
		B	C	A	D	D			
		D	A	D	B				
		D			B	D			
		C	C			D			
present									
present		C					x		
		C							
		D		D					
					D				
	25	4	2	3	5	5	1	6	16
		340	518	124	335	342	99	1680	10,806

Sesklo (Kroll 1991): * species indicated with reference to J. Renfrew 1979, but which may in fact correspond to the Initial Neolithic sample. *Achilleion:* ** given as *Hordeum vulgare* in Renfrew 1979. *Argissa:* The plant remains from Argissa (Hopf 1962) come from level XXIX (the 'Hut'). The grain of *Panicum miliaceum* is probably intrusive. *Servia:* The list does not give the complete range of species. *Franchthi:* there are almost no plant remains from securely dated EN contexts.

Prodromos, and to slightly less than 50 per cent at Nea Nikomedeia, where lentils are especially abundant. At Giannitsa B, the seeds and by-products of the cereals alone amount to 90/95 per cent of all the cereals, pulses and fruit (Valamoti 1992).

The importance of cereals is confirmed by their frequency of occurrence in the different samples, a measure of relative abundance preferred by several specialists (Dennell 1974, 1976; Kroll 1981): *T. dicoccum, T. monococcum* and *Hordeum* are present in every site and every level studied. *T. dicoccum* and *Hordeum* are present in a large majority of the samples themselves (see table 8.1).[12]

Conversely, legumes vary from about 10 to 50 per cent by number of seeds, but their presence in the different samples is much less systematic: only the lentil, the most common legume, is found in almost all sites and levels, with the curious exception of Sesklo EN2 and EN3. *Pisum, Vicia* and *Lathyrus* have much more irregular distributions and are not found in all levels of occupation or even in all sites.

Pulses do not require heating before threshing, and are consequently considered less prone to carbonization than cereals (Halstead 1981: 317). Yet pulses are normally stored for winter consumption, and the carbonization of seeds can frequently be due to accidental conflagrations rather than to intentional heating. Since cereals predominate in every site sampled except Nea Nikomedeia and come from all kinds of contexts – cooking areas, burnt floors, midden, etc. – this systematic over-representation may nevertheless indicate that cereals were produced and stored on a larger scale than legumes (*contra* Halstead 1981: 317). The 'traditional divorce between extensively grown cereals and intensively grown, labour-intensive pulses' (Halstead 1989b: 30) could well be anchored in Early Neolithic agricultural practices.

The exploitation of wild plant resources

Cultivated species amount to 80 to 100 per cent of the seed assemblages when quantified data are available. To what extend does this reflect the actual predominance of cultivated species over that of wild plant resources?

Leaves and tubers are not preserved in archaeological assemblages, wild fruit can be eaten raw, away from the village, and wild plant seeds need not be stored for sowing. Thus, they have fewer chances than legumes or cereals of being recovered in archaeological assemblages. Furthermore, recovery techniques introduce systematic biases against the smaller seeded wild species: it is noteworthy that a large diversity of wild plants is found only in Kroll's samples, that is, where flotation has been practised (table 8.1). Wild plants may thus be severely under-represented in the seed assemblages, and their importance in

[12] Except for a few samples at Nea Nikomedeia and Prodromos that yielded fewer than five seeds, and a few pure caches of legumes at the latter site.

the diet may accordingly be underestimated. Björk (1995) recently argued that wild plant resources could in fact have represented the bulk of the diet in EN Greece, agriculture being only small-scale and of limited importance.

The list of wild Early Neolithic seeds does contain several edible species. Small-seeded fruits, such as figs, are present only in the most carefully collected samples (Sesklo, Otzaki and Argissa), but they are well represented in frequency of occurrence. *Vitis* is only sporadically present and there is no indication that it was cultivated (Renfrew J. 1995). Curiously, fruits with larger pips or nutshells – *Prunus, Pistacia, Quercus, Cornus, Crataegus* – less susceptible to recovery biases, are found in only one to three assemblages at the maximum and always in small quantities. In Macedonia, at Giannitsa B, fruits amount to only 0.8 per cent of the total remains from cereals, legumes and fruit (Valamoti 1992). Wild fruits were occasionally collected, but there is no indication that they were consumed regularly, except possibly for figs.

Most of the other species are typical field weeds and are considered as such by several specialists (see Jones G. 1987; Kroll 1981 or Valamoti 1992). This concerns, for instance, *Lithospermum, Fumaria, Avena, Galium spurium, Lolium, Bromus* or *Agrostemma*. However, *Buglossoides arvensis* (= *Lithospermum*)[13] *Avena* and *Bromus* may have been collected as fodder or as complementary food and the leaves or buds of *Portulaca, Galium* and *Stellaria*, and so forth are also edible. There is thus no doubt that the list of wild species contains several edible species. But whether they constituted a staple diet is another matter. All are present in a very small number of samples only and in very small quantities, and I doubt that taphonomic biases alone can explain their under-representation.

Many wild plants must be processed before being eaten (Stahl 1989). Vetches and acorns, for instance, are toxic unless thoroughly cooked. All dried legumes must be cooked, and many wild fruits (such as *Pyrus*) are too hard to eat without first being boiled. Nuts and acorns, brought back to the village for eating, cooking or storing, would leave recoverable remains, as would the pips of fruits. If wild plant resources represent a staple in the diet, or if they are used as fodder, they have to be stored and/or processed in a settlement occupied year-round. In this case, accidental carbonization during cooking, the rejection of nutshells in hearths, or accidental burning down of houses would have given ample opportunity for the preservation of wild cereals, legumes and fruits. It is precisely when they are secondary products that they are most amenable to the taphonomic biases mentioned above. In many western European Neolithic settlements wild plants are indeed well represented, and a comparison between the data from Greece, and, for instance, Great Britain (Moffet *et al.* 1989) shows striking contrasts that probably represent extreme opposite situations.

More likely, wild plants in early Neolithic Greece did not play a significant role in the diet. First, it is unlikely that the available species would have been

[13] *Buglossoides arvensis* was found as a pure cache in MN levels at Achilleion, which shows it was intentionally collected or stored.

abundant enough and have had enough caloric value to constitute a staple diet, especially the leaves. Tubers and bulbs grow mostly on open stony ground on hills and lower mountains, and would not have been easily accessible to peasants in the large alluvial basins. According to Hather's detailed study (1994: 721), it is in fact unlikely that roots and tubers could have provided a staple diet of carbohydrates anywhere in the Mediterranean areas of the Near East and Europe. Halstead (1981a: 315, 1984: 2.8) also considers that the use of wild plants, as a whole, was limited in the main alluvial basins by their dispersion, low density, low yields and seasonality.[14] Examination of the seed assemblages certainly confirms a low and irregular representation of wild plant resources, and unless one postulates special processing techniques in Greece, Early Neolithic peasants must have eaten fewer wild plants than their western European counterparts. All the wild species that could leave abundant remains, such as *Quercus*, *Cornus* or *Corylus*, which are found in quantity in other European sites, are here very scarce or even absent. In this respect, most of the wild plants recovered in EN settlements thrive in open, dry places. No shade-loving species suggests the systematic exploitation of tree groves or forests. Some regional differences may have existed, however: non-weedy wild species seem better represented in sites marginal to the areas of densest settlement, where access to more varied natural environments would have been easier. But even in these cases they are usually represented by a very low number of seeds and cannot be taken as evidence of systematic consumption and storage. This tallies with Halstead's argument, according to which the very size of the human communities[15] would have precluded the use of wild resources as a subsistence basis in such environments (Halstead 1989b: 31).

To the contrary, cultivated species are far more abundant and, above all, far more regularly present in the various samples. There is thus little support for the hypothesis of a diet based on wild resources, as suggested by Björk (1995). But even as complementary food, wild plants appear surprisingly scarce. The data on plant exploitation hint to a deliberate ignorance of wild resources, which the study of faunal remains will further emphasize.

Agricultural system

Reconstruction of the agricultural system and potential crop yields confirm that a systematic exploitation of wild species would not have been a necessity. Given the permanence of the settlements and small-scale territories, crop rotation, especially between cereals and pulses, would have maintained soil fertility and restricted weed growth (Dennell 1984: 98, 1992: 80; Halstead 1981b:

---

[14] Limited resources in the large alluvial basins may find support in the absence of Late Palaeolithic or Mesolithic sites in the very same areas.
[15] More than the actual size, I would consider the density of settlements in Thessaly as the determining factor.

319–20). This traditional Mediterranean alternance was probably coupled with short-term fallow and manuring of the fields by the grazing of animals on stubble and fallows (Amouretti 1991: 121; Jones and Halstead 1995). Since lakes and marshes were abundant in some regions it was also possible to fertilize the fields by spreading wild plants such as reeds, rushes, sedges, wild irises, and so forth.

The occurrence of pure or almost pure deposits of seeds (over 80 per cent of a given cultivar) at Prodromos and Nea Nikomedeia, for instance, suggests the separate cultivation of emmer wheat, einkorn, pea, grass pea and bitter vetch (Jones and Halstead 1995; Halstead 1989b: 30). Intentional maslins of cereals or legumes, characterized by variable proportions of each cultivar (Jones and Halstead 1995), cannot be investigated in our samples because of lack of contextual data.

Given the climatic conditions, seeds were most probably sown in the autumn (Amouretti 1992; Barker 1985: 63, 254), but spring-flood agriculture may have been practised along the main rivers, lakes and springs (van Andel and Runnels 1995). According to Jones' observations in Assiros and Amorgos (Jones 1992), few weeds in our samples are actually characteristic of either winter or spring sowing: *Lolium temulentum* and *Agrostemma githago* belong to the Secalinetea group, and would indicate spring sowing. *Portulaca oleacera*, and possibly some *Bromus* and Chenopodiaceae, would be more characteristic of the Chenopodietea group and indicate winter sowing, row crops or waste grounds.

Cereal yields under traditional techniques over the Mediterranean area vary from about 300 to 600 kilos per hectare, the latter figure being more frequent (Davis 1991; Whitelaw 1991; Wilkinson 1992). Halstead has argued that such figures are probably too low for the Neolithic,[16] since modern ploughs and draught animals facilitate extensive cultivation on soils of secondary fertility. He thus suggests that more intensive practices during the Neolithic may have given yields of up to 1000 kilos per hectare (Halstead 1981a: 317–18). But even with a 'low' figure of 600 kg/ha, and assuming an annual consumption of *c.* 200 kg of cereals and pulse per person, a figure in the high values of the range provided by Davis (1991: 162, 166), 50 to 60 hectares of cultivated land would have been sufficient each year for a settlement of 200 inhabitants. Allowing for alternate year fallowing and for a higher population – *c.* 300 to 400, following Gallis' estimates of settlement sizes –, the total agricultural area need not have been over 250 ha, a figure still below the theoretical territories computed for eastern Thessaly (see ch. 7). These estimates, which would imply the exploitation of about 1 ha per person, allowing for fallowing and storage of seeds for sowing, are below the figures given for historical periods: 2.6 ha of land per person in Bintliff 1989: 91; a maximum of *c.* 2 ha in various Aegean islands,

---

[16] They are also below most figures for natural stands of wild cereals (see Harlan 1989; Zohary 1969).

sometimes less, in Davis 1991: 183. The difference could correspond to a more intensive system of production with no draught animals. But even if higher figures are retained, a territory of *c.* 450 ha, as calculated for Eastern Thessaly, would have sufficed for a population in excess of 200. According to both options, all fields could have been located within easy reach of the village, 5–10 minutes walk, but expanses of forests could not have been very large in the most densely settled regions. Available land could also be used for the production of fodder crops. Bitter vetch (*Vicia ervilia*) and grass peas (*Lathyrus sativus*) are, today, typical fodder crops in Greece. In addition, both can also be eaten by humans if necessary. Yet, as pointed out by Halstead (1993: 65), the recognition of fodder crops is difficult, and would require specific analysis.

Cereals, legumes and dried fruit must have been stored for winter consumption. The form of storage for cereals – whole spikelets or free grains – is not yet securely known. The storage of grain as whole spikelets gives better protection against insects and fungi, and the absence of spikelet bases in seed samples may be related to recovery techniques (Hillman 1981; Jones 1987). Early Neolithic pots are generally too small for long-term storage (Björk 1995; Vitelli 1989), and storage pits develop only in the Late Neolithic. Consequently, Björk argues that storage was very limited. But storage is a necessity in a sedentary economy and in regions of marked seasonal contrasts. Built granaries are known in the Near East as early as the Pre-pottery Neolithic A (Cauvin 1994: 64), but most of the traditional storage facilities typical of the Mediterranean area would have left no archaeological traces. All could easily have been used as early as the EN: silos of unbaked clay, wooden chests, reed baskets, clay-lined reed jars, containers in animal skin, woven bags, and so forth (see Kanafani-Zahar 1994).

Storage is not related only to the need for winter provisioning. As recently emphasized by Halstead (1989a, 1990b) and Forbes (1989), surplus production is an inherent risk-minimizing device in areas where annual yields can fluctuate widely. This 'normal surplus' has important implications, since it provides for an in-built means of exchange and leads the way to specialization (Runnels and van Andel 1988: 101).

Animal husbandry

From the very beginning of the Early Neolithic, sheep, goats, pigs, cattle and dogs are present in the faunal remains, with sheep being the most abundant in number of remains (see table 8.2). As with plants, the quality of recovery is unequal and often not up to modern standards. In addition, the effects of differential survival of bones have seldom been assessed.[17] But, here again, strong and constant patterns give grounds for some levels of generalization.

---

[17] For discussion see Greenfield 1988; Payne 1985; Trantalidou 1990; for an exception, see Halstead and Jones 1980.

Ovicaprines are always predominant in number of remains, in spite of their smaller size and the potential effects of differential bone preservation. Their proportion ranges from 50 to 88 per cent, but is generally between 55 and 70 per cent. When the distinction was possible, sheep were usually shown to be more frequent than goats.[18] Halstead (1987) considers the overall predominance of sheep as surprising, since the other domestic animals, goats, pigs and cattle, are better adapted to a wooded environment. He takes this as an indication that animal husbandry was restricted in scope and limited to cleared agricultural lands (Halstead 1987, 1989b). But I have already argued in favour of a more open environment than that claimed by Halstead, and sheep are in fact the animals best adapted to dry conditions (Bökönyi 1974: 95; Helmer 1992: 114).

At any rate, the importance of sheep should not be overestimated: the live weight of a cow is nearly thirty times that of a sheep and four times that of a pig. In terms of meat yields, *Bos*, which represents 10 to 41 per cent of the rest, would have predominated in most sites, with the exception of 4 per cent at Achilleion. Though the estimation of meat yields with Vigne's refined MOW method[19] has not been applied to our series, the latter has been shown to be consistent with the estimates based on the weight of bones. At Prodromos 1, 2 and 3 the weight of cow bones in all samples is always above 55 per cent of the total (and up to 67 per cent), whereas the weight of ovicaprid bones is always under 32 per cent and usually under 25 per cent. In the EN1A of Knossos, cattle would have provided 50 per cent of the total meat. Though large cow bones would tend to preserve better than the smaller ovicaprid bones, it is unlikely, as stated by Vigne (1991), that Early Neolithic populations from Greece (or elsewhere) were primarily 'sheep eaters'.

The important variations in the proportions of bovids are difficult to explain, since the extreme figures come from Prodromos 3 and Achilleion,[20] two sites located in western Thessaly and in comparable environments (table 8.2). Even at Prodromos the percentage of *Bos* varies from 30 per cent (Prodromos 1 and 2) to 41 per cent (Prodromos 3), the latter figure possibly being related to the smaller size of the sample. The figures for pigs are on the whole more stable, ranging from *c.* 10 to 25 per cent,[21] and pig is sometimes more abundant than cattle (*contra* Bökönyi 1973: 167).

Comparisons of Prodromos' mortality profiles with S. Payne's models (Payne 1973) indicate an exploitation of sheep predominantly tuned to the production of meat. The highest mortality peak is between six months and three years of age, with nearly 60 per cent of the animals killed before two years.[22] The sex

[18] Otzaki (EN2 and EN3) appears as an exception (Boessneck 1962: table 4).
[19] Meat and Offal Weight (Vigne 1991).
[20] Even if one includes the 'auroch' from Achilleion in the domestic *Bos*, the total proportion of bovids remains very low: 5.7% in number of remains for each phase.
[21] There is no apparent relation between the proportion of pigs and the abundance of acorns in the floral remains.
[22] The scarcity of infants (as opposed to juveniles) is problematic. It could be due to differential bone preservation, or to the slaughter of some lambs away from the settlement (Halstead and Jones 1980; Payne 1985).

Table 8.2 *Faunal remains from Early Neolithic strata in number of rests.*

		Argissa, c. XXVc to XXIX (EN1, EN2)	Otzaki (EN2)	Otzaki (EN3)	Prodromos 1 and 2 (EN2, EN3)	Prodromos 3 (EN2, EN3)	Sesklo (EN1)
Domestic fauna	Sheep	12	46	108	718*	125*	427
	Goat		57%	49%	56%	49%	64%
	Bos	11	27	65	388	105	92
			33%	30%	30%	41%	14%
	Pig	17	7	44	171	26	144
			9%	20%	13%	10%	22%
	Dog		1	2			3
			1%	1%			0.5%
	Total domestic	40	81 100%	219 100%	1277 100%	256 100%	666 100%
	% domestic of total fauna		c. 100%	98%	98.3%	97.3%	92.4%
Wild mammals	Red deer	2		3	22**	7**	14
	Roe deer						7
	Fallow deer						
	Ibex						
	Auroch						
	Wild swine		1?				
	Wild cat						1
	Badger						1
	Hare			1			30
	Fox						
	% wild mammals	<1%	2%	1.7%	2.7%	7.5%	4%
	Indet. fragments	4	6	30			
	Total mammals	46	88	253	1299	263	720
Other wild species	Tortoise/ turtle				present		1
	Birds				present		
	Fish				present		
	Shellfish				present		
	Total						721
	Sources	Boessneck 1962	Boessneck 1955	Boessneck 1955	Halstead and Jones 1980; Halstead 1984	Halstead and Jones 1980; Halstead 1984	Schwart 1981

Notes:
* Ratio sheep/goat for Prodromos 1, 2 and 3, based on postcranial bones, is 5:1.
** Includes red deer and roe deer (Halstead 1984; table 7.1).

Percentages have been rounded to the nearest decimal

Sesklo (EN2)	Sesklo 1972 excav.	Achilleion (phase I)	Achilleion (phase II)	Servia V	Nea Nikomedeia 1961 excav.	Lerna I	Knossos EN Ia
	291	788***	1157***		310	87 + 3 Ovis sp.	332****
2%	67%	88%	83%	c. 60%	71%	63%	75%
	58	36	61		64	17	29
%	13%	4%	4%	c. 15%	15%	12%	7%
	85	62	152		65	34	82
4%	20%	7%	11%	c. 15%	15%	24%	18%
	3	9	17		1	1	1
0.5%	1%	1%	1%		0.2%	0.7%	0.2%
	437	895	1387		439	142	444
	100%	100%	100%			100%	100%
6%	93%	93.5%	93%		c. 93%	88%	c. 100%
3%	13	15	30		frgts.***	2	
	7	7	8		frgts.***		
		2	1		frgts. ***		
		5	3				
		16	20			8	
	5	6	15			4	
		1					
	1		1				
	17	10	21		common	3	1
						2	
%	6.5%	7%		c. 7%	11%	<1%	
							65
51	470	957	1486			161	510
			2		1		
			1		present		
					present		
chwartz 985	Schwartz 1981	Bökönyi 1989	Bökönyi 1989	Watson 1979	Higgs 1962	Gevjall 1969	Jarman and Jarman 1968

*** On the limited number of diagnostic bones, the percentage of sheep and goats is respectively 64 and 36% in phase I, 80 and 20% in phase II.

**** The percentage of goats is about 10% (Jarman and Jarman 1968: 256).

ratio shows a heavy bias in favour of the longer survival of females: there was a marked preference for the killing of male lambs under one year (Halstead and Jones 1980; Halstead 1987). Though the sample is small, the analyses from Prodromos further suggest that sheep and goat herds may have been managed differently, with goat being culled later than sheep and with a more balanced ratio of males and females. Meat exploitation is also suggested for pig and cattle at Prodromos and this overall pattern is confirmed at Lerna, Knossos and Achilleion.[23] At Achilleion, during the Early and Middle Neolithic, 60 to 90 per cent of the domesticates were killed before reaching maturity. Here again, goat is an interesting exception since 54 per cent of the goats survived to adulthood (Bökönyi 1989).

The culling of the animals at Prodromos spread over a large part of the year, with no marked seasonality. This indicates that the animals were killed when needed, and not at an 'optimal' meat yield (Halstead 1992: 25). This mode of exploitation would have enhanced herd stability rather than productivity (Halstead 1989b: 29) and tends to confirm the use of flocks as a store of food (Halstead 1993). Only a limited number of animals could have been maintained year-round on the small territories calculated for Thessaly. On Keos, modern-day traditional farmers sustain about one animal per hectare of land, so that a family of five persons kept about eight animals on their 8–10 hectare farm (Whitelaw 1991). Though the exact figures doubtless vary,[24] small-scale herding is the most plausible, especially in regions of dense settlement (Halstead 1981a, 1984, 1987). A village territory of c. 450 ha could have supported at least 450 animals – probably more because Thessaly is more fertile than Keos – that is, 10–15 animals per family if the population estimates are accurate.

The exploitation of wild animals

As obtains for plants, wild mammals are strikingly scarce relative to domesticated animals despite much less acute taphonomic bias.

The proportion of wild vertebrates in EN sites varies from less than 2 per cent to 7 per cent only, with one exception at Lerna I (11 per cent) but on a very small sample. Deer – mostly red deer – and hares predominate in the wild fauna, but their number of rests is always several times smaller than for the least represented domestic species, dog excepted. The good relative representation of hare, more abundant than wild boar, auroch, fallow deer or roe deer, is noteworthy, since it demonstrates that the apparent scarcity of wild game cannot be attributed to a problem of differential bone preservation.

---

[23] Bogucki (1984), in particular, has convincingly argued in favour of milking and cheese production in the Early Neolithic Linearbandkeramik, much before the postulated 'Secondary Product Revolution'. But none of his arguments or evidence holds for the Early Neolithic of Greece, possibly because natural conditions differ, but also because the Early Neolithic in Greece is much earlier than the Linearbandkeramik.   [24] Especially when animal exploitation is intensive.

Auroch has been identified only at Achilleion and Lerna. Since Bökönyj, who studied the fauna from Achilleion, has remained a strong proponent of the local domestication of *Bos* (Bökönyi 1989),[25] one wonders whether other specialists would have given the same identification. Indeed, at nearby Prodromos where bovid remains were even more numerous, Halstead could not confirm the presence of aurochs (Halstead and Jones 1980: 101). The remaining wild species, mostly *Ibex, Meles, Felix, Vulpes* and *Sus*, are also very rare. This underlines the absence of systematic exploitation of fur-bearing animals. The apparent lack of interest in hunting is a choice, not an environmental constraint. This is demonstrated by the fact that in Thessaly, for instance, after several millennia of Neolithic exploitation, the relative and absolute proportion of wild game increased at the beginning of the Bronze Age (see Driesch 1987).

Until recently, Thessaly additionally offered rich possibilities for fishing and fowling (Halstead 1989b: 29). There is little doubt that Neolithic farmers occasionally enriched their diet with such resources. Remains of birds, reptiles, fish, shellfish and tortoises are found on most inland sites in small quantities, and at Pyrassos, one of the few EN settlements near the sea coast, large fish bones, shells and remains of crustaceans were found alongside the usual domestic fauna (Theocharis 1959). Fishing, however, seems to have been of limited scope throughout the Neolithic (Powell 1996; Stratouli 1996).

On a general level, the importance of these smaller wild resources is difficult to assess since their remains are affected by 'acute taphonomic biases', not the least being poor recovery (Halstead 1989b: 29; Trantalidou 1990). One may wonder, nevertheless, why taphonomic biases against wild resources in general should be systematically more acute in Greece than elsewhere, or more acute during the Early Neolithic than during later prehistoric periods.

Conclusion

I consider, instead, that the available data indicate a deliberate emphasis on domesticated plants and animals, in a symbolically and economically coherent system. Far from being 'natural', the Early Neolithic environment in Greece was a social construct based on newly introduced species and new forms of exploitation. The limited exploitation of wild plants and animals, together with the permanent and sedentary settlements, exemplifies what Chapman called the 'domestication of space' (Chapman 1988). The opposition between the domestic and the wild worlds (Hodder 1990: 164) is well illustrated by the neglect of large game: it is not until the end of the Neolithic that some wild species, especially deer, will acquire, or reacquire, a symbolic value of their own. This selectivity against wild resources is rooted in a very ancient attitude of Neolithic farmers. Already by the PPNA, 'Ce qui étonne le plus, en fait, c'est

---

[25] Despite the scarcity of wild aurochs in the Later Pleistocene and Early Holocene of Greece.

moins l'ensemble des végétaux et animaux effectivement consommés que la liste de ceux qui l'étaient naguère et ne le sont presque plus', (The most surprising, actually, is less the list of plants and animals that were effectively consumed than the list of species that were exploited until recently and no longer were.) (Cauvin 1994: 89). This shows that the factors underlying this attitude cannot be explained solely in economic terms. It underscores the importance and the symbolic value given to domesticated resources, a symbolic value that was retained several centuries later when they had gained undeniable economic value. Most, if not all, the domestic species in Greece are of exogenous origin; thus the opposition between wild and domestic is reinforced by an opposition between local and non-local, which will also be clearly expressed in the technical domain.

The permanence of the Early Neolithic settlements, most of which continued to be occupied during a large part of the Neolithic, demontrates that this 'artificial' economic system was completely successful.[26] It is now impossible to agree with the statement that 'among neolithic people, especially, the margin of subsistence was frightfully narrow and an ever-present threat to survival' (Caskey and Caskey 1960: 160).

---

[26] EN populations were nonetheless affected by health problems. Bisel and Angel (1985) report a mean age of death for EN adult females of Greece and Turkey of 29.8 years, and 33.6 for males. Altogether, 43% of the individuals were affected by porotic hyperostosis, but the sample includes sites located in particularly unhealthy environments such as Lerna. It is also now known that the age of death of adult females tends to be systematically underestimated (Masset 1971).

CHAPTER 9

THE EARLY NEOLITHIC VILLAGE

In many societies, architecture directly reflects the social organization and symbolic conception of space. The distribution of houses within a settlement, their size and building techniques, the structuring of space and activities within the house, can all relate, to a greater or lesser degree, to the social and sexual relations within the group and to its ideological background. 'L'architecture domestique – structuration et codification spatiale par excellence – produit et reproduit, dans le temps et pour chaque maisonnée, la vision partagée que la société a du monde' (Domestic architecture, which implements by excellence a structuration and codification of space, produces and reproduces through time, for each household, the shared vision of the world of the society) (Coudart 1994: 228). At the same time, individual houses materialize the divisions within the group: they emphasize the importance of the lineage, the household or the individual as a discrete unit. Differences in status, wealth or role can thus be expressed in the size, layout or ornamentation of the house. Village architecture thus results from an interplay between collective norms, collectively accepted variations, and individual differentiation.[1]

The respective strength of these three components can vary, however, as do the architectural features that reveal them. I shall argue here that Early Neolithic architecture in Greece is characterized by an unusually high level of intersite variation and change through time. Because of the limited scale of most excavations, intrasite variability is more difficult to assess, but may also have been important. Contextual factors and individual choices seem to predominate over collective norms and the affirmation of common traditions.

However, this variability of architectural techniques contrasts with the stability of the settlements themselves. Almost all Early Neolithic settlements known to date were occupied over many generations. The stability and identity of the group itself may thus have been expressed by the very permanence of the settlement, rather than by the buildings of which it was composed.

---

[1] 'Car *l'uniformité* – par laquelle l'unité domestique affirme et confirme son appartenance au groupe culturel – est forcément compatible avec les *différenciations* à travers lesquelles la maisonnée exprime ses particularités' (Coudart 1994: 229).

The nature of the settlements: mound settlements or flat sites?

Because the majority of Neolithic settlements in Greece, from the Early Neolithic on, show themselves as conspicuous tells – locally known as *magoules* or *toumba*[2] – it is generally assumed that the formation of tells started in the Early Neolithic. The formation of tells, or mound settlements, requires not only the use of mudbricks, daub or pisé in the construction of the walls – therefore resulting in thick deposits when the walls disintegrate – but also repeated rebuilding over the foundations and debris of older buildings. Tells, as opposed to short-lived villages or 'flat sites', with lateral shifts of the built areas, reflect both a *permanence* of the settlement over generations and a *constricted* concept of the village space.

Lichardus-Itten recently challenged the existence of mound settlements in the EN of the Balkans, arguing that the formation of tells did not start until the (Balkanic) Middle Neolithic[3] (Lichardus-Itten 1993). Because the oppositions between permanent and shifting settlement, or between constricted and open settlements, have had economic, sociological and symbolic implications, the reality of 'tells' in the Early Neolithic of Greece thus requires discussion.

On the whole, EN settlements of Greece possess all the characteristics of *permanent* settlements put forward by Kaiser and Voytek (1983): traces of heavy architecture, thick and rich deposits covering long periods of time, evidence of varied activities, internal differentiation of activity areas, year-round occupation, and so forth. Even in the Early Neolithic, there is little doubt that settlements were occupied over several generations. Proving that they also reflected a restricted conception and use of space is more difficult, given the absence or limited scope of the excavations.

The height and surface of unexcavated sites can only be indicative, since they are determined not only by the duration and nature of the settlement, but by the architecture and site formation processes. Only four EN settlements of eastern Thessaly were never reoccupied afterwards (Gallis 1992: nos. 40, 218, 286, 325). They presently have a visible height of 1 to 4 metres above the plain, and an estimated surface of 0.5 to 3 ha (Gallis 1992). These figures tally with the depth of EN deposits in excavated sites, which vary from *c.* 2 metres or less – Sesklo, Soufli, Elateia, Nea Makri, Achilleion, Nessonis I – to *c.* 4 metres at Gediki, Magoulitsa, Otzaki, Sesklo C, with a maximum of 6 metres at Prodromos 3. Only these last figures are high enough to be taken, by themselves, as safe indications of mound settlements.[4]

Evidence of repeated rebuilding on the same spot or on the same foundations is more reliable, since it is less dependent upon site formation processes. Where

[2] Respectively in Thessaly and Macedonia.
[3] That corresponds to the Late Neolithic of central and southern Greece.
[4] The average rate of tell formation is about 1 m per century in the Balkans. Given the duration of the Early Neolithic, thicker deposits could have been expected. However, the study of architectural remains (below) indicates that the rate may have been lower during the earliest phases of the Early Neolithic.

excavations have taken place, successive occupation levels are indeed the norm: the maximum is reached again at Prodromos 3, with ten successive Early Neolithic levels (Hourmouziadis 1971a: 175), but examples of successive house floors or superimposed stone foundation walls are also found at Achilleion (Gimbutas *et al.* 1989), Gediki (Theocharis 1962b: 74), Otzaki (Milojčić-von Zumbusch and Milojčić 1971), Elateia (Weinberg 1962), Lerna (Caskey 1957: 160; 1958: 139) and Giannitsa B (Chrysostomou 1991). Sesklo provides a good example of the contrasts between continuously settled areas, the Acropolis and the sector B, and areas of shorter occupation, Sesklo A and C (see sections in Wijnen 1981 and Wijnen 1992). The available data thus support the hypothesis of tells, that is, of permanent settlements *rebuilt over generations over the same, limited area*. If one follows Lichardus-Itten's argument, Early Neolithic Greece would then present an interesting contrast *vis-à-vis* the Balkanic regions. It demonstrates the importance given to tight communities and to continuity through generations. It also demonstrates that environmental conditions and agricultural techniques permitted a permanent hold on the land.

Excavations and soundings are usually located near the centre of the site, or at least away from its tapering extremities. It is therefore difficult to determine whether the limitations of the village space were marked by actual physical boundaries. Surrounding walls and ditches were claimed at Nea Nikomedeia and at several later settlements,[5] but the evidence is far from compelling, at least for the Early Neolithic. According to Rodden (1965), Nea Nikomedeia was initially surrounded by a pair of walls that were quickly replaced by a deep ditch, once filled with water. In the final monograph, however, Pyke mentions only ditches, with the 'deep ditch' cross-cutting two narrow, parallel ditches (Pyke and Yiouni 1996: 29, 52). In addition, the ditches were uncovered in one sector only and over a very small area. It is thus impossible to determine whether they actually 'surrounded' the settlement. Even if they did, various interpretations could be put forward. The largest ditch has been related to the necessity for drainage (Jacobsen 1981) but, according to Bintliff (1976a; *contra*: Rodden 1964b), Lake Giannitsa was already dry; Nea Nikomedeia was surrounded by an open plain covered with silts. Other functional explanations include the protection of the harvests and animals against predators, the control of flocks, the control of access to the village, and so forth. A delimitation of the inner village space, of purely symbolic value, is also a possibility: surrounding walls, fences, ditches, 'fortifications', and so on, are a common feature of early sedentary villages, especially in the early phases of settlement in a region.[6]

[5] The large 'fortification ditch' from Soufli, initially published as EN (Theocharis 1958: 80), has been subsequently reattributed to the Middle Neolithic (Theocharis 1973b: 65 and n. 69).

[6] e.g., Jericho in the Levant (Bar-Yosef 1986), PPN villages of Cyprus (Le Brun 1984, 1989), Early Neolithic sites of the Tavoliere in Italy (Tinè 1983), and, more controversially, early Linearbandkeramik sites in Belgium (Cahen and Jadin 1996; Keeley 1992). B. Woodcock, commenting on an earlier version of this typescript, remarked that 'A little paranoia never hurts anyone in a new and strange land!'

Not all settlements, however, exemplified this restricted conception of space. Large, extensive, so-called 'flat' sites are also recorded. Whereas all Neolithic phases are recorded on the Acropolis of Sesklo, the surveys, soundings and excavations around the Acropolis reveal a shifting settlement pattern. Sector C, on the slope opposite the Acropolis to the west, yielded only remains of the 'preceramic' and Early Neolithic 1. Sector A (trench B 1972), approximately 60 m to the south of the Acropolis, yielded remains of the Early Neolithic 3. Sector B, more than 150 m to the south-west of the Acropolis, showed a longer sequence covering all phases of the Early and Middle Neolithic. Elsewhere, only Middle Neolithic finds were recorded (Wijnen 1981). Nea Makri, in Attica, is also considered a 'flat' site, with lateral shifts in settlement. It covers several hectares and presents a shallow stratigraphy of no more than three metres from the Early to the Late Neolithic (Theocharis 1956; Pantelidou-Gkofa 1991). Finally, the Early Neolithic level at Sidari, although known only from a natural section, demonstrates the probable existence of short-term Early Neolithic occupations (Sordinas 1969).

These few examples are sufficient to reveal a range of settlement types, from the most permanent and well-delimited villages to small, short-lived settlements. Since site recognition is strongly biased in favour of the most permanent settlements, the few examples of 'flat' sites are important. They demonstrate that the permanent *'magoula'*, although an important characteristic of the Greek Neolithic, is not an exclusive feature.

Conversely, the lack of interest in caves by EN populations remains striking. As suggested earlier, this may be related to the limited role played by transhumance; but it is noteworthy that caves were apparently not used, either, as hunting camps.[7] The lack of interest in caves may be a consequence of the general lack of interest in wild resources. But it could also be part of a deeper symbolic opposition between the domestic and the wild, whereby dwelling places themselves, the 'domus', had to be artificially created and man-made.

Village size and population

The spatial extent of Early Neolithic settlements remains conjectural, since the majority are known only through surface surveys. Furthermore, in the few settlements that were sounded or excavated, the EN strata were usually exposed on a very limited surface. Surface distributions of artefacts can lead to gross overestimations, due to ploughing, erosion and the use of domestic refuses as manure in surrounding gardens and fields. Conversely, estimations based on the diameter of the presently visible mound tend to underestimate the size of the settlement when its base is buried under sediments.[8]

---

[7] For a good example of an Early Neolithic shelter used as a hunting camp, see Binder 1991.
[8] As demonstrated by van Andel for Plateia Magoula Zarkou (van Andel and Runnels 1995; van Andel *et al.* 1995).

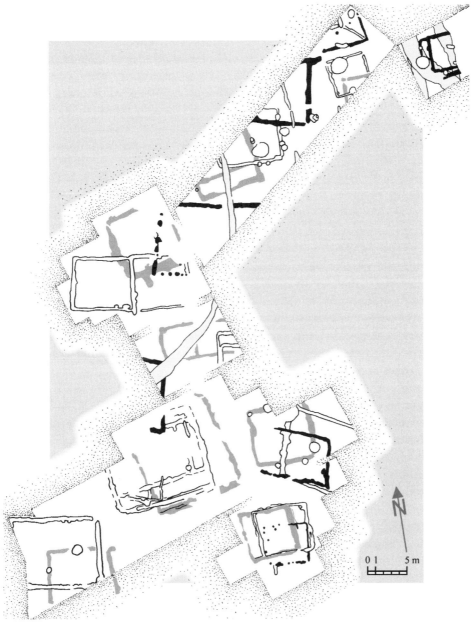

Fig. 9.1 Plan of the excavations at Nea Nikomedeia, with all successive
building phases. The ditch in the centre is from a later date, the
ditches at the top left date from the Early Neolithic (after Pyke and
Yiouni 1996).

Accordingly, size estimates vary substantially from one author to another. According to French (French n.d., quoted in Halstead 1984: table 6.3), most Thessalian *magoules* cover from 1 to 2 hectares, whereas Gallis gives estimates ranging from 3 to 4 ha as a mean (Gallis 1992: figs. 11, 235 and 14, 236). Gallis' larger estimates, though based on the surface distribution of artefacts, remain, nevertheless, plausible for the period. Nea Nikomedeia covered approximately 2.4 ha in the Early Neolithic (Pyke and Yiouni 1996: 47). The major PPNA tell settlements in the Near East already extend over 1 to 3 hectares (Bar-Yosef and Belfer-Cohen 1991: 190) and sites up to 12 ha are known as early as the PPNB (Abu Hureyra, Ain Ghazal, Basta). Three hectares is by then a current figure (Balkan-Atli 1994; Bar-Yosef and Belfer-Cohen 1991: figs. 1–8; Cauvin 1997) and Roodenberg considers the 2.5 ha Early Ceramic Neolithic tell of Ilıpınar (western Anatolia) as 'middle sized' (Roodenberg 1993: 251). The figures quoted for the four purely EN sites of eastern Thessaly (0.5 to 3 ha) may thus be within the actual range.

Uncertainties pertaining to the size of the settlements necessarily rebound on population estimation, in itself a notoriously hazardous exercise. The discussion will focus again on Nea Nikomedeia, which provides the only relatively large-scale excavation of an Early Neolithic village in Greece. Its representativeness is difficult to assess; all that can be said is that no obvious differences in the organization of village space have been revealed by the more limited excavations in other sites.

EN sherds were scattered all over the surface of the tell and the EN occupation at Nea Nikomedeia can be estimated at about 2.4 ha (Rodden 1965). About 1700 m^2 were excavated, less than one-eighth of the site. Pyke identified the remains of eight buildings in the earliest building phase, spread 2 to 5 metres apart. Seven of them are considered to be domestic houses, grouped around a larger building of presumed collective function (see below, ch. 12). The second building phase showed the same number of structures, whereas only six were uncovered from the third building phase (Pyke and Yiouni 1996).

If the density of buildings is held constant over the whole site, their total number can be estimated at between 50 and 100 at any one time. Pyke retains the higher figure and suggests a total population of 500 to 700 for the first and second building phases (Pyke and Yiouni 1996: 47–8). But strict contemporaneity of all the buildings, even within a single 'building phase', is doubtful. In a rather conservative estimate, Halstead (1981a: 312) considered that 25 to 30 per cent of the surface of the site was built over, and that only 20 to 30 per cent of the houses were occupied simultaneously. Using Narroll's figure of 10 square metres of built area per person (Naroll 1962), he estimated the total population to be between 120 and 240 inhabitants – well below the figures of 360 or more suggested by Renfrew or Angel (Angel 1972; Renfrew 1972: 238). Halstead's estimate tallies with Jacobsen's, who finds Renfrew's density of 200 persons per hectare too high and uses instead an estimate of 100 persons per hectare, based

Fig. 9.2 Schematic representation of the successive building phases at Nea
Nikomedeia (after Pyke and Yiouni 1996).

on Near Eastern ethno-archaeological studies.[9] He thus suggests a population of *c.* 200 to 250 people at Nea Nikomedeia (Jacobsen 1981: 313).

On the basis of Nea Nikomedeia's density figures, Halstead has suggested an average density of *c.* 100/300 persons per hectare of settlement in the Greek Neolithic. Relying on French's low estimates for the superficies of the Thessalian settlement, he considered that the population would have ranged from 40 to 80 inhabitants in the smallest sites (0.4 ha) and from 120 to 240 in the largest (0.8 ha) (French n.d.; Halstead 1981a). Jacobsen (1981: 313), however, considered that the size of Neolithic villages in Greece was underestimated and more in line with the figures later published by Gallis (1992). These figures, often in excess of 1 to 2 hectares and up to 10 hectares, would still correspond to populations of 100 to 300 persons on average if the lower estimate of 100 inhabitants per hectare is retained. Despite their small size, the theoretical territories reconstructed from the distribution of settlements in eastern Thessaly could perfectly support such population densities on an agricultural basis.

The general layout of the village

As already observed, most Early Neolithic occupations are covered by several metres of later prehistoric deposits. Consequently, the earliest building levels were usually exposed over a very limited area.[10] These small soundings yielded at most the partial remains of one or two buildings, so that the general layouts of the settlement are impossible to assess. It seems, however, that most villages were composed of rectilinear detached buildings, located close to one another – 2 to 5 m, for instance, at Nea Nikomedeia. They show no common walls or bounded courtyards. This contrasts with the clustered plan of the central Anatolian villages of the same period, which Roodenberg (1993: 254) attributes in part to the use of gable roofs that require freestanding walls. Buildings were scattered over the settlement, and although their orientation seems to have been approximately parallel – roughly east–west at Nea Nikomedeia and Achilleion – no real planning can be brought to light.

The architecture of the buildings

Only a dozen sites yielded remains of Early Neolithic architecture, with several superimposed building phases (see table 9.1). With one or two exceptions that will be discussed later, these buildings contained evidence of varied activities, yielded abundant domestic equipment and were associated with internal and/or external hearths or ovens. Given their dimensions, they could have

[9] Broodbank (1992: 43) also takes 100 persons per hectare as the lower density limit.
[10] Significantly, at Nea Nikomedeia, the only Early Neolithic site excavated on a fairly 'large' scale, the later levels had been partially quarried away.

Table 9.1 *Summary of architectural remains from the Early Neolithic*

Site	Foundations	Materials	Techniques	Dimensions	References
Lerna, AP	Stone walls	Stones, mudbricks		Rectangular houses	Caskey 1958: 139
Nea Makri, lower strata	Entire house(s) slightly buried, 0.35–0.40 m deep	Light wattle and daub probable		One rectangular house, at least 5×4 m	Theocharis 1956: 4
Nea Makri, upper EN strata	Stone walls, 0.35–0.40 cm wide	Stone, mudbricks	Mudbricks walls, roof supported by wooden posts	Rectangular houses, c. 2.5 m wide	Theocharis 1956: 4–5
Elateia	None	Posts, wattle and daub	Wattle and daub on posts		Weinberg 1962: 166
Halai	Stone walls	Stone and mudbricks	Mudbrick walls		Pariente 1993: 825
Achilleion Ib	Stone walls, dug into trench	Stones, compact 'pisé'			Winn and Shimabuku 1989a: 34
Achilleion IIa	None	Posts, wattle and daub	Three rows of post-holes lined with pebbles, posts secured by hard clay packing		Winn and Shimabuku 1989a: 36
Achilleion IIb	None	Posts, wattle and daub	(as above)		Winn and Shimabuku 1989a: 38–9
Magoulitsa		Mudbricks			Papadopoulou 1958
Prodromos 2	None	Posts, pisé, branches, reeds, clay	Walls of pisé with posts, wooden roof	10 m×10 m (?), partitioned into smaller rooms	Hourmouziadis 1971b, 1972
Otzaki, earliest stratum	None	Mudbricks, 30 cm long	Mudbrick walls, wattle and daub roofs?		Milojčić-von Zumbusch and Milojčić 1971

Table 9.1 (*cont.*)

Site	Foundations	Materials	Techniques	Dimensions	References
Otzaki, later EN strata	None	Wattle and daub, no posts, light structures		Houses *c.* 4 m wide, and more than 5 m long	Milojčić-von Zumbusch and Milojčić 1971
Argissa EN1	None	Posts, reeds, daub (clay mixed with chopped plant remains)	Wattle and daub on posts	*c.* 5 m wide, length preserved on 4 m, rectangular	Milojčić *et al.* 1962
Argissa EN2, EN3	None	Mostly posts, wattle and daub	Post-houses with wattle and daub dominant		Milojčić 1959b: 9
Argissa, EN3	None	Mostly mudbricks	Mudbrick houses dominant		Milojčić 1959b: 9
Gediki	Stone walls	Stone, twigs, branches, reeds, daub	Wattle and daub		Theocharis 1962b
Sesklo A and C (EN1)	Stone walls	Stones, 'pisé'			Wijnen 1992
Sesklo B[I]E (EN1)	Stone walls	Stones, mudbricks?			Wijnen 1992
Sesklo A (EN2, EN3)		Mudbricks, beams, branches, worked clay	Mudbrick walls, roofs of beams and branches covered with worked clay		Wijnen 1992: 63
Sesklo B (EN2, EN3)	Stone walls	Stones, etc.?		Length of one house 7.5–8 m?	Wijnen 1992
Pyrassos		Posts, wattle and daub, mudbricks	Post houses and mudbrick houses		Theocharis 1959: 38
Giannitsa B		Posts, 'pisé'	Posts set in pairs, with wattle and daub or pisé walls	Ellipsoidal house?	Chrysostomou 1991, 1993

Site				Shape	Size	References
Giannitsa B	Trenches	'Pisé', limestone slabs	Pisé walls with lining (?) of limestone slabs			Chrysostomou 1991
Nea Nikomedeia	Trenches	Oak posts, wattle and daub, 'pisé'	Frame in oak. Posts set 1 m to 1.5 m apart in the centre of foundation trenches. Walls: sapplings and bundled of reeds plastered inside with mud mixed with chaff and outside with white clay	Square	from 6×8 m to 12×12 m	Rodden 1962, 1965, Rodden and Rodden 1964a, Pyke and Yiouni 1996.

accommodated a large nuclear family and can be considered as domestic houses according to classical criteria (e.g., Levy and Holl 1987).

Two basic architectural types, each with several variants, can tentatively be recognized: post-houses, with a heavy timber frame and wattle and daub walls, and mudbrick or 'pisé' houses, without vertical timber frames. The latter type, found for instance at Argissa and Otzaki, Pyrassos, Nea Makri and Lerna, seems to appear slightly later than the former, although sample biases cannot be ruled out. The difference between the two types is probably less clear cut than suggested here: the analyses that follow will show the correlation between building techniques and raw materials is far from strict. However, before we discuss them in more detail, a third and supposedly earlier type has to be considered: the so-called 'pit-houses'.

A first stage: pit-houses?

Though rectilinear buildings clearly prevail during the EN, some of the earliest constructions, which would date, for the most part, to the EN1, have been described as oval or round 'pit-houses'. If this holds true, it would signal a major transformation in architectural traditions during the Early Neolithic that strongly evokes the shift from round to rectilinear houses in the earliest phases of the Near Eastern Neolithic. As this shift is considered of major sociological importance (Cauvin 1997; Flannery 1972; Saidel 1993), the evidence for similar transformations in Greece is worth considering in some detail.

The problem proves to be rather difficult since, as Theocharis aptly described them, the earliest architectural remains in Greece are 'few and rather wretched' (Theocharis 1967: 174–5). At Argissa, the only well-documented building is a rectangular house of probably EN1 date, on the surface of the planum XXXVIIIb. But Milojčić also refers to 'pit-houses', and claims that they had disappeared by the EN2 (Milojčić 1959b: 9; Weinberg 1970: 576). However, no published document can warrant this affirmation. A 'pit-house/storage-pit' is also mentioned at the base of trench B at Achilleion. It is tentatively dated from phase Ia, but the section (Gimbutas *et al.* 1989: fig. 2.1) indicates that it belongs to the early part of phase Ib. Only partially excavated, it is a roughly circular pit of slightly more than 2 m in diameter that is apparently very shallow. Its small size and the absence of any architectural features – postholes, daub, beaten clay floor, hearth, etc.– hardly support its interpretation as a pit-house. Weinberg (1970: 576) similarly mentions 'pit-houses' at the bottom of the Lerna sequence, but Caskey had, probably rightly, interpreted these small and irregular pits as clay-digging pits (Caskey 1958: 138).

Thus far, the most convincing evidence for 'pit-houses' comes from Theocharis' excavations at Nea Makri, in Attica. In the lowest Early Neolithic stratum, several 'houses', cut into the virgin soil, were uncovered under later EN buildings on stone foundation walls. Only one has been described in some detail: it was rectangular, measured more than 5 m by 4 m, and was cut 0.35–0.40 m deep into the subsoil. Its straight walls were presumably made of a light material such as branches. Its size and regularity preclude its interpretation as a rubbish pit, whereas the presence of a cobbled hearth in its central part reinforces that of a house (Theocharis 1956: 4). The 'pit-houses' found in the second trench have not been described in detail and their interpretation remains problematic. Several pits, spaced close to one another, were cut into the virgin soil at a depth of 0.50–0.60 m. They were apparently of a circular shape, and one reached 3 m in diameter. No hearths have been reported. They were overlain by mudbrick houses on stone foundations, and the interpretation as clay-digging pits seems more plausible than that of houses. Similar pits were later uncovered at Nea Makri by Pantelidou-Gkofa in the restricted area she explored during rescue excavations. In her opinion, these were not pit-houses but storage pits (Pantelidou-Gkofa 1991: 191). One should also mention the earliest construction at Giannitsa B, supposedly of oval shape (Chrysostomou 1991). This, however, could be a misleading impression due to the circular shape of the deep pit later dug in the centre of this building. The disposition of the post-holes could fit equally well with a rectangular construction.

Significantly, the only acceptable example of a 'pit-house', that from Nea Makri, already consists of a large *rectangular* building. Although it emphasizes the variety of building techniques in Early Neolithic Greece, it does not suggest any drastic shift from small, round houses to large rectangular ones. It is probably safer to consider most 'pit-houses' as clay digging pits, as did Wijnen for the earlier 'pit-houses' at Sesklo (Wijnen 1992: 57). Large pits are present at the bases of most sites, even when they were founded later: they correspond to the initial phase of settlement, when the need for fresh building material would have been most acute.

That large quantities of clay were needed is demonstrated by the presence of wattle and daub walls in several settlements dated to the EN1. Stone foundation walls with traces of 'pisé' were uncovered on the Acropolis and in sector C of Sesklo, while mudbricks seem to have been used in sector B(I)E (Wijnen 1992: 58). The excavation trenches are too small to make out the plan or function of the buildings, but they are all clearly of a square or rectangular shape. Similarly, the EN1 'hut' uncovered at Argissa was a rectangular building, with large post-holes and wattle and daub walls (Milojčić 1960).

The limited remains from the earliest ceramic Neolithic strata reveal square or rectangular constructions that already made use of a variety of materials and assembly techniques. The diversity observed in the better known remains of the later phases of the Early Neolithic is thus rooted in an old tradition and no conceptual break can be brought to light. The hypothesis of round 'pit-houses' at the base of the ceramic Neolithic in Greece and the subsequent shift to quadrangular buildings seems to derive from an unconscious parallel with the Near East, more than from the excavation data from Greece itself.

The typical EN buildings: plans and dimensions

With the few possible exceptions mentioned above, all buildings are square or rectangular. These rectangular plans, together with the frequency of a central row of posts or the examples of Middle Neolithic house models, suggest pitched (or gabled) roofs. However, flat roofs have also been suggested for some early buildings at Otzaki, but without any determining argument[11] (Milojčić-von Zumbusch and Milojčić 1971: 16).

Though often described as 'small' houses (e.g., Demoule 1993: 3), some of these buildings can reach a respectable width and length. The smallest houses at Nea Nikomedeia ranged from 6 m×8 m to about 8 m×8 m. One measured at least 9 m×11 m, while the so-called 'shrine' of the first building phase reached 11.8×13.6 m (Pyke and Yiouni 1996). These dimensions are not unique: one building from Prodromos 2 also seems to have measured at least 10 m×10 m.

Although one-room houses are common, two-room houses are not unusual. A large house from Prodromos 2 was divided into small rooms by wattle and daub walls (Hourmouziadis 1971b) and several houses at Nea Nikomedeia were partitioned across the long axis into two communicating rooms. The general plan of these two-room houses is reminiscent of the pier-house plan from the PPNB of the Levant (Cauvin 1994: 134), with the partitions running perpendicular to the long axis of the building; it also announces the 'megaron' plan of later periods. The rooms probably had different functions: in one of the best-preserved examples, at Nea Nikomedeia, a raised 'plaster' bench or platform had been built along one of the narrow walls of the smaller room. A hearth and a storage bin were sunk into it, which suggests the room was used for food storage and preparation (Rodden 1965: 85).

Some houses, exemplified at Nea Nikomedeia, opened on to fenced-off porch areas or timber surrounds. These extensions seem to have been an integral part of the domestic space: a three-sided lateral surround along the northern wall of a house, made of large timbers, sheltered two ovens, while the two-room house already described opened on to a porch that covered a nest of complete pots (Rodden 1965; Rodden and Rodden 1964a).

The number and position of the doors remains unclear. Large hollowed stones found at Elateia and Sesklo (Weinberg 1962: 166–7; Wijnen 1992: 58) have been interpreted as door pivots. At Elateia at least, this interpretation is incompatible with the position of the post-holes and the hearth: the 'door pivots' should probably be considered as deep mortars, associated with the heavy pounder found nearby.

---

[11] Flat-roofed buildings have also been suggested at Achilleion, for the beginning of the Middle Neolithic (phase IVa) (Winn and Shimabuku 1989a: 63).

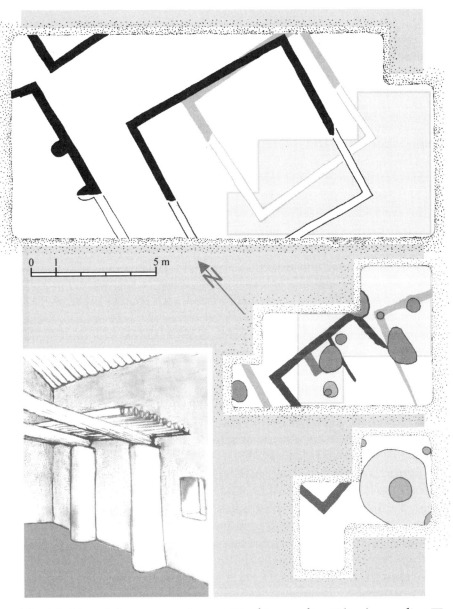

Fig. 9.3 Map of the constructions at Otzaki, sounding II (top), sounding III, planum 4–6 (centre) and planum 10g-h (bottom) (after Milojčić-v. Zumbusch and Milojčić 1971). Bottom left, proposition of reconstitution of the interior of a buttressed house.

Raw materials and building techniques

If the house plan showed a limited range of variations, building techniques on the contrary are extremely variable from site to site or within sites. Several variants can be distinguished both for mudbrick and post houses in the treatment of the foundations. At Magoulitsa and Otzaki, mudbrick houses were laid directly on the ground. Elsewhere mudbrick or daub constructions were erected on a stone foundation wall, which could itself be set in a trench (Achilleion Ib) or, more frequently, laid directly on the ground (Lerna, Nea Makri, Gediki, Sesklo, Halai). Similarly, post houses were set directly on the ground at Elateia, Achilleion II, Prodromos 2, Argissa and Pyrassos, or into trenches at Giannitsa B and Nea Nikomedeia. In the latter example, the trenches were 0.35 to 0.50 m deep, 60 cm wide, and 'either packed with dry, permeable soil, or, more commonly, lined with clay-marl, which was left to dry to cement hardness in the sun before the walls were built' (Rodden and Rodden 1964a: 564). Unlike the outside walls, the internal partitions, also supported by posts, were not dug into trenches (Rodden 1962). At Achilleion, the bases of the post-holes were also packed with hard clay and occasionally lined with cobbles in phase IIA (Winn and Shimabuku 1989a: 36).

The posts were sometimes set in pairs, as at Giannitsa B, or more frequently, singly. At Nea Nikomedeia the diameter of the posts, probably made of oak, varied from 8 to 20 cm and their spacing from 1 to 1.5 m. The techniques used for felling large trees and preparing the timber are not easy to identify. Polished axes, especially large ones, are conspicuously rare (see ch. 11), indicating that trees were probably felled by fire or bark-cutting. They could afterwards be split and shaped with the bone 'gouges' or 'chisels' that abound in these sites and are well adapted to the task (Sidéra 1993).

For particularly large houses, internal rows of posts were needed to support the roof. One of the largest buildings at Nea Nikomedeia, at least 8 m × 11 m, presented a line of 'outsized' post-holes, perpendicular to the long axis of the house (see the 'pier-house' plan mentioned above). The larger building called the 'shrine', 12 m wide, was divided by two parallel rows of very large posts that were slightly inclined towards the centre of the structure. An important feature of both houses is the presence of internal 'buttresses' set by opposite pairs along the long walls to help support the heavy roofs[12] (Rodden and Rodden 1964a). The use of internal buttresses recalls early eastern Anatolian architecture: they were already used in several PPNB buildings at Çayönü and Çafer Höyük (Aurenche *et al.* 1985; Balkan-Atli 1994; Braidwood *et al.* 1981).

Other settlements yielded no traces of posts. Mudbrick houses do not normally require timber frames of heavy vertical posts, so the absence of vertical posts is probably real at Magoulitsa, Otzaki and in the later EN of Argissa. In

---

[12] Buttresses are wrongly considered characteristic of the Middle Neolithic.

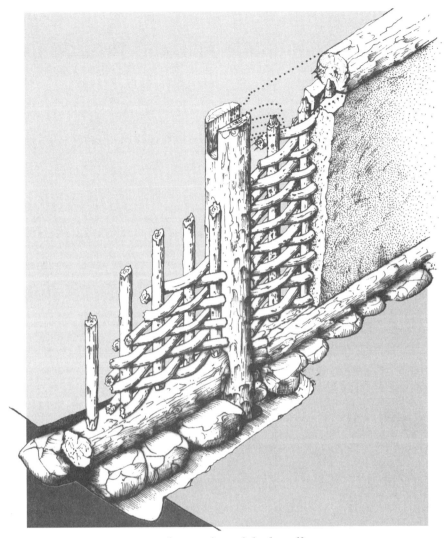

Fig. 9.4 Reconstitution of a wattle and daub wall.

other cases, especially when the walls were built of 'pisé', as at Achilleion Ib, or wattle and daub, as at Gediki, posts set within or on stone foundation walls may have disintegrated without leaving recognizable traces.

The absence of strict correlations between the foundations, the frame and the raw materials used for the walls is striking. Post-houses are normally associated with wattle and daub walls, as at Elateia, Achilleion IIa and b, Prodromos, Argissa, Nea Nikomedeia, but 'pisé'[13] or mudbrick walls are also

---

[13] Given the presence of posts, the use of pisé *sensu stricto* (i.e., of packed earth between timber shuttering) can be ruled out. The term *pisé* probably refers here to daub or walls made out of lumps of clay.

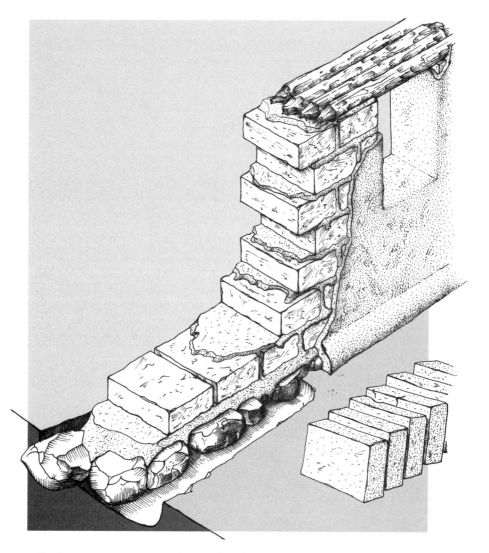

Fig. 9.5 Reconstitution of a mudbrick wall.

mentioned (Prodromos 2, Pyrassos). Houses set on stone foundation walls were built of mudbricks at Lerna and Nea Makri, of so-called pisé at Achilleion Ib,[14] or of wattle and daub at Gediki. But mudbrick walls could also be erected without any stone foundation wall or apparent frame, as was the case at Magoulitsa, Otzaki and Argissa.

---

[14] Here again, the use of the real pisé technique is doubtful: it is extremely rare in Antiquity, and the low remaining elevation of the wall would not allow the preservation of the characteristic marks left by the shutters. In the absence of mudbricks, a wall made out of packed lumps of clay appears more probable.

In all cases, however, clay was the most important building material for the walls. Neither the amount of clay used for each building phase, nor the numerous clay-digging pits thus needed seem to have been correctly evaluated in Greece.[15] The clay was mixed with chaff, another easily available raw material. Some of the so-called 'sickle-blades', with their characteristic polish, were most probably used to cut the chaff (e.g., Anderson 1994b). The prepared clay was then shaped into mudbricks, or applied to a wattle frame. At Nea Nikomedeia, the saplings were set upright 3 to 4 feet apart and the space between them was filled in with bundles of reeds standing on end. The inside surface was then plastered with mud mixed with chaff, the outside with white clay (Rodden 1965: 84).

The raw materials used for roofs apparently varied. A large water-logged wooden feature, thought to be part of a roof, was uncovered at Prodromos 2. It has not been published in full detail, but seems to demonstrate an early knowledge of carpentry techniques, with split planks up to 30 cm wide and wooden pegs (Hourmouziadis 1971b). More recently, evidence of wooden roofs has also been discovered at Giannitsa, but these also await detailed publication (Chrysostomou 1991). At Otzaki, where the use of wood seems to have been rather limited, a flat roof of wattle and daub, set over mudbrick walls, has been suggested for the oldest building (Milojčić-von Zumbusch and Milojčić 1971: 16). Gabled(?) roofs made of beams and branches covered with worked clay have also been reported from Sesklo (Wijnen 1992: 6), while Rodden suggests the use of thatch at Nea Nikomedeia (Rodden 1965: 87).

The floors of the houses at Prodromos, Gediki, Elateia and Nea Nikomedeia for instance were usually carefully laid with hard beaten clay and regularly redone: at Elateia, four successive layers were observed in a single EN house (Weinberg 1962: 167). In the largest building at Nea Nikomedeia, the 'shrine', a layer of broad-leaved marsh grasses or reeds had been spread between the natural clayey subsoil and the beaten clay floor (Rodden and Rodden 1964a),[16] while at Nea Makri, some floors were underlain with small pebbles to reinforce the mud coating (Theocharis 1956: 6). 'Plastered floors' have been reported at Achilleion already in the earliest levels (Winn and Shimabuku 1989a: 33–4), but whether this refers to real, gypsum-based, plaster, or to lime plaster, white clay or ground chalk is unknown. White-coloured prepared floors were also found recently at Halai (Pariente 1993: 825).

---

[15] Lerna and Nea Nikomedeia, where clay-digging pits have been identified, constitute rare counterexamples (Caskey 1957: 138; Rodden 1962: 270). They must have been present everywhere, however. To cover the walls of a wattle and daub post-house, Pétrequin and his collaborators used 2200 kg of clay (Monnier *et al.* 1991).

[16] Weinberg (1970: 578) also mentions a 'wooden floor raised on posts', but I have not traced the original reference.

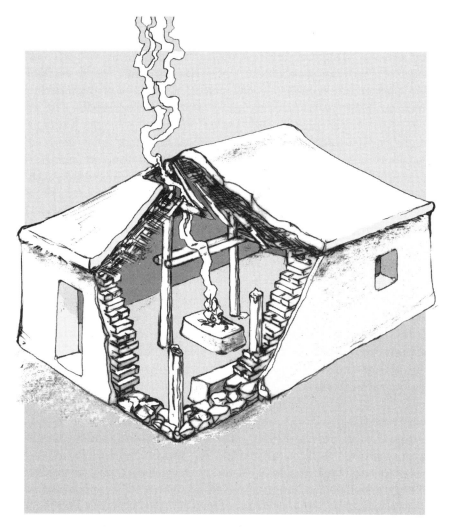

Fig. 9.6 Hypothetical reconstitution of a mudbrick house, based on
excavation remains and house models.

Internal features

Worked clay was also used for varied domestic features inside the houses:
shelves, benches, raised platforms, complex hearths, storage bins, and so forth.
The raised bench in a small room at Nea Nikomedeia, with a hearth and storage
bin sunk into it, has already been mentioned. In the building phase that followed,
clay-lined basins were found in two of the houses. They were filled with ashes
and charcoal, and one of them was surrounded by scattered cereal grains, suggesting that they were used for parching the grain (Rodden and Rodden 1964a).
Hearths were a common feature inside the houses, but their location and nature
seems to have varied even within a single site. In one of the Nea Makri houses

(Savvopoulos sounding) the hearth was flat and raised on a platform; in another house, from the Marinaki sounding, it was surrounded by stone slabs and set into the ground (Theocharis 1956: 6). At Argissa, a rectangular fireplace, laid directly on the ground, was found inside the 'hut' from level XXVIIIb. A small adjacent pit filled with ashes and burnt clay may be have been part of the cooking installation rather than a post-hole, as suggested by Milojčić (Milojčić *et al.* 1962: 6). At the other corner of the house was a later fire-pit, cutting through the floor of the 'hut'. It was surrounded by a regular alignment of post-holes that suggests either a shelter, or technical activities such as the smoking of skins. The most complex internal hearth published so far comes from a post-house of Achilleion (phase IIb). It consisted of a circular fire-pit, some 30 cm deep and 60 cm wide, backed on one side by a horseshoe-shaped protection of 'bricky earth'. The fire pit itself was lined with a layer of cobbles, and contained many bones mixed with cobbles, ash and charcoal (Winn and Shimabuku 1989a: fig. 4.9).

Around the houses

Many daily domestic and artisanal activities seem to have taken place outdoors. Where excavated, the areas between the houses reveal a great variety of associated features, such as pits, basins, prepared floors, hearths and ovens. Achilleion and Nea Nikomedeia provide the most detailed examples, though the exact nature and role of these associated features are often difficult to assess.

'Storage pits', or clay-digging pits?

Pits were ubiquitous around the houses, and their uses must have varied. However, since little attention has been paid to the exact shape of the pits or to their content and distribution, their 'functional' attributions are, in most cases, mere guesses. The presence of discarded domestic artefacts indicates that most pits were used as 'rubbish pits', but this does not imply that they were originally dug for this purpose. For instance, the repeated association of a pit, an oven or hearth and numerous scattered stones at Achilleion, phase IIa, squares A and B, recalls 'Polynesian pit ovens' with their nearby hearth to heat the cooking stones.

'Storage pits' have been claimed at several sites. At Nea Nikomedeia three large clay-digging pits, apparently surrounded by a heavy timber frame, were later reused as rubbish pits and fragments of the same ceramic vessel were dispersed in several pits; however, Rodden suggests they may also have been used for a while as storage pits (Rodden 1962: 270). The 'storage pit or pit-house' from level Ib at Achilleion has already been mentioned: neither interpretation is convincing considering its size and shape. Another 'storage pit', with a plaster coating, comes from level IIIa (Winn and Shimabuku 1989a: 46). It does not appear on any published section, thus its exact shape remains unknown. But neither its dimensions – about

5 metres wide – nor its contents – several querns, grinders, figurines, vessels, etc. – support this interpretation. Finally, not much is known of the 'storage pits' from the base of Nea Makri (Pantelidou-Gkofa 1991: 191), and their function remains conjectural. Without any analysis or convincing morphological evidence, the very existence of storage pits in the Early Neolithic remains undemonstrated.

Outdoor work-areas

At Achilleion, the pits often cross-cut artificially prepared floors, thought to be outdoor work areas. In layer Ib, two 'plastered floors' and a hardened surface with traces of chalk are considered work areas; one was limited by a 'pisé' wall on a stone foundation wall set in a trench, which may in fact correspond to the collapsed remains of a house. A 'work and food preparation area' was uncovered in level IIa, spreading over a 'plastered floor'. The artefacts on this floor include two antler tools, a palette, fourteen pottery discs, a female fig-urine and an animal figurine (Winn and Shimabuku 1989a: 37). In level IIb, a rich 'workshop' 'littered with bone tools' was possibly roofed, as suggested by the presence of post holes and burnt clay construction rubble (Winn and Shimabuku 1989a: 39). Slightly later (phase IIIa), a large rectangular reed mat impression was covered with piles of pottery sherds, as though all had been dumped together in what is thought to be a refuse area (Winn and Shimabuku 1989a: 44). Many other 'work areas', 'workshops' and 'food preparation areas' are mentioned in each stratum, usually associated with hard packed floors or plastered floors. But the functional identification relies in a large part, if not exclusively, on the nature of the remains found on or around these floors. This procedure is questionable, as there is no evidence that the objects were used where they have been discarded. The functions attributed to the objects them-selves are also arbitrary and often quite problematic. Even if the importance of outdoor activities cannot be doubted, their precise identification would require thorough analyses of depositional contexts and spatial distributions. This holds true even for the most conspicuous, and apparently least ambigu-ous outdoor features, such as hearths, fire-pits and ovens.

Hearths, fire-pits and 'ovens'

In level IIa at Achilleion, an outdoor hearth, with traces of two posts on its margin, was located just outside a post-house. Further away, in what is consid-ered a courtyard, a 'domed oven' was found. It is described as a domed fireplace made of a complex layering of clay, earth and plaster, with a lateral bench extending on one side. The 'dome' and lowermost part of the bench were built of brown clay. The bench was then covered by a thick layer of black earth that was overlaid by burnt yellow clay. Both the bench and oven finally received a thin 'plaster' coating (Winn and Shimabuku 1989a: fig. 4.10). If fully domed,

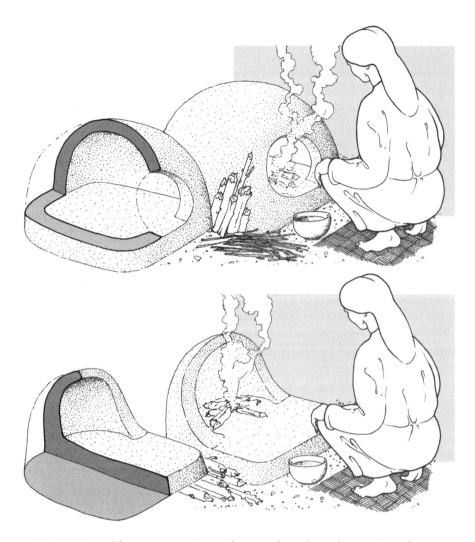

Fig. 9.7 Possible reconstitutions of ovens, based on observations from
Achilleion and Nea Nikomedeia.

this oven would be one of the earliest 'true' ovens found in Europe.[17] However,
from the published text and illustrations alone, this cannot be confirmed. The
low raised 'wall' appears to be intact since its top was covered by 'white
plaster', and no other traces of the presumed dome can be recognized. Given
the published section, a low earthen protection, comparable to that described
for the indoor hearth of phase IIa, seems just as plausible. In this respect, the
reconstruction of the 'semi-domed' oven from phase IIb (Winn and
Shimabuku 1989a: fig. 4.14) appears more convincing, even if the exact height

[17] Built ovens of various types are already well known in the Near East (Molist 1986).

and curvature of the surrounding 'wall' remain approximate. The latter enclosed a heavy, raised platform, also made from a homogeneous mixture of clay, abundant chaff, large and small stone grit and small pottery sherds.

A similar mixture of clay with large quantities of straw and vegetable temper had been used for the walls of the so-called ovens at Nea Nikomedeia. Badly preserved, they were located outside two houses and are described as 'probably open at the top, roughly cylindrical in form, and set in or on a basin scooped out of the sub-soil' (Rodden 1962: 270–1). According to the description, they may in fact resemble the open hearths surrounded by a protecting wall from Achilleion that we have just described. At any rate, none of them can be taken as definite evidence of fully domed ovens in the Early Neolithic and Pyke has recently pointed out many inconsistencies in the original descriptions of 'ovens' at Nea Nikomedeia (Pyke and Yiouni 1996: 51–2).

Simple outdoor hearths were also common at Achilleion, but the most interesting combustion feature is a large circular hearth from level IIb that seems to have reached 4 m in diameter. It was set in a slightly depressed basin and consisted of alternating layers of yellow chalky and dark ashy material. Because of its unusually large size, it has been considered a 'communal' hearth, perhaps used for firing pottery (Winn and Shimabuku 1989a: 40). But the presence of chalk instead evokes the preparation of 'plaster', so frequently mentioned for the floors, benches and pits at Achilleion.

The variety of combustion features, inside and outside the houses, strongly suggests varied uses. These could include the preservation and preparation of food, the firing of pots, the preparation of 'plaster', the preparation of resins, glues and dyes, the smoking of skins, and so forth (Prevost 1993). But, for the most part, these activities were common to all Neolithic societies. The diversity of fire-related features in Greece, as opposed to western Europe, cannot be explained solely in terms of function. It also denotes different traditions in the way fire-related features were conceived, used and integrated in the house.

The variability of Early Neolithic architecture in Greece: a few remarks

In the concluding insert of her essay on architecture as social and technical choices, Coudart stated that

On a admis que ce qui relevait de l'identité culturelle et des représentations collectives était stable et participait du mouvement lent et structurel de l'histoire, et que ce qui dépendait du registre culturellement moins déterminé des faits individuels et des évènements contingents relevait de conjonctures courtes et d'une diversité souvent impossible à classer dans une typologie. (Coudart 1994: 233)[18]

---

[18] 'We have admitted that what pertained to cultural identity and collective representations was stable and participated to the slow structural movement of history. To the contrary, what pertained to the culturally more flexible domain of individual acts and contingent events varied quickly and was often too diversified to fit into any typology.' In order to discriminate between the three levels of stability/variability that she revealed in archaeological and ethnographic con-

Our review of the available data has certainly revealed 'a diversity often impossible to classify in a typology', to use Coudart's own words. Few architectural features can be considered to be 'stable' and indicative of 'common norms'. The predominance of rectilinear buildings and the abundant use of clay as a building material are probably the clearest examples. The 'stable variations' are equally few: one could cite mudbricks versus post-houses as general archetypes, one-room houses versus two-room houses with a transversal division, and the presence of varied but usually complex combustion features. Few as they are, these stable features are, nevertheless, especially important: they all present strong Near Eastern affinities.

Mudbricks are typical of the Near East, and their use in Europe is mostly restricted to Greece. On the contrary, wattle and daub constructions, which are rare in the Near East, are characteristic of Europe and Treuil considered them a local invention (Treuil 1983). Yet, wattle and daub walls have been found in the earliest subphase of Çayönü (Braidwood *et al.* 1981: 252; Schirmer 1990) and post-houses with 'pisé' or wattle and daub walls have recently been uncovered in the lower Early Neolithic strata of Ilıpınar in western Anatolia (Roodenberg 1993). All are older than the European examples, and a common origin for both building techniques can now be suggested (Demoule 1993: 3). Though much rarer, the internal buttresses in pairs and the flat wattle and daub roofs, if confirmed at Otzaki and, slightly later, at Achilleion, would also constitute strong arguments in favour of direct derivation of Greek from Near Eastern architecture.

Similarly, the prevalent use of clay, the hard-packed clay and the 'plastered floors', the integration of parts of the domestic 'furniture' into the architecture itself – 'benches' or platforms, for instance – certainly imparted a 'Near Eastern' aspect to these houses. In this respect, combustion features deserve special mention. Ovens and complex hearths are typical in the Near East (Molist 1986), but extremely rare or non-existent during the Neolithic in Europe outside the Balkans. There, simple hearths in scooped-out basins or flat hearths on a clay lining prevail.[19] In Greece, on the contrary, great care and much energy were devoted to the construction and maintenance of complex combustion features. I shall argue later that, among other factors, this variety and complexity of combustion features is related to different cooking traditions. In Greece as in the Near East, contrary to what occurred in temperate Europe, food was not boiled in pots but more generally grilled, roasted and baked.

In sum, the most basic and stable features of the Early Neolithic architecture in Greece, which, according to Coudart, ought to show the slowest rate of change through time, all display strong Near Eastern affinities. Rather than

texts, she uses a systematic grid of analysis that has proved too detailed for our context, given the low overall quality of the data and their heterogeneity.

[19] Hodder (1990: 107) reflected on the paucity of evidence for hearths or ovens in the Linearbandkeramik, and suggested they had limited significance for these groups. It should be remembered, however, that the actual floor of the LBK houses is usually not preserved.

repeated contacts, this might indicate a common origin and the maintenance through time and space of basic social and architectural concepts.

However, these common concepts cannot be considered, strictly speaking, as collective or restrictive cultural *norms*. Wherever building techniques are described in any detail, they systematically display important intersite and intrasite variability. Admittedly, the latter does not refer to 'synchronic' variations, which are impossible to analyze given the present state of the data. But rapid diachronic change is exemplified in almost every site: no two superimposed buildings are exactly comparable, and they sometimes differ quite substantially from one building phase to another (e.g., Achilleion, Nea Makri, Giannitsa B, Argissa). This corresponds well to what Coudart predicted for 'individual decisions and contingent events', as opposed to the expression of collective representations and cultural identity.

Differences in local resources are part of these 'contingent' factors. They may explain part of the intersite variability: heavy timber with daub filling is usually predominant in wooded environments and mudbricks in drier environments, where large timber is more difficult to obtain. Accordingly, one would expect mudbrick buildings to be prevalent in drier southern Greece (Guest-Papamanoli 1978). It is also tempting to relate the rapid decline of post-houses in eastern Thessaly to the progressive depletion of large timber in an area of dense settlement. At Argissa, post-houses are progressively outnumbered during the EN by mudbrick houses, and mudbrick houses are the rule in the late Early Neolithic of Otzaki (Milojčić 1959b).[20] Environmental constraints can also be perceived in the treatment of the foundations: stone foundations, a sound protection against the effects of rainfall or seasonal flooding, are absent in the centre of alluvial basins where suitable stone was difficult to find.

However, local resources do not explain everything: within a single settlement – Sesklo, Argissa, Otzaki, Achilleion, Nea Makri or Pyrassos – walls made of mudbricks, wattle and daub or 'pisé' coexist in different buildings. Light wattle and daub constructions with saplings, branches, reeds, rushes, and so on, are especially versatile and can be found everywhere. Interestingly, the lack of standardization in Neolithic constructions is echoed in present-day vernacular architecture: mudbricks, wattle and daub and stone or even sherds are often freely combined in a single building according to what is available at a given time, to architectonic constraints and to stylistic preferences.

The predominance of individualization over normalization in house building is thus a significant feature of the Early Neolithic architecture in Greece. Even in a phase of geographical expansion and land colonization, different architectural techniques and plans could be combined and recombined at will. Individual differences were not only possible, but socially accepted. This contrasts with what obtains in other early European Neolithic traditions, espe-

---

[20] A similar shift is seemingly observed at Nea Makri (Pantelidou-Gkofa 1991).

cially in the Linearbandkeramik. In the latter case, the structure of the houses followed well-defined rules and was clearly used as a strong affirmation of identity (Coudart 1998; Modderman 1988). To find a similar degree of collective normalization in Greece, one may have to change the level of analysis. First, common norms could have occurred in the organization of space and activities within the house, rather than in its architecture proper.[21] Second, it is possible that the *magoula* itself, rather than the houses of which it was composed, was the strongest focus and expression of collective identity.

Though sampling biases may partly account for the predominance of *magoules* – or mound-settlements – their very number demonstrates that the clustered permanent settlement was firmly embedded in the collective representations of the village and village life. These villages were conceived from inception as stable topographical and social units. Ancestral continuity was physically expressed and materialized by the progressive elevation of the settlement (Chapman 1989). By itself, the conspicuousness of the *magoula* revealed the strong and stable links of a given community with its territory and with past generations. At the same time, the constricted concept of village space it materialized underlined the physical reality of the village community. Consequently, the affirmation of collective identity may not have needed a re-emphasis by strict adherence to traditional norms in house building. In this sense, the very permanence of the settlement may actually have contributed to making individual differences socially acceptable. In turn, the spatial promiscuity of the different households, the second characteristic of mound settlements, may have been what promoted the desire for differentiation.

[21] It can be hoped that future excavations will allow testing of this hypothesis.

CHAPTER 10

CRAFT SPECIALIZATION: THE CONTRASTING CASES OF CHIPPED-STONE TOOLS, POTTERY AND ORNAMENTS

In Greece, as elsewhere, archaeological traditions have paid little attention to the organization of Neolithic craft productions. The 'German School', headed by Vl. Milojčić, concentrated on chrono-cultural classifications, based on the shape and decoration of potteries.[1] The 'British School', led by E. Higgs and C. Renfrew, took a more resolutely economic orientation. Yet, until Torrence's pioneering study (Torrence 1986), the latter did not include the production of domestic tools and implements. Following Childe's models, the organization of production was assumed to be village-based and simple (Childe 1951a). Few questioned that the technical options could be explained in purely utilitarian terms, disregarding the new demands, new possibilities and new constraints that sedentism and farming set on craft production.

On the whole, artefacts were studied not as the product of an 'art', but as 'finished objects', from purely formal or aesthetic points of view. The knowledge, skills and technical choices involved in their manufacture were basically ignored, and so were, consequently, the cultural, economic and social choices that underlay the organization of production. Yet, how the artefacts were produced and what they were used for was an integral part of social strategies: 'the Neolithic is not an "economy" but a mode of human behaviour, in which socially transmitted ideas about what kind of raw materials and what species of plants and animals to exploit, and in what way to do so, are applied both to subsistence and non-utilitarian ends' (Nandris 1990: 12).

Technological studies are only beginning in Greece. Excepting a few very pioneering studies, they have mostly concerned ceramics and chipped stone tools and remain restricted by a near-absence of functional analyses. It is still impossible to discuss bone, stone or shell artefacts according to the spheres of activities in which they intervene. Technical systems and the relations between, for example, stone and bone tools in woodworking, or between chipped stone tools and polished-stone tools, cannot be fully comprehended. Accordingly, we will emphasize production techniques and the organization of production rather than functional perspectives. Despite these limitations, this technological approach reveals economic transformations that were just as important in the technical domain as they had been in the subsistence domain. They illustrate

---

[1] Compare, for instance, the number of pages devoted to pottery classification and to all other artefacts in site reports such as Otzaki or Argissa (Milojčić 1959; Milojčić-von Zumbusch and Milojčić 1971; Mottier 1981).

the importance of social choices in technical productions, and the irrelevance of simple autarkic models.

The three craft productions explored in this chapter, chipped-stone tools, pottery and ornaments, may seem to have little in common. But all three provide us with good insights concerning the emergence of craft specialization, the varied forms of organization and the different finalities of craft production.

The production of chipped stone tools

Chipped stone tool assemblages of the Early Neolithic have frequently been described as 'simple.'[2] This is true from a typological perspective,[3] but what has escaped recognition is that this very simplicity rests upon complex strategies of raw material exploitation and sophisticated methods of production. On both grounds, Early Neolithic chipped stone tools depart radically from the Mesolithic assemblages known in Greece (Perlès 1990a).

The raw materials

From the onset of the Neolithic, several raw materials, each with different physical properties, were worked by different techniques for the production of different classes of tools. Tools could afford to be 'simple' – that is, not much modified by retouch – precisely because the blanks were produced according to well-defined norms, in order to fulfill specific functional requirements.

The most common pattern,[4] which allows for some local variations, is characterized by the predominant use of *non-local* raw materials often obtained from considerable distances (Kozłowski *et al.* 1996; Moundrea-Agrafioti 1980, 1981; Perlès 1989b, 1990b). The predominance of exotic raw materials may in part explain why chipped stone tool assemblages are generally far less abundant in Greece than in Neolithic assemblages from central and western Europe.

From the Peloponnese up to Thessaly, Melian obsidian is usually predominant in number of pieces (Perlès 1990b). It was introduced in the villages as pre-formed or partially flaked cores, and served for the production, by pressure-flaking,[5] of light blades and bladelets with sharp, usually unretouched,

---

[2] 'Lacking both in variety and invention', says Weinberg (1970: 581). I agree with the first term, not with the second!

[3] i.e., if one considers the range of formally retouched tools.

[4] The following analyses rely mainly on A. Moundrea-Agrafioti's studies of Prodromos and Sesklo, and on personal examination of the material from Franchthi, Lerna, Elateia, Argissa, Soufli, Achilleion, Nea Nikomedeia and Chaeronea in particular. I sincerely thank all excavators for giving me access to their collections. Unless the analyses have been developed in more detail elsewhere, no references will be given.

[5] This does not imply that all blades/bladelets are pressure-flaked. The first stages of preparation and production include direct and indirect percussion, before pressure-flaking.

The origins of pressure-flaking in Greece had remained unclear for a long time. It is present in the Late Mesolithic of Europe and in the PPNB of the Taurus, associated with the typical Near Eastern 'naviform core' method. If pressure-flaking had been introduced from the Taurus, why were naviform cores completely absent from Greece? The recent discoveries from

cutting edges. In some sites, such as Argissa or Achilleion, fine-grained cherts are worked in a similar fashion and seem to have complemented the obsidian production.

Larger, heavier 'sickle-blades' of honey or yellow flints were also imported, but in much smaller quantities and always as blades rather than cores.[6] They were produced by indirect percussion and also by pressure-flaking. When so, the method was different than with obsidian, since the forces involved were much higher (Pelegrin 1988). Their characteristic gloss indicates that they were mostly used for plant or hide processing. The origin of these blades is still unknown: the west coast is the most likely candidate, but the quarries have still to be found.[7]

Fine quality jasper blades, usually produced by indirect percussion, appear to be functional equivalents to honey-flint blades. Although jasper, or, more generally, radiolarite is ubiquitous in Greece, the extremely fine-grained jasper, often referred to as 'chocolate flint',[8] comes from very specific and restricted deposits. I have found some of these high in the Pindus Range.

Local raw materials – cherts and radiolarites of inferior quality – are usually a minority, unless the site is located near chert sources or far away from the coast like Achilleion or Prodromos. When a minority, they consist mainly of flakes and irregular blades. The techniques of production – direct percussion, often with a hard hammer, more rarely indirect percussion – are then strikingly simpler than with imported raw materials. Besides casually retouched flakes and blades, they mostly provided borers, beaks and sturdy little points.

Obsidian did not reach western Macedonia during the Early Neolithic. There, the artisans used a wide range of flints and cherts, often of good quality. Some flints belong to the above-mentioned categories of imported 'honey-flint' and 'blond flint', introduced into the site as finished blades. The other varieties appear to have been found and worked locally.[9] But here flint and cherts do not constitute 'secondary' raw materials. The craftsmanship, unlike when local flints and chert supplement obsidian tools, is of a superb quality: the flint blade-lets from the deposits of the 'shrine', which amounted to more than 400 pieces (Rodden and Rodden 1964a, 1964b), present a degree of standardization that I have never encountered in any other Neolithic assemblage.[10]

footnote 5 (cont.)
> Shillourokambos (Cyprus, eighth millennium cal. BC) shed light on this problem: the naviform core technique is used on flint, but never on obsidian. The method of production of the obsidian blades (made on Cappadocian raw materials and imported as already flaked products) is exactly that found in EN Greece. An Anatolian origin thus becomes more plausible than a European one, for chronological and technical reasons. The absence of the naviform core technique on flint in Greece would, to the contrary, confirm the Western origin of this raw material and associated techniques of production.

[6] See good colour photographs in Moundrea-Agrafioti 1996: figs. 55–9.

[7] Considering the size of the blades, the quality of the flint and the nature of the cortex, I assume that the raw material was quarried and not merely collected on the surface or in rivers.

[8] See Moundrea-Agrafioti 1996: fig. 55.

[9] Moundrea-Agrafioti (personal communication 6/96).

[10] I am grateful to the British School of Archaeology at Athens and to R. J. Rodden for permission to look at the material. The latter is to be published by A. Moundrea-Agrafioti.

Techniques of production

The techniques of production are best known for obsidian, which reveals highly standardized procedures.[11] The irregularities of the natural block were removed with a hard hammer and the core was then preformed by indirect percussion. Obsidian cores typically presented three crests. After the removal of the frontal crest, the cores were worked frontally in small alternating series of four or five blades/bladelets, first by indirect percussion, then by pressure-flaking. The detachment of each blade was carefully prepared: the overhang was removed, the point of pressure was isolated by careful microchipping on the flaking surface, and the edge was ground down for more resistance. EN (and MN) obsidian blades are therefore characterized by a small, flat butt, with traces of preparation on the dorsal surface. Because the platform itself was left intact during the preparation, few rejuvenation flakes were needed. Most of the blades, especially during the full production phase, the 'plein temps de débitage', were of high quality, with regular, parallel ridges and edges.[12]

Formal and informal tools

The toolkit consists mostly of obsidian, flint and jasper blades. Obsidian blades were often left unretouched. Retouching in the Early Neolithic was not frequent, and was limited in extent. It consists mostly of short abrupt or semi-abrupt retouch of the edges. The large invasive pressure-flaked retouch was not yet in use, contrary to what occurred during the same period in Anatolia.

Most flint and jasper blades were also left unretouched, but a fair proportion shows the characteristic gloss often attributed to 'sickle-blades'. They constitute the dominant 'typological tool' in Early Neolithic assemblages. The flint and jasper specimens are characterized by limited, unilateral or bilateral gloss (e.g., Perlès and Vaughan 1983: fig. 1, nos. 3–8). The distribution of the gloss suggests a parallel or oblique insertion into what must have been wooden handles, since no bone or antler hafts have been recovered in EN contexts. When retouched, the blades bear only a short, direct, marginal retouch. Contrary to later specimens, they almost never show evidence of repeated resharpening or transformation, and were discarded at an early stage of use. Some obsidian blades also bear a well-defined gloss, overlaying a striated and matt surface produced by use. Others, on the contrary, show the same matt surface, but with no developed gloss (e.g., Perlès and Vaughan 1983: fig. 1, nos. 9–10 and 11–12). In both cases, these blades were resharpened by a deep, mostly inverse, denticulated retouch.

---

[11] And, consequently, much less standardization in the products themselves! If the same procedures are used all along the production phase on the core, the nature and morphology of the blades will vary according to their position on the flaking surface and their size will diminish as the flaking goes on.

[12] Until microchipping of the fragile edges, the fragmentation and the frequent reuse of blades as splintered blades obscured their original regularity!

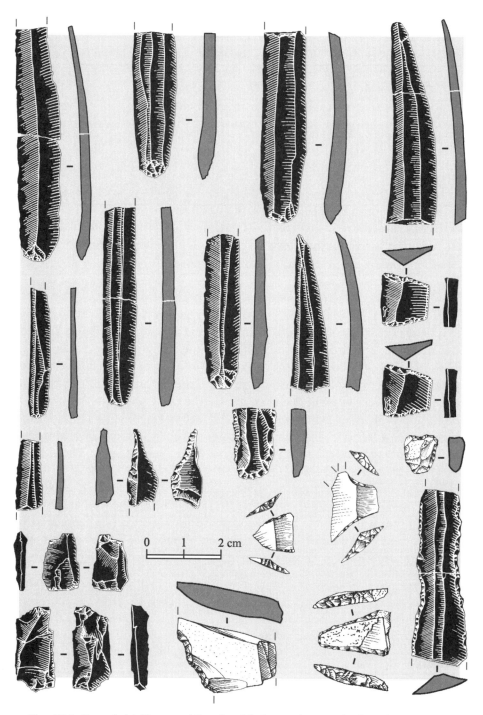

Fig. 10.1 Franchthi Cave and Paralia: blades and retouched tools of obsidian and flint.

Microwear analyses at Franchthi concluded that all these tools were used on plants, but under slightly different conditions for the flint blades, glossed obsidian blades and matted obsidian blades (Perlès and Vaughan 1983). Varied uses were suggested, in relation with matting, basketry, weaving, fodder and straw collecting. The harvesting of cereals was considered to be the less likely. Since then, progress in microwear analyses have confirmed that the harvesting of cereals was only one of the many uses of the so-called 'sickle-blades': reed and rush work is often more common, and even skin working or clay working can produce a macroscopically similar gloss (Anderson 1994a, 1994b).

The latter hypothesis could apply to small flakes characteristic of the Early Neolithic and usually made of local raw materials. They present a steep curved back, natural or retouched, and a gloss on the opposite edge or corner. They are analogous to flakes that, according to Gassin's experiments and microscopic observations, were used as small finger-held knifes to remove the excess of clay on the rim of a pot (Gassin 1993). However, the few pieces that have been submitted to traceological analyses in Greece (e.g., Kozłowski *et al.* 1996: fig. 3, no. 3; Perlès and Vaughan 1983: fig. 1, nos. 1 and 2) have so far revealed only plant polish and can be compared to similar sickle inserts from Cyprus (Astruc, in prep.).

Some rare and large trapezes, shaped by abrupt truncations on pressure-flaked blades, constitute the only type that could be related to the class of (transverse) projectile inserts. The highly elaborate pointed arrowheads, typical of the Near East, are absent from Early Neolithic assemblages in Greece.[13] End-scrapers, truncated blades, notches or denticulated blades are never abundant and burins even rarer. Functional analyses performed on the assemblage from Lerna I suggested a wide range of uses, both for retouched and unretouched pieces (Kozłowski *et al.* 1996). Besides the 'sickle inserts', blades and flakes would have been used to cut, scrape and incise wood and bone, to process hides, to carve meat and crush minerals.

The quantity of borers, drills and points varies substantially from site to site. At Franchthi, during the second part of the Early Neolithic, thousands of small borers and points were manufactured on a specific local chert, in clear stratigraphic relation to the production of cockle-shell beads (see below, pp. 223ff). The larger beaks are never numerous but they are regularly present: they were needed to make mending holes and to make the perforation on sherd spindle whorls (see ch. 11). Finally, mention should be made of the splintered blades: their proportion varies, but they are usually not as numerous in Early as in Middle Neolithic asscmblages. These splintered blades are the characteristic by-products of technical activities (probably involving both wood and bone working) in which a broken fragment of a blade was reused as a wedge in indirect percussion. When splintered blades are abundant, many of the initial blades become almost unrecognizable.

---

[13] One specimen was found at Lerna (Kozłowski *et al.* 1996: illus. 3.3) but the chances are high that it is intrusive.

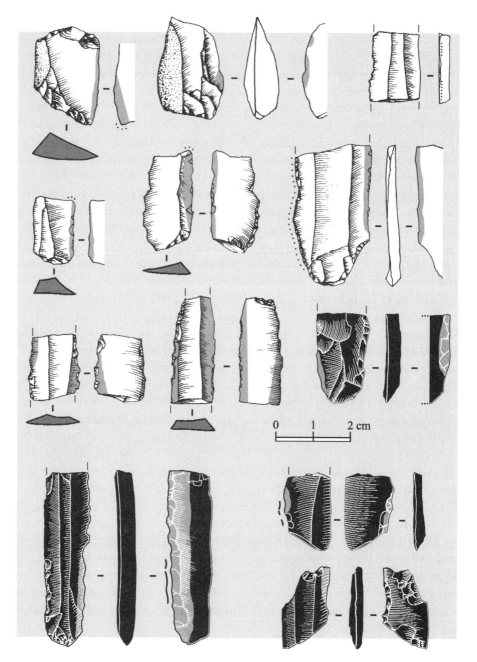

Fig. 10.2 Franchthi Cave and Paralia: glossed elements of flint and obsidian.

Unlike the case with ceramics, so far no regional variability has been observed. The techniques of production are similar everywhere, and the types appear to be directly linked to their function, leaving little space for stylistic variations. This homogeneity over a very large area raises the problem of who procured the raw materials and who produced the tools.

The organization of raw material procurement

I have argued in detail elsewhere why direct procurement of obsidian and honey-flint at the sources seemed most unlikely (Perlès 1989b, 1990b, 1992). Honey-flint was never worked in the settlements, and the number of imported blades in each assemblage – often less than a dozen – was too small to warrant expeditions to the sources. Conversely, obsidian cores were flaked in the villages, but the acquisition of Melian obsidian, from Thessaly for instance, required trips over lands and seas of several hundred kilometres. This in turn required a specialized knowledge of boat construction and sea-faring, the Aegean Sea being notoriously unpredictable. That such a seafaring knowledge would have been maintained and transmitted from generation to generation in inland peasant communities appears very unlikely. In addition, the Aegean islands were still uninhabited, and the time, energy and risks involved with individual trips of several months to Melos would hardly be warranted by the few hundred grams of obsidian exploited in each site every year, or even decade.[14] Direct procurement from the sources is even more unlikely if one considers that obsidian, flint and jasper came from totally different regions[15] and that other exotic raw materials, again from different sources, were often required for grinding tools or polished axes. Indirect acquisition through exchange accords better with the procurement of partially or totally flaked products and the small absolute quantities found in each village.[16]

However, the distribution of obsidian or honey-flint in the different sites does not correspond to a pattern of down-the-line trade (Renfrew 1984). Obsidian is well represented and usually predominant in most sites of eastern Greece as far north as Thessaly. Only the sites nearest to the Pindus, such as Achilleion, Prodromos or Magoulitsa, have a smaller proportion of obsidian. At Achilleion at least, this is due in part to a higher absolute quantity of local and regional raw materials, and in part to the introduction of obsidian cores at a late

[14] Given that one kilogram of obsidian can yield several hundred bladelets through pressure-flaking.

[15] Even though the flint sources are not yet precisely localized, a Cycladic origin can be ruled out. On geological and archaeological grounds, the west coast of Greece or the Adriatic eastern coast are the most likely origins. I have never seen either fine-grained jasper in the Cyclades.

[16] In her detailed study of obsidian distribution, Torrence (1986) had concluded, to the contrary, in favour of direct procurement. But her sample did not include EN assemblages, and I agree with her conclusions for the (later) series she had observed. By then the Cycladic islands were settled, and the trip to Melos was far easier.

stage of production, when very few flakes were produced.[17] Further north, in western Macedonia, obsidian disappears completely (Perlès 1990b) and it is also absent from the few EN assemblages that I have seen in western Greece.[18]

The abundance of obsidian far from the sources, followed by a very rapid decline, corresponds to Renfrew's model of distribution by itinerant 'middle-men' (Renfrew 1984). In our case, given the requirements of seafaring, the most plausible hypothesis is that of specialized seafaring groups,[19] which would have procured and distributed obsidian all over eastern Greece up to Thessaly. A single trip to Melos, bringing back several kilograms of obsidian, could easily fulfill the yearly needs of many villages.

How the flint blades were distributed will remain problematic until the sources have been precisely identified. The pattern appears to be a concentration in north-western Greece, followed, behind the Pindus Range, by a very wide-ranging distribution in very small quantities. Itinerant craftsmen can also be envisioned, but I would not preclude, considering the walking distances and very small quantities, that down-the-line trade was also operating.

In any case, the wide-ranging distribution of obsidian and other exotic raw materials demonstrates an extended geographical knowledge and the will to undertake long – and certainly hazardous – expeditions. As suggested earlier, the initiative may have come from the former local hunter-gatherers, rather than from the first sedentary peasants of inland Greece (Runnels and van Andel 1988: 101).

The organization of production

Procurement through exchange does not necessarily imply specialized production. However, the latter hypothesis accounts for many features of the obsidian and honey-flint assemblages, better than that of individual production. First, it accords with the very nature of pressure-flaking: this is a demanding technique, which requires a long apprenticeship and regular practice (Clark 1987; Clark and Parry 1990; Pelegrin 1984, 1988). Even if the detachment of the blade is not difficult in itself, strict control of the volumetric and angular parameters of the core must be maintained throughout the reduction sequence. Considering the low number of blades produced every year at each site, it seems unlikely and certainly unnecessary that everyone would undergo this demanding apprenticeship. Had they done so, the rate of production would not have

---

[17] Elster 1989 and personal observations. I thank M. Gimbutas and E. Elster for allowing me access to this material.

[18] In particular Ayios Nikolaos at Astakos and Choirospilia.

[19] 'Specialization' is here defined as an activity done by a limited number of groups or individuals, in order to redistribute the products (or services) within a wider community. It usually, but not necessarily, rests upon knowledge, skills or equipment not possessed by the others. Craft specialization, thus defined, can go hand in hand with other subsistence activities and need not be full time. In this precise case, full-time specialization can be ruled out since navigation in the Aegean has always been restricted to summer times.

allowed each knapper to 'keep their hand in'. Yet, observation of thousands of blades shows an almost null rate of conceptual or gestural errors. In addition, the hypothesis of itinerant specialists accounts for the introduction of obsidian into the villages as already preformed cores or even partially exploited cores, rather than raw nodules.[20] The cores themselves are very rarely found in the assemblages. When present, they are usually in a state of exhaustion[21] and their number is well below what would be expected from the blade production. I expect that at least some were taken away for further exploitation in the next visited village, a conclusion also reached at Lerna by Kozłowski and his collaborators (Kozłowski *et al.* 1996: 299). Finally, the contrasts between the quality of the production with local raw materials and with obsidian make it very unlikely that they were done by the same knappers.

Imported blades of flint and jasper indicate another mode of specialized production: they were not produced in the settlements, and must have originated from production centres that exported their products far away. Even more than with obsidian, the production of these large and regular honey-flint blades required special skills and equipment (Pelegrin 1988, in prep.).

The diversity and complexity of the exploitation of raw materials cannot be explained solely by mediocre local resources. Technically adequate sources of chert or jasper, for instance, could have been and often were found at much shorter distances from the settlements. The selection of raw materials was a deliberate choice, whereby the most immediate 'natural' and local resources were again neglected (see above ch. 8 and Perlès 1992). The preference was given to goods of exotic origins, perhaps because the use of obsidian was embedded in secular traditions deriving from Anatolia (Demoule 1993), perhaps also because their very exoticity gave them an added value (Helms 1988). However, this would not have been possible if the social and economic organization had not allowed, or even favoured, group specialization and intergroup exchanges. The exploitation of exotic raw materials was indeed a costly choice, both in terms of both procurement and production.[22] It would hardly have been compatible with the daily tasks of an inland farmer, and certainly not justifiable in terms of productivity. Part-time (seasonal) specialization and trade appear to have been embedded very early within the Neolithic economy of Greece. This would explain the choice of production methods that were demanding in terms of apprenticeship and technical investment, but that relied afterwards on standardized procedures and that allowed a high productivity per block.

These characteristics of production are not specific to chipped stone: they can also be found in ceramic production (Costin 1991; Costin and Hagstrum

---

[20] As indicated by the conspicuous under-representation of cortical flakes, crest and platform preparation flakes, primary crested blades (Perlès 1990b).

[21] See Moundrea-Agrafioti 1996: fig. 55c.

[22] Pressure-flaking and indirect percussion allow high productivity and minimal waste, but require higher technical investments than direct percussion.

1995). Thus the organization of pot production in Early Neolithic Greece could, in theory, have been organized along similar lines: high skills, standardized procedure and high productivity. However, this is not the case, and the contrasts that will appear concerning all these criteria between Early Neolithic pots and chipped-stone tools become all the more significant.

The ceramic production

Unlike the production of stone tools, pottery manufacture was still a new craft in the seventh millennium. The Early and Middle Neolithic appear to be, according to a few, important technological studies, fascinating phases during which the main aspects of ceramic technology were being progressively explored. Technological studies are still limited to a few sites of the Peloponnese,[23] of Thessaly[24] and of western Macedonia.[25] Archaeometric analyses are even more restricted[26] but the results of both approaches are consistent enough to provide a basis for preliminary generalizations. They also immediately reveal important contrasts with chipped-stone production: pottery production was village-based, it relied on the exploitation of local raw materials, and the rate of circulation of the products between villages was very low.

On the other hand, as with chipped-stone tools, Early Neolithic pottery has been qualified as 'simple'. This qualification is, on the whole, more apt than for lithics: both the shapes and dimensions of the pots are within the range of the easiest ceramic productions.[27] Early Neolithic pots have even been considered by some as 'coarse', by comparison with later Neolithic productions. But, as argued by Vitelli,

The EN pots in Greece are made with the loving care and extended effort of most beginning potters, and they are crude and coarse in the same ways and for many of the same reasons. The EN pots are coarse not by the potters' choice, as were the pots of later Neolithic potters, but because of the limitations imposed by their experience and knowledge of relevant technology. Viewed in the context of the available technology, they are excellent products. (Vitelli 1995: 60)

Manufacture of pots

The relative lack of technical sophistication can be perceived at all stages of the manufacturing process. Varied local clay sources were exploited, including, in rare cases – Sesklo, Achilleion, Nea Nikomedeia and Giannitsa B – a fine clay

---

[23] Vitelli 1974, 1984a, 1984b, 1988, 1989, 1993; Weinberg 1937.
[24] Björk 1995; Gardner 1978; Kotsakis 1983, 1986; Wijnen 1981, 1993, 1994.
[25] Pyke and Yiouni 1996.
[26] Björk 1995; Jones R. 1986; Maniatis and Perdikatsis 1983; Maniatis *et al.* 1988; Schneider *et al.* 1991.
[27] The small or medium sizes and rounded shapes limited the problem of wall collapse during the building of the pot (Roux 1990; Vitelli 1995).

that gave almost white, very fragile 'porcelain wares'. A wide range of nonplas-tics, often naturally present in the clay, served as temper: predominantly crushed limestone or calcite followed by quartz in the Peloponnese, mica and micaschist at Sesklo, quartz at Achilleion. Rarer non-plastics included andes-ite, serpentine, feldspar, schist and possibly grog or plant fibres.[28] Significantly, at Franchthi, Lerna, Sesklo, Achilleion and Nea Nikomedeia, even when it was intentionally added[29] the amount or nature of the temper varies independently from the nature of the vessel – size, wall thickness, shape – and thus presum-ably of its function (Björk 1995; Pyke and Yiouni 1996; Vitelli 1993; Wijnen 1994). 'There is therefore no proof that the potters knew that functional reac-tions in the pottery could be changed by adding different tempering material' says Björk in her study of EN pottery from Achilleion (Björk 1995: 87). However, one should beware of making too strict correlations between the characteristics of the biscuit, the temper and potential uses. The 'theoretical' expectations are often contradicted by actual uses in present-day pottery using communities (Gosselain 1995, 1998).

The predominant shape is a convex bowl of relatively small size, with a rounded or more rarely flat bottom to which a circular ring-foot or flat base was frequently added. The bottom of the pot was first moulded, but two different traditions have been recognized for building the walls: coiling and building with slabs. Vitelli identified coil building at Franchthi and Lerna, with small coils 2 to 3 cm thick (Vitelli 1984b, 1993: 96). Wijnen, to the contrary, recog-nized slab building in Macedonia, Thessaly, central Greece and Corinthia, and reflected on the possible origins of these two different traditions (Wijnen 1993, 1994). But Yiouni identified coil building at Nea Nikomedeia, not slab building (Pyke and Yiouni 1996: 60) and Björk mentions the use of slabs at Achilleion only for very open shapes (Björk 1995: 97). Different interpretations by the ana-lysts, rather than different 'traditions', may be at stake.

Close observations of the variations in coiling techniques may indicate dif-ferent motor habits, and therefore different learning contexts and traditions (Gosselain 1995, 1998). At Nea Nikomedeia and other later Macedonian settle-ments, the potters placed their coils on top of each other. In most other sites the coils partly overlapped. Pinching from a lump of clay was also used, but appears to have been restricted to very small or miniature vessels (Pyke and Yiouni 1996: 61). A foot and very small lugs could then be added.

When dried, the pots were scraped down inside and out in order to smooth the surface and thin the walls: walls as thin as 3 to 5 mm were already common in the Early Neolithic.[30] Occasional variations in thickness and irregularities

---

[28] Vegetal temper was mentioned at Achilleion (Winn and Shimabuku 1989c) but not found in the samples later analyzed by Björk 1995; it is also mentioned at Prodromos (Hourmouziadis 1971a: 176–9).

[29] Such as quartz at Achilleion, crushed calcite at Franchthi, or grog at Nea Nikomedeia.

[30] Five to seven mm as a mean at Franchthi, 4 to 10 at Achilleion and Elateia, 3 mm for the finer pots at Corinth, 15 mm for the largest.

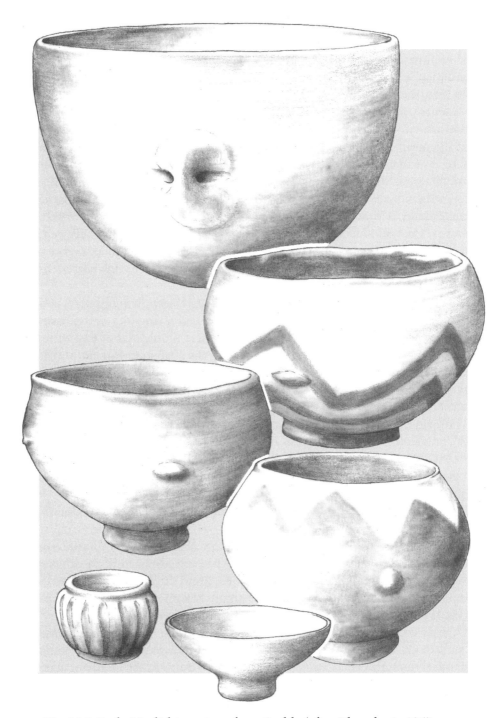

Fig. 10.3 Early Neolithic pottery from Sesklo (after Theocharis 1967, Theocharis 1973 and Papathanassopoulos 1996).

of shape indicate that at least some potters lacked regular practice (Vitelli 1993: 98–9).

The following manufacturing stages, which gave the pot its final appearance, also demonstrate intensive, careful work. The pots were smoothed and sometimes slipped, either using the same clay, or with a red or white firing clay in the later phases of the Neolithic (Wijnen 1993: 322). They were occasionally painted, then burnished. The resulting fine gloss is characteristic of careful, time-consuming burnishing (Vitelli 1993: 97; Weinberg 1937; Winn and Shimabuku 1989c). Its quality must be underlined: it is very seldom attained in European Neolithic pottery and constitutes a distinctive feature of the Greek Early Neolithic pottery. The use of a thick mineral coating, identified at Nea Nikomedeia, remains exceptional. It underlies, once more, the peculiarities of the western Macedonian pottery tradition (Pyke and Yiouni 1996: 65–9). Decorations, which were applied to a small minority of the pots, mostly included linear geometric designs painted with iron-oxide-rich pigments, or occasionaly white paint, finger-made impressions, incised dots or small clay pellets.

Detailed examination of thousands of sherds from Franchthi revealed no evidence for stacking or for firing more than one pot at a time (Vitelli 1993), although Weinberg reported limited evidence of stacking at Corinth[31] (Weinberg 1937: 495). The firing was done in an open bonfire or in a pit, in a reducing or oxidizing atmosphere, at temperatures variously estimated at between 650 and 900°C (Björk 1995; Maniatis and Tite 1981; Overweel 1981; Vitelli 1991; Pyke and Yiouni 1996). SEM examination and thermogravimetric analyses realized by Björk indicate that five sherds from Achilleion, baked in a reducing atmosphere, were fired between 700 and 850°C, while eighteen others, baked in an oxidizing atmosphere, were fired between 700 and 950°C (Björk 1995: 67). Considering the wide range of temperatures attained within a single 'open' bonfire,[32] one should be cautious of giving too much significance to such variations.

The pots were placed in direct contact with the fuel and this resulted in frequent 'clouding'. Weinberg noted that many superficially oxidized sherds still presented a black core, which he considered as an indication of incomplete firing (Weinberg 1962: 168). This appears to hold true at Achilleion (Björk 1995: 47), but even pots fired at a high enough temperature will show a black core if the firing was brief. Many sherds, however, do not present this black core, and Vitelli did not find evidence at Franchthi of systematic underfiring. The dominant ware, the Lime pots,

were fired in a direct fuel firing, with ready access to oxygen during most of the firing. Very smoky fuel, such as straw, seaweed, dung and green wood are not likely

---

[31] As evidenced by the presence of a firing circle at the base of the pots.
[32] Gosselain 1992, 1995.

to have produced the light colors of the mass of sherds. The large firing clouds were caused by direct contact with the coal and ashes in the final stages of firing. Thick sherds with dark cores and light surfaces suggest a certain amount of organic matter in the raw clay body was not fired to a hot enough temperature to oxidize fully. The more usual uniformly light core on sherds of average thickness (5–7 mm) suggests a firing both long enough and hot enough to burn out most of the organic matter, while staying below the temperature of decomposition of the calcium carbonates. (Vitelli 1993: 98)

Interestingly, other wares, found in much smaller quantities, were fired under different conditions. The sand-tempered 'Sandy Ware' appears to have been fired in a constantly reduced atmosphere, covered by a thick stack of fuel, possibly dung (Vitelli 1993: 106). The andesite-tempered wares were first fired in an oxidizing atmosphere, then a reducing one (Vitelli 1993: 112).

Different firing techniques were thus already known and practised. Yet Wijnen (1993: 323) remarked that there remained a problem with painted decorations: the iron oxides frequently turned reddish, and there was often very little contrast between the decoration and the background.

Rate and organization of production

The suggestion that pots were usually not stacked during firing tallies with estimates of a very low annual rate of production. At Franchthi, Vitelli estimates the annual EN production to have been about 12 to 13 pots (Vitelli 1993: 210). Wijnen suggests even lower figures for the sites she studied in Thessaly: around 5 pots per year (Wijnen 1993: 324). At Achilleion, Björk also favoured a limited number of potters (Björk 1995: 137) and, following Winn and Shimabuku's figures for this site (Winn and Shimabuku 1989c) one can suggest a deposition of about 100 sherds only per year in the excavated sectors. At Nea Nikomedeia, Yiouni arrived at figures she considers substantially higher: 25 to 90 pots a year for the eight houses of each building phase (Pyke and Yiouni 1996: 186). Nea Nikomedeia is on the late side of the Early Neolithic, so that a higher production rate would not be surprising. However, using the data she provides – a total of 1,115 pots for an occupation that lasted 50 to 150 years – I estimate the annual production at only 7 to 22 pots. Whatever the case, all these figures remain low in terms of total annual production. Even if the lowest estimates were multiplied by a factor of three or more, a single experienced potter could easily have handled the entire village production in a few days or weeks at most.[33]

Given this limited output, the evidence for several contemporaneous potters in a single settlement is all the more intriguing. Yet, this is the conclusion reached by Vitelli at Franchthi:

[33] The lowest production rate I know of for potters working (what they call) full-time is four pots a day, of a size twice that of Early Neolithic pots in Greece (observations by S. Gueye, Senegal river. Personal communication 7/96). Even at such a leisurely pace, ninety pots could have been made in three weeks.

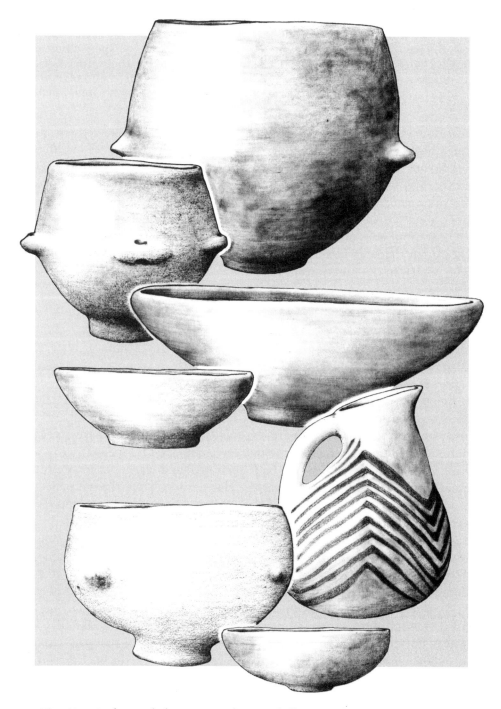

Fig. 10.4 Early Neolithic pottery from Achilleion and spouted jar from Nemea (after Theocharis 1967 and Papathanassopoulos 1996).

At Franchthi, five distinctive wares occur throughout the Early Neolithic deposits. All were made in the same basic shapes and sizes, but each ware was using different nonplastics. The pots in each ware were scraped differently, burnished with different tools and at different angles, had their rims finished with different motions, their lugs and bases added in subtly different ways, and were each fired using different procedures and, probably, fuels. (Vitelli 1995: 60)

At least four of the wares were locally made and their proportions remain stable through time (Vitelli 1993: 208–9). This shows that the coexistence of different wares did not result from the temporary presence of potters of different origins, and even less from random procedures. It implies the transmission through generations of different techniques and 'recipes' among several distinct lines of potters. Since we know that the exchange of goods was a current practice, and since the output does not justify several potters, this may imply that one could not use a pot made by just anyone (Perlès and Vitelli 1994; Vitelli 1995). Can this be related to the functions of the pots?

The use of pots

Archaeometric and technological analyses converge to demonstrate that most pots were *not* used for cooking on an open fire, as currently assumed for the Neolithic. The different analyses conducted on sherds from Achilleion led Björk to conclude a low resistance to 'thermal shock' (Björk 1995: 80–1). Björk based her conclusions on the use of quartz as temper,[34] the insufficient firing, the low porosity, especially in the earliest phases, and the high frequency of ring-bases that would have detached if repeatedly exposed to fire. The same conclusions had been reached earlier by Vitelli for Franchthi, where she had noted that the clay composition, the near-absence of coarse-grained pottery, the added circular feet, the lack of soot deposits on the pots and the good burnishing gloss retained on the bases precluded their use as cooking pots (Vitelli 1989, 1991, 1993: 214). On similar bases, Wijnen also rejected the use of pots on open fires in Thessaly, western Macedonia and central Greece (Wijnen 1993: 324).[35] Yiouni's observations at Nea Nikomedeia remained inconclusive, but provided few definite evidence for the use of cooking pots (Pyke and Yiouni 1996: 191). There is no evidence, either, in favour of indirect cooking with heated stones. In all probability, the food was not cooked in pots but rather baked, grilled and roasted. This, in turn, would explain the importance and complexity of the hearths found inside and outside the houses.

[34] An ambiguous criterion: quartz-tempered cooking pots are in fact more than common in Africa.
[35] Yet, she told Björk that 'vessels that looked suspiciously as if they had been used over a fire' seem to emerge in the EN3 at Sesklo. This has not been confirmed, but these vessels would have still remained a minority (personal communication, quoted in Björk 1995: 6).

Bulk storage in pots is no better an alternative to explain their function: the small number of vessels, combined with their relatively small size,[36] would not have allowed the storage of grains for a single family over the year (Björk 1995; Pyke and Yiouni 1996; Vitelli l989). Using Halstead's estimate of *c.* 200 kg of cereal per person per year, Yiouni calculated that in the excavated part of Nea Nikomedeia a storage capacity of 7,500 to 12,500 litres would have been needed every year. This 'annual' figure is not far below the total storage volume of the Nea Nikomedeia pots, but for the whole duration of the EN occupation (Pyke and Yiouni 1996: 191–2). As already mentioned, there are many other means of storing grain (see above ch. 8). Amongst these, a possibility to be considered is the use of unbaked clay containers: their preservation is exceptional, but one was discovered at Sesklo, in an unspecified context (Tsountas 1908: 167, fig. 82).

If they were neither used for cooking nor for bulk storage, the pots may have been used for storing 'special goods' in small quantities (Wijnen 1993: 324),[37] for serving, drinking and eating on special occasions, or for ceremonial and ritual uses (Björk 1995: 128–32; Theocharis 1973b: 40; Vitelli 1993: 213–19). It is easy to envision pots being made especially for marriage or death ceremonies, celebration of agrarian rituals, festive occasions or offerings to the gods. The main point, however, is that pottery, far from being rapidly and widely adopted for daily domestic uses, remained limited in quantity, was produced with time-consuming techniques and was used infrequently.[38] There is here a clear opposition with the daily used stone tools, for which highly standardized and productive methods had been developed. This opposition results from social choices, not from technical constraints: cooking pots do not require elaborate procedures (Gosselain 1995) and the production could easily have been adapted to this function. In nearby Albania, fine wares predominated only in the Podgorni I culture, nearest to the present-day Greek border. Everywhere else, as in the Starčevo world, coarse pottery was predominant (Manson 1995; Prendi 1990). Similarly, cooking and storage pots constitute the vast majority of Early Neolithic ceramic assemblages of Bulgaria, even in settlements close to the present-day Greek border (Demoule and Lichardus-Itten 1994).[39] The

---

[36] Most of the EN pots at Franchthi seem to have ranged from approximately 20 x 20 cm to 30 x 30 cm in width and height, with a slightly smaller diameter at the rim (Vitelli 1993: figs. 1–13). At Achilleion, 95 per cent of the pots had a rim diameter of under 26 cm (Winn and Shimabuku 1989c: tab. B.11).

[37] Three sherds from Achilleion revealed traces of uncooked lipids and proteins through chromatography and spectrophotometry (Isaksson, in Björk 1995: 83–7). None could be interpreted without ambiguity.

[38] Otherwise, the rate of breaking would have been higher. It is difficult to find figures for the life expectancy of serving pots, so we have to rely on cooking pots. In a wide survey of thirty-eight villages in the Niger delta, Mayor found that cooking pots had a mean life expectancy of 2.5 years, and serving pot/storage pots 5 years (Mayor 1994). Small- and medium-sized pots, as found in the Greek EN, last even less: 1 to 2 years. In a completely different context, Graves also finds a life expectancy of less than two years for medium-sized cooking pots (Graves 1991).

[39] Having seen ceramic assemblages from both areas, I can testify that the opposition is not due to different analytical categories or interpretations. Amongst other things, it should be noted that in the Balkanic regions the predominance of cooking pots and storage jars leads to much larger ceramic assemblages.

preference given to fine wares in Greece thus appears as a cultural idiosyncrasy that individualizes Greece from most of the Balkans. Because it has bearings not only on the conception and role of pottery but also on feeding habits – a notoriously conservative domain – I believe it underlines different origins of the Neolithic groups and different processes of Neolithization.

In view of the 'special' uses and quality of these fine wares, both Vitelli (1993: 217; Perlès and Vitelli 1999) and Björk (1995: 132–4) see pottery-making in the Early Neolithic of Greece as a prestige or status-loaded activity, possibly resting on some esoteric knowledge. Theocharis (1973b: 40) for his part did not hesitate to speak of 'employed' specialist craftsmen and specialized centres of production. Later provenance analyses did not confirm the existence of specialized centres of production and showed, to the contrary, that the majority of the production was local. However, the presence of several potters in a village does not mean that each woman (or man) was a potter. The low output would rather suggest the contrary, and pottery-making may well have been, as suggested by Björk and Vitelli, restricted to particular individuals within the community. The strong indications in favour of specialized pottery production in the Middle Neolithic (Perlès and Vitelli 1994; Vitelli 1993: 216–17) could then be seen as the outcome of a social process already engaged during the Early Neolithic.

However this does not necessarily entail, by itself, that Early Neolithic potters possessed a *higher* status than other members of the village. Undoubtedly, they produced artefacts that were socially and/or ritually valued, and they did possess the special skill of mastering firing procedures. In many present-day traditional societies, transforming clay into pottery remains a process fraught with risks of failure, and to which innumerable restrictions and taboos are attached (e.g., Gosselain 1995). It would be surprising if, at the very beginning of pottery production when pyrotechnology was in its very early stages, this had not been even more true. Whether this led to them being set apart, or, on the contrary, to them being given prominence, potters would have been, at least, considered as powerful individuals.

I have no doubt, however, that with passing time – the EN lasted several centuries – potters could have increased the range of shapes and sizes as well as their productivity, had they wanted to.[40] In this respect, many technical characteristics of the EN pottery must be again considered as social choices. The relative 'inexpertness' is not only a consequence of a low output: it also reflects the lack of incentive for more difficult or more abundant productions. As will become even clearer in the Middle Neolithic, pottery was deliberately downplayed in daily utilitarian usage, as though it was considered more useful as a ceremonial or festive artefact than as a mere cooking pot or storage jar.[41]

[40] Theocharis (1973b: 39–40), Weinberg (1970: 584), Winn and Shimabuku (1989c) all note that 'skills' improved during the EN, but the interesting point is that this concerns the firing conditions and the final appearance of the pots rather than the range of shapes, sizes and functions.

[41] The alternative being the production of distinct wares for specific social or ritual uses, as is commonly done in Africa nowadays.

Pottery and group identity

Probably because of this lack of incentive for more diversified productions, the classical role of pottery as an expression of group identity does not appear to be strongly developed. The homogeneity of techniques, shapes and functions of the pottery all over Greece predominates over regional variations. Wijnen (1993: 324) aptly notes the apparent contradiction between local productions and the parallel development, all over Greece, of similar shapes, surface treatment and firing techniques. She thus suggests that the pots were exchanged between villages, an hypothesis hardly supported by petrographic analyses (see below), or that potters intermarried between different villages and exchanged their knowledge.[42] The latter hypothesis is more than plausible, since most village communities would have been too small for complete endogamy. It is, however, insufficient to explain the strong homogeneity noticed by Wijnen herself. Some degree of exogamy must also be postulated in the Middle or Late Neolithic, since communities were of a similar size or sometimes smaller, yet regional or micro-regional differences are strongly developed (Demoule and Perlès 1993). Whether or not pottery is used to express identity and differences is not a mechanical consequence of alliance and residential rules, but a social choice.

The highest degree of homogeneity corresponds to the earliest, 'Monochrome' phase, perhaps because the affirmation of common norms was more important, ideologically and sociologically, in the earliest phases of settlement. After several generations, these norms seem to have relaxed. Regional stylistic differences come to light, and the later phases of the Early Neolithic are more differentiated than the earlier phases (see for instance the early Incised/Impressed from western Thessaly, the distinctive painted wares of Macedonia or the Black-Burnished ware of Boeotia). But the distribution of these wares shows no sharp regional boundaries: it corresponds to what Halstead called an 'overlapping distribution' (Halstead 1984: 4.3.2). This may be related to open networks of relations, in which regional differences were expressed but not deliberately manipulated. In this respect, a contrast has already been mentioned between the densely settled Thessaly and the sparsely settled Peloponnese. Whereas in Thessaly both regional and chronological variations develop after a while, the variation is so limited in the Peloponnese that even chronological differences could not be brought to light (Vitelli 1993; Weinberg 1970: 586). A comparable situation has been observed by Coudart (1993) with the Linearbandkeramik architecture, where collective norms were especially stringent: the respect of these norms was stronger in regions of dispersed settlement, as though the dispersion of the communities made it all the more necessary to reassess a common identity.

---

[42] An hypothesis that would be reinforced if, as occurs frequently nowadays, potters belonged to an endogamous social category of craft specialists.

The circulation of pottery

Whatever the social mechanisms involved, the overall homogeneity of pottery in Early Neolithic Greece was clearly related to the circulation of ideas or potters rather than pots. At Elateia, only three sherds of Corinthian Variegated ware were considered by Weinberg as imports (Weinberg 1962: 169). The few possible imports at Franchthi correspond to the same ware. It is a very minor ware, amounting to 0 to 2 per cent of the total, ungritted and similar to the Rainbow ware from Lerna. It possibly originates from Corinthia, where compatible clay deposits are known and where this ware is abundant (Vitelli 1993: 209). At Corinth itself, Weinberg singles out a few fragments of red-on-white painted wares that might be imported from central Greece. At Sesklo, only a few impressed sherds may have been imported from north-eastern Thessaly (Wijnen 1981: 37), but the very special 'porcelain ware' produced at Sesklo may have circulated up to Kypseli and Karditsa in the western Thessalian plain (Schneider *et al.* 1994: 64). On the whole, however, the circulation of pots appears to have been limited in quantity and the distances of circulation far smaller than for stone tools.

Two very different systems of production have thus been brought to light by the study of chipped stones and pottery. Each corresponded to objects to which different social roles and values had been attributed. Dependency on exotic raw materials, and its corollary dependency on specialized groups, had been accepted (or chosen?) for the daily-used stone tools. Although 'exotic' and of a probably high acquisition cost, there is little evidence that they were used, or rather discarded, in ritual or symbolic contexts. Pottery production, conversely, remained a village craft that exploited local raw materials. Several potters were apparently involved in each village, even though the rate of production was so low that a single potter could probably have answered the needs of several villages. But pottery, contrary to stone tools, was not a purely utilitarian artefact: it was still denied the mundane role of a cooking or a storage pot[43] and its uses must have been restricted to special functions or occasions. Pottery in particular, and ceramic in general, was frequently associated with ritual activities (see below, ch. 13). Under these conditions, it may have been socially unacceptable to entrust the production of ceramic artefacts to potters who were not part of the community, or even of a definite subgroup within the community. This would explain the presence of several potters in each village, as well as the very low rate of circulation between villages, in constrast with the production and distribution of the more utilitarian stone tools.

---

[43] Even during the Middle Neolithic, when a few cooking and storage pots are present, they remain a minority (Perlès and Vitelli 1994; Vitelli 1993).

Ornaments and carved stone artefacts

Ornaments show a spectacular development in the Neolithic of Greece, in terms of both quantity and craftsmanship. In Early Neolithic contexts, however, the number of beads and pendants reported in the publications remains rather low. Whether this reflects a limited use of ornaments or deficiencies in recovery techniques, especially for the smaller beads, is debatable. The other carved artefacts such as 'earstuds', stone vessels or 'stamp-seals' are equally rare but have more abundant and more easily made counterparts in clay. In this case, their small number does reflect, in all probability, a limited rate of production and a special value.

Early Neolithic ornaments fall into two distinct categories: first, beads produced and threaded in series, and second, finely carved pendants, each somewhat different from the other. The skills required and the technical constraints in the production of these two categories are different and must therefore be discussed separately. On the other hand, the production of carved and polished pendants is based on the same basic techniques and requires the same skills as the production of earstuds, stone-seals, carved stone figurines and stone vessels. They could have been produced by the same artisans, whether gifted individuals or craft specialists.

Carved stone and shell artefacts

Pendants are made from a variety of raw materials besides clay: marble, 'greenstone', 'blackstone', porphyry, alabaster, shell and bone. Most pendants are unique pieces, often of simple schematized or geometric shapes, though froglike pendants are known from Achilleion and Nea Nikomedeia. They are usually finely carved and polished, though they display variation in details of shapes and care in their manufacture. They were certainly made individually by artists who were familiar with stone working, but there is no indication that they were produced in large series in specialized workshops.

The same variability is found with stone vessels. Small stone vessels have been found in a limited number of sites, and six only have given indisputable EN specimens.[44] The number of settlements that yielded stone vessels is thus very limited. Interestingly, however, wherever stone vessels have been found, several specimens were usually recovered. Nea Makri stands out from

---

[44] Definite EN stone vessels were found at Achilleion, Nessonis, Sesklo, Gediki, Nea Makri and on an EN surface site, Magoula Karaïkia 1. The chronological attribution of the fragments from Tsoungiza, Dendra, Franchthi and 'the region of Sparta' is more problematic. Stone vessels have also been found in surface sites where EN is represented along with other periods: Nikaiai 1, Chara 1, Mandra 1, Larissa 8, Kypseli, Magoula Tourkoyefira, Elateia 1 (oriental Thessaly), Ayios Georgios 1 (see Gallis 1992). They probably correspond to the 'EN' vases published in the Goulandris catalogue (Papathanassopoulos 1996: nos. 169–74).

all other sites, with fragments of more than twenty pieces in various raw materials.

Stone vessels were made from 'marble' or from 'greenstone', as well as from gypsum and sandstone at Nea Makri (Theocharis 1954, 1956). Local work has been suggested only in the latter site[45] and systematic analyses of the provenance of raw materials would most certainly demonstrate the occasional importation of already-made vessels.[46]

The EN1 pieces from Achilleion and Nessonis I (Theocharis 1967: 120–1, figs. 67–70, pl. XXVIIA) are characterized by their small size, simple shapes and very thick walls. Their manufacture required some patience but no particular skill. Later pieces display a higher craftsmanship, with regularly convex walls that are sometimes fine enough to become translucent (see Theocharis 1973b: fig. 239). The shapes are varied, from convex bowls to open cups and flat dishes. These open shapes could have been simply pecked out, then scraped and polished, and a small drill was also used on the finely carved (EN?) pierced miniature stone vessel from Karamourlar (Theocharis 1973b: fig. 275). The most outstanding piece, however, comes from an early context: level Ia at Achilleion. It is a fragment of a superb round greenstone dish, elaborately carved and polished, with slightly convex walls, a ring foot and a small lip under the rim (Gimbutas et al. 1989: 256, fig. 8.18). This dish must have required a block of raw material quite exceptional in its dimensions and qualities. If it is as regular as depicted in the publication, it probably also required the use of a turntable and an exceptional mastery of stone-working techniques.

Equally impressive in terms of workmanship are two remarkable polished spheroid 'mace heads', found close together at Sesklo (Theocharis 1973b: fig. 273; Wijnen 1981: 41). A fragmentary piece, of similar quality, was found at Franchthi in the same chronological context. They demonstrate that the techniques needed to drill large holes in stone were already well mastered, although this technique will not become common until the Final Neolithic.

The finest stone 'earstuds' and marble pins, the hemispherical stone 'buttons' with transverse perforations or the steatite 'stamp-seals', especially those characterized by a square meander design,[47] also display good workmanship. However, their manufacture would not have required the degree of practice and skills shown by the above-mentioned greenstone dish. On the other hand, the long marble pins are specific to Nea Nikomedeia and several stone 'stamp-seals', from Early and Middle Neolithic Thessalian settlements, display

[45] But the expression of a 'stone bowl industry' (Phelps 1975: 114) goes beyond the limited indications given by Theocharis (1954, 1956).

[46] Analyses of a small marble vessel from Franchthi, initially considered as Early Neolithic, indicated that the marble came from the southern Peloponnese or from the Cyclades (Herz 1992). But its stratigraphic context is now considered Middle Neolithic.

[47] Most of these are dated to the Middle Neolithic but one was found in the middle part of level 1 at Pyrassos. In the initial publication, the stamp is firmly dated to the EN (Theocharis 1959: 64–6) and Theocharis later confirmed this attribution (Theocharis 1967: 149). Yet, Pilali-Papasteriou attributes it to the MN, probably on stylistic grounds.

strong analogies in the complex meander design as well as in such details of manufacture as the small circular depressions at the end of the straight grooves. Both instances suggest production by a few artisans within a small region, sharing and transmitting their specific technical traditions.

There are thus some hints that the production of carved stone and shell arte-facts may have been in the hands of specialists. The high technical and artistic level displayed in ornaments led Kyparissi-Apostolika (1992) to suggest a spe-cialized production, and the high number of broken stone vessels, conceivably broken during manufacture, has been taken to indicate a specialized workshop at Nea Makri (Phelps 1975: 114). It is indeed doubtful that everyone had the skill required to produce these finely carved and polished artefacts. On the other hand, most of them probably required more dexterity and patience than a specific technical knowledge or equipment. Consequently, the hypothesis of individual production cannot be a priori rejected. Detailed work on the origins of the raw materials would certainly clarify the problem, if only to indicate whether or not these artefacts were produced locally. Unfortunately, spondylus ornaments, which were later traded over vast distances, seem to have remained very rare in the Early Neolithic[48] and cannot inform us on this problem.

The restricted number of carved stone and shell artefacts demonstrates, at any rate, that they were not produced for personal use by every member of the community. Whether they were made by a few motivated individuals, or whether they were produced in specialized workshops remains unclear and probably varies from one category of artefacts to the other. In some cases at least, the technical achievements preclude a purely occasional, personal pro-duction.

Beads: discussions around a specialized workshop at Franchthi

The discovery of complete bead necklaces remains exceptional in the Early Neolithic of Greece, in part because human burials did not contain such funer-ary gifts (see discussion in ch. 13). Nevertheless, two necklaces were uncovered at Nea Nikomedeia. One was composed of twenty-seven cockle-shell beads, while the second was composed of sixteen 'very small fusiform shells', prob-ably *dentalia* (Rodden and Rodden 1964b: 604). But the regular discovery of small marble, steatite or shell discoid beads presumably indicates that small bead necklaces were rather common.

The production of such small beads, to be threaded in series, presents com-pletely different technical problems than the production of studs, pins or pen-dants. Individually, the shell (or stone) beads display less technical investment than the pendants or other carved objects, but their production in larger quan-tities may have rested on more standardized and time-efficient procedures.

---

[48] A perforated spondylus was found at Sesklo (Wijnen 1981: 47) and unworked spondylus shells were present as far inland as Achilleion (Gimbutas *et al.* 1989: 252).

I have suggested elsewhere that a specialized workshop for the production of large quantities of small cockle-shell beads was operating at Franchthi during the Early Neolithic (Perlès 1992). This was based on the discovery, in late EN contexts of the Paralia, of hundreds of cockle-shell bead blanks, broken or discarded during manufacture (Shackleton 1988: appendix D).[49] They were concentrated in two distinct *loci* of the Paralia, L5 NE and Q5-Q/R5, 30 metres apart, and were very clearly associated, stratigraphically and spatially, with hundreds of small chert points and borers rapidly made from a specific local raw material.

Microwear analyses (Vaughan, in prep.) showed that these micro-points and borers had been used on a hard raw material. Many bead blanks themselves show traces of micro-chipping on the broken edges, of the kind experimentally produced when shaping the blank with a hard point. A point was also used, at least in some cases, to initiate the perforation and stabilize the borer. The micro-borers show clear rotative use marks and were presumably used for the central perforation.[50] I thus concluded that the points and borers were not only stratigraphically, but also functionally related to the production of shell beads. Furthermore, the discrepancy between the very high number of small flint points and drills on the one hand, and the number of finished beads on the other, indicated, in my opinion, a mass production for export.

Miller (1996) recently challenged this interpretation and reversed the argument. By comparison with her own experiments and rates of breakage, she concluded that 'the great amount of cockle shell bead manufacturing debris found at the site results more from manufacturing errors than from a large output of finished products' (Miller 1996: 27). Indeed, she wondered at the very low proportion of finished beads – 4 per cent, some chipped or broken – versus rejected blanks, broken blanks and unfinished beads.[51] She suggested that this was in part, but in part only, 'a result of technical inexpertise and human error, wherein a low percentage of beads were completed in the production process without breaking' (Miller 1996: 20; see also 26). Since she envisions all-around necklaces made of cockle-shell beads only, which would have required *circa* 300 beads for a small necklace, this low output would have corresponded to a few necklaces at most, nothing 'beyond the needs of the Franchthi community' (Miller 1996: 29).

The divergences between the two interpretations rest on two factors. First, on what serves as a basis for estimating the production: the chert micro-points and borers, the complete beads, or the rejected, unfinished specimens. Second, on the status given to Miller's own experiments, rates of breakage and discard. Can the latter serve as a measure of what may be expected from the prehistoric artisan?

---

[49] Miller recorded 600 worked elements of *Cerastoderma glaucum*. This figure must be below the actual number since the shell residues from several Paralia trenches have remained unsorted.

[50] Judging by the presence of asymmetrical perforations, I doubt, however, that a bow drill was used (*contra* Miller 1996).

[51] Miller (1996: 24) gives a total of 543 bead blanks and unfinished beads from the Paralia.

Fig. 10.5 Shell beads produced at Franchthi, with associated tools.

Since Miller's study was published, I have re-examined the unfinished beads from Franchthi and remain convinced that the small chert micro-points were indeed used to carve, by flaking around, a circular preform out of the initial chips. It may not have been necessary (Miller did not think so), but the micro-chipping scars on the edges of the bead blanks leave little doubt that percussion was indeed used.[52] The advantage of regularizing the blank by indirect percussion would have been to diminish the time and effort required for grinding it down to an almost perfect circle, the stage of manufacture that Miller precisely found the most time-consuming.

The very high number of micro-points, which can each be used to produce several rough-outs, thus remains, in my opinion, a fair measure of the total scale of the production. The latter can, consequently, be estimated in the thousands. In turn, this implies that the artisans would have been well practised and their rate of breakage and failure necessarily lower than Miller's.[53] Miller lacked practice, and chose one 'chaîne opératoire' amongst several equally plausible ones. Consequently, her figures for breakage and discard, or her timing of the different stages, can hardly serve to estimate the total production and the time it required in an Early Neolithic context.

It is also possible that Miller overestimated the number of beads needed for a single necklace: more often than not, ancient and traditional necklaces are strung with beads of varied shapes and raw materials (e.g., Dubin 1987). Furthermore, the only 'complete' one known so far, from Nea Nikomedeia, had only twenty-seven cockle-shell beads. Franchthi thus remains, in my opinion, a good example of a production that exceeds the needs of the resident community, that is, of a specialized production.

The concentration of micro-points, borers, bead blanks and unfinished beads in two distinct areas of the Paralia[54] further suggests that several individuals were engaged in this production. We would thus have an instance of group specialization, some inhabitants of Franchthi profiting from their spare time to produce large quantities of beads, from a locally available and abundant raw material. This would constitute yet another case of craft specialization that was village-based, as with pottery, but distributed outside the original community, as with chipped-stone tools. Undoubtedly, all these conclusions need to be further tested and may be altered by subsequent studies. What cannot be doubted is that the principles that underlied the production of chipped-stone tools, pottery, carved artefacts and beads *were* different, that the organization of craft production in the Early Neolithic was already differentiated, and that, in some cases, it rested on complex strategies of raw material exploitation.

---

[52] This is not a 'surprising' discovery. Exactly the same procedures and stages of manufacture are found in other Neolithic cockle-shell bead workshops (e.g., Laporte *et al.* 1998).

[53] She started to manufacture 32 beads, but was able to complete 7. The others broke or presented an off-centred perforation that led to their rejection before grinding and polishing.

[54] Miller claims that these *loci* were dumps rather than actual working areas. I can find no specific data or observation in favour of this claim in L5 and Q/R5. To the contrary, it is probably the case in Q6N, a small concentration not far from Q/R5.

CHAPTER II

A VARIETY OF DAILY CRAFTS

The importance given in the previous chapter to flaked-stone tools and pottery should not delude us: especially for the case of chipped-stone tools, it reflects their importance for the prehistorian more than their importance for the pre-historic villager! Functional studies have indeed begun to make clear that many tasks formerly performed with chipped-stone tools, such as wood and skin working, were now performed with implements made from polished stone, bone, or even shell and teeth. These 'transfers' within traditional crafts, together with the introduction of new activities, resulted in a complex techno-logical system that was highly sensitive to local idiosyncrasies, traditions and even fashions.

Bone tools, grinding tools, pounding tools, polished celts or the miscellane-ous sherd-discs, sling bullets, spools, spindle whorls, and so forth, all classified as 'small finds' in traditional excavations, are now just beginning to receive the attention they deserve.[1] Until recently a lack of systematic studies, a reli-ance on traditional approaches and morphological classifications, and a near-absence of functional analyses have all drastically limited our understanding of 'small finds'. These varied artefacts cannot be satisfactorily analyzed either from the point of view of their production or from the point of view of their use. Even the traditional groupings such as 'bone tools' or 'ground stones' are mostly artificial. They do not correspond to homogeneous categories in terms of manufacturing techniques, nor, necessarily, to functionally related groups of artefacts.

But the problem does not only lie in the lack of detailed studies. Categories of material that have been studied in depth, that is with a conjunction of tech-nological, morphological and functional analyses, have been shown to display very varied functions, with no straightforward relation between raw material, shape, manufacturing technique or metrical attributes. I believe this relates to a fundamental attitude of the Neolithic artisan, at least in the regions under study, which our traditional categories of analysis are poorly equipped to appre-hend. We have indeed tended to classify all these 'small finds' according to broad 'natural' raw material categories: bone, stone, shell, and so forth, as though the latter constituted meaningful functional categories. Yet it is becoming clear

---

[1] Do they really? See the three pages altogether allotted to chipped-stone tools, polished stone tools and bone tools in the catalogue of the Goulandris exhibit on 'Neolithic Culture', compared to the twenty-four pages devoted to pottery.

that prehistoric artisans had both a more flexible and a finer perception of raw material categories. On the one hand, not all stones are equal, and stones were not randomly selected for specific tasks. On the other hand, if shells or bones presented comparable functional properties, the prehistoric artisan did not hesitate to use either stone, bone or shell for a given task.

The immediate consequence is that neither the raw material, in its broadest definition, nor the shape of the tool are sufficient to assign it a definite function. In addition, technical traditions and cultural preferences complicate the picture: similarly shaped tools can be used for different functions in different cultural contexts, and the same functions can be performed by tools of different raw material and shape.

However, given the near-absence of detailed studies of these artefacts in the Early Neolithic of Greece, the following discussions will be constrained by traditional categorizations and descriptions. Their primary aim is to point out problems and future fields of inquiry. Indeed, despite the grouping of these artefacts into the category of 'small finds', I believe them to be of primary importance: all together, they define the technological system of a given Neolithic community. Even at the most superficial level, this system reveals deeply rooted traditions. For instance, several of the artefact categories discussed below are, in Europe, specific to Greece and the Balkans. Understanding their role would contribute to our understanding the deeper structural contrasts between the different expressions of the Neolithic in Europe.

War weapons or shepherds' implements? The ubiquitous sling bullets

Amongst the artefacts characteristic of Greece and the Balkans are the numerous 'sling bullets' or 'slingstones', usually considered as fighting or hunting weapons. Sling-bullets are made of clay[2] and often found clustered within the houses. In trench 3 at Elateia a cluster of twenty-eight sling bullets was found near the hearth of a house floor at 2.80 m, a second one on a floor at 2.95 m, again near a hearth, and a cluster of six, associated with spools, on a floor at 3 m (Weinberg 1962: 166, 202).[3]

Sling-bullets are fairly standardized in shape, length (average 6 cm) and diameter (average 3 cm). They present the classical ovoid shape, with two more or less pointed butts, and often show a small flattened surface on which they can rest without rolling over. The Neolithic clay sling bullets from Greece, like those of the Near East, are often simply dried or half-baked[4]. Weinberg (1962: 202) explains their clustering near hearths by the need to dry or half-bake them.

---

[2] I have not found stone sling bullets from secure Early Neolithic contexts. There is one 'EN' specimen at Franchthi, but the unit it belongs to is contaminated by later material.
[3] There are some slight contradictions in the distribution of the sling bullets between page 166 and page 202.
[4] This was noted, for EN or later similar specimens, by Rodden (1962: 285), Tsountas (1908: 344–5), Wace and Thompson (1912: 125), Weinberg (1962: 202) and Wijnen (1981: 47).

However, they frequently disintegrate when excavated, which suggests that they were even more abundant than the specimens actually recovered.[5]

Childe was the first to draw attention to the presence of sling bullets in Greece. According to him, they demonstrated that Neolithic Greece belonged to what he called the 'sling area' (Childe 1951b), extending from the Middle East to Greece. Because of the well-known use of the sling as a war weapon in Classical times, he considered the Neolithic specimens also to be weapons. In the 'sling area', slings would have long been more important than the bow as war weaponry. To my knowledge, this interpretation has not been subsequently questioned. A recent paper on slings and sling bullets, significantly entitled 'David's weapon', offers no other interpretation (Voutiropoulos 1996).

Yet, in our context, it raises several problems: why would weapons be made from light, unfired or poorly baked clay? Why choose such a fragile material for shooting? Why should they be found so regularly *within* the house, next to the hearth? Finally, why are they so abundant and so regularly present, when we have no evidence for warfare?

They could, of course, have been used for hunting rather than fighting. Slings are a familiar weapon for shooting at birds, for instance. But most of the abovementioned objections still hold true here. In particular, why would they be frequent, when bird bones are almost absent from the faunal assemblages?

Despite their association with hearths, the raw material precluded any use as cooking stones or boiling stones.[6] I had thus suggested elsewhere that several of their characteristics corresponded to that of loom weights (Demoule and Perlès 1993: 375). They were clustered within house, unfired or poorly baked, rather standardized, and in numbers that could fit light weights for narrow looms. However, it must be admitted that their shape is especially awkward for this use and that this hypothesis was not really convincing.

Since then, a much more satisfactory interpretation was offered to me by J.-M. Geneste.[7] Geneste had personally observed young shepherds in the Near East use sling bullets to bring back stray sheep to the herd, when they had no sheep dog with them. An interpretation of clay sling bullets as shepherds' implements fits all their observed specificities: the use of rapidly manufactured clay sling bullets rather than natural pebbles would be a gain of time in alluvial

---

[5] Clay sling bullets are recorded in many EN sites, such as Nea Nikomedeia, Magoula Koskina, Prodromos, Otzaki, Sesklo, Pyrassos, Elateia, Nea Makri, Dendra, Lerna. They are also very frequent in surface collections of sites with EN occupations (Gallis 1992). In some sites, such as Nea Makri and Pyrassos, they were found only in EN levels (Theocharis 1956: 24; 1959: 66). But they continue to be used in the MN at least in other sites (Ayios Petros and Tsangli for instance).

[6] I wondered what Theocharis had in mind when he referred to them as 'checkers' in the English version of 'Neolithic Greece' (Theocharis 1973b: fig. 274)? It seems to be a simple mistranslation of the Greek.

[7] Geneste, oral communication 10/96. This interpretation was supported by J.-J. Hublin, who had seen his grandmother use sling stones to keep her sheep in northern Africa and was confirmed through personal inquiries in Syria. In Morocco, sling stones are also used to protect the crops against the birds (Monthel, oral communication 5/00). As also remarked by Monthel, David, in the Bible, is specifically referred to as the young shepherd of the family (First Book of Samuel).

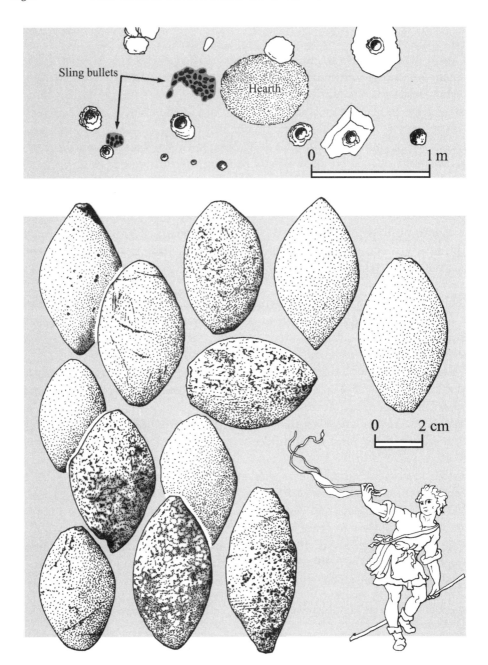

Fig. 11.1 Clay sling bullets from Sesklo and Elateia, and their location near the hearth on a floor at 2.8/2.9 m deep in trench 3 from Elateia (after Weinberg 1962 and Theocharis 1973).

plains, where pebbles have to be collected from the river-bed itself. Since they are not collected after throwing, their daily use and daily loss imply they would have had to be manufactured frequently. This, in turn, explains why they have been found on several occasions left drying near the hearth. Their standardization in size and weight would have given the shepherd a good regularity and precision in the throw, and their relative softness is best suited to uses where the aim is to hit but not to harm.

In turn, this may also explain their uneven distribution amongst sites: only one was found by Gimbutas in her excavations at Achilleion, and none at Franchthi. Of course, they could simply have disintegrated completely. But both sites are located in environments where small pebbles are readily available, and may have been used instead. This could also have been the case on the stony island of Ayios Petros, where several clusters of stone pebbles were found in MN domestic contexts (Efstratiou 1985).

Forest clearance or multipurpose tools: the polished stone blades

If the sling bullet may have been the shepherd's implement, the polished axe has always been considered, in turn, the farmer's most important tool for clearing his land. However, Theocharis noted long ago that polished stone blades, or 'celts', were in fact very rare in the earliest phases (EN1) of the Greek Neolithic (Theocharis 1967: 111). Though they progressively increase in number, they remain poorly represented during the entire Early Neolithic: in most excavations, the total number of celts barely reaches a dozen. Only 8 specimens were recovered from EN strata at Achilleion, 13 at Sesklo (sector C), 5 in the EN levels from Franchthi, and one in the soundings of Elateia.[8] It is thus difficult to concur with the statement that, in Greece, 'the stone axe was the most useful and necessary working tool in the life of the Stone Age' (Sugaya 1992: 76).

On the contrary, the small number of celts in general, and of celts large enough to fell trees in particular, immediately raises the problem of forest clearance. We are dealing here with the initial settlements in Greece, in an environment that was still wooded. Intriguingly, the relation between initial settlement, forest clearance and abundance of sturdy axes that is well established in other regions (Pétrequin and Jeunesse 1995; Pétrequin and Pétrequin 1988) does not hold true in our context. But the relative scarcity of polished celts in Greece is not unique: Ricq-de Bouard (1996: 232) remarked that polished stone blades were far fewer in Mediterranean France than in eastern France or Switzerland.

Several factors can account for this relative scarcity: the nature of the vegetation, the permanence of the settlements and the architectural traditions.

---

[8] Weinberg (1970: 581) refers to more than 100 celts at Nea Nikomedeia, but no figure is actually given in Rodden's publications.

Celts are a primary clearing tool in regions of dense forests and rapid rejuvenation. In Greece, the more open original forests of the lowlands could have been cleared by fire or by debarking the larger trees. Once opened, rejuvenation was slow and consisted mostly of shrubs for which large axes are ill-suited (Pétrequin and Jeunesse 1995; Pétrequin and Pétrequin 1993). Second, the permanence of most settlements over generations limited the need for new clearance. In this respect, it is certainly significant that the proportion of large axes increases in the Late and Final Neolithic, precisely when the exploitation of the still forested hills became more systematic. Finally, the use of clay as a major building material diminished the need for wood in domestic architecture.

Most EN polished stone tools are also of very small size compared with their counterparts in western or northern Europe. The illustrated EN specimens at Achilleion are under 4 cm long (Gimbutas et al. 1989: fig. 9.6) and the majority of the celts at Franchthi, for the whole Neolithic, do not exceed 5 cm in length. Specimens between 2 and 3 cm long are common at Franchthi, as they are in all other long-term settlements. Rather than woodcutters' tools, the polished blades, especially in the Early Neolithic, must be seen primarily as light-duty domestic tools, best fitted for a variety of tasks such as light carpentry, skin-working and bone-working.

Raw materials

This is confirmed by the choice of the raw materials, where the soft serpentinites[9] are especially well represented. Unfortunately little attention continues to be paid to raw materials (e.g., Sampson and Sugaya 1988/9; Sugaya 1993), despite their importance for the classification and understanding of the celts (Moundrea-Agrafioti 1981; Moundrea-Agrafioti and Gnardellis 1994). The fact that most polished stone tools in Neolithic Greece were made on very soft raw materials immediately narrows down the possible range of functions and points to sharp contrasts with western and northern European countries.

Microcrystalline or fibrous igneous and metamorphic rocks were the most widely used (Moundrea-Agrafioti 1996). The latter comprise serpentine, serpentinites, so-called 'jadeites', schistoserpentinites, andesite, granodiorite, basalt, but also, occasionally, hematite, marble, hard limestone, steatite, and so forth. The local availability of these raw materials varies but detailed studies of provenance remain to be conducted. Flint was never used in the Early Neolithic of Greece, as usually occurs when tenacious rocks are available.[10] The latter,

---

[9] Their hardness on the Mohs scale is only about 3 to 4.

[10] *Contra* Papathanassopoulos 1981. Appropriate flint would have been hard to come by in most regions, but this alone does not explain the absence of flint axes: high-quality flint blades were already traded over hundreds of kilometres in the Early Neolithic. I have seen flaked and polished flint axes in museum collections from the Kozani region, but they are probably later in date.

   In any case, I am tempted to think that the flint axe, far from being the 'typical' Neolithic axe, was mostly manufactured when other suitable raw materials were not available. No flint axe is

however, differ in hardness and resilience, and this influenced both the manufacturing techniques and the functional properties of the tool.

Flaking, as the first stage of manufacture, has never been recognized in Greece
to this date.[11] Microcrystalline and other hard raw materials were shaped out by
pecking, then ground and polished. The time-consuming polishing was often
restricted to the working edge (Moundrea-Agrafioti 1996). The softer rocks, in particular the serpentinites, were sometimes shaped by sawing, but more often
directly ground down and completely polished (Moundrea-Agrafioti 1981;
Moundrea-Agrafioti and Gnardellis 1994; Winn and Shimabuku 1989b: 262). Small
hand-held and medium-sized mobile polishers, as found in most sites, would have
been sufficient to polish most blades or the cutting-edge of the larger tools.[12] The
numerous intersecting polishing facets on the small Franchthi celts confirm that
they were polished step by step, not in a continuous motion on a large polisher.[13]

These manufacturing procedures leave little in the way of archaeological signatures, unlike the shaping of chipped flint axes. Consequently, the extent of
local manufacture is unclear. Specialized axe production workshops are
common in the European Neolithic, but it impossible to say whether the same
is true in Greece. Specialized production would have entailed the exploitation
of primary sources of raw material, a high output and wide trade networks
(Pétrequin and Jeunesse 1995). It is possible that the limited demand for celts
in Greece could be satisfied by the exploitation of suitable river pebbles, in the
context of a domestic production. But I suspect that at least some of the longer
and finer specimens came from quarried material, not from river pebbles.

Whatever the case, the maintenance of the tools was done within the settlements: the small size of many tools can, in part, be related to frequent resharpening, especially necessary with the soft serpentines. The tools were valued
enough that broken or splintered specimens were not infrequently cut into
halves longitudinally to produce one or two miniature 'chisels' (see Gimbutas
et al. 1989: fig. 9.6, no. 6). Many damaged specimens also show traces of reuse,
such as pecked and smoothed working-edges or pecked surfaces.[14]

Axes, adzes and chisels

Even if river pebbles were used as raw material, they were not picked up randomly. Raw materials of different mechanical properties were selectively used

known from Anatolia, at least before the sixth millennium, even in sites where good quality
flint was widely used for chipped-stone tools (Balkan-Atli 1994). Flint axes were used in the late
PPNB of the Southern Levant, but were absent from the Northern Levant even though the majority of the stone tools were made on large nodules of good-quality flint (Cauvin 1994: 200).
Similarly, in southern France, no flint axe is known despite good sources of high-quality 'yellow
flint' (Ricq-de Bouard 1996). In eastern France, the hard quartz mudstone was preferred to flint
(Pétrequin *et al.* 1993).

[11] But it must have been used for the rare flint axes mentioned above.
[12] Non-portable polishers, on large boulders or on rocks, are unknown in Greece.
[13] Stroulia, in prep. and personal observation.   [14] Stroulia, in prep.

for tools of different size or morphology, and presumably, function (Moundrea 1975; Moundrea-Agrafioti 1981; Moundrea-Agrafioti and Gnardellis 1991, 1994; Winn and Shimabuku 1989b: 262–6).

Polished stone tools are commonly classified as axes, adzes and chisels, depending on their shape and presumed mode of action.[15] No celt from the Early Neolithic in Greece has been found hafted and the distinction between axes and adzes relies on the classic criteria of edge symmetry. Axes are considered to have a straight, symmetrically bevelled working edge, whereas adzes would have a concave or asymmetrical working edge. According to this distinction, both axes and adzes would have been present in Greece during the earliest phases of the Neolithic.[16] This is not always the case: the Early Neolithic Danubian tradition, for instance, contains only adzes, and Pétrequin considers the simultaneous presence of axes and adzes to be a distinctive southern characteristic (Pétrequin and Jeunesse 1995: 19).

The earliest classification of celts in Greece comes from the pioneering work of Tsountas (1908), who relied on several morphological criteria to establish four types and various subtypes. This classification has been widely used since, and, in one way or another, the morphology of the blade, to the exclusion of other criteria, has remained prevalent in most subsequent essays (Mylonas 1929; Sampson and Sugaya 1988/9; Winn and Shimabuku 1989b). However, as early as 1975 Moundrea-Agrafioti showed significant correlations between raw materials, manufacturing techniques, dimensions and shape (Moundrea 1975; Moundrea-Agrafioti 1981). This multivariate approach was later sustained by multidimensional statistics, which led to the definition of four main groups (Moundrea-Agrafioti and Gnardellis 1991, 1994):

- the very large 'axes', always made from hard, often micrograined rocks, which are always pecked and present a fusiform shape, a circular transverse section, a pointed butt and a symmetrically bevelled cutting edge
- the large 'axes', manufactured from the same raw materials and by the same techniques, but of a smaller length, oval transverse section and with a rounded butt.
- the medium- and small-sized tools, made either from hard or soft rocks, relatively wide in proportion to their length, triangular or trapezoidal in shape, with a rectangular transverse section. They are often directly ground and polished all over. Almost all the 'adzes', with an asymmetrical working edge, fall into this category but small 'axes' are also present
- the chisels, characterized by their elongation, very small length, sawn edges, narrow butt with distinct traces of percussion.

[15] Chisels are characterized by their elongated shape and their use in indirect percussion. Axes and adzes are used in direct percussion and share similar overall shapes: axes are hafted with the working edge parallel to the haft, whereas adzes, used in a perpendicular motion, have their working edge perpendicular to the haft. Both can be used to fell trees.
[16] But hafted archaeological pieces from lacustrine sites and ethnographic specimens have revealed instances of asymmetrically bevelled 'axes', and symmetrically bevelled 'adzes' (e.g., Pétrequin and Pétrequin 1993: 35–42); this flexibility could account for the lack of one-to-one correlation between the shape of the working edge and wear traces (see below, p. 235).

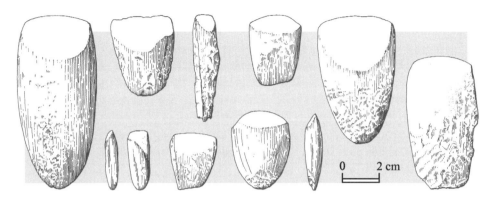

Fig. 11.2 Stone celts ands and chisel from Elateia, Sesklo and Achilleion (after Gimbutas *et al.* 1989, Papathanassopoulos 1996 and Weinberg 1962).

These groups are considered to be functional rather than chronological (Moundrea-Agrafioti and Gnardellis 1994), but the relation between morphology, technique and function appears to be somewhat loose. Moundrea (1975) observed at Prodromos than some 'axes' and most 'adzes' showed traces of use on the butt, as though they had been used in indirect rather than direct percussion. In turn, the microwear studies conducted by Christopoulou (1992) on the Sesklo celts allowed her to recognize three functional categories based on the direction of the microstriations. Again these functional groups cross-cut both dimensional and morphological categories.

The lack of relations between morphology and wear traces was also remarked in Mediterranean France by Ricq-de Bouard. She suggested that the main classes were related not to different functions or chronological phases but to different manufacturing techniques. The latter would have, in turn, depended on the nature of the raw material and the state under which it was collected (Ricq-de Bouard 1996: 64). Moundrea-Agrafioti (1981: 219) concurs that the raw material may have been more discriminant in terms of function than the overall shape or symmetry of the cutting edge.

Unfortunately, these classifications tell us little about the actual uses of these tools. Polished stone blades have traditionally been considered primarily as woodworking tools. There are no reasons to doubt they have been used as such, though this was certainly not their only function. The medium-sized celts of Greece would have been well adapted to the carving of tenons and mortises,[17] to the manufacture of wooden containers[18] or of wooden hafts and handles. Their use at various stages in the manufacture of bone tools has also been demonstrated elsewhere, and could well apply in our context. Finally,

[17] This technique has been reported on the wooden 'roof' from Prodromos (Hourmouziadis 1971b, 1972).
[18] None has been preserved in Greece, but the superb examples from Çatal Hüyük give an idea of the superior craftsmanship attained at that time (Mellaart 1967).

recent experiments have shown that small polished adzes, not necessarily made out of hard raw materials, were especially well adapted to the defleshing and scraping of skins.[19] This usage could explain the scarcity of chipped-stone scrapers, usually associated with this task.

The occasional presence of wear traces on the butts would indicate that the tools were sometimes hand-held and used by indirect percussion. Most, however, were probably hafted. Antler sleeves, although present in Anatolia at the same period, appear only later in Greece (Moundrea-Agrafioti 1987; Stordeur 1987). Wooden hafts, or hafts made of sheep/goat horns, could easily have been used instead.

Diachronic perspective

All classifications, whether morphological, functional or mixed, have failed to reveal clear chronological trends (Moundrea-Agrafioti and Gnardellis 1991, 1994; Winn and Shimabuku 1989b: 266). All classes or types are present from the Early to the Final Neolithic, although the largest axes are rarer in the earlier periods. This represents a vivid contrast to what obtains in other regions, where axes present a distinct evolution in production techniques, shapes and sizes, both in the long term and short term. Interdisciplinary studies of settlements in eastern France even allowed the demonstration of a correlation between the size and morphology of the axes and the state of the forest under exploitation (Pétrequin and Jeunesse 1995; Pétrequin and Pétrequin 1988). Conversely, the lack of significant chronological variation was noted in Mediterranean France by Ricq-de Bouard (1996).

The absence of clear chronological patterning in both areas is revealing: it suggests that the function and mode of functioning of the tools did not change through time. This makes sense if one considers, as argued above, that most tools were used for domestic crafts and had little to do with forest clearance: no modification of the blades and hafting would have been needed to adapt to the different stages in forest exploitation. But it also implies that there was no incentive for technical improvements and that the social and symbolic status of these implements remained unchanged.

Indeed, the attribution of the celts to light domestic crafts raises the problem of their status and value. The high symbolic value of the large forest clearance axe, used exclusively by men, is well known from ethnographic contexts (e.g., Pétrequin and Pétrequin 1993). In archaeological contexts, an exclusive relation between large celts and male burials appears to be confirmed by funerary data from the Linearbandkeramik Neolithic (Farrugia 1992). The evolution of the axe in Western Europe also shows that this symbolic value and demonstra-

---

[19] Collective experiments made at Chalain in 1995 by P. Pétrequin and his collaborators, on an auroch skin. Personal communication by V. Beugnier, 9/97.

tion of power progressively led to the manufacture of 'ceremonial' or 'prestige' axes of exceptional craftsmanship and dimensions (Pétrequin *et al.* 1993; Pétrequin and Jeunesse 1995).

But was the axe less valued in Greece because it was related mostly to domestic crafts? Not entirely. Two of the 'fine greenstone' celts uncovered at Nea Nikomedeia in the 'shrine', a building of unusual size that yielded a whole array of exceptional artefacts, were more than 20 cm long, four to five times the length of the usual celt of greenstone (Rodden and Rodden 1964b: fig. 11). A few other unusual deposits of celts are known from later contexts in Greece[20] and curious clay replicas of axes have been uncovered at Achilleion (Gimbutas 1989a: 213). If it can be ascertained that they had no technical function, they may indicate, like the Nea Nikomedeia axes, that, in Greece also, axes could have had more than a strictly utilitarian value.

Bone: a versatile raw material

The relative paucity of chipped and polished stone tools may be contrasted with the abundance of bone tools.[21] The latter are diverse, and often of high craftsmanship (e.g., Theocharis 1973b, 1973c: fig. 16). Their functional range must have been very wide, and bone may in fact have been preferred to the soft serpentine blades for some of the tasks traditionally associated with polished stone tools.

The selection of species and anatomical parts

Because 'bone tools' are, by definition, made out of bone, antler, or more rarely teeth, a more detailed study of the selection of the raw materials has often been neglected. However, bones from different anatomical parts or from different species have different mechanical properties (Liolios 1992). These were often exploited by prehistoric artisans, who selected different species through time, adapted the production methods to the different bones and used different anatomical parts for specific categories of tools (Sénépart 1991, 1992; Sidéra 1993).

In the Early Neolithic of Greece, the preference was for small domestic mammals, most specifically to ovicaprids. Pig and cattle bones were used more rarely, whereas wild animal bones and antlers remain exceptional. This would seem to directly reflect the relative abundance of the different species in the faunal assemblages (see ch. 8). However, the situation is more subtle: in southeastern Thessaly, ovicaprid bones amount to more than 80 per cent of the Neolithic bone tools (Moundrea-Agrafioti 1981: 268), an exceptionally high figure in the faunal assemblages. In addition, Payne had noted at Franchthi that the proportion of goat over sheep bones seemed more important in the bone

---

[20] For instance, the hoard of eleven polished celts found in a (probably MN) house from Lerna (Caskey, 1957).   [21] This is especially striking at Knossos (see Evans 1964).

tools than in the faunal assemblage.[22] This was based on preliminary observations only, and the matter should be further investigated. It may confirm that prehistoric artisans did not simply pick up the bones most readily available after meat consumption.

Some variations in the choice of anatomical parts can be documented from site to site, and would also deserve further investigation. For instance, in the EN of Sesklo, awls were manufactured on tibias and ribs of ovicaprids and pigs and in one case on a tibia of hare, rather than on the more commonly used metapodials (Moundrea-Agrafioti 1981: 322). Pig bones were used also for spatulas, chisels and 'burnishers' (Wijnen 1981: 43ff.), whereas at Nea Nikomedeia, most of the spatulas, points, needles and awls appear to have been made of sheep and goat bones (Rodden and Rodden 1964b: 604).

Manufacturing techniques

Our knowledge of EN bone tool manufacturing techniques is primarily based on Moundrea-Agrafioti's studies of Prodromos and Sesklo (Moundrea 1975; Moundrea-Agrafioti 1980, 1981) and the following information is mostly derived from these sources.

Long bones were broken into two fragments by percussion to remove one epiphysis or split lengthwise by grooving. Ribs were first cut transversally, then frequently split into two halves along the diploe. Large splinters produced by percussion were also frequently used when no epiphysis was needed as a natural handle. Points and awls made from long-bone splinters are particularly abundant during the Early Neolithic.

The proximal end of the tool, an epiphysis or a fracture, was variously shaped: condyles from metapodials were usually left intact, condyles from tibias were thoroughly ground down. The distal or working end was also shaped according to different techniques: bilateral convergent grooving for pointed tools or abrasion, in particular for all the tools with a transverse working edge. The finishing consisted of scraping and polishing. Most tools were polished on whetstones, either the active end only or the whole tool. Needles and large 'spatulae' were sometimes perforated. The perforation was usually done with a pointed tool in a circular motion[23] rather than by bifacial longitudinal grooving, a technique that Stordeur (1988a) considers characteristic of the Near East. On the whole, these manufacturing techniques preserved intact a large part of the original bone or splinter, a characteristic of Neolithic bone working.

Moundrea notes that at Prodromos, a majority of the tools showed dark traces, indicative of soil staining or contact with fire (Moundrea 1975). Given the frequency of these traces, intentional fire treatment, a technique long

---

[22] S. Payne, oral communication, 1982.
[23] See the unfinished perforation on a tool published by Moundrea-Agrafioti 1996: fig. 67h.

known in the Levant (Stordeur 1988b: 83–9) and widespread in the European Neolithic (Sénépart 1991), appears quite plausible.

The range of tools is wide: awls, points, needles, spatulae, gouges and burnishers. Most are common to all sites, but some variation can be detected. At Prodromos, awls and unperforated needles are the most common, followed by gouges and burnishers or chisels. Two heavily burnt shoulder blades may have been used for scooping ashes. Three 'chisels' were manufactured from deer antler. Though the Prodromos assemblage is fairly typical of EN bone tool assemblages, some of the rarer types are not represented. For instance, perforated 'needles', unknown at Prodromos, were found at Argissa, Soufli and Achilleion (e.g., Winn and Shimabuku 1989b). Similarly, large bone hooks are known at Nea Nikomedeia (Rodden 1965) and possibly at Franchthi (Jacobsen 1976) but are absent from most other sites.[24]

Theocharis (1967: pl. XX, C) interpreted a unique slotted bone shaft from Sesklo as a sickle or saw handle. The interpretation is not altogether convincing, since both epiphyses are preserved, and the piece could be an unfinished bone awl from a split metapodial. This underscores an interesting point raised by Nandris (1971a): the striking absence in Greece – with dubious exceptions from the 'aceramic' of Knossos and a few later specimens from Sesklo and Rachmani – of slotted bone sickles and bone spoons, two types well represented in the Early Neolithic of south-eastern Europe[25] and Anatolia. The absence of these distinctive artefacts can be considered as an indication of different traditions and origins.

No functional analysis has yet been published of Greek Early Neolithic bone tools. However, the types found in Greece are fairly standard, and we can probably transfer the conclusions reached from other assemblages. Microwear analyses, experiments and ethnographic comparisons show that Neolithic bone tools were used for a wide array of tasks and on a wide range of raw materials. They could have been used to remove the bark from poles and branches, split, scrape, and shape wood, for defleshing and scraping hides, for softening leather ties, for sawing hides and textiles, for scraping, burnishing and polishing pots; they were also used in basketry and weaving, and as digging tools (Maigrot 1997; Sénépart 1992; Sidéra 1993). Unfortunately, the shape of a tool is not sufficient to assign it a specific function, and microwear analyses are, here, an absolute necessity. However, bone tools are especially abundant in Greece and carefully manufactured, so that there is no reason to suppose that their use was more restricted than elsewhere. Given the paucity of polished stone tools in the Early Neolithic levels, I would assume, for instance, that most wood and hide working was actually done with bone tools, and that bone was a prominent raw material in the technological system.

[24] Most bone hooks from Franchthi are MN, however. They were also plentiful at Youra in the Northern Sporades (Sampson 1996a, 1996b), but in contexts that remain to be confirmed. Their abundance in this coastal site would appear to confirm their interpretation as fishing hooks, but it should be recalled that some were also found in the Initial Neolithic levels of Soufli, far from the sea.   [25] And also in some provinces of the Cardial: see Sénépart 1992.

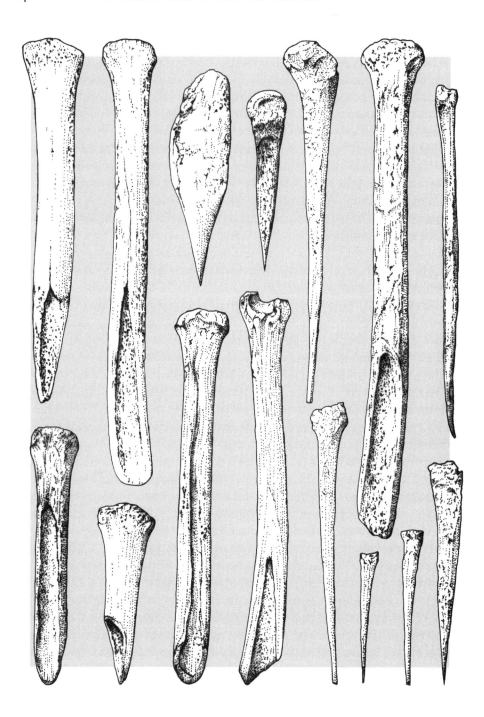

Fig. 11.3 Bone tools from various Thessalian sites (after Gimbutas *et al.* 1989, Papathanassopoulos 1996, Theocharis 1967 and 1973).

Shell tools

As stated earlier, I suspect much flexibility in the choice of raw materials for a given tool, even if one raw material may predominate. In this respect, it is worth mentioning shell tools, although, to my knowledge, no technological study has yet been published.

The Neolithic strata of the coastal site of Franchthi have yielded many worked shells. Most are ornaments, but some were manufactured and used as tools. The predominant category consists of 'scrapers' or 'burnishers' with a well-worked, abraded and rounded edge, made using a variety of species such as cowrie shells, pinna and spondylus. These tools display a large variety of sizes, and probably correspond to different uses. Their working edges are often comparable to that of bone or polished stone tools, and they may have served similar functions. In particular, they would appear to be well adapted for scraping soft materials such as clay and skin. At least two come from EN (or EN/MN) contexts at Franchthi, one made from a cowrie shell, the other from spondylus. Like several other spondylus specimens, the latter is ground down and polished on the outer surface, so that it resembles a carefully made little cup. However, wear traces on the distal edge suggest these were instead used as tools.

Grinding, pounding and polishing

The stone artefacts used for pounding, grinding and polishing are variously classified as pestles, pounders, handstones, grinders, palettes, mortars, polishing stones, whetstones, querns or millstones.[26] They cover two broad functional categories: tools used by percussion – pounders, mortars – and tools used by friction – millstones, polishers, burnishers, whetstones, and so forth. In terms of manufacturing techniques, they range from natural pebbles bearing only traces of use to artefacts completely shaped by flaking and pecking. They also include rare carved and polished artefacts. The study of this composite category of artefacts is notoriously difficult and the few specialized studies conducted thus far have dealt with the more elaborate but also rarer artefacts, such as millstones (Runnels 1981).

Precisely because these tools were often used after little or no modification, their physical characteristics were all the more important. Their use involved a wide range of actions that relied on different mechanical processes, from the coarse breaking of nuts or minerals to the reduction of cereals into gruel or flour. Rocks with different mechanical properties had to be used to respond to these varied mechanical constraints (Runnels 1981; Schoumacker 1993). Even

---

[26] The terminology is all but systematic in the publications about Greece, and I shall not attempt to give a proper classification. Wright (1992) has recently published a classification, which, though rather synthetic, could be used as a basis in Greece. A more systematic classification is currently elaborated by de Beaune (1999).

the most cursory examination of the rather poor literature provides indications of a differential use of raw materials and shows that Early Neolithic villagers did not pick up pebbles randomly.

Petrographic requirements are especially stringent for grinding tools: abrasive grains must have a specific hardness according to the material worked, they must be neither too resilient to fracture nor too fragile, and they must present naturally sharp angles. Similarly, the size of the grains and the cohesion and porosity of the cement influence the working properties of the tool (Schoumacker 1993). An empirical understanding of these parameters explains the selection of different raw materials for the different types of grinding tools. At Pyrassos and Sesklo, volcanic rocks from the old Mikro Thive volcano, 5 to 10 km from the sites, were used for the 'coarse' grinding slabs, whereas local schist was chosen for the finer-grained grinding slabs of Sesklo (Wijnen 1981). Volcanic rocks are often well suited for grinding flour, which may explain their use in sites even more distant from the sources: imported vesicular basalt was used at Achilleion, for instance, as early as the phase I (Winn and Shimabuku 1989b: 271). At Franchthi, none of the andesite or basalt millstones from the Saronic Gulf that Runnels had studied (1981) can now be assigned to the Early Neolithic,[27] according to Vitelli's (1993) stratigraphic attributions. Yet, crushed andesite is present as a temper in a few wares. Some andesite implements may thus have been imported to the site and later reused as grit in the production of pots (Runnels 1981: 103; Vitelli 1993: 111, 208–9).[28] Sandstone, which also offers varieties well suited for millstones, was most widely used at Franchthi, Lerna, Elateia and Argissa. It is presumed to be local, but precise sources have not been identified and, at Argissa at least, I do not see how sandstone could be 'local'. Millstones in the Early Neolithic were small (less than 30 cm), rather flat, and elliptical (Runnels 1981) or quadrangular (Milojčić-von Zumbusch and Milojčić 1971). In either case, they were carefully manufactured, first by flaking then by pecking and grounding.

A wide range of 'local' rocks were also used for the more common conical pestles, handstones or pounders. Again, deliberate selection of raw material can be perceived. At Prodromos, Moundrea observed that spherical and cubic grinders were manufactured mostly from quartzitic rocks, whereas conical or cylindrical pestles were made from granitic rocks (Moundrea 1975: 100).

Physical requirements for polishers are altogether different: they must have a regular granulometry, a medium hardness, and grains of a size appropriate to the degree of polish required (Schoumacker 1993). Microcrystalline rocks and schist hand polishers, used in the manufacturing of bone and stone tools as well as grooved polishers, possibly used for bone needles or points, are known from

---

[27] According to Vitelli's (1993) re-examination of the stratigraphy.
[28] The possibility remains that a more local source had been exploited for tempering the pots (Vitelli 1993: 208–9). The on-going studies of the grind-stones from Franchthi by A. Stroulia may bring new data on this issue.

several sites, such as Prodromos, Sesklo, Otzaki, Magoulitsa (Moundrea 1975: 95). 'Palettes', small rectangular, flat polished stones appear to be rather rare (see Winn and Shimabuku 1989b: fig. 9.12, no. 2). Moundrea-Agrafioti (1975: 95) has suggested that they may have been used for working hides.

The variety of artefacts, their abundance and the choice of specific raw materials all demonstrate that grinding and pounding tools were used in a great variety of domestic tasks. Though they are frequently found near hearths and ovens (Weinberg 1962; Winn and Shimabuku 1989a, 1989b), their use was certainly not restricted to food preparation: the preparation of clay, temper, pigments, vegetal fibres, hides, bone tools and pottery, all required, at one point or another, the use of grinding, pounding and polishing stones. Whether one considers the choice of raw material, the manufacturing techniques or their usage, 'grinding tools' do not constitute a homogeneous category. Detailed investigations will probably reveal a thorough understanding of their mechanical properties by prehistoric artisans, and more complex provisioning strategies than is usually assumed. Appropriate raw materials could not always be found in the alluvial plains. This holds true especially for millstones, a prominent implement in the daily preparation of food and for which, to this day, no effort is spared to obtain adequate raw materials (Runnels 1981, 1985).

Matting and basketry

The production of mats, basketry and especially cloth has long been considered associated with the advent of the Neolithic. Yet, much earlier imprints of textiles or fine mats have now been reported from the Upper Palaeolithic sites of Pavlov and Dolni Věstonice, in Moravia (Adovasio *et al.* 1995; Soffer *et al.* 1998). Together with the abundant evidence for matting and basketry in Mesolithic and PPNA sites (Stordeur 1989), they demonstrate the great antiquity of these crafts. Matting, basketry and weaving were certainly fully developed in the Early Neolithic of Greece, and fine textiles may have constituted one of the 'invisible' elements of the earliest trade systems.

Few testimonies have survived from our context of study and all direct evidence relates to matting rather than basketry or cloth. A superb imprint of a tightly flat-woven rush mat, apparently a two-by-two canvas weave, was uncovered at Soufli on, or rather 'in', the everted rim-sherd of a large pot (Gallis 1982: 32 n. 13). Similarly, more than thirty impressions on the bases of ceramic pots were found at Nea Nikomedeia (Rodden and Rodden 1964b: 605). Amongst these was an impression of twill matting and two examples of a two-by-two weave, apparently made from rushes half a centimetre wide. However, the mat impressions at Nea Nikomedeia are remarkable for the predominance of the twenty-eight samples of closed twine, with the weft threads invariably sloping downwards towards the left. Most samples showed two to three warps and four to five wefts per centimetre, but two finely woven specimens had up to five

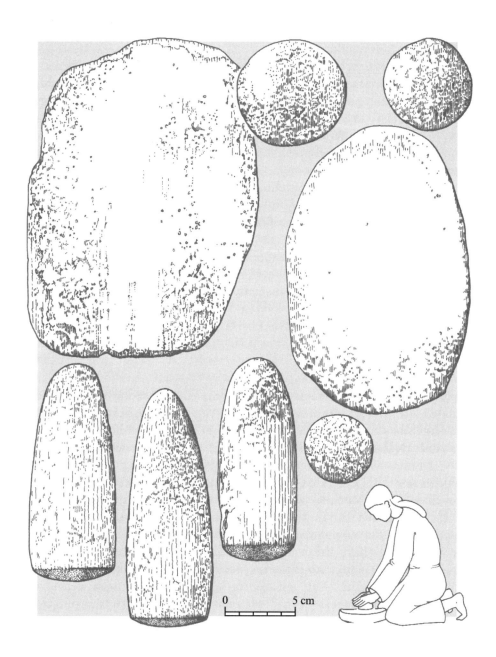

Fig. 11.4 Grinding and pounding tools from Elateia (after Weinberg 1962).

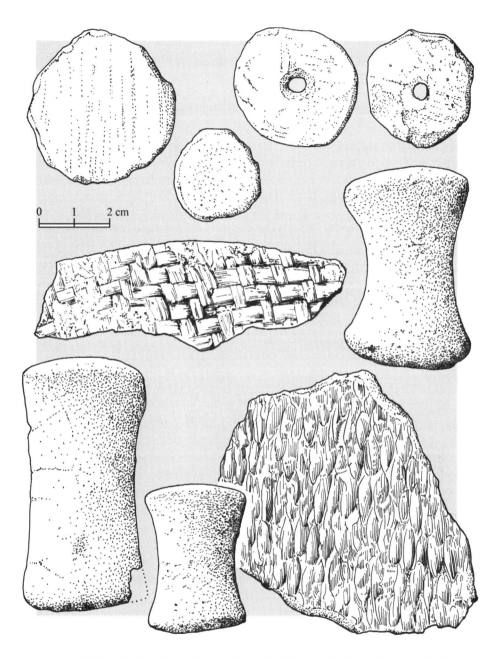

Fig. 11.5 Sherd-discs from Franchthi, spindle whorls from Knossos, bobbins from Elateia and mat impressions from Soufli Magoula and Nea Nikomedeia (after Gallis 1982, Rodden 1965, Weinberg 1962 and personal photographs).

warps and eight to nine wefts per centimetre (Rodden and Rodden 1964b: 605). When Rodden published these observations more than thirty years ago, he was intrigued by the predominance of twined specimens, since none were known in the Old World before 3000 BC. Ironically, it has now become the earliest construction technique known in Europe, where it predominates in the Upper Palaeolithic samples from Moravia. Several fragments of twined matting have also been found in the PPNB deposits of Nahal Hemar, and twine weaving is reported from Çatal Hüyük (Schick 1989: 51). Yet, according to Schick, twine weaving remains rare in the Near East, and is mostly associated with cultic contexts. In Greece, on the contrary, the use of twine woven mats in pottery-making and its predominance throughout the Neolithic indicate that it was not restricted to special functions or contexts.

The material used for the twined mats or fabrics remains uncertain: Rodden suggests 'grasses', without any further precision. 'Grasses', rushes, reeds and sedges were easily available locally, and could be harvested with the numerous flint and obsidian 'sickle-blades' found in all sites. Their 'cereal gloss', as demonstrated by traceological studies, was in fact frequently produced by work on reeds and rushes (e.g., Anderson 1994a, 1994b; Gassin 1993).

Spinning and spindle whorls

In contrast to matting, direct evidence is almost completely lacking for cloth weaving, or true weaving.[29] A fragmentary, loosely woven cloth of unknown raw material is mentioned at Prodromos but has not been reported in detail (Hourmouziadis 1972: 396). Weinberg (1970: 582) also refers to two 'fine textiles, possibly woollen' from Nea Nikomedeia, but they probably correspond to the two finer twined specimens already mentioned. Though twining is sometimes used for cloth (Geijer 1979: 6; Wilson 1979: 70) this is rare and there is no definite indication that we are dealing here with actual cloth rather than fine matting.

In order to investigate weaving practices in EN Greece, indirect evidence must be used. According to Rodden, 'the evidence for bone needles with eyes, spindle whorls made from potsherds and loom-weights suggest that the people of Nea Nikomedeia were familiar with weaving' (Rodden and Rodden 1964b: 605). This is perhaps true, but there remains nevertheless a high degree of ambiguity in all the evidence that can be brought forward.

Spinning is usually the most easily documented stage of the process, due to the ubiquitous spindle whorls. Yet even the latter are problematic in the Early Neolithic: the typical conical, semi-spherical or biconical spindle whorls are hardly ever found. The very few specimens mentioned[30] are so rare that, if their

---

[29] i.e., for weaving soft, spun fibres that, being flexible, require a loom to provide tension.
[30] Carington Smith, in 1975, could only refer to a few specimens from Corinth (Kosmopoulos 1948: 41) and Nemea (Blegen 1975) but their context is insecure. I can only add one to the list: a 'classical' spindle whorl seems to be illustrated at Prodromos (Hourmouziadis 1972: pl. 335).

stratigraphical context is confirmed, they probably ought to be interpreted as perforated pendants or weights rather than spindle whorls. On the other hand, centrally perforated clay discs, cut out of sherds, abound in EN sites[31] and most certainly represent the earliest form of spindle whorls (Carington Smith 1975: 119; Weinberg 1970: 582). Barber, a specialist of prehistoric textiles, considers them as typical of prehistoric Greece and Anatolia (1991: 59–60), but sherd spindle whorls are still widely used nowadays, in particular in Africa (Lebeuf 1962: 50).

These sherds range from about 4 to 6 cm in diameter, with a central hourglass perforation typical of bifacial holes bored into an already hardened material. However, not all centrally perforated sherds are necessarily spindle whorls. To be functional, the perforation must be centred and the whorl balanced. Roughly circular-shaped sherds were also used to steady the top or bottom of rotating drill shafts. They present a central, conical depression, sometimes surrounded by circular scratches (Theocharis 1967: fig. 20B).[32] If the sherd was turned around and reused in a similar fashion, it ended up with an hour-glass perforation and can thus be confused with a spindle whorl, were it not for the lack of balance and symmetry or the circular scratches.

Bow drills also can be weighted with a whorl, which then displays the same characteristics as a spindle whorl. But the rather rarer instances of rotative perforation in the Early Neolithic, mostly for ornaments, would not account for the abundance of whorls. Consequently, the majority of perforated sherd-discs can be considered as spindle whorls.

Experiments conducted by Bocquet and Berretrot (1989) on Neolithic whorls from Charavines (Isère) showed that the moment of inertia of flat discoid whorls was, on the whole, higher than that of bi-convex or bi-conical whorls. They would thus give long-lasting slow spins, allowing for the fabrication of rather loose threads (Barber 1991: 52; Carington Smith 1975: 120).

This raises the question of the nature of the fibres that were spun. The presence of perforated sherd-disc spindle whorls, together with the abundance of sheep bones, has been taken as evidence for wool-spinning (Papaefthymiou-Papanthimou 1992: 80). However, at this early stage of domestication, sheep are not yet supposed to have produced wool (Ryder 1969).[33] In addition, the

---

[31] For instance at Sesklo, EN1 (Wijnen 1981), Otzaki (Milojčić-von Zumbusch and Milojčić 1971) Magoula Koskina (Hourmouziadis 1969a and b), Prodromos (Hourmouziadis 1972: pl. 335), Pyrassos (Theocharis 1959), Nea Nikomedeia (Rodden 1964a), Servia V (Carington Smith 1975: 120), Achilleion Ib (Gimbutas *et al.* 1989), Nea Makri (Theocharis 1956: 26), Elateia (Weinberg 1962: 203–4), Corinth (Kosmopoulos 1948) and Franchthi (Carington Smith 1975: 120).

[32] I have seen them classified as unfinished or semi-perforated spindle whorls.

[33] The problem is not entirely settled, however (see discussion in Barber 1991: 20–30). Bone evidence is mute on this question, so that only animal figurines or fragments of cloth could solve the problem. Preliminary identifications of wool textiles at Çatal Hüyük in the seventh millennium (Helbaeck 1963) were later contradicted by analyses (on different samples) where the textile was recognized as flax (Ryder 1965: 176). However, some doubts remain for another fragment, which displays under microphotography the typical scales of wool, but was not further tested. Ryder also discusses an early figurine of a woolly sheep, identified at Tepe Sarab around 5000 BC uncal. (Ryder 1984: 70).

culling patterns of sheep in Early Neolithic Greece do not indicate a regular exploitation of the animals for wool. But spindle whorls could just as well have been used to spin goat hair, flax, many other textile fibres and bast. An early use of goat hair could explain why goats, though not numerous, were seemingly culled at a later age than sheep (see ch. 8); however, there is no definite proof. Flax, on the other hand, is known to have been woven as early as the eighth millennium BC in the Near East (Bower 1993; Schick 1989; Stordeur 1989), and later became a predominant textile fibre in Neolithic Europe. Since linseeds have now been found in the Early Neolithic of Greece, the weaving of flax seems a plausible hypothesis.

In order to produce very fine fibres, flax must be uprooted while still green. When stronger threads are required, or when seeds are needed for the next crop, it is processed only after it has seeded (Wilson 1979: 11). In recent rural Greece, flax was uprooted when ripe. The seeds were immediately beaten out in the fields and were stored in a pot for the next season's sowing. The flax bundles were then put in water for retting (Carington Smith 1975: 22ff.). Neither alternative would leave many stray seeds within a settlement itself, which can explain why linseeds remain rare in these contexts.

The hypothetical use of flax in Early Neolithic Greece may account for the characteristics of the spindle whorls. The ancient Egyptians used high-whorl drop spindles, that were set spinning by rolling the bottom of the shaft on the thigh. This naturally produces an S-twist, well adapted to the natural S-spin of the flax that they used to the exclusion of any other fibre. An examination of the depiction of Egyptian spinners (see, for instance, Barber 1991, 1994) shows these high-whorls to be rather large and flat. The early sherd whorls from Greece may thus correspond to a period when mostly flax was in use, and spun on high-whorled, thigh-rolled spindles. It is also tempting to relate the introduction of the smaller conical whorls, in the Late Neolithic, with the progressive introduction of other fibres more frequently spun with a Z-twist, on a low-whorl drop spindle, such as wool.[34]

Weaving: of elusive loom-weights, bobbins and sherd-dics

The production of thread by spinning necessarily raises the question of the loom, whether for the production of cloth or of woven carpets. The vertical

[34] Carington Smith also suggested a relation between spinning methods and the material used, but she referred to the later and smaller spindle whorls from Greece: 'It may be no accident that ancient Egyptians, producers of fine linen from the earliest times, used spinning methods likely to produce an S twist, and probably also prehistoric Greece used one that is more likely to give the Z twist which is unsuitable for flax, but so often found in wool.' (Carington Smith 1975: 79) However, as pointed out by Barber, wool can be spun both ways, and the spinning direction seems to be determined by the type of spindle in use.

Treuil (1992b: 124–30) suggests that the small clay spindle whorls of the Late Neolithic at Dikili Tash were still used as high whorls, for spinning wool. To the contrary, the heavier bi-convex or bi-conical whorls of the Bronze Age would have been used as low whorls for the spinning of flax.

warp-weighted loom is considered the characteristic loom of prehistoric Europe (Barber 1991: especially pp. 80ff., 113, 249, 299; Hoffman 1974) and is claimed to have been already in use in the Early Neolithic Körös culture of Hungary (Barber 1991: 93–4). A warp-weighted loom may also have been used at Çatal Hüyük, so that both Anatolia and Central Europe have been considered as possible origins (Barber 1991: 254). It could have then spread throughout Europe from either of these centres, while the ground loom still prevailed in the Near and Middle East as well as Egypt.

Accordingly, one would expect to find evidence for the warp-weighted loom in Greece as early as the seventh millennium. However, typical loom-weights are extremely rare, and this casts doubts on their very existence. A 'loom-weight' – seemingly a discoid pebble with an unfinished shallow gauge – is mentioned at Prodromos (Moundrea 1975: 109), but waisted weights can serve a large variety of other purposes and the very fact that the piece is unique renders this interpretation doubtful. 'Loom-weights' are also mentioned at Nea Nikomedeia, but no description is given and this may refer to the spools and bobbins (Rodden and Rodden 1964b: 605). The only weight of characteristic shape and clay body, a pyramidal, perforated clay weight painted with horizontal stripes, was found in a pit dug into the hard pan at Corinth, on the south side of the Temple of Apollo (Weinberg 1974). The associated pottery is mostly of a typical EN shape and clay body[35] but, again, the piece is unique and cannot constitute a case for the use of weighted looms in the Early Neolithic.[36] In all other sites, perforated loom-weights are clearly lacking: they do not become common in Greece until the Late Neolithic. Either the warp-weighted loom was not yet in use in Greece as suggested by Carington Smith (1975), or loom-weights did not conform to the most classic shapes and raw materials.

It is possible, indeed, that the weights have disappeared or that they were not correctly identified. Loom-weights are often only partly baked: incomplete firing is actually so common that Barber considers this a good criterion to discriminate loom-weights from fish-net weights or 'cooking stones' (Barber 1991: 97 n. 11, 98). One could thus hypothesize that loom-weights are absent because they were made of unbaked clay and have disintegrated. Yet, other categories of artefacts, such as the sling bullets, were made of unbaked clay and did survive in Early Neolithic sites. It would be surprising if the heavier loom-weights, and they only, had totally disappeared.

In addition, perforated loom-weights of clay are the most usual, but perforation is not a necessity. In Central Africa, unperforated loom-weights are tied in small bags or nets, so that their number can be adjusted to the tension of the warp required for each new weaving.[37] In western Africa, some vertical looms

---

[35] John Lavezzi confirmed that the context was a good Early Neolithic (personal communication 7/96).
[36] It is also very close in shape and decoration to two weights from Phthiotic Thebes, attributed to the Late Neolithic.   [37] E. de Dampierre, personal communication 1994.

are weighted with small stones tied directly to the warp threads (Gauthier 1989: 96). The traditional Scandinavian vertical warp-weighted loom used mostly stone weights, often waisted but unperforated (Hoffman 1974). To compensate for the variable weight of the stones that were collected in the fields, they were tied to a different number of warp threads according to their weight.

But the distribution of stone pebbles in Early Neolithic houses, as reported through publications, does not correspond to the spatial distribution expected for loom-weights. According to Barber's study, looms are usually stored away when not in use, and loom-weights are often found within houses in small clusters of about 6–30, frequently associated with spindle whorls (Barber 1991: 98, 99, 102).

This typical distribution would in fact fit better with other categories of clay artefacts that have also been associated with weaving. 'Spools', or bobbins, were first discovered at Elateia, where about twenty small half-baked and unbaked clay 'bobbins' where inventoried in mostly EN contexts. They were typically found in clusters, not far from hearths: eleven were found together on a house-floor at 2.10 m (trench 3), associated with spindle whorls and sling bullets (Weinberg 1962: 203). Since then, thirty-eight were found in EN levels at Sesklo (Papaefthymiou-Papanthimou 1992), fourteen were found in a small EN sounding at Servia (Carington Smith 1975: 124) and many others at Nea Nikomedeia (Rodden and Rodden 1964b), Prodromos (Hourmouziadis 1972: pl. 335), Achilleion (Gimbutas 1989b: 252) and Otzaki (Milojčić-von Zumbusch and Milojčić 1971).

The bobbins and spools were named as such by analogy with contemporary objects. Yet, as noted by Carington Smith (175: 123–5), they are usually not hollow enough to hold any great length of thread, and often too roughly made to be used for winding thread.[38] Despite their lightness (37 to 68 g at Servia), she instead suggests that they were used as unperforated loom-weights. Some of the 'spools' from Elateia (Weinberg 1962: pl. 69) and Achilleion (Gimbutas *et al.* 1989: pl. 8.4) are certainly heavy enough to be used as such, and the Middle Neolithic ones even have an axial perforation. But the variety of sizes is difficult to explain if these were intentionally made as weights.

Unperforated clay discs, cut out of sherds, have also been occasionally interpreted as loom-weights.[39] This is the case at Achilleion, where clay discs were usually found in domestic contexts, clustered on a bench or in the corner of the house: seventy-five altogether come from the EN levels, including a group of eleven, outside a house, in level Ib (Björk 1995: 145; Gimbutas 1989a: 254). Winn and Shimabuku (1989a: 34) remark that the latter context is unusual,

[38] Barber also said that, as a weaver, she would never use the 'shuttles' or bobbins from Knossos, of a slightly different shape than the ones discussed here, but also coarsely made and poorly fired (Barber 1991: 107, n. 17).

[39] Some were found at Franchthi (Vitelli 1993: pl. 4), Sesklo (Wijnen 1981), Otzaki (Milojčić-von Zumbusch and Milojčić 1971), Achilleion (Gimbutas 1989b: 254–5) or Elateia (Weinberg 1962: pl. 69).

since clay discs are normally found *within* houses. It is precisely their presence in houses, together with the absence of typical, perforated loom-weights, which led Gimbutas to interpret them as loom-weights. However, no weights are given, and the smaller and thinner specimens, besides their awkward shape, are probably too light to be used as 'weights'.[40]

However, few alternatives are satisfactory to account for the regular presence of sherd-discs, usually 4 to 6 cm in diameter: they are sometimes used as pot lids, but the EN specimens in Greece are much smaller than the average pot opening. Similarly, they are too small to be used as turntables to make pottery or stands for pots and they do not show the expected wear traces (Gebauer 1995: 105). Their use as pot scrapers is no more convincing: they do not show extensive use-wear, and K. D. Vitelli finds subcircular scrapers rather difficult to handle (Vitelli, personal communication 7/96), although this use is documented in ethnography. Sherd-discs have also been interpreted as 'tokens' or game pieces, but these interpretations are just as unverified as the others.[41] A personal examination of many sherd-discs did not help me solve the problem. I could find no indication that they had been tied (as for loom-weights), and the occasional wear facets I could occasionally observe were very limited and showed no systematic patterning. So far, no hypothesis seems to satisfactorily account for the numerous sherd-discs, a characteristic implement of Early Neolithic settlements in Greece and the Balkans.

This critical evaluation of the evidence possibly related to warp-weighted looms leads to inconclusive results: no category of artefacts can be reliably determined to be ancient loom-weights, although 'bobbins' and sherd-discs may *possibly* have been used as such. This leads us back to the second alternative, that is, that the warp-weighted loom was introduced to Greece in a later phase of the Neolithic. In a recent synthesis of textile production north of the Alps, Winiger (1995) concluded that warp-weighted looms used for weaving large textiles were not in use before the Bronze Age, when wool became the predominant yarn. He remarks that all of the Neolithic textile fragments whose borders have been preserved were narrow linen strips of simple weave, which could have been produced with a freely suspended back-strap platter. Larger weighted frames would have been used to produce bast warp fabrics, such as the cape worn by the Hauslabjoch man.

We have argued earlier that many techniques used in the Early Neolithic of Greece derive directly from the Near East. There, the ground loom is documented in the early phases of the Neolithic (Akkermans *et al.* 1983; Maréchal 1989; Stordeur 1989). It is possible that it was the first type of loom used in Greece also. The warp-weighted loom would have been introduced later, during

---

[40] Sixty to 100 grams is normally considered a minimum (see Carington Smith 1975; Bocquet and Berretrot 1989).
[41] Among several other uses, sherd-discs are used by children, in the Lake Chad region, to play ducks and drakes (Lebeuf 1962)! But they also served as pot-scrapers or to smooth down the walls and floors of houses.

the Late Neolithic, possibly from central Europe. However, the problem cannot be considered as settled.

Even ground looms or freely suspended looms require heddle tools or beaters. Carington Smith notes that two fragmentary tools made from polished ribs, both perforated at the tip and found in the Initial Neolithic strata from Argissa (see Milojčić et al. 1962: pl. 20), could have served as needle shuttles. Similarly, Moundrea-Agrafioti (1996) associates the highly polished and sometimes perforated spatulae made on large ribs with weaving. It is possible that these 'spatulae' were used as shed sticks or sword beaters, even in the absence of a warp-weighted loom. Yet the most usual shedding tool and beater in primitive looms, with their limited shed, is the pin beater: a well-polished bone 'awl' or point, of the type that is so plentiful in any Early Neolithic bone tool assemblage.

Seals or textile stamps?

Weaving is not necessarily the last step in textile manufacture. Woven cloth, especially when made of flax whose fibres do not dye well, can be subsequently decorated with motifs printed with mineral or vegetal dyes. Mellaart (1967: 220) interpreted the clay 'seals' from Çatal Hüyük as textile stamps, and referred to similarities of motifs between the seals and the decorated textiles represented on the frescoes. This interpretation has also been suggested, amongst others, for the clay stamp-seals of Greece – strikingly similar to Anatolian or Balkanic seals – and also for the beautifully carved stone specimens, unique to Greece (Pilali-Papasteriou 1992). Clay stamp-seals have been found in stratified contexts from a few Early Neolithic settlements: Argissa, Sesklo, Nessonis (Pilali-Papasteriou 1992) and Nea Nikomedeia (Rodden and Rodden 1964a). Only two stratified stone specimens can be attributed to the period, one from Pyrassos (Theocharis 1959), the other from Sesklo (Pilali-Papasteriou 1992: no. 2; Theocharis 1973b: pl. 20).

Detailed observation of some of the so-called 'stamp-seals'[42] shows that, here again, the category is probably artificial (the ambiguity of this double denomination is by itself revealing). All are small-sized artefacts with a flat decorated surface and, usually, a small handle above. A few specimens are probably true 'seals', the motif being created by the negative imprint on a soft material. Most, however, can be considered as 'stamps'. The high-relief motif – triangles, zigzags, crosses – is carved to a well-defined, absolutely flat surface, whereas the negative grooves are left rough and unfinished (see Papathanassopoulos 1996: catalogue nos. 271, 273, 274). These stamps are indistinguishable from textile stamps I have collected from various ethnographic contexts, or observed in archaeological contexts where their use was confirmed by decorated cloth

---

[42] As they are called, for instance, in the overall study of Makkay (1984).

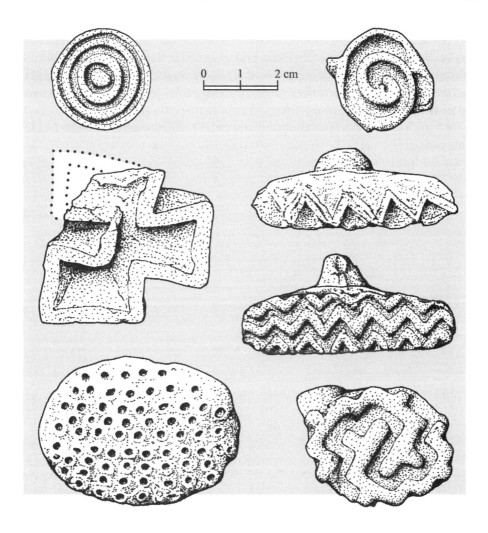

Fig. 11.6 Clay stamps from Sesklo and Nea Nikomedeia (after Rodden 1965 and Papathanassopoulos 1996).

remains.[43] Their small size would accord well with the production of narrow linen strips or ribbons, but they could also have been used to decorate the borders of large pieces. The variety of designs in a single site and the striking similarity of designs over large areas, the Balkans, Anatolia and the Near East, could then be accounted for by a common background of geometric motives, not necessarily invested with high symbolic significance.

Several categories of clay and bone artefacts may thus be plausibly related to weaving and textile production. Yet in no case is the relation unambiguous. This uncertainty deprives us of any insight into the organization of what must

[43] In particular from Turkey and South America.

have been a significant craft production. If all the classes of artefacts we have considered above were actually related to weaving, the latter would have to be considered as a widespread domestic craft. On the other hand, if it is assumed that only some of the above-mentioned artefacts were related to weaving, then a rather different organization of production might be considered. The distribution of these artefacts amongst settlements is uneven, and this could indicate a differential distribution of weaving activities, either within or between settlements.

CHAPTER 12

RITUAL INTERACTION? THE MINIATURE WORLD OF 'DOLLS OR DEITIES'

According to some recent essays on the Neolithic, the latter should be viewed primarily as a mental, symbolic mutation: a new conception of the supernatural world, a different way of interacting with 'divinities' (Cauvin 1997; Hodder 1990). Whether or not this 'symbolic revolution' is considered as a driving force, it cannot be denied that the technical, economic and social transformations were sustained by transformations in the symbolic and ritual domains. The latter are often expressed in spectacular ways: the early PPNB monumental buildings such as the 'Skull building' at Çayönü (Özdoğan and Özdoğan 1990), the 'temples' with greater than life-size anthropomorphic pillars at Nevali Çori (Hauptmann 1993), the 8-metre high tower of Jericho (Kenyon 1957). These early collective monuments are echoed, in later contexts, by the equally monumental graves and megalithic buildings of the Atlantic façade. In parallel, the highly structured representations on the house walls at Çatal Hüyük demonstrate that this 'symbolic revolution', whatever its exact interpretation (e.g., Cauvin 1997; Forest 1993; Hodder 1990), had also penetrated within the more private, domestic sphere.

Yet, no equivalent of these spectacular symbolic expressions has thus far been found in the Neolithic of Greece.[1] If a spiritual mutation is to be recognized, it can possibly be sought in the profusion of small, 'non-utilitarian' objects – miniatures, models, ornaments, precious stone artefacts, incised clay tablets, and so forth – that characterize the Neolithic of Greece and that of its Near Eastern and Balkanic counterparts. But the evidence is profoundly ambiguous, and even the apparent proliferation of these small objects may be misleading: rather than a new system of beliefs, the abundance of figurines, for instance, might simply reflect the shift from wood to a new and more durable raw material, baked clay. 'More durable' to our eyes, but also more easily worked and even more easily broken! A feature that, as I shall argue, must be taken into account in their interpretation. In this respect, the ubiquity of figurines in domestic contexts suggests that at least some participated in domestic rituals, whereas their variability would indicate different roles or meanings. Yet, interestingly, if domestic rituals involving figurines were of any importance, their importance was restricted to definite regions: the distribution of figurines is strikingly uneven across Greece.

---

[1] For a rare but later exception, see the recently discovered plastered bull's skull from LN Dikili Tash (Darcque and Treuil 1997).

Strictly speaking, the miniature clay objects are for the most part of unknown meaning and function. By analogy with later remains, they are usually thought to have had symbolic functions such as the expression of individual status, or for magical, religious and ritual practices. However, the tendency to attribute 'ritual' functions to any artefact of unknown use has been contradicted in an equally abundant literature that suggests more mundane or utilitarian roles.

I have not, any more than others, found the key that would reveal the meaning of this miniature world of figurines, vases, house models, 'altars', and so forth. I do not intend to go into extensive discussions or summarize an already prolific literature. I am not, either, especially interested in their interpretation. On the other hand, I am convinced that their very abundance in certain Neolithic socio-contexts and their absence from others is significant, and can tell us something on the functioning of these societies.

The anthropomorphic figurines

The abundance of figurines in domestic contexts is a characteristic of the Greek Neolithic, which is shared with the Balkans and the Near East. In these regions, anthropomorphic figurines – overwhelmingly feminine – are a new feature: none had been recovered in earlier prehistoric contexts. According to Gimbutas (1989a: 220) the ubiquity of figurines in and around houses demonstrates the importance of domestic cults of various 'feminine goddesses'. Following Marangou, it reflects, on the contrary, a large variety of uses, including that of toys (Marangou 1986, 1992; Treuil 1983, 1992a).

'Dolls or deities'? This question, borrowed from the title of Talalay's study of the Franchthi figurines (Talalay 1993), aptly summarizes the two extreme interpretations classically evoked for figurines. They have indeed been interpreted as idols depicting gods and goddesses (Cauvin 1997; Gimbutas 1982; Rodden and Rodden 1964b); as toys (cf. Marangou C. 1992; Treuil 1983, 1992a; Ucko 1968); as fertility symbols, representations of ancestors or individual 'portraits' (Bailey D. 1994); as shamanistic devices, amulets (Marangou C. 1992), charms (Morris I. 1985), as childbirth aids (Bolger 1996); and also as means of social communication (Hourmouziadis 1973a).

While it is true that we have no actual 'proof' of the ritual use of Neolithic figurines in Greece, I consider it difficult to argue that figurines only had purely mundane uses, and that all were simply toys or 'pedagogic devices'.[2] Greek Neolithic figurines, with their different shapes, degree of elaboration,

---

[2] One could expect the figurines to be more thoroughly fired than is frequently the case if they were to be manipulated daily by children. Second, their very abundance in some sites (up to 150 fragments were recovered from the sounding at Prodromos 2) and their absence in others makes me doubt they were mainly toys, as though the use of toys was restricted to the children of some very specific sites or regions.

sexes and positions, probably covered a range of meanings and functions (Marangou C. 1992; Orphanidis, in Gallis and Orphanidis 1996; Talalay 1993). In an ethnographic study devoted to small wooden figurines from Africa (Fagg 1970), I listed no less than fifteen different functions, all magical or ritual, and no feature could help us differentiate the ancestor's representation from the amulet for a safe pregnancy. In a single Chadian village, Lebeuf (1962) recorded at least four very different meanings and uses for the clay figurines: some represented divinized ancestors and were put in sanctuaries, others represented masked dancers, and others represented enemies: they were made and buried when enemies attacked the village. Some, of a smaller size, were indeed children's toys.

Ritual uses of anthropomorphic representations are known from all over the world, and are well exemplified in the Mediterranean Chalcolithic and Bronze Ages.[3] Figurines are also present in the only house foundation offering recognized in Greece, a small LN house model from Plateia Magoula Zarkou uncovered by Gallis (Gallis 1985). Rejecting the possibility that figurines had ritual uses seems, on the whole, a more costly hypothesis than the reverse. However, going beyond such a general statement has always been and remains extremely difficult.

The emergence of the human figure

Human figurines do not appear immediately in their fully developed, 'naturalistic' form. The EN1 figurines from Sesklo (Theocharis 1976a, 1977; Wijnen 1981: fig. 14) resemble the Initial Neolithic specimens and are quite distinct from the later, more familiar clay figurines. The human body remains indistinct or highly schematized. Diagnostic sexual features are absent, and the schematization is sometimes so extreme that the very identification as anthropomorphic can be debated (i.e., Theocharis 1973b: fig. 206 and pl. XXII, Theocharis 1977: fig. 92). At Sesklo the EN1 clay figurines are very small: 2 to 4 cm for the intact specimens. Some are seated, broadly conical or pear-shaped; all body parts merge together, with no distinct head, neck, breast, arms, and so forth. (Wijnen 1981: 45–6). Because of their large buttocks, an attribute that is constant in later feminine figurines, these clay figurines can be considered feminine. However, other distinctive sexual attributes are lacking. Other small clay figurines may have been standing, although it remains unclear whether the legs were actually represented (Wijnen 1981: 45). The body parts are barely more distinct than in the previous type, with the arms indicated by small protuding butts. EN1 stone anthropomorphic figurines were found at Sesklo, where they consist of a carved pebble (Theocharis 1976b: fig. 83) and a schematized marble head (Wijnen 1981: 45). The pebble figurine from Sesklo can be

[3] See for instance the figurines in the miniature shrines in Chalcolithic and Bronze Age Cyprus or in the Balkans.

likened to another pebble figurine found at Karamourlar, but this site is too disturbed to ascertain its exact dating (Theocharis 1973b: fig. 14).

Several EN1 figurines have close parallels in the Near East, but from earlier periods. They seem to derive from an early system of representation in which features remained somewhat blurred, and in which clearly defined feminine attributes were not yet overwhelmingly predominant.

During the later phases of the Early Neolithic ('EN2 and EN3'), as the figurines became more abundant, the human shape emerged more clearly from the clay. Pear-shaped schematic figurines continued to be produced,[4] but they now coexisted with more 'naturalistic' figurines showing well-defined body parts: head, neck, arms, legs. In parallel, diagnostic sexual features are well marked and leave no doubt that the vast majority of figurines were feminine. The EN2 thus witnesses the appearance of the 'classic' feminine figurines, whose variations in types, styles and modes of representation should not mask a fundamental unity of conception.[5] Four broad types can be distinguished: the above-mentioned pear-shaped figurines, the 'stand-type' figurines truncated below the torso, the sitting figurines and the standing figurines. In Thessaly, from where most figurines have been uncovered, all types share a special emphasis on overdeveloped belly, hips and thighs.[6] A deeply incised, reversed 'triangle' often underlines the lower part of the belly, the hypogastrium and the inguinal folds, below a well-marked navel. Standing and naturally sitting figurines are the more naturalistic. The arms are usually folded over or under the breast, whilst the legs are straight and slightly set apart on standing figurines, and straight or folded on sitting figurines. Given the systematic emphasis on the waist and belly, the variability in the treatment of the breasts is interesting: they are either hidden by the arms, represented in a natural way, or completely absent.

On both 'naturalistic' and 'schematic' figurines, the upper part of the body, neck and head, is highly schematized. The face is either pasted on to a cylindrical or pointed rod, or topped by a protuding and very characteristic knob (see Gimbutas 1989a; Nandris 1970). Slightly oblique incised eyes and a pinched nose stand out as the most conspicuous features on these triangular or oval faces. The well-known 'coffee-bean' eyes,[7] pasted on the face and frequent on Middle Neolithic figurines, seem to appear only at the end of the Early Neolithic (Wijnen 1981: 45). The mouth, contrary to the eyes, is not systematically indicated[8] and consists of a small slit or round hole.[9] There is clearly no

---

[4] See for instance the figurines from Otzaki (Milojčić-von Zumbusch and Milojčić 1971).
[5] See Hourmouziadis 1973a, Talalay 1993 or Ucko 1968 for comprehensive studies; Gallis and Orphanidis 1996, Theocharis 1967: pls. XXV and XXVI, for illustrations.
[6] In this respect, the narrow-waisted figurines from Nea Nikomedeia stand out as clearly different. Generally speaking, the published figurines from Nea Nikomedeia differ stylistically from those of Thessaly.
[7] Which Weinberg relates to the cowrie shells plastered on some PPN skulls at Jericho (Weinberg 1970: 580).
[8] At Nea Nikomedeia, Rodden notes that only two figurines show the mouth (Rodden and Rodden 1964b: 604), but the total number of figurines is unknown.
[9] Was vision, thus, more significant than speech?

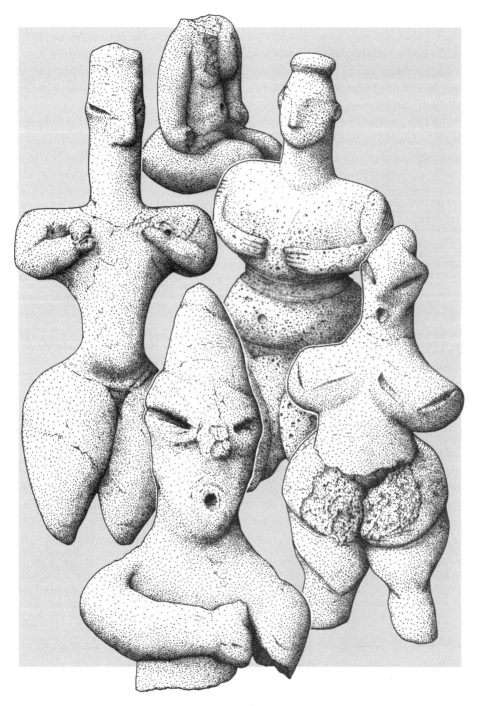

Fig. 12.1 Clay feminine figurines and flat-topped marble figurine from Nea Nikomedeia, Prodromos, Ayios Petros and Sparta (after Theocharis 1973 and Papathanassopoulos 1996).

attempt at rendering individual features. They seem to express a more general-ized and abstract feminine concept, in which the notions of prosperity and/or fertility seem to have been paramount.

The restricted number of types in EN feminine figurines,[10] and even more, their restricted geographic distribution (see below), lead me to think that their meanings and roles did not cover the whole range of variation previously envi-sioned. Together with their overall homogeneity, their clear-cut geographic dis-tribution would point, instead, to an integrated set of functions, beliefs or rituals, which were enacted only in specific socioeconomic contexts.

Distribution between sites and regions

Almost 300 EN figurines[11] are recorded from a dozen excavated sites in Thessaly and western Macedonia, a figure below the actual number since detailed counts are not systematically given in preliminary reports. Within this broad region, their relative density may have varied from site to site: western Thessalian settlements such as Prodromos or Achilleion appear richer in figurines than eastern Thessalian settlements such as Argissa, Otzaki or Sesklo. However, the disparities in the quality of recovery and publications make it difficult to pursue this issue without a more precise database.

Macro-regional contrasts are far more conspicuous (Talalay 1993). South of Thessaly, the number of figurines known to date is strikingly small: two frag-ments are dated to the EN at Elateia (Weinberg 1962: 201) and two legs, pos-sibly belonging to anthropomorphic figurines, were found at Nea Makri (Theocharis 1954: figs. 42 and 43). Franchthi, with three to five fragmentary fig-urines (Phelps 1987; Talalay 1993), had been considered an exception in the Peloponnese, otherwise devoid of figurines (Talalay 1993: 58). However, with a better grasp of the site chronostratigraphy (see Vitelli 1993), no figurine can now be definitely attributed to the Early Neolithic.[12] One can also mention the five marble specimens from 'the region of Sparta' (see Papathanassopoulos 1981: fig. 27; Theocharis 1973b: figs. 17, 200, 226), also attributed to the EN, but without any solid ground.[13]

[10] Feminine figurines departing from the four types previously mentioned are exceptional. One can mention, for instance, the figurine holding a load on its head found at Prodromos (Hourmouziadis 1973a).

[11] See Hourmouziadis 1973a, Talalay 1993. This figure is based on Hourmouziadis (1973a) and on my own files. It includes the following sites: Achilleion, Daudza, Magoula Karamourlar, Magoulitsa, Myrini, Nea Nikomedeia, Nessonis, Pyrassos, Otzaki, Sesklo, Soufli and Tsangli. More have been reported from other sites, but no illustrations are given.

[12] Of the three figurines retained by Talalay (1993: table 1), two come from disturbed or later con-texts (FC 11 from A 31 and FC 122 from H2B: 59). The earliest securely dated figurine (FC 190, from Q5S: 186) comes from the Ceramic Interphase I/II (Early to Middle Neolithic), but its clay body is unlike any EN clay body from the site (Vitelli, quoted in Talalay 1993: 24).

[13] Hauptmann (1971: 350) and Phelps (1975: 115) attribute the Spartan figurines to the site of Koufovouno, but no EN has been identified at Koufovouno (Renard 1989).

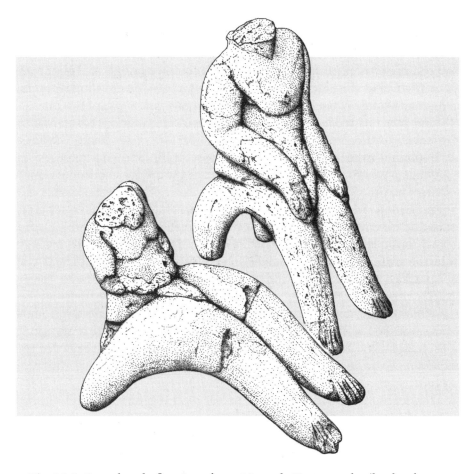

Fig. 12.2 Seated male figurines from Magoula Karamourlar (back; after
Theocharis 1973) and Sesklo (front: after Papathanassopoulos 1996).

How can this irregularity be accounted for? Talalay evokes the possibility
that most figurines were unbaked and were not preserved (Talalay 1993: 59).
However, why would differential preservation create such a strong geographical pattern?

Regional discrepancies of a similar magnitude can in fact be found in the
Middle Neolithic, when figurines were even more abundant. This would rather
indicate systematic differences in the role and importance of figurines between
the two regions. Figurines are especially abundant in regions of dense settlements and rare in the sparsely populated Peloponnese. As suggested by Talalay
(1993: 62): 'Could the ostensible permanence and stability of EN communities
in the north have encouraged the production of figurines, while the more
tenuous existence and possibly sporadic occupation of villages in the south
have precluded the use of such images?'

I doubt, in fact, that the answer lies in the economic background, since there is little evidence for substantial differences in the economic system between Thessaly and the Peloponnese or central Greece. To the contrary, we have already pointed out the important sociological differences induced by the presence or absence of close-by neighbouring villages. Obviously, a higher population density would, by itself, create more occasions for the use of figurines, but this alone does not account for such a contrasted distribution. Observing that in present-day Africa the production and use of masks, statues and figurines is more important in regions of dense population, some colleagues[14] suggest that the difference was linked to the composition of the village community and/or the power relations between communities.

Going beyond this suggestion is 'shear and wild speculation',[15] yet I find it worthwhile having a try. In the sparsely populated Peloponnese, the community may have been mainly composed of close relatives, whose role and status within the community were already defined by filiation and alliance. There may have been no need to redefine their status on a *sociological* basis, through collective rituals cross-cutting kinship affiliation. The situation may have been obverse in the close network of Thessalian villages, where the need to counteract potential conflicts may have led to widespread alliances with non-kin groups. In the latter situation, the individual's status would have needed to be redefined on social grounds, through collective rituals that served simultaneously as a means of integration between the different – and potentially centrifugal – segments of the community. In addition, power rivalries within or between village communities may have induced a redundancy of rituals and symbolic expressions of power. From this perspective, figurines could be seen as an element of various rituals that ultimately served in the definition and integration of a complex, dynamic and tense *society*. Under very different sociological conditions, such rituals would not have been needed in the dispersed and smaller Peloponnesian groups.

Context of recovery and modalities of use

Does contextual information provide any clue concerning the exact nature of such rituals? As it turns out, the context of recovery is too ubiquitous to be of much help in this matter. At Nea Nikomedeia, five figurines were recovered in the largest building of the earliest phase, which Rodden called 'the shrine'. Three were found together in its NE corner and were broken in pieces as though they had fallen on the floor when the building caught fire (Rodden and Rodden 1964b: 604). However, numerous fragments of figurines were also found scattered in the rest of the settlement. At Achilleion, figurines were found inside and outside

---

[14] Eric de Dampierre, Eric de Garine and Manga Bekombo, specialists of central and western Africa.
[15] B. Woodcock, *in litt*. 3/2000.

houses, near hearths, ovens or work areas, on built platforms or in pits, associated with other 'rare' items such as miniature vessels, or, on the contrary, mixed in with the usual domestic garbage in the dump (Gimbutas *et al.* 1989).

The figurines found in the burnt down 'shrine' from Nea Nikomedeia are possibly the only instances of EN figurines found in what can be considered their primary context of 'use' or deposition. Everywhere else, they were found in and around the houses, probably mostly in secondary depositional contexts, and almost always broken. Though this may hinder a contextual interpretation, it should, nevertheless, be taken as relevant information.

In the preceramic site of Khirokitia in Cyprus, Le Brun noticed that the figurines, made out of stone, were, first, absent from the numerous burials, and second, discarded everywhere or even re-employed in wall constructions (Le Brun 1989: 79–80). This strongly suggests that the figurines had in fact lost their value when discarded. As aptly stated by Le Brun: 'une telle négligence, un tel désintérêt montré à l'égard des représentations anthropomorphes inclinerait à penser que leur utilisation devait être limitée dans le temps; après quoi, vidées du sens dont elles avaient été investies, elles étaient abandonnées' ('such neglect, such patent lack of interest towards anthropomorphic representations, leads us to think that they have been used only briefly; after which, having lost the meaning they had carried, they were abandoned').

In other words, the figurines would have had no intrinsic value or permanent status, but only a 'use-value', on and for specific occasions.[16] Having lost all value or importance after being used, they would then have been discarded anywhere, either broken during use or through taphonomic processes after discard. If clay figurines were made for a specific use and discarded shortly afterwards, their rapid manufacture and poor firing are better explained. The different parts of the body were made separately, often around a clay or stone pellet, and pegged or stuck together without much care. Consequently, they frequently broke apart. If it is assumed that they were initially conceived as short-lived artefacts, the high frequency of 'split-legs', for instance, need not be invested with special social significance (*contra* Talalay 1987).

However, this would not apply to all figurines. The marble figurines that later became more abundant were obviously meant to be seen or to last longer. They remain extremely rare in the Early Neolithic,[17] but other figurines also

---

[16] This recalls the fired-clay figurines from the Palaeolithic settlements of Moravia. Despite thorough firing, these numerous animal figurines were nearly all found broken into small fragments and scattered around the hearths (Vandiver *et al.* 1989, 1990). I was also interested to read, when writing this chapter, that the Jomon clay feminine figurines were also considered to have been intentionally broken (Dōi 1998: 27).

[17] One stone specimen only has been recovered from a reliable stratigraphic EN2 or EN3 context, again at Sesklo (Theocharis 1962a: fig. 13d, 1962c: fig. 57). A second one, from the Athens Agora, is reproduced in the recent Goulandris Museum catalogue (no. 235) but Talalay did not include it in her exhaustive catalogue (Talalay 1993) and it cannot be considered as secure. Several surface finds, including the already-mentioned specimens from 'the region of Sparta', are attributed to the EN, but on stylistic grounds only. A stone figurine was recently reported from Nea Nikomedeia (Touchais 1989) but it could be Early or Late Neolithic in date.

show an unusually high degree of care in their manufacture. This applies, in particular, to the carefully modelled and much rarer 'enthroned' figurines, several of which have definite EN dates.[18] Nandris called them 'Integral Seat Figurines' and described them as 'usually male, seated with hands on thighs on a seat which is an integral part of the piece, whose own legs form the front legs of the seat' (Nandris 1970: 200–1).

Together with some equally rare elongated standing figurines, these seated figurines constitute the whole sample of male figurines. The differences in representational standards as well as the numerical discrepancy suggest different roles and function than for the feminine figurines. However, the male figurines do not, any more than the feminine figurines, provide grounds for the hypothesis of a drastic 'revolution' in religious beliefs in the Neolithic. A prominent feminine deity might well have been emerging (Cauvin 1997),[19] but it remains invisible in our context. The numerous figurines can evoke representations of ancestors, spirits, small divinities or fertility concepts, just as they can evoke transcendent deities. In addition, we have seen that the short-lived clay figurines seemed, on the whole, to be characteristic of densely settled agglomerations or regions. This, I believe, precludes both an interpretation as dolls and as deities: why should children in the less densely settled areas be deprived of toys? Why would the cult of transcendental deities be absent from regions of sparser settlement?

Human representations on vessels

Human representations are not restricted to free-standing figurines. Though much rarer, anthropomorphic representations on vessels are varied and often quite spectacular. In one instance, at Prodromos, a very small figurine was modelled on a flat clay dish, standing as a sort of ship 'figurehead' (Theocharis 1973b: 44, fig. 12). Also found at the same site was a fragmentary feminine figurine carrying an open container on her back, possibly the modelled spout of a vase (in Papathanassopoulos 1996: no. 208).

Human representations are also found modelled and coated with slip under the rims of clay vessels. In several instances, the emphasis is not on the body but instead on the face, as on the ten sherds bearing a human face from Nea Nikomedeia (Rodden and Rodden 1964a: figs. 7 and 8; Theocharis 1973b: fig. 219–20; Pyke and Yiouni 1996: 88). As with the figurines, the eyes, the nose and the ears are sharply modelled, but the mouth can be missing. On the other hand, the strong features evoke men's faces rather than women's, and the addition of beards in three cases confirms that, on vessels, masculine representations may predominate over feminine ones.

---

[18] From Magoulitsa, Achilleion, Sesklo, Pyrassos for instance. For an illustration, see Theocharis 1973c: fig. 15.

[19] Its presence is indisputable later, in megalithic art for instance (L'Helgouach 1997/8).

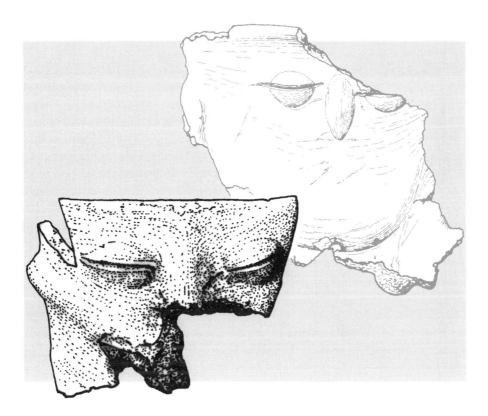

Fig. 12.3 Anthropomorphic vessels from Nea Nikomedeia (after Rodden 1965 and Theocharis 1973). The front figure is approximately 12 cm wide, the back one slightly larger.

In the same site were also found two exceptional sherds with human silhouettes, modelled on monochrome vessels (Pyke and Yiouni 1996: 88). One of them, which is fragmentary, depicts the lower part of a feminine body with the legs bent outward at right angles, at the level of the knees (Rodden and Rodden 1964a: fig. 3). This unnatural position, for which I know no equivalent in Greece except, perhaps, on some 'frog-like' pendants, immediately recalls the 'birth-giving goddess' depicted on the walls of houses at Çatal Hüyük. It again suggests that western Macedonia had stronger links with Anatolia than with the rest of Greece.

Zoomorphic figurines

According to Cauvin (1994), the primordial feminine symbol of the Near East incarnates the ideas of fecundity, maternity, power and dominance over the

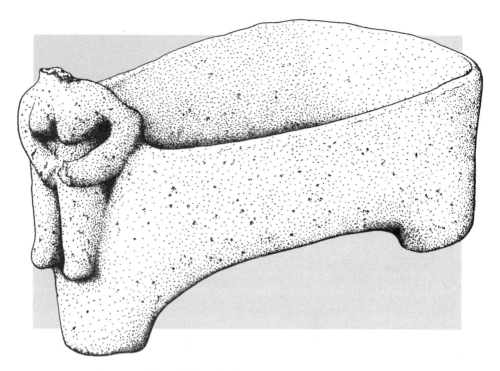

Fig. 12.4 Clay vessel with female figurine from Prodromos (after Theocharis 1973).

wild world. It is accompanied by a male symbol, initially expressed in zoomorphic representations: the wild bull or wild predators in particular.

It is difficult to find a parallel to this symbolic association in Greece. Animal figurines are much rarer than anthropomorphic figurines (Toufexis 1994).[20] They are also quite distinct in their conception, and I doubt that they functioned as complementary pairs within a single symbolic system. However, their small number and undiagnostic features precludes any attempt at interpretation.

Sexual characteristics are never emphasized on animal figurines: all animals appear to be 'unsexed'. Whereas feminine figurines conform to a few stereotypes, underlying probable symbolic functions – exaggeration of the buttock, hips and thigh – there is no particular emphasis on any part of the body with animals.[21] The representation is more 'neutral' (Cauvin 1994: 143), often so 'neutral' that species determination becomes awkward. Yet, at least some of the figurines were painted (see the painted calf head in Theocharis 1973b: fig.

[20] Gimbutas, for instance, identified only seven zoomorphic figurines among a total of over 200 figurines in the Early and early Middle Neolithic at Achilleion (Gimbutas 1989a: 178).

[21] The two figurines interpreted as pregnant by Toufexis are exceptions (Toufexis 1994).

217). It is thus possible that species indications were given by the details of the painting rather than by the overall shape. In the meantime, the difficulties of identification lead to diverging views of the categories of animal represented. According to Theocharis (1973b: 46), Orphanidi (1992) or Toufexis (1994), most of them were domestic. Weinberg, on the other hand, mentions several wild species (Weinberg 1970: 580). But how could we decide whether the fine suid from Nea Makri (Theocharis 1954: fig. 5), for instance, is a wild boar or a domesticated pig?

Among the wild animals are three exceptional frog figurines from Nea Nikomedeia, made not from clay but from carved and polished stone (Rodden 1964b). The choice of this taxon for these unique and very finely manufactured pieces may seem odd: they belong neither to the sphere of domestic animals, nor to the classic symbols of the wild world: bulls, deer, predators and raptors. However, I would not be surprised if frogs did have a special symbolic meaning in the Neolithic of Greece. The frogs from Nea Nikomedeia are clearly frogs, but there are also, in Greece and the Near East, a few (deliberately?) ambiguous representations, that can evoke either schematized frogs and/or feminine representations. In the latter case, the women would be highly pregnant, or in a birth-giving position. Instances of these representations can be found at Achilleion (Gimbutas *et al.* 1989: 228), at Malthi Dorion (Valmin 1938: pl. 1) and at Chara 1 (Gallis 1992: 192). They are present in Turkey in the seventh millennium site of Kösk Höyük (Silistreli 1989), and I am tempted to interpret in a similar way the enigmatic central low-relief representation held by two clearly anthropomorphic beings at Nevali Çori (see Cauvin 1997: pl. III). Frogs belong to symbolic representations in many areas, and seem to relate everywhere to the Creation or to birth and fertility.[22] The unique pieces from Nea Nikomedeia may, consequently, be more than exquisite animal representations.

Miniatures and replicas

The 'miniature world' of the Early Neolithic in Greece is not limited to zoomorphic and anthropomorphic representations. It also includes artefacts, some that recall daily-used objects, some that may possibly exist only in a miniature version. The clay replicas of polished axes found at Achilleion (Gimbutas *et al.* 1989: 213) have already been mentioned, and have no equivalent elsewhere that I know of. On the other hand, clay and more occasionally stone miniature replicas of ceramic vessels are frequent. They constitute a rare instance where a

---

[22] According to the *Dictionnaire des Symboles* (Chevalier 1969) as J. Cauvin kindly pointed out to me (*in litt.*, 11/94).

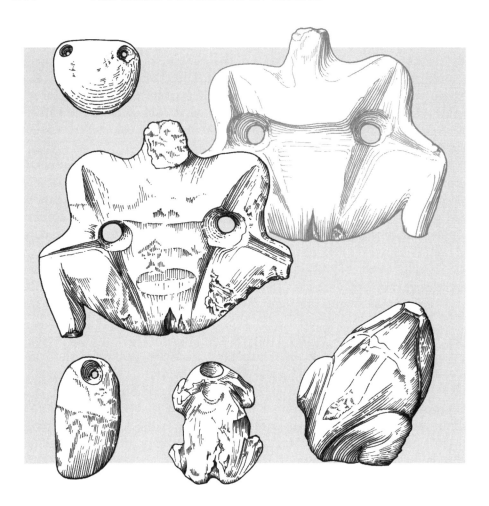

Fig. 12.5 Clay pendant (top left) and polished stone pendant (bottom left) from Achilleion, 'frog-like' or anthropomorphic figurine from Achilleion (both faces), frog figurines from Nea Nikomedeia (after Gimbutas *et al.* 1989 and Rodden 1964a).

ritual use can be demonstrated, since miniature clay vessels were deposited with human cremations at Soufli (see ch. 13). A miniature marble bowl was also deposited with a child burial at Franchthi, but the latter, initially considered as EN, is now dated to the MN (Vitelli 1993). Carefully made miniature clay tables, with three or four feet, have also been found in several sites: Prodromos, Achilleion, Magoulitsa 1, Nea Nikomedeia.[23] Some bear a large per-

---

[23] At Achilleion intact 'offering tables' have only been found in subphase IVa, but comparable feet were recovered from levels Ia, II and III (Gimbutas *et al.* 1989).

Fig. 12.6 Animal heads from Sesklo (top) and Nessonis I (bottom) (after
Theocharis 1973). Double animal figurine from Magoulitsa I (after
Papathanassopoulos 1996).

foration on their surface, and have been interpreted as 'offering tables' or
domestic altars. A fragment of what may have been a miniature armchair, possibly a seat for a figurine, was also found in the Early Neolithic of Achilleion
(Gimbutas 1989a: fig. 7.16).

These miniatures are carefully made, never found in large quantities, and
show a limited range of themes. This, I believe, rules out the hypothesis of
simple children's toys, and their use in ceremonial or ritual contexts appears
plausible. The same may apply to the well manufactured clay ladles and spoons
(see Prodromos: Hourmouziadis 1972; Achilleion: Gimbutas *et al.* 1989:
210–11; Sesklo: Theocharis 1973b: fig. 213). These objects are too rare for daily-
used utensils, and are known as 'elite funeral pottery' in some megalithic

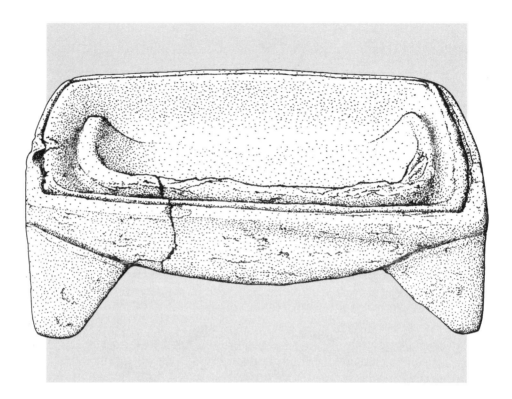

Fig. 12.7 Small clay table (length 17 cm) from Sesklo (after
Papathanassopoulos 1996).

tombs of Western Europe (Gebauer 1995: 105). Gimbutas believed they were
used for ritual offerings (Gimbutas 1974: 210–11), but, as usual, more mundane
uses, such as their use during social gatherings or collective meals, can also be
suggested.

The interpretation of these miniatures and replicas thus poses the same problems as the interpretation of the figurines. Rituals were certainly instrumental
in the regulation of relations between social units, between humans and the
natural world, between the natural and the supernatural worlds. However, no
single category of artefact can be *unambiguously* associated with ritual practices. Several categories of artefacts may *plausibly* be associated, in part or in
totality, with ritual practices. So far as the evidence goes, the widespread distribution of these artefacts in domestic surroundings suggests that most rituals
would then have taken place in or around the houses, rather than in specially
dedicated ceremonial buildings.

Collective ritual buildings?

A possible counter-example to the latter proposition comes from the extensive excavations at Nea Nikomedeia. There, the houses from the first two building phases[24] were grouped around two unusually large, superimposed buildings. The earliest one measured 11.8×13.6 m and covered a surface of 160 square metres. The later one, partially excavated, measured over 10.85×9.05 m and covered more than 100 square metres (Pyke and Yiouni 1996). These two buildings differ from the others not only by their larger size but also by some architectural features and by their content. The earlier one was divided into three parts by parallel rows of heavy timber. Five female figurines, already mentioned, were found in a corner of the earliest building, together with 'two outsized greenstone axes, two large caches of unused flint blades, two very unusual gourd-shaped pottery vessels, and several hundred clay "roundels" of unknown function' (Rodden 1964b: 114). The flint blade caches contained several hundred pieces each, which were extremely standardized, but contained no corresponding core or flakes. This building burned down and was then rebuilt on a similar tripartite plan, but with a larger central section, two lateral aisles and internal buttresses (Rodden and Rodden 1964a: 564).

Pending a detailed publication of these buildings and their content, their interpretation remains conjectural. Rodden implies they had cultic functions by calling the earlier one the 'shrine' (Rodden and Rodden 1964a), a suggestion retained by Pyke (Pyke and Yiouni 1996). Halstead, to the contrary, suggests they could be the houses of a family that was especially successful in long-distance trade, as indicated by the caches of so-called 'exotic flint' (Halstead 1995: 13, n. 19). Both alternatives could be defended by analogy with other Early Neolithic contexts. The distinctness of the architectural features recalls the specificity of the collective 'sanctuaries' found in Levantine and Anatolian sites (see discussion in Cauvin 1994: 155ff.). On the other hand, they can also be compared to the unusually large buildings found, always singly, in many Linearbandkeramik settlements. Various interpretations have been offered, such as clubhouses, men's houses or ceremonial houses (Soudsky 1969). It has also been suggested that they were built for and by households with especially large networks of relations or that housed individuals with special responsibilities within the community (Coudart 1991).

The data from Nea Nikomedeia are currently too limited to warrant any conclusion before full publication. However, the discovery of buildings of unusual sizes and architecture in one of the only two extensive excavations for the period should make us wary of considering all EN settlements as composed of

---

[24] Three 'phases' have now been suggested at Nea Nikomedeia (Pyke and Yiouni 1996), but it remains unclear that they constitute occupational phases rather than successive rebuildings of the different buildings.

domestic buildings of equivalent sizes and function. The possibility that the Nea Nikomedeia buildings served collective functions should not be rejected too quickly: their size is indeed impressive – almost 150 square metres – and, to my knowledge, neither the flint 'caches' nor the outsized polished axes have any equivalent elsewhere in Greece. On the other hand, one function at least can be ruled out: contrary to some of the collective 'sanctuaries' of the Near East, the Nea Nikomedeia buildings did not contain human remains.

CHAPTER 13

INTERACTING WITH THE DEAD: FROM THE DISPOSAL OF THE BODY TO FUNERARY RITUALS

All societies have to deal with the practical, psychological and social problems created by death. The responses vary widely and depend as much on beliefs as on the organization of the living society. A primary reading of the available data on EN funerary customs reveals a pattern shared with the Balkans: no organized necropolises, no conspicuous monuments, but a variety of 'domestic' funerary rituals comprising primary burials in pits, secondary burials, cremations and bone scatters. The interpretations have converged in pointing out the lack of sophistication and 'simplicity' of the funerary rituals, the latter being, in turn, considered as the expression of a simple, 'egalitarian' society (cf. Demoule and Perlès 1993; Gallis 1996a; Hourmouziadis 1973b). Yet, I shall now argue that we have all been misled in our reading of the data: we have considered the exception to be the rule.

More than twenty years ago, Hourmouziadis already pointed out that the populations of the large settlements of Sesklo and Dimini had obviously been disposed of in unexcavated cemeteries or outside the settlements. No burial had been uncovered, despite the vast areas covered by the excavations (Hourmouziadis 1973b: 209–10).[1] Since then, only one burial, of EN1 date, has been found at Sesklo: that of an adult, in sector C below the Acropolis (Theocharis 1977: 88–93). More generally, the sample of Early Neolithic burials has remained extremely meagre in spite of further excavations and the discovery of several cremations at Soufli (Gallis 1975, 1982). Altogether, the remains of no more than 50 to 60 intentionally buried individuals can be attributed to the EN.[2]

---

[1] Cavanagh and Mee recently made the same observation for the Neolithic of Greece as a whole (Cavanagh and Mee 1998).

[2] I have retained here the following burials: about 25 inhumations from Nea Nikomedeia (1962 and 1963 excavations) (Rodden and Rodden 1964b), two inhumations and 14 cremations from Soufli (Gallis 1982), the partial remains of 11 individuals in the collective burial at Prodromos (Hourmouziadis 1971, 1973b), one inhumation each at Kephalovrysso, Argissa, Sesklo (Hourmouziadis 1973b; Milojčić et al. 1962; Theocharis 1977).

Despite Gallis' cautionary note (Gallis 1996a), at least three of the five burials attributed to the EN at Lerna (Caskey 1956, 1957, 1958) can be considered as intentional burials. But whether they should be dated from the EN or the MN remains unclear (Vitelli in litt., 7/96). Similarly, the cremations from Prosymna (Blegen 1937) remain poorly dated. Gallis (1996a) attributes them to the MN. The situation at Franchthi is equally problematic. After revision of the stratigraphic context and associated ceramics by Vitelli (1993), the four burials from within the cave, previously dated to the Early Neolithic or Early/Middle Neolithic (Jacobsen and Cullen 1981: table 1), should now be considered as early Middle Neolithic. The four 'EN' baby burials from the Paralia yielded no ceramics and cannot be assigned to a specific phase of the Neolithic (Vitelli 1993: 47, n. 7), although the possibility that they are Early Neolithic cannot be rejected either.

To this small number should be added an unspecified (but equally small) number of individuals found as 'bone scatters'.

I must admit that it was not until I read Morris' study of burial rituals in Classical Greece (Morris I. 1992) that I realized the full implications of this situation:[3] we do not know how the vast majority of the population was treated after death. What we know about are the *exceptions*, these very rare, probably atypical cases, in which individuals were buried in a special way that led to their recovery. And it is as *exceptions* that they should be apprehended, for instance, to understand why they were denied typical burial rituals, not as a reflection of the norm.

'Normal'[4] funerary rituals were such that the remains are not found during 'normal' excavations. Hourmouziadis (1973b: 210) long ago raised the most probable alternatives: corpses could have been disposed of in nature, cremated, or buried in cemeteries outside the settlements.

The norm? Burial ground and cremations at Soufli

The small cremation burial ground from Soufli (Gallis 1975, 1982) would appear to confirm Hourmouziadis' hypothesis. It was discovered by chance, after a drainage ditch cut through the eastern end of the *magoula*. A small excavation of *c.* 10×5 m revealed fourteen cremation burials plus a dubious one and two burning pits, or pyres, interpreted as crematoriums. Another cremation was uncovered 8 m to the north, whilst two pit-burials were found in strata above the cremations.

The two larger features, interpreted as 'crematoriums', consisted of shallow circular pits, 1.10 to 1.30 m in diameter and about 0.30 m deep, with heavily burnt walls and abundant remains of intense combustion (Gallis 1982). Burnt bricks (pyre B) and post-holes (pyre A) may have been related to platforms supporting the corpses. Many small fragments of charred human bones were scattered in the pits but Gallis noted that, in 'Crematorium B', the bones found at the edge of the pit were only partially cremated (Gallis 1982). No pottery or grave goods were found in these pits.

The other pits are of smaller dimensions: *c.* 0.60 m in diameter and 0.20 m in depth. They contained charcoal and many fragments of charred human bones. Traces of burning on their sides would indicate that the charred remains were deposited in the pits while still hot. The undisturbed pits[5] yielded two

footnote 2 *(cont.)*
　　I shall not take into account the supposedly EN burials from Pan's Cave at Marathon (mentioned by Hourmouziadis 1973b) and from Koutsouria (Deïlaki 1973/4, Protonotariou-Deïlaki 1992) for lack of any reliable contextual information.
[3] Hence the very different interpretation offered here from that in Perlès and Demoule 1993.
[4] In the etymological sense of *normal*, i.e., as referring to the norm.
[5] Most cremations were partly destroyed by the irrigation ditch that led to their discovery (see Gallis 1982).

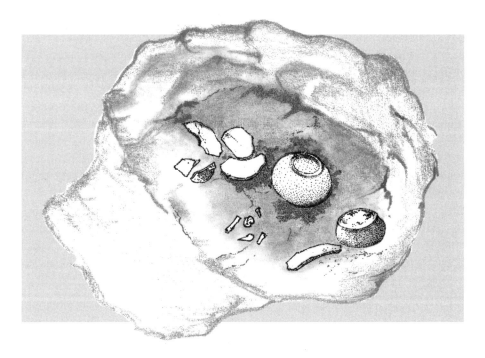

Fig. 13.1 Cremation pit with human ashes and pots from Soufli Magoula
(after Gallis 1982).

kinds of pottery: first, typical EN monochrome pottery, which was found either
unburnt or heavily burnt (Gallis 1982). According to Gallis, 'the broken monochrome vases mixed with the bones were evidently smashed intentionally, and
indeed in some cases over the funerary pyre' (Gallis 1996a: 172). In addition to
the EN Monochrome, the pits also contained from one to three crudely made
miniature vessels of about 5 to 6 cm in diameter that seem to have been fired
in the funeral pyre itself (Gallis 1982, 1996a). Other than the pots, which
include finely made fruit-stands and bowls, grave goods were limited to fragments of animal bones and to a rubbing stone found in a double cremation (no.
10). Fragments of human bones were found in all pits. In several cases the bones
belonged to different individuals, but this could be due to accidental mixing
from the pyres. Not much precision could be given as to the sex or age, but the
cremations seemingly concerned adults of both sexes as well as juveniles and
one infant.

Several features are noteworthy in the example of Soufli: the concentration
of burials in a special burial ground[6] on the side of the settlement, the complex
funerary rituals, and the presence of indisputable grave goods that include specific offerings like the miniature vessels.

---

[6] Gallis (1996a: 171) considers it cannot be called a cemetery, but the reason is unclear.

These cremations recall finds from the small cave of Prosymna, near the Argive Heraion. There, several shallow pits dug into the cave floor contained charcoals and, in three cases, fragmentary burnt human bones (Blegen 1937). Though the cave contained EN material (Phelps 1975), these cremations should probably be dated to the Middle Neolithic (Cavanagh and Mee 1998: 8; Gallis 1996a: 176; Hourmouziadis 1973: 209). Yet both instances are revealing: Prosymna is located in a cave related to a settlement that has not yet been discovered. The Soufli burial ground is located at the periphery of its tell, in an area that is rarely reached in small-scale excavations. There is thus a distinct possibility that such cemeteries, located away from the core of the settlement, constituted a regular feature rather than an exception.[7]

Since the practice of cremation is demonstrated in the Early Neolithic, another alternative put forward by Hourmouziadis, that of ash dispersal, also becomes plausible. However, other funerary practices also could account for the scarcity of intramuros burials. Cremations and inhumations are usually not exclusive in the European Neolithic, and cemeteries with regular pit-burials, a few hundred metres away from the settlements, could also have gone unrecognized.[8]

Accounting for the exceptions: intra-settlement pit-burials

Considering the duration of the Early Neolithic and the population estimates (see ch. 6), it is clear, conversely, that intra-settlement burials are a rarity. Looking at the situation in retrospect, one cannot see how it could have been otherwise: if every inhabitant of these long-duration settlements had been buried in a pit, within the precincts of the living, the whole space would have been rapidly filled with funerary pits![9]

As the single burial from Sesklo clearly demonstrates, very few individuals were buried directly around the houses. Can we, thus, make sense of these rare exceptions to the rule? Discussing the Sesklo, Starčevo and Karanovo I cultures of the Balkans, Gimbutas (1991: 331) observed that intramuros burials mainly comprised children, adolescents and females. Burial sites for males were conspicuously lacking. This, in her opinion, demonstrated the high status of women and children and their strong ties to the house. But I believe that the obverse interpretation is equally, if not more, plausible.

Amongst intra-settlement burials, the most frequent in Greece are primary pit-burials.[10] With two exceptions, they consist of single burials. At Nea

---

[7] Let us recall that the LN cemetery of Plateia Magoula Zarkou was also discovered by chance, thanks to a drainage ditch, a few hundred metres away from the *magoula* (Gallis 1982).

[8] It may be relevant that the only two LN cemeteries known to date, from Soufli and Plateia Zarkou Magoula, also contained cremations only. Cemeteries with inhumations have not yet been found before the Final Neolithic.

[9] For an excellent discussion of the spatial problems involved in 'funerary rituals', i.e., by the double process of treating the corpse in its materiality and taking care, through rituals, of the affective shock and social trauma, see Leclerc 1997.

[10] The other instance, illustrated by Prodromos, will be discussed below.

Nikomedeia more than twenty individual graves were uncovered (Rodden 1962; Rodden and Rodden 1964b).[11] One Early Neolithic pit-burial each was also found at Soufli, Sesklo, Argissa and Kephalovrysso. Five more were reported from the deepest levels at Lerna, of which three at least seem to be regular pit-burials rather than bone scatters (Caskey 1956, 1957, 1958). However, their date is difficult to ascertain as they could have been dug from early Middle Neolithic strata. Finally, the four possibly Early Neolithic infant burials from Franchthi are all pit-burials, some of the pits being lined or capped with stones. The only exceptions to the norm of single burials are two triple burials from Nea Nikomedeia, one of a woman holding two children, the other one with three children.

The pits are usually located outside the houses or, more rarely, in collapsed buildings. In two instances only, at Soufli and Kephalovrysso, the burial was found under a house floor but nothing in the available data indicates more than a random association. The burial pits are shallow and irregular. They were dug without care, and it seems clear that in most instances clay digging-pits or rubbish pits, too small to hold an extended body, were re-employed as burial-pits.[12] This would explain the flexed position of the bodies, which can hardly be considered as part of a ritual expression: there is no regular pattern in the degree of flexion, orientation or position of the body. The dead variously lay on their side, their back or their face, sometimes in rather awkward positions imposed by the shape of the pit.[13] None was adorned (Kyparissi-Apostolika 1992), and one child only, at Lerna, was accompanied by a small ceramic vase of EN type.[14] Otherwise, scattered animal bones that could easily be part of the rubbish fill are the only possible 'grave goods'.

As pointed out by Rodden (1962) and Jacobsen and Cullen (1981), there is, on the whole, an absence of emphasis on the visibility of the dead and little indication of ritual elaboration: 'remarkably little attention appears to have been focused on the disposal of the dead' (Rodden and Rodden 1964b: 607). Needless to say, considering the amount of time, fuel and care required for the complete cremation of a human body, the contrast between these casual intramuros inhumations and the Soufli cremations could not be stronger.

A further contrast is underlined by the absence of noticeable grave goods. Both observations would appear to confirm that these burials are 'atypical', and that they concern individuals who were denied normal funerary rituals.

---

[11] The higher number of burials from Nea Nikomedeia partly reflects the more extensive excavations.

[12] Here, for instance, is how Hourmouziadis describes the burial from Kephalovrysso: 'The corpse was found buried in a shallow pit with the legs extended and crossed, the right one over the left one. It seems that the body had to be folded in order to fit into the pit, which had certainly not been dug to its size' (Hourmouziadis 1973b: 210).

[13] See the triple burial of children at Nea Nikomedeia, illustrated in Rodden and Rodden 1964b: fig. 14.

[14] But K. D. Vitelli points out that these dark burnished monochrome vases continue into the Middle Neolithic and cannot provide a definite dating for the burial (*in litt.*, 7/96).

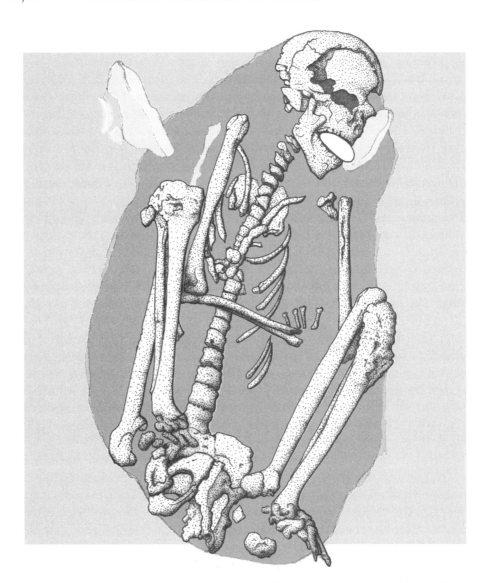

Fig. 13.2 Male burial in a pit from Nea Nikomedeia, with a pebble stuck into the mouth (after a photograph by J. Rodden, published in Theocharis 1973).

Ethnographic data provide ample evidence of individuals who could not be buried according to the normal rituals, either because they did not reach the required age or status, or because of the conditions of their death (violent death or illness, for instance). The pebble stuck into the jaws of the tightly flexed male adult at Nea Nikomedeia (Rodden and Rodden 1964b: fig. 21) certainly suggests that there was something unusual about this man or about his death.

Statistics by sex and age of the pit-burials cannot be provided until the burials from Nea Nikomedeia have been published in detail. But it is noteworthy that, according to the presently available data, children predominate over adults.[15] If the data from Nea Nikomedeia confirm this age distribution, it could give strong support to the hypothesis of individuals denied normal funerary rituals, most often because they had not reached the required age or social status.

Ossuaries, secondary burials or ancestor cults?

As stated earlier, pit-burials are normally found outside, not inside houses. In this respect, as in many others, the 'multiple secondary burial' found below a house floor at Prodromos 1 appears quite exceptional.

Hourmouziadis, who excavated it, describes it as follows:

Here, beneath the floor of a large neolithic house, three successive deposits of skeletal remains were found, consisting of eleven human skulls and a few other broken thigh and rib bones. Scattered among them were sherds of plain coloured pots as well as three silica tools. These skeletal remains had not been arranged in an orderly fashion, a fact which leads to the conclusion that they were not connected with a funerary rite. In the excavator's opinion, the eleven skulls as well as the other bones had been transported into the house from some other site where the dead had lain for their preliminary burial. In other words, in Neolithic Prodromos we have a case of exhumation and reburial. (Hourmouziadis 1973b: 210)

What Hourmouziadis meant by stating that the bones 'were not connected with a funerary rite' is slightly unclear. 'Exhumation and reburial' certainly belong to 'funerary rituals', including those of contemporaneous Greece. Or did he mean that the bones were simply thrown away? The human bone deposit from Prodromos can indeed be interpreted in two different ways. Given the disorderly distribution of the bones, it could be considered, minimally, as an ossuary.[16] Alternately, it could represent secondary burials. Broadly speaking, mixed human bones in secondary position can be deposited in two drastically different situations. In the first case, the bones have lost all relations to specific individuals; they have become 'reified', that is, dishumanized, and are disposed of all together in ossuaries, usually to make more space for the incoming deceased in the initial burial ground (Leclerc 1997: 400). In the other case, to the contrary, selected and symbolically meaningful bones of known individuals are collected and preserved, either openly displayed or deposited in special locations. Ossuaries, *sensu stricto,* are normally required when restricted burial chambers are used repeatedly for collective burials, a pattern unknown

---

[15] Three adults are reported so far from Nea Nikomedeia (including the woman with two children), one at Sesklo, one at Soufli and one at Kephalovrysso. Five children so far are reported from Nea Nikomedeia, one at Soufli, one at Argissa. The five 'burials' from Lerna were all of children, and the four possibly EN burials from the Paralia at Franchthi were all babies' burials.

[16] In the sense of bones from several individuals mixed together and set aside or thrown away (Leclerc 1997: 399–400).

in Greece. Thus, at Prodromos the selection of bones, the over-representation of skulls and the location of the deposit beneath a house floor would rather indicate the deliberate preservation of meaningful remains.

The deposition of skulls under house floors recalls the well-known Near Eastern practice, otherwise strikingly absent in Greece. The presence of eleven skulls together (and the mention of a 'large' house?) further evokes the separate deposits of skulls in ceremonial buildings, such as the 'house of the dead' at Çayönü (Özdoğan and Özdoğan 1990). Unfortunately, Prodromos has never been published in detail: it is thus impossible to pursue this line of inquiry and determine whether this 'large' house presented other unusual features.

At any rate, the discovery from Prodromos reflects practices quite different from the pit-burials or from the cremations from Soufli. In many societies, the exhumation of selected bones from a deceased corresponds to a change of status, from deceased to ancestor. But if some sort of ancestor cult or, more generally, of selective secondary burial, was practised in Early Neolithic Greece, why would Prodromos stand out as an exception? Should we attribute it, again, to the chance discovery of a collective ritual locus, not usually brought to light by limited excavations?[17]

In fact, individual 'secondary burials' have been mentioned at other sites, in particular at Franchthi (Jacobsen and Cullen 1981). 'Bone scatters', their logical complement if some bones have been left aside, have been found at Nea Nikomedeia (Rodden 1962), Tsoungiza (Blegen 1975) and Franchthi (Jacobsen and Cullen 1981). But Collins Cook and Cullen, working on the Franchthi human bones, now wonder whether 'secondary burial' and 'bone scatters' do not simply represent disturbed primary burials (Collins Cook and Cullen, in prep.). Given the casual treatment of primary burials within settlements and the apparent absence of grave markers, such disturbances would have been inevitable (Cavanagh and Mee 1998: 6). On the other hand, the evidence from Prodromos demonstrates, at least, that exhumation and manipulation of the bones were indeed practised during the Early Neolithic in Greece. The hypothesis that secondary burials existed at that time should not be altogether rejected.

Discussion

This reanalysis of 'funerary rituals' has allowed us to distinguish at least three different patterns: the first, exemplified by the cremations from Soufli, is characterized by the existence of a distinct sepulchral area, by complex rituals, by the presence of grave goods and, seemingly, the predominance of adults. The second, found in many settlements, is characterized by the absence of a distinct sepulchral area, by burial practices reduced to the minimum, by the absence of

---

[17] It took many years of *extensive* excavations before the exceptional 'house of the dead' at Çayönü, which contained the remains of about 400 individuals, was discovered.

grave goods and the apparent predominance of children. The third, exemplified by Prodromos 1, implies the exhumation and reburial of selected parts of the skeleton. It relates to a later stage of the death rituals, and may indicate the existence of ancestor cults.

I have argued that only the first case reflects, albeit certainly partially, the 'normal' funerary rituals that were applied to the majority of the population. If this argument is accepted, then earlier conclusions about the domestic character of funerary rituals, their important variability, the lack of grave goods and the lack of emphasis on death rituals (e.g., Demoule and Perlès 1993) are unwarranted, if not straightforwardly wrong.

This has a bearing on two fundamental issues, one pertaining to ideology, the other to social structures. First, if it is admitted that the vast majority of people were *not* buried within or near houses, then the strong symbolic association between the house and the dead, claimed for the early periods of the Neolithic in the Near East and Balkanic Europe (Cauvin 1997; Chapman 1994a, 1994c; Hodder 1990), would not hold true in Greece.[18] To the contrary, the abundance of figurines and rarity of burials might tentatively suggest an opposition between fertility, or 'life' rituals, performed within or around houses, and funerary rituals, performed in collective spaces outside the living area.

However, if the deceased were not usually associated with the *house*, they were still associated with the *village*, that is, with the community of the living. The burial ground from Soufli, if representative, was close enough to the core of the settlement to underlie the strong links between the living and the dead. The skull and bone deposit from Prodromos further suggests that selected individuals were brought back within the living quarters, again collectively. The strongest relation thus appears to be not between individuals, live and dead, but between the deceased, taken collectively, and a collectivity of live individuals. Whether the latter comprised the whole village, or only segments of the community such as lineages, is impossible to ascertain. The excavation at Soufli was too limited to determine the extent of the burial ground and the number of cremations. The discovery of a cremation 8 metres from the main concentration suggests a more extended burial ground, possibly divided into discrete quarters. There is no way to tell, in fact, whether this was the only burial ground associated with the village, or whether each of its main components had its own separate burial ground.

The second consequence of this reanalysis of funerary rituals pertains to the social structure: intra-settlement pit-burials, and in particular the absence of grave goods, can no longer be used, *per se*, to infer an absence of social differentiation.

---

[18] Chapman suggests, concerning the intramuros pit-burials of the the Körös culture of Hungary, that, 'Most inhumations are deposited within the settlement, in pits or on unoccupied parts of the site, so as to include some of the ancestors in the local settlement context of living' (Chapman 1994c: 80). In the case of Greece, the apparent predominance of children in pit-burials would rule out this interpretation.

The systematic absence of grave goods appears to be directly related to the special way the dead were disposed of, not to the way the living society was organized. However, where grave goods are present – the cremations from Soufli – they are indeed remarkably consistent in nature and number in the different deposits. Thus far, the Early Neolithic society in Greece would indeed appear to be fairly 'egalitarian', a problem that will be explored in more detail in the following chapter.

CHAPTER 14

INTERACTIONS AMONG THE LIVING

In the densely settled regions of northern Greece, interaction between individuals, families and groups was not only a necessity, but also an unavoidable consequence of settlement patterns. Interactions, willingly or unwillingly, peacefully or aggressively, were constantly taking place at many different levels: within the household, within the village community, with neighbouring communities or with more distant groups. 'How to deal with others', when 'others' were both numerous and variously related – or unrelated – to oneself, was probably the most difficult problem these early Neolithic societies had to solve. How and to what degree this universal problem was solved depends in large part on the social structures in general and, in particular, on the nature of the institutions developed to regulate conflicts.

Early Neolithic societies have long been considered 'simple', lacking status and role differentiation as well as hierarchical institutions. But some time ago Sherratt had already opposed Childe's vision of Neolithic societies as 'simple', arguing that the ability to organize large-scale exchanges without hierarchical control was, by itself, indicative of some form of complexity (Sherratt 1982: 15). There is indeed no sociological reason why a 'complex' society should necessarily be organized along hierarchical lines, even if hierarchy is a frequent outcome of socioeconomic differentiation. Early Neolithic Greece provides evidence for differentiated status, roles and functions, and for intense interaction at all levels of society. Yet, there is no evidence that the organizing principles were of a hierarchical order.

The status of the individual

There are indeed few *conspicuous* elements to suggest that some individuals or families possessed an institutionalized superior status, that is, that there existed a stable and transmittable hierarchy.

The latter is often expressed in architecture, and we have indeed insisted on the variability in building techniques. However, these techniques, *per se*, can hardly be taken as evidence of hierarchical differences. All the techniques employed are costly in terms of manpower, energy and time, and none can be singled out as more demanding than the others. Conversely, the size of the houses also varies and the construction of larger houses obviously required that larger taskforces were assembled. Yet, aside from the largest and somewhat problematic buildings from Nea Nikomedeia, we are apparently dealing with a continuum, and there is no evidence that each settlement contained domestic houses that were *systematically* larger than the other ones. No privileged location, either, can be singled out, and as far as one can tell the content of the houses did not drastically differ in abundance and wealth. 'In other words, while domestic architecture may reflect marked inequalities in the size and success of individual households, these villages may have been technically "egalitarian" in that inequality was achieved and transient rather than ascribed or institutionalized' (Halstead 1995: 13). This lack of direct evidence, however, is far from compelling: no settlement has been excavated in its totality, no detailed comparison of the content of individual houses can be made from the published data. One can legitimately wonder, for instance, whether the systematic presence of a single large building in Linearbandkeramik settlements would have been recognized if the latter had been excavated on the small surfaces characteristic of most excavations in Greece.

The funerary data are not of outstanding quality either, but they too support the hypothesis of basically egalitarian societies. A negative feature may be the most revealing in this sense: there are no monumental graves sheltering the remains of single or few individuals enriched by exotic grave goods.[1] Burial rituals did not require the participation of more than a few persons at a time, and the graves either lacked grave goods, or displayed a similar array of fine pottery and miniature vessels (see ch. 13). Ornaments are, unfortunately, conspicuously absent from these burials (Kyparissi-Apostolika 1992). Nor do the location and modalities of burial indicate differences of treatment or of status between men and women. Only young children seem to have been treated differently, but this may only mean they had not reached the required social status for normal burial rituals.

So far, the data that are usually called for as indexes of social differentiation do not allow discrimination of more than the obvious age groups. When more indirect information is called for, a more nuanced situation is brought to light. It suggests that status was indeed differentiated, though not necessarily hierarchically organized.

A first potential axis of differentiation was craft specialization. Technological data have clearly indicated a distribution of tasks and some degree of craft specialization, both between groups and within settlements (see ch. 10). I have already suggested, following Helms (1988), that the knowledge of distant places possessed by those who procured obsidian and honey-flint blades may have given them a special prestige. In parallel, Björk (1995: 134) and Vitelli (1993: 217) both envisioned pottery-making as a prestige or status-loaded activity because of the ceremonial and cultic functions they attribute

---

[1] As in the Carnacean or Cerny monumental graves, for instance.

to Early Neolithic pottery in Greece. In addition, Vitelli underlines the special powers conveyed by the mastery of fire and the transformation of dry, brittle clay into permanently hard vessels (Vitelli, in Perlès and Vitelli 1999). The notion that potters had a special status accords well with numerous ethnographic examples, where potters often belong to endogamous castes or professional groups. The latter are frequently of low or marginal status, unless pottery carries a powerful social or ritual symbolism (Arnold D. 1985: 198), as seems to have been the case in Early Neolithic Greece. Similarly, J. Arnold remarked that the importance of shell beads among the Chumash Indians conferred a fairly high status to the specialized bead makers (Arnold J. 1995: 95), and this is precisely a domain where we have found indications of craft specialization. More generally, craft specialists on the north-west coast of North America possessed a high status, which was in part linked to a secrecy concerning their techniques (Ames 1995). Elsewhere on the contrary, most notably in India and Africa, artisans often belong to castes of inferior status. Thus, whether higher, lower, or simply different, even part-time craft specialization may have been conducive to status differentiation in the Early Neolithic of Greece. It is, in fact, one of the factors considered determinant in the development of heterarchical social organizations, with their 'flexible hierarchy and lateral differentiation' (White and Pigott 1996: 151).

Another line of evidence pertains to artefacts that can be considered 'valuables' because of their rarity, the skills and time required for their manufacture, and the quality of the raw material selected. Stone vessels, stone discs, earstuds, pins, stamp-seals, large perforated polished spheres, elaborate ornaments in stone or shell are the most conspicuous artefacts that fit this definition. Most indeed have clay counterparts, much more easily and quickly manufactured. Consequently, the use of such hard and often lovely looking raw materials is a deliberate choice, not an intrinsic attribute of these categories of artefacts. The point is not to claim that they all had a similar function, which they clearly did not, but to underline that there existed artefacts that not every individual or household possessed.

Fragments of stone vessels and dishes from secure Early Neolithic contexts were found in only six sites (see ch. 10). Aside from Nea Makri, which yielded numerous fragments, one to three specimens only were recovered in each site. Despite the small size of most excavations,[2] it is thus doubtful that stone vessels were present in each settlement and each household. One of them, found in the earliest occupation level at Achilleion, is of breathtaking craftsmanship, and must have required quite an exceptional block of raw material (Gimbutas *et al.* 1989: fig. 8.18). It was found broken, as were almost all the other specimens. This is indeed an intriguing feature of stone vessels: they were rare and certainly valued possessions, yet, they are very rarely found intact. The

---

[2] Curiously, no stone vessel has been reported from Nea Nikomedeia.

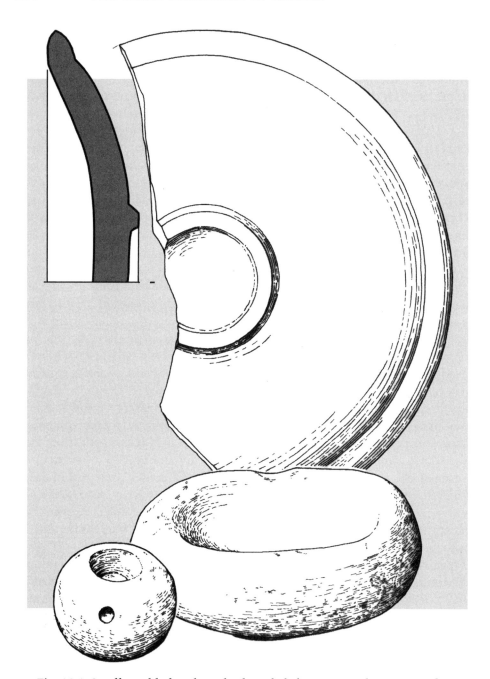

Fig. 14.1 Small marble bowls and schist dish from Magoula Tourcoyefira, Magoula Mezourlo and Achilleion (after Gimbutas *et al.* 1989 and Papathanassopoulos 1996).

'marble vessels' cited in the literature often turn out to be small and disappointing fragments. Only the very thick EN1 pieces appear to be largely intact, but even this is not certain.

Why should stone vessels break so systematically, and in such small fragments? Even if dropped on hard beaten clay floors, they would not break easily. Why are there no mending holes either, when the latter are frequent on broken clay vessels? Do we only find the remnants of vessels broken during manufacture? In that case, why should they be so rare and why have no complete specimens been found?

Dikaios considered that the stone vessels he found at Khirokitia in human burials were intentionally broken (Dikaios 1953: 219, 230, quoted in Le Brun 1989: 75). Le Brun himself concurs that the flat spouted stone dishes were specifically associated with burial practices (Le Brun 1989: 75–6). Our data, in Greece, are much less informative: no specific context emerges from the literature, but at least one small (MN) stone vessel was indeed associated with a child burial at Franchthi (Jacobsen and Cullen 1981).[3] Yet, their state of preservation remains puzzling. Was their breakage part of a ritual use? Or should we evoke, alternatively, the socially required destruction of valuable possessions?

The longer and finer earstuds are also usually fragmentary. Rodden suggested the smaller specimens were possible ear ornaments and the larger specimens pins (Rodden and Rodden 1964b). Nandris, for his part, considered them headpins, by analogy with figurines from Nea Nikomedeia (Nandris 1970), while their French denomination, 'labrets', suggests they were inserted into the lip. A plausible interpretation, considering the differences in sizes, is their use for holding woven or leather clothes. All indeed are characterized by a prominent head, but otherwise they vary in length and shape.[4] Besides the clay specimens,[5] they are made of various fine rocks – steatite, serpentine, quartz, marble – which were finely carved and polished. They demonstrate a clear continuity of traditions with the Initial Neolithic earstuds, but EN specimens display higher craftsmanship and more varied shapes than their earlier counterparts. Rodden considers that, given the time and care involved in their manufacture, they must have had a special value (Rodden and Rodden 1964b: 604).[6] Interesting possibilities of long-distance trade have been raised by Nandris (1977b: 296), who stated that the 'green serpentine' from which earstuds from Soufli, Argissa,[7] and Nea Nikomedeia were carved was in fact a nephrite,

---

[3] It too had a large fragment missing on one side.
[4] Papaefthymiou-Papanthimou and Pilali-Papasteriou 1997: fig. 11; Theocharis 1963b: fig. 37, 1967: pl. XII B; Wijnen 1981: 46–7.
[5] Found at Sesklo and Giannitsa B, in particular. One had also been found in the Initial Neolithic at Argissa.
[6] On the north-west coast of America, labrets, as our earstuds are called there, were worn only by high-status women. Ames (1995: 165, n.1) notes that most were broken when recovered, and wonders whether this could be related to the will to maintain the value of labrets as status-markers. Rodden and Rodden (1964b) also note that the tips of the small earstuds at Nea Nikomedeia were broken.   [7] Nandris must be referring here to the 'Initial Neolithic' earstuds.

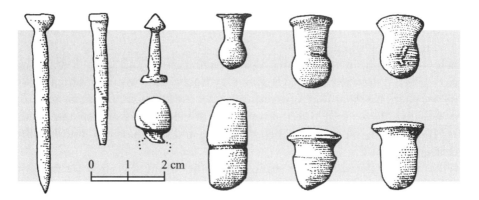

Fig. 14.2 Stone earstuds and pins from Soufli, Sesklo, Achilleion and Nea
Nikomedeia (after Gimbutas *et al.* 1989, Rodden 1965 and
Theocharis 1967).

coming from the high parts of the Pindus Range. This contradicted Rodden's
observation, according to which the earstuds from Nea Nikomedeia were
carved on a green or blue serpentine coming from outcrops of the Vermion
mountains that back the Macedonian Plain. Unfortunately this issue, to my
knowledge, has not been pursued.

Earstuds can hardly be considered as 'frequent' (*contra* Nandris 1970: 198) or
distributed 'all over Greece' (Wijnen 1981: 46–7). To the contrary, they show a
well-differentiated geographical distribution: of the ten Early Neolithic sites
where I have recorded earstuds, eight are located in Thessaly[8] and two in
Macedonia (Nea Nikomedeia and Giannitsa B).[9] In Thessaly they seem to be
restricted to the early phases of the EN, but they are well represented in
western Macedonia in later EN contexts. If earstuds are to be thought of as personal ornaments or pins for clothes, their restricted geographical distribution
and limited number[10] clearly indicates that few individuals in fact wore them.
Interestingly, the geometrically engraved stamps, which have sometimes also
been considered as a way to adorn oneself, follow an identical geographical distribution.

Stone 'stamp-seals' are not only rare, but, on first reading, they would seem
to be good candidates for individual identification. Unfortunately, this is the
one interpretation that can be thoroughly rejected: the motifs consist of a
small range of geometric patterns that can be found from the Indus to the
Carpathians. There is clearly no attempt at any individualization of the motifs,

---

[8] Gediki, Magoula Koskina, Sesklo, Soufli, Achilleion, Zappeio 1, Ayios Georgios Larisas 2,
Elasson 2. I do not believe my list to be exhaustive, but it is certainly representative.
[9] The only stud I know in southern Greece is from Dendra, in the Argolid. It was on display at the
Archaeological Museum of Nafplion, but could be of earlier date.
[10] About fifty stone specimens have been recovered altogether, but half come from Nea
Nikomedeia.

and therefore, of their owner. One motif, however, appears to be specific to Thessaly: it is a complex design of interlocking meanders, more commonly found on stone than on clay. This elaborate pattern is characteristic of the MN, but was already found on an EN specimen at Pyrassos (see ch. 11). It is the only instance of a motif that may characterize, if not specific individuals, at least a regional community.

Steatite, marble, or even clay stamps are very rare in the Early Neolithic of Greece (Makkay 1984; Pilali-Papasteriou 1992). They come, again, from Thessaly and western Macedonia exclusively, and only two stone specimens can be attributed to Early Neolithic stratified contexts at Pyrassos[11] and Sesklo[12]. If their interpretation as stamps for the decoration of woven cloth is correct, this would imply that the majority were in fact made of wood.[13] Since stone and clay specimens share the same motifs and technical characteristics, and thus, presumably, the same function, the rarity and exceptional craftsmanship of the steatite and marble specimens[14] must be seen as deliberate. The possession and use of stone stamps must have been restricted to a few individuals or occasions.

Other stone objects worth mentioning in this context are the outstanding greenstone axes from Nea Nikomedeia, and the superbly polished and perforated spheres found at Sesklo (Theocharis 1973b: fig. 273) and Franchthi, again, in a broken state. Rare stone 'sling bullets' also exist, but none, to my knowledge, has been recovered from a reliable EN context.

All of these stone artefacts had their equivalent in clay, and certainly also in wood. Yet, on rare occasions, the trouble was taken to produce them in raw materials far more difficult to work, but also more durable. Their possession and use probably conferred or confirmed a special role or status to the owner. Whether this pertained to wealth, to social or to ritual functions, will probably remain unknown. However, it can be considered as indirect evidence of status differentiation within the community.

It is also noteworthy that most of the artefacts discussed above showed a restricted geographic distribution: with few exceptions, they came only from Thessaly and western Macedonia. Since the far more abundant clay figurines follow a similar pattern, it is unlikely that this distribution can be attributed solely to excavations biases. It may, to the contrary, confirm the hypothesis of

[11] This beautiful seal is firmly dated from the middle EN stratum in the original publication (Theocharis 1959: 64–6) and this attribution is retained in Theocharis 1967: 149. Pilali-Papasteriou (1992: 21) attributes it to the MN, probably on stylistic grounds since it is very close to MN specimens. Yet I see no stratigraphic reason to doubt the original dating.

[12] This specimen (Pilali-Papasteriou 1992: no. 2; Theocharis 1973b: pl. XX, bottom row, right) bears an unusual linear pattern of three parallel grooves that evokes a needle polisher. However, a clay seal from Nea Nikomedeia (Rodden 1964b: top row, right; Makkay 1984: no. 169) bears a fragmentary design of a similar kind, which can support the former interpretation.

[13] Actually the most common raw material for textile stamps.

[14] Perhaps the most outstanding is an MN marble specimen from Achilleion, called a 'game board'. It shows the typical Thessalian meander pattern, but drawn obliquely (Gimbutas *et al.* 1989: fig. 7.73).

a more complex social differentiation in regions of denser settlement and higher demography (see ch. 12). More intense social relations would have thus led to increased heterarchy (Ehrenreich *et al.* 1995) and to an increased use of items of personal identification and social display.

Interaction within the village community

Because the settlement was repeatedly rebuilt on its own foundations, it constituted a stable, permanent physical entity that corresponded to a social 'node', according to Chapman's expression (Chapman 1994c). One way or another, the village had to function as a community. Precisely how, is what may help us define the social and economic relations within Early Neolithic societies.

There is no doubt that a village of more than 100 to 200 inhabitants would have been composed of several discrete social units, such as age classes, sub-clans or lineages. They would have constituted an intermediary level, or a series of intermediary levels, between the household and the village community in many technical, economic, social or ritual activities. One can assume, for instance, that the building of a house entailed the co-operation of a large taskforce for which kinsfolk and affines were recruited, or that any death entailed collective rituals performed by specific segments of the families concerned. Yet, in the present state of our data, these various levels remain impossible to distinguish. Not surprisingly, only the extreme ends of this continuum of embedded social units, the household and the village as a whole, can somehow be individualized.

As a consequence, Neolithic villages are often casually taken as an economic unit in terms of subsistence strategies. In more argumented cases, they are considered, more plausibly, as an aggregation of economic units larger than the household. However, when discussing the nature of socioeconomic units within a village community, a distinction should be made between production and consumption (Holl 1990). In our context, the situation seems clear as far as production is concerned: there is no evidence for a collective organization of production. There are no collective granaries, no recognizable collective animal pens, no concentrations of agrarian implements in specific areas of the settlement. As remarked by Halstead, 'architectural evidence from neolithic Greece suggests that a family household, whether nuclear or extended, was literally walled off as the basic unit of residence, production and consumption' (Halstead 1995: 20). Indeed, the presence of the whole range of domesticates in each house, together with that of hearths and ovens, suggest that the household was also simultaneously the unit of production and, to a large extent, the unit of consumption.

Yet, Halstead also considers that individual households would not have been viable economic units in the long term, and that the 'tendency to domestic iso-

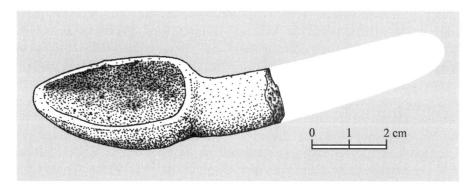

Fig. 14.3 Clay spoon from Achilleion (after Gimbutas *et al.* 1989).

lation' had to be counteracted by mechanisms that reinforced solidarity at the level of the village community (Halstead 1995: 16). Precisely such mechanisms would have been at play at the level of food consumption. The presence of hearths and ovens outside the houses, in open courtyards, would have entailed an obligation to share food with one's neighbours not only on special occasions, but on a regular basis. The community would thus have functioned in a system of reciprocal obligations that simultaneously balanced individual risk and maintained equality between households (Halstead 1989a: 74).

This might well be the case, but the basis of the argument is unconvincing: hearths are located inside houses as often as outside (see ch. 9), and even when cooking is done outside and in full view of other inhabitants, it is clear from numerous ethnographic observations that no compulsory sharing is necessarily required. Furthermore, the theory of widespread sharing as a risk-reduction strategy amongst farming groups has recently been challenged by Plog (1995: 196–7), who states, concerning Pueblo groups, that 'exchange intensity increased when conditions for agriculture were better and surpluses were more likely', and not when risk was at a maximum. Other motives for sharing and other categories of shared goods are indeed equally plausible. The exchange between households of breeding animals, in particular, would have been a genetic necessity if the estimates concerning the size of the herds are correct (see ch. 8). Halstead points out that 'to maintain genetic diversity in the long term, a breeding population of several hundred individuals of each species would be needed' (Halstead 1992: 23). As a consequence, 'exchange of livestock would have integrated a number of herds small enough to be manageable at a household level into breeding populations large enough to be demographically viable', the latter requiring not only exchanges between households within the same village, but also occasionally between different villages.

Another occasion for exchanging food or goods between households would have been reciprocal co-operation for agricultural tasks. Co-operation during the most demanding phases of the agricultural cycle, such as field clearing and

harvesting, is basically a necessity in non-mechanized agriculture. Such temporary co-operation, based on filiation, alliance and individual association,
entails not only reciprocity, but usually also some collective feasting or food
and drink consumption. The larger hearths and pit-hearths already described
may well have served in these occasions, and the consumption of cattle may
plausibly have taken place during these collective festive meals.

Co-operation for house-building or agricultural work would not have
required the presence of the whole village community: subgroups constituted
of particular kinsmen, affines or friends would have sufficed. On the other
hand, the village must have occasionally functioned as a unit for collective
tasks such as digging the ditches at Nea Nikomedeia or building the terracing
walls on the Paralia at Franchthi. This entailed collective decisions and co-
ordination, probably taken at the level of a village council, though the presence
of a village chief cannot be ruled out. Such a council, possibly constituted of
elders or of heads of lineages, would have had to deal also with 'invisible' but
equally important issues such as settling land disputes, managing water
resources, sending delegations to other villages, and so forth. In addition, it
could also have had ritual functions.

Whether the village as a whole constituted a ritual unit for specific cremo-
nies can be debated.[15] There is no definite evidence for collective ceremonial
buildings (see ch. 12) but collective rituals can take place anywhere within or
around the village. Many spectacular dances and ceremonies that involve the
whole village are documented ethnographically; in most cases, they leave no
archaeological trace.

The burial ground from Soufli Magoula (ch. 12) demonstrates that collective
loci did exist however, at least for funerary rituals. However, whether it concerned the whole village or only a smaller fraction remains uncertain. The small
size of this rescue excavation does not allow us to discriminate between a village
and a lineage burial ground, for instance. In all probability, rituals were taking
place at different levels of the village social and ritual organization. Without a
clearly identifiable central authority, collective rituals would have been a powerful integrative mechanism. Sherratt's discussion of the fifth-millennium communities of the Hungarian plain seems perfectly appropriate for our context:

Control within the community, however, was a problem common to all. This
control may have been accomplished by ritual and ideological means rather than
by more overt expressions of power. The elaboration of cult objects at this period
indicates the existence of ritual codes shared by all communities of the area.
Relations within groups could thus have been regulated by ritual; those between
groups by selective alliance. (Sherratt 1982: 22)

The issue of alliances raises the question of the village as a genetically viable
population. The answer is most probably negative, if only for demographic

[15] As it does nowadays as a parish, for instance.

reasons: if the population estimates are right, a mean of *c.* 100–200 inhabitants, including children and aged individuals, would have been insufficient to sustain a viable endogamous breeding network in the long term. In smaller settlements, exogamy would have been even more of a requirement. Sociological reasons also would have reinforced the need for external alliances: in densely settled areas, alliances, whether through intermarriage or through individual partnerships, would have helped to offset potential conflicts between closely spaced villages.

Interaction between communities

Trade or warfare?

Intermarriage between families is a classic means of settling inter-family feuds, just as trade, on a more general level, is usually considered the alternative to war (Dalton 1977). Yet Keeley recently argued that marriage, through conflicts over the bride-price or dowry, and trade, through lack of perceived reciprocity, are just as much *causes* for conflicts than means of avoiding them (Keeley 1996). In the context of closely spaced villages, conflicts concerning land exploitation, water resources and animal grazing would also have been inevitable. Propinquity invites interaction, interaction increases the chances of dispute (Keeley 1996: 122–3).

A priori, the density of human population and settlement in Thessaly would thus lead to a high risk of conflicts. Unless intra- and inter-group institutions were powerful enough to impose pacific solutions, these conflicts could easily have escalated into physical violence.

However, we have no evidence of the latter. None of the skeletons recovered in the Early Neolithic showed traces of violent, traumatic death. Bone and stone projectile points are conspicuously scarce in the Early Neolithic. The only known case of an EN settlement surrounded by walls or ditches, Nea Nikomedeia, may correspond to the 'frontier situation' described by Keeley (1996: 131–8): Nea Nikomedeia is the northernmost settlement sharing some Thessalian pottery styles, and it is contemporaneous with the earliest settlements of Balkanic influence founded on the other side of the Giannitsa Gulf. However, other explanations can be offered (see ch. 9), and extended excavations of other settlements may also reveal a will to delimit the village space. Finally, although some buildings have been destroyed by fire, there is no evidence for a complete destruction by fire of any Early Neolithic village.

'One social reason for war is that peace is too costly to maintain', says Keeley (1996: 159). Yet in contexts such as ours, the reverse may well have been true. If the regular, multidirectional network of villages was paralleled by a similar network of alliances, any conflict between two local groups would have rapidly degenerated into a regional, large-scale conflict. I thus agree with Halstead that 'early Greek villages invested heavily in maintaining peaceful co-existence rather than a state of "warre" or latent hostility between communities.' (Halstead 1995: 14).

Frequent and peaceful interaction between the different village communities is indicated by the strong stylistic homogeneity of the pottery. Early Neolithic pottery production relies on a limited repertoire of technical knowledge and practices, but this alone does not explain the similarities in shapes, sizes and surface treatment all over Greece. There clearly existed shared norms that prevailed over the tendency to individualization (Perlès and Vitelli 1994). Since these norms were not maintained through a wide circulation of pots (see below), a frequent circulation of people, or maybe itinerant potters, seems implied. The case is even more clearly exemplified in the Middle Neolithic, where the rapid technical and stylistic transformations of the Urfirnis wares are immediately transmitted over the whole of the Peloponnese, probably by the potters themselves, who alone could pass on the 'tricks of the trade' (Perlès and Vitelli 1994, 1999).

The restricted use of pottery, which mainly seems to consist of fine serving dishes, is certainly further evidence of the importance of interaction between different households or communities. In many ways, the 'refusal' to use cooking pots was a costly choice, and one that can only be justified if the social importance of fine 'table ware' was paramount (Halstead 1995; Perlès and Vitelli 1994). However, reciprocal visits between communities do not normally limit themselves to the offering of food and drinks. They are normally accompanied by reciprocal exchanges of goods, which are essential to the establishment and maintenance of social ties (Dalton 1977; Lemonnier 1990; Pétrequin and Pétrequin 1993; Mauss 1960; Sahlins 1974).

Trade and exchange

I have argued elsewhere (Perlès 1992) that the Greek Neolithic offered exemplary data for the distinction of several spheres of exchange, that is, for a multicentric economy according to Bohannan and Dalton's definition (Bohannan and Dalton 1962). In this context, the social function of exchange is best exemplified by the circulation of Middle or Late Neolithic fine wares over short or medium distances, between communities that all produced wares of equivalent quality. Later on, the circulation of arrowheads in the Late and Final Neolithic seems to have played a similar role. In both cases, no economic or technical need could by itself account for the circulation of the products. Interestingly, however, evidence for this kind of interaction remains very limited during the Early Neolithic.

At Franchthi, the only ware that appears to have been imported during the Early Neolithic is an ungritted ware, similar in biscuit to the 'Rainbow Ware' from Lerna and to common pottery at Berbati, Nemea and Corinth. It is rare at

Franchthi and never amounts to more than 5 per cent of the pottery (Vitelli 1993: 113–14 and 209). At Elateia, only three sherds of 'Corinthian Variegated Ware' are thought to be imports (Weinberg 1962: 169). At Sesklo, all the production is now thought to be local, including the fine EN3 White Ware, once considered possibly as a north-eastern Thessalian production (Wijnen 1993: 323). The same occurs at Nea Nikomedeia, where Yiouni found that the clay body of the rare White on Red and Porcelain wares was compatible with clays of local origins (Pyke and Yiouni 1996: 77). The circulation and exchange of pottery was evidently very limited in the Early Neolithic, though some have undoubtedly escaped recognition.

Reciprocal exchanges between communities could obviously have concerned goods that leave no archaeologically recognizable signature, such as grain, live animals, mats, baskets or woven cloth. We have already seen that the exchange of live animals within and between communities can be considered a necessity, both to maintain viable herds (Halstead 1992) and as a means of 'social storage' (Halstead 1981b; Halstead and O'Shea 1982). On a broader scale, Sherratt has suggested that Thessaly as a whole could have been 'a node of exchange between lowland and hinterland through exchange of cattle' (Sherratt 1982: 23). This could have been true for the few settlements located in the high valleys of the Penios and its tributaries, but the sparse settlement outside the main alluvial basins would have limited the role of Thessaly or Boeotia as suppliers of cattle to more arid or rugged countries. If term-to-term exchange was used as a means to sustain alliances between neighbouring communities, it thus mainly concerned goods that are presently 'invisible'.

There is, however, another socioeconomic option that could have preserved long-term peaceful interaction between the different communities: 'arbitrary village specialization'. In this economic pattern, different villages and groups specialize in the production of various goods that they trade with others, although each could have produced the same goods. Ethnographic examples are known in North America (Ames 1995), South America (Keeley 1996: 150–51), New Guinea (Pétrequin and Pétrequin 1993: 345) and Africa (Launay 1982, 1988). In archaeological contexts, similar situations are known in the Early Neolithic Rössen, Danubian and Lengyel cultures (Bogucki 1988), and in the Szakalha/Tisza culture of Hungary (Sherratt 1982). Amongst frontier Danubian communities of Belgium, the differential distribution of manufacturing debris indicates an inter-village specialization in the production of stone axes, flint blades, certain types of ceramics and finished hides (Keeley 1996: 152). The reciprocal dependence thus created impedes the development of conflictual or hierarchical relations, and constitutes the basis for a 'horizontal integration' of households and communities (Bogucki 1988).

Early Neolithic settlements in Greece have not been published in a way that renders such a detailed analysis possible. There are, however, some indications that a similar situation, *mutatis mutandi*, could have obtained.

Several categories of clay artefacts have a seemingly uneven distribution between sites. Sherd-discs, spindle whorls, bobbins and sling bullets, for instance, are reported in abundance from some sites, but appear to be scarce or absent in others. Until we can rely on more extensive excavations, it will be difficult to ascertain whether this may indicate intra-site specialization, inter-group specialization, or, more simply, unsystematic archaeological publication. Meanwhile, the available evidence opens the possibility of inter-group 'arbitrary' specialization, in particular for the production of textiles and hides. This situation seems frequent enough elsewhere in European Neolithic contexts to warrant further investigation and detailed technological study in Greece.

The case for the trade in stone tools, which is more easily documented, is slightly different since some groups could have specialized in their production because they – and they only – had access to the sources of raw materials. There would be no 'arbitrariness' in deciding to specialize in seafaring trips to Melos. In addition, it is more than doubtful that the groups that specialized in obsidian procurement were neighbours of the Thessalian villagers. Trade was thus taking place between socially distant groups, and did not serve, primarily, to maintain a balance within a given region. However, even obsidian trade could have been used to reinforce ties between related communities if some degree of redistribution was involved. This can neither be proved nor disproved for the Early Neolithic, but the obsidian dribbling out of Macedonia suggests it took place at least in the Late and Final Neolithic.

Interactions between groups also probably dealt in rarer and probably more valuable goods. There is little doubt that detailed analyses of raw materials would demonstrate the circulation of several categories of stone artefacts, such as earstuds, stamp-seals, stone vessels and pendants. In this respect, shell ornaments present a more accessible situation. A few spondylus artefacts have been uncovered not only in near-coastal sites like Franchthi, but also in inland sites: unworked spondylus are mentioned at Achilleion (Gimbutas *et al.* 1989: 252), a pierced spondylus shell was found at Sesklo (Wijnen 1981: 47) and spondylus beads are reported from Prodromos (Moundrea 1975). This demonstrates that inland communities acquired ornaments or at least the raw material that came, directly or indirectly, from coastal communities.

All the above-mentioned artefacts circulated in small quantities, and most of them were manufactured as unique pieces by time-consuming procedures. In this respect they differ fundamentally from the production of obsidian blades and clearly relate to a different kind of specialization and exchange. Their distribution easily fits the model of down-the-line exchanges of prestige goods (Renfrew 1984). Even if the latter are only modestly developed during the Early Neolithic, they must also have contributed to the various modes of interaction between individuals and communities.

Conclusion

Despite their limits, the currently available data indicate that socioeconomic differentiation was already developing along distinct lines in the Early Neolithic. Some individuals or families possessed objects that few others possessed, whether for ritual, social or cultic reasons. Some individuals practised crafts that others did not, and different status may have been attached to these different crafts. Some individuals were exhumed after burial, and their skulls grouped together.

None of this, however, indicates 'social inequalities' in a classic sense. I am certainly not suggesting here that Early Neolithic society in Greece was based on any kind of institutionalized, hereditary hierarchy. Indeed, Halstead noted that there were 'powerful constraints on the maximum size of Neolithic settlements in Thessaly', with a maximum figure of about 300 inhabitants. This figure would have been precisely the limit of an egalitarian society, in order to avoid internal conflicts (Broodbank 1992; Halstead 1984: 6.4.3, 1995 and references therein).

What I am suggesting, however, it that Early Neolithic society was organized along different lines, with complementary roles and status, and that the latter included specialized economic functions. Part-time craft specialization, embedded within subsistence tasks, would have served not only a more efficient technological organization, but above all a more efficient social organization. It is indeed noteworthy that none of the raw materials or artefacts traded in the Early Neolithic of Greece can be considered as strictly indispensable: even for chipped-stone tools, local or regional substitutes were available. Without denying its technical and economic benefits, trade should be viewed here primarily as a social mechanism (Mauss 1960; Sahlins 1974).

In densely settled areas, each village community would have been faced with the problem of avoiding conflicts with neighbouring communities. In the sparsely settled areas, each community would have been faced with the problem of maintaining contact with more distant neighbours. In both cases, 'arbitrary specialization' between communities could have provided a framework for balanced interaction and co-operation.

Yet, if this constituted a shared answer to radically different problems, it could not, by itself, have provided the whole solution. The propinquity of Thessalian communities and the isolation of the Peloponnesian ones clearly also called for different integrative mechanisms. It is as yet difficult to discern what the latter could have been. The only relevant indication is the relative abundance, in the more densely settled areas, of rare artefacts such as stone stamp-seals, earstuds, incised clay tablets, 'altars', and the like. Their distribution follows that of the anthropomorphic figurines, which suggests that prestige-related and ritual ceremonies were more intense in the more densely settled areas, both because society was more complex and because competition more intense.

Since rituals imply ritual specialists, we have here again an element of status and role differentiation. Altogether, Early Neolithic society in Greece appears to have relied on a broad range of economic, social and ritual functions, each requiring specialist roles to be fulfilled by different individuals and groups. Each interacted fully with each other, and this clearly maintained balanced relations in the long term. Considering the variety of interacting roles and functions, these societies can be considered 'complex'; possibly all the more complex given that, in the absence of central authority, many different institutions and groups had to intervene in order to regulate the flow of people and goods.

CONCLUSION

'How to deal with others', when, due to sedentism, 'others' had become more numerous and could no longer be chosen or changed at will, was, I have suggested, one of the most fundamental problems facing Neolithic societies. Obviously, the first farmers in Greece were not the first folk anywhere to face this problem. Several solutions had already been implemented, in particular in the Near East during the several millennia that witnessed the development of sedentary life.

Nevertheless, our first farmers in Greece may have had, or wanted, to implement new solutions and develop new mechanisms of social regulation. After a farming economy was introduced in continental Greece, the first villagers created, in the most favourable areas, a dense network of closely spaced settlements that had little or no equivalent in the Near East. They had to experiment with sedentary life in small or medium-sized, but densely distributed, communities. Compared with life in some of the largest PPNB or Early Pottery Neolithic agglomerations of the Near East, such as those that reached 12 hectares of densely packed houses at Abu Hureyra or Çatal Hüyük, this necessarily entailed a different socioeconomic organization.

The size of the largest Near Eastern prehistoric agglomerations precludes, according to decision-making theories (Johnson G. 1978, 1982; Reynolds 1984), an egalitarian organization, or a purely horizontal mode of integration. Successive levels of decision would have been necessary in communities grouping hundreds, perhaps thousands of people. Some form of hierarchical control would also have been necessary for the organization of such formidable collective tasks as the building of the walls and tower of Jericho, the 'Skull building' of Çayönü, or the sanctuaries of Nevali Çori and their monumental sculpted pillars. In parallel, a hierarchical organization of the settlements themselves is perceptible. The largest centres are surrounded by smaller-sized villages and hamlets, for which the former appear to have played the role of economic, social and ritual centres (Bar-Yosef and Belfer-Cohen 1991; Kuijt 1994).

None of this obtains in Early Neolithic Greece. All settlements appear to be similar in nature, consisting of medium-sized villages, and no dispersed farms or hamlets have been identified. In a given region, all villages exploit similarly favourable environments, and all are, apparently, of comparable size. According to population estimates (see ch. 9), all would have remained under the threshold at which a pyramidal organization would have become necessary. No sign of institutionalized hierarchy, within or between the communities, is perceptible. The smaller size of the population in each village would have, indeed, reduced risks of internal conflicts and facilitated collective decisions. On the other hand, the proximity of the different villages, in particular in Thessaly, would have greatly enhanced the risks of conflicts between neighbouring communities. Thus a redefinition of social and economic relations, within, and above all, between communities was required. I have suggested that the latter was based, in large part, on a horizontal differentiation of economic roles and social status, institutionalized interdependency and a balanced reciprocity of obligations between individuals and groups.

The precocious development of craft specialization in Neolithic Greece and the widespread exchange of utilitarian goods must be viewed in this context. The Early Neolithic of Greece provides very strong evidence of craft specialization, even if the latter was probably still seasonal and embedded in other subsistence activities. This was revealed, albeit under different forms and for different purposes, when detailed technological studies were carried out on chipped-stone tools and pottery. Immediately, the myth of autarkic, domestic productions had to be questioned, and the same will certainly occur when detailed studies of other non-perishable goods are undertaken. It is also logical to deduce that craft specialization occurred with perishable goods, such as textiles or hides.

The important point, however, is that neither craft specialization nor the exchanges that ensued can be deemed as strictly necessary in economic or technical terms. Pottery-making could have become a craft practised in every household. Similarly, locally or regionally available raw materials could have been used for the production of stone tools. Thus, even the production of daily-used tools had been socially redefined to serve social as well as technical needs. A honey-flint sickle blade served to cut plants, but also to maintain reciprocal obligations with those who procured it. The deliberate 'definition' of pottery as an item of ritual or social value, rather than as daily-used cooking pots or storage jars, can be seen as a deliberate choice to sustain a parallel system of obligations and integration through social and/or ritual practices.

Even the more classic domain of rituals can ultimately be seen as profoundly linked to social aims. The abundance of figurines in the most densely settled areas, and their quasi-absence elsewhere, indeed suggests that, whatever their precise meaning and function, their very production and use was linked to specific social conditions. Figurines were needed where social entities were larger, and were probably instrumental in regulating more complex social interactions.

The importance of social and ideological choices has been shown also in the realm of subsistence economy. Natural resources were seemingly neglected to such an extent that their deliberate refusal has to be postulated. In a similar way, the quasi-absence of cave occupations during the Early Neolithic may result both from an emphasis on man-made dwellings and the choice to restrict the areas exploited to the man-made territory that surrounded the village.

In all respects, the Early Neolithic way of life in Greece seems to have been based, indeed, on an unusually anthropogenic and anthropocentric context, where the 'natural' environment had been artificially recreated, and where many, if not most, technical activities were socially mediated. The same could probably be claimed for many other Neolithic societies. However, the dynamic of the Neolithic in Greece shows that the early Neolithic groups went further in this direction than their successors. In the following millennia, hundreds of caves were reoccupied, settlement spread on the barren hills, wild fauna was increasingly hunted even in the most densely settled areas, while local raw materials were more commonly exploited. The emphasis on a man-made and socially mediated environment can thus be considered as a characteristic of the early Neolithic system, resulting from ideological choices more than economic or technical necessities.

According to some very well-known authors (e.g., Gimbutas 1991; Hodder 1990), the early Neolithic ideology not only insisted on the dichotomy between the natural and the domesticated worlds, but also on the social or symbolic predominance of the feminine element. Yet, the reader will certainly have noticed the quasi-absence of reference in this analysis to the respective roles of men and women in the organization of society. The major reason is that I see little in the data that would shed light on this problem, or indicate any inbalance in favour of one or the other gender. Hodder (1990: 68–9, 137) has underlined the emphasis on the 'domus', on nurturing and rearing in the south-eastern European villages, and hence on the feminine elements of society. However, as he himself indicates, this does not imply that women 'played a central role in production' or had any 'real power' (Hodder 1990: 68). To the contrary, Vitelli (1993) and Björk (1995), basing their interpretation on their familiarity with Early Neolithic pottery from Greece, have suggested that potters enjoyed an especially prestigious status. According to Vitelli, pottery making was done by women, who also mastered the knowledge of medicinal plants and drugs. Accordingly, she believes that women-potters would have been endowed with a high status and special healing powers, akin to shamanistic powers.

This is a possibility to be considered, although numerous ethnographic examples show that such healing powers are frequently shared by individuals of both sexes. On the other hand, highly skilled stone-working is a masculine activity in the few historical cases known to us. Thus the production and exchange of exotic stone tools can be considered more probably a masculine activity. Since stone artefacts are, among the recoverable remains, the most widely traded during the Early Neolithic, the control of long-distance trade, and the prestige attached to it, can be more plausibly attributed to men.

Thus, here again, the scant evidence upon which we can rely – or rather, the most plausible inferences – points to a differentiation of masculine and feminine roles, rather than to the predominance of one sex. Elster's view of a balanced distribution of tasks within a Bronze Age household, if no more demonstrable than other models, fits the available data better (Elster 1997).

On the other hand, the marked predominance of feminine figurines might support the hypothesis of a special symbolic power attributed to women as life-givers and bearers of fertility. Yet, the presence of male figurines cannot be ignored, and the particular features displayed by some, such as the 'enthroned' male figurines, could alternately be taken as an indication of a dominating status. The disparity in number between male and female figurines might simply reflect different modalities of use, most female figurines being frequently but briefly manipulated, while the few male figurines would have been of long-lasting use and value. Aside from the difference of frequency, there is, at any rate, no convincing element that suggests a predominance of feminine symbols.[1] Taken at face value, the presently available data suggest that the same basic principle was operating at all levels of society, from the household to the regional population: a principle of complementarity and balanced reciprocity.

This Early Neolithic socioeconomic system would necessarily have taken several generations to reach its full development and equilibrium. Yet, no successive stages can be documented. This is in part due to lacunae in the data, but in part only. The location of settlements, the exploitation of farm animals or the production of stone tools, for instance, show no marked changes during the initial phases of the Neolithic. In many respects, the Neolithic in Greece appears already fully formed from the beginning, without 'transitional' or 'progressive' phases.

Equally specific is the fact that the socioeconomic system of the Early Neolithic remains essentially stable throughout the two millennia that follow, during the entire Middle and Late Neolithic. Sherratt pointed out that 'early agricultural communities were on occasion capable of operating large-scale exchanges in the absence of developed hierarchies, and that such societies may have undergone cycles of increasing complexity and devolution that defy characterisation as stages in a unilinear progression' (Sherratt 1982: 15). Yet, despite perceptible tensions and transformations in the Middle and Late Neolithic (Vitelli, in Perlès and Vitelli 1999), major socioeconomic transformations did not take place until the Late Neolithic in the Peloponnese, or the Final Neolithic in Thessaly.

One may wonder about the mechanisms that ensured such long-term stability. There is no doubt that Greece was no more idyllic than anywhere else, and that tendencies to break the system were just as strong as in any other society. How, then, did Neolithic societies in Greece escape the major disruptions,

---

[1] Yet is true that, had Çatal Hüyük not been excavated, we would have had no clue regarding the symbolic predominance of a feminine representation in that part of the world.

breaks and emergence of new socioeconomic systems that rhythm Neolithic dynamics in Western Europe with a much higher frequency?

I am tempted to think that the rapid integration of local hunter-gatherers and the very permanence of the settlements are parts of the answer. Already by the Early Neolithic, all traces of earlier Mesolithic traditions had disappeared, and there is no evidence of conflicts or competition between farmers and hunter-gatherers. There was no need to create new forms of settlements – by or because of hunter-gatherers – when farming later spread out of the core areas. No need either to create such conspicuous symbols as the monumental tombs and mega-liths, whether these are considered as displays of power by, or for, the local groups (Sherratt 1990, 1995). Second, the village itself constituted a permanent and conspicuous reference to the past. Individuals were rooted in their own ancestral land, with constant physical and psychological reference to their ancestors and to the social, economic and ritual rules they had established. This may have favoured the self-reproduction of a traditional organization and counteracted tendencies towards change and innovation. A third and parallel factor may have been the relative fertility of the land that did not entail crises and adjustments of the economic system, just as the demographic stability already reached by the EN2 postponed the need to exploit environments of secondary value until late in the Neolithic.

The latter statement may seem to contradict claims for the spread of the farming economy from Greece to the Balkans and the Adriatic during the Early Neolithic. The south-eastern Balkanic Neolithic indeed shares many common features with the Greek one, and this has been taken as an indication that it originated in Greece (Halstead 1989b: 26; Dolukhanov 1983: 476; Renfrew 1986: 480). The most explicit statement is perhaps that of Lichardus:

Le matériel archéologique de cette région [Grèce du Nord] entretient en effet des rapports d'évidence avec celui des pays balkaniques et l'on considère en particulier que la Grèce septentrionale a constitué un centre originel de la diffusion du Néolithique vers les Balkans, et par là, vers l'Europe centrale. (Lichardus, in Lichardus *et al.* 1985: 228–9)[2]

I believe, however, that the problem is far from settled. Many of the shared features, such as the permanent settlements,[3] may derive from common origins and similar environmental potentialities, rather than from direct filiation. To the contrary, the radical contrasts not only in the decoration of the pottery but, above all, in the very conception and role of pottery (see ch. 10), persuasively argue, in my opinion, against a direct filiation. Choosing to use massive amounts of coarse pottery for storing and cooking food, or, to the contrary, to

---

[2] 'The archaeological remains from this region [northern Greece] bear obvious relations with those of the Balkans and northern Greece in particular is considered as an original centre of diffusion of the Neolithic towards the Balkans and , therefore, towards central Europe.'

[3] Although it will be recalled that Lichardus-Itten disclaims the presence of tell settlements in the Early Neolithic of the Balkans (Lichardus-Itten 1993).

restrict the production of pottery to fine wares, are social options that are too radically opposed to postulate a direct continuity. It will be remembered, in addition, that such differences entail profoundly different cooking habits, a domain that is amongst the most conservative in human behaviour. The pre-Starčevo and Starčevo groups of Bulgaria may thus have come directly from Anatolia and Thrace, with whom they share many common cultural elements, a few hundred years after Greece was first settled by farmers. The Greek Macedonian settlements, whose idiosyncratic features have been noted throughout this study, may bear witness to the interaction between two different traditions, at a late phase of the Early Neolithic, in the Thessalian sense. Rather than constituting an original centre that later spread to the Balkans, they may even *derive* from a southward movement, from the Balkans to Greek Macedonia. Similarly, the few Early Neolithic sites from the north-west of Greece, with their *Impressa* ware, can be better viewed as the southernmost settlements of the Adriatic coast tradition, rather than as a development of the Thessalian tradition.

I see little indication, in fact, that the Early Neolithic farmers from Greece spread outside their original *oecumene* in the eastern part of Greece. This may be due, in part, to the close adaptation of the socioeconomic system they had created to the land itself. Had they crossed the Pindus to the west, or the Rhodopes to the north, they would have gradually met with increasingly different climatic conditions, which would have required important adaptations of the cultivated plants and thus of farming and husbandry pratices (Halstead 1989b; Nandris 1970, 1977a). For instance, in the Balkans and central Europe, 'winter cold progressively replaces summer drought as the principle climatic factor on plant growth' (Halstead 1989b: 26), thus favouring an extended vegetative period rather than an early maturation. Until cereals and pulses were fully adapted to these new conditions, the annual yields would have been less predictable, which probably led to a more important reliance on stock-breeding, in particular on cattle.

There is no doubt, however, that these problems could have been overcome, had the will to expand further been a sufficient incentive. Yet, for reasons that remain unclear, the early farming communities from Greece apparently did not chose to pursue their 'wave of advance' once they had settled in Greece. Was it, very simply, due to the success and stability of the socioeconomic system created by the earliest farming communities in Greece?

Different factors have been suggested to explain this stability. Yet, they represent only a partial answer to the problem, as indicated by the important transformations that occurred elsewhere in comparable human and natural environments, the Tavoliere in Italy or Bulgaria, for instance. Even after in-depth examination of the available data, many fundamental aspects of these Early Neolithic societies still escape us. This is due in part to the inadequacy of the database and the need for modern, extensive excavations. I am afraid, however, that even if (or when) we can rely on a larger and more detailed corpus, more fundamental problems may continue to limit our understanding of these first Neolithic societies.

Throughout this work, I have tried to show that the notion of 'simple' Early Neolithic societies can no longer be accepted, both for logical and archaeological reasons. Early Neolithic societies in Greece – and, doubtless, everywhere else – were 'complex' societies that had created a completely anthropogenic environment, solved the problems of cohabitation and competition in densely settled areas, and succeeded in sustaining long-distance trade over more than a millennium. Yet, as far as the evidence goes, they achieved this without having recourse to any form of institutionalized hierarchy or control. All the evidence points, instead, to a heterarchical organization, based on a differentiation of social and economic roles. However, we reach here the limits of our interpretative possibilities. This is a form of complexity that we can hardly apprehend, for lack of reference models. Early Neolithic societies were the first farming communities to exploit rich and unspoilt lands. In Greece at least, they were not threatened by outsiders, whether hunter-gatherers or other farmers like themselves. The land was rich enough and the demography such that they could create surpluses, without having to pay a tribute to civil or ecclesiatical powers. They had developed widespread exchange systems that were not controlled by a minority, so that they could acquire exotic goods not only for social display, but also more simply for daily use.

These constitute exceptional socioeconomic conditions that, by definition, elude later historical comparenda. We have few, if any, models of reference that correspond to this unique combination of economic and political features. Any reference to later prehistoric or historic contexts is bound to distort our perception of these societies, and reduce them, illegitimately, to the more familiar and far more constrained peasantry, derived from yet other millennia of history.

BIBLIOGRAPHY

Adovasio, J. M., Soffer, O. and Klima, B. (1995) Paleolithic fiber technology: data from Pavlov I, Czech Republic, c. 27,000 BP. Paper presented at the 60th annual meeting of the Society for American Archaeology, Minneapolis, Minnesota, 3–7 May 1995, 10 pages.

Akkermans, P. A. et al. (1983) Bouqras revisited: preliminary report on a project in Eastern Syria. *Proceedings of the Prehistoric Society* 49: 335–72.

Allen, H. (1990) A Postglacial record from the Kopais Basin, Greece. In S. Bottema, G. Entjes-Nieborg and W. van Zeist (eds.), *Man's Role in the Shaping of the Eastern Mediterranean Landscape*, A. A. Balkema, Rotterdam, pp. 173–82.

Alram-Stern, E. (1996) *Die ägäische Frühzeit. 2 Serie. Forschungsbericht 1975–1993*, vol. I, *Das Neolithikum in Griechenland*, Verlag der Österreichischen Akademie der Wissenchaften, Wien.

Ames, K. M. (1995) Chiefly power and household production on the Northwest Coast. In T. D. Price and G. M. Feinman (eds.), *Foundations of Social Inequality*, Plenum Press, New York, pp. 155–87.

Ammerman, A. J. (1989) On the Neolithic transition in Europe: a comment on Zvelebil and Zvelebil (1988). *Antiquity* 83: 162–5.

Ammerman, A. J. and Cavalli-Sforza, L. L. (1984) *The Neolithic Transition and the Genetics of Populations in Europe*, Princeton University Press, Princeton.

Amouretti, M.-C. (1991) Les rythmes agraires dans la Grèce antique. In M.-C. Cauvin (ed.), *Rites et rythmes agraires*, diff. de Boccard, Lyon, pp. 119–26 (Travaux de la Maison de L'Orient 20).

Anastassiades, P. (1949) General features of the soils of Greece. *Soil Science* 67: 347–62.

Anderson, P. C. (1994a) Insights into plant harvesting and other activities at Hatoula, as revealed by microscopic functional analysis of selected chipped stone tools. In M. Lechevallier and A. Ronen (eds.), *Le site de Hatoula en Judée Occidentale, Israël*, Association Paléorient, Paris, pp. 277–96 (Mémoires et Travaux du Centre de Recherches Français de Jérusalem, 8).

Anderson, P. C. (1994b) Reflections on the significance of two PPN typological classes in light of experimentation and microwear analysis: flint 'sickles' and obsidian 'Çayönü' tools. In H.-G. Gebel and S. Kozłowski (eds.), *Neolithic Chipped Stone Industries of the Fertile Crescent*, Ex Oriente, Berlin, pp. 61–82 (Studies in Early Near Eastern Production, Subsistence and Environment, I).

Andreou, S., Fotiadis, M. and Kotsakis, K. (1996) Review of Aegean Prehistory V: the Neolithic and Bronze Age of Northern Greece. *American Journal of Archaeology* 100: 537–97.

Angel, J. L. (1969) Human skeletal material from Franchthi Cave. Appendix II. In

T. Jacobsen, Excavations at Porto Cheli and vicinity, preliminary report II: the Franchthi Cave, 1967–1968. *Hesperia* 38: 380–81.

Angel, J. L. (1972) Ecology and population in the Eastern Mediterranean. *World Archaeology* 4(1): 88–105.

Arnold, D. E. (1985) *Ceramic Theory and Cultural Process*, Cambridge University Press, Cambridge.

Arnold, J. E. (1995) Social inequality, marginalization, and economic process. In T. D. Price and G. M. Feinman (eds.), *Foundations of Social Inequality*, Plenum Press, New York, pp. 87–103.

Astruc, L. (in prep.) Analyse fonctionnelle et spatiale de l'industrie lithique de Khirokitia (Néolithique Précéramique, Chypre), Thèse de doctorat, Université Paris X.

Auda, Y., Darmezin, L., Decourt, J.-Cl., Helly, B. and Lucas, G. (1990) Espace géographique et géographie historique en Thessalie. In *Archéologie et espaces. Actes des Xèmes rencontres internationales d'archéologie et d'histoire d'Antibes, 1989*, Editions APDCA, Juan-les-Pins, pp. 87–126.

Augereau, A. (1993) Evolution de l'industrie du silex du Vème au IVème millénaires avant J.-C. dans le sud-est du Bassin Parisien, Thèse de doctorat, Université Paris I, 2 vols.

Aurenche, O. (ed.) (1977) *Dictionnaire multilingue illustré de l'architecture du Proche Orient ancien*, Maison de l'Orient Méditerranéen Ancien, Lyon.

Aurenche, O., Calley, S. and Cauvin, J. (1985) L'architecture de Çafer Höyük (fouilles 1982–1983). Rapport préliminaire. *Cahiers de l'Euphrate* 4: 11–34.

Aurenche, O., Evin, J. and Gasco, J. (1987) Une séquence chronologique dans le Proche-Orient de 12 000 à 3 700 BC et sa relation avec les données du radiocarbone. In O. Aurenche, J. Evin and F. Hours (eds.), *Chronologies in the Near East. Relative Chronologies and Absolute Chronology 16,000–4,000 B.P.*, British Archaeological Reports, Int. series 379, Oxford, 2 vols., pp. 21–37.

Bailey, D. W. (1994) Reading prehistoric figurines as individuals. *World Archaeology* 25(3): 321–31.

Bailey, G. N. (ed.) (1997a) *Klithi: Palaeolithic Settlement and Quaternary Environments in Northwest Greece*, Vol. I: *Excavations and Intra-Site Analysis at Klithi*, McDonald Institute for Archaeological Research, Cambridge (McDonald Institute Monographs).

Bailey, G. N. (ed.) (1997b) *Klithi: Palaeolithic Settlement and Quaternary Environments in Northwest Greece*, vol. II, *Klithi in its Local and Regional Setting*, McDonald Institute for Archaeological Research, Cambridge (McDonald Institute Monographs).

Bailey, G. N., Adam, E., Panagopoulou, E., Perlès, C. and Zachos, K. (eds.) (1999) *The Palaeolithic Archaeology of Greece and Adjacent Areas: Proceedings of the ICOPAG Conference, Ioannina, September 1994*, British School at Athens Studies 3, London.

Bailey, G. N., Carter, P. L., Gamble, C. S. and Higgs, H. P. (1983a) Asprochaliko and Kastritsa: further investigations of Palaeolithic settlement and economy in Epirus (north-west Greece). *Proceedings of the Prehistoric Society* 49: 15–42.

Bailey, G. N., Carter, P. L., Gamble, C. S. and Higgs, H. P. (1983b) Epirus revisited: seasonality and inter-site variation in the Upper Palaeolithic of north-west Greece. In G. N. Bailey (ed.), *Hunter-Gatherer Economy in Prehistory: a European Perspective*, Cambridge University Press, Cambridge, pp. 64–78.

Bailey, G. N., Gamble, C. S., Higgs, H. P., Roubet, C., Sturdy, D. A. and Webley, D. P. (1986) Palaeolithic investigation at Klithi: preliminary results of the 1984 and 1985 field seasons. *Annual of the British School at Athens* 81: 7–35.

Balkan-Atli, N. (1994) *La Néolithisation de l'Anatolie,* Institut Français d'Etudes Anatoliennes d'Istanbul, de Boccard, Paris (Varia Anatolica 7).

Bar-Yosef, O. (1986) The walls of Jericho: an alternative interpretation. *Current Anthropology* 27(2): 157–62.

Bar-Yosef, O. and Belfer-Cohen, A. (1991) From sedentary hunter-gatherers to territorial farmers in the Levant. In S. A. Gregg (ed.), *Between Bands and States: Sedentism, Subsistence and Interaction in Small-Scale Societies,* Center for Archaeological Investigations, occasional paper 9, Southern Illinois University, Carbondale, pp. 181–202.

Barber, E. J. W. (1991) *Prehistoric Textiles. The Development of Cloth in the Neolithic and Bronze Age with Special References to the Aegean,* Princeton University Press, Princeton.

Barber, E. J. W. (1994) *Women's Work: the First 20,000 Years. Women, Cloth and Society in Early Times,* W. W. Norton, New York.

Barker, G. (1985) *Prehistoric Farming in Europe,* Cambridge University Press, Cambridge.

Baxter, M. S. (1983) An international tree ring replicate study. *Pact 8*: II.8: 123–32.

Beaune, S. A. de (1999) *Apport du matériel lithique non taillé à la compréhension du progrès technique dans les sociétés préhistoriques,* Habilitation à diriger des recherches, Université Paris X, 3 vols.

Beeching, A., Binder, D., Blanchet J. C. *et al.* (eds.) (1991) *Identité du Chasséen,* APRAIF, Nemours (Mémoires du Musée de Préhistoire d'Ile de France 4).

Bialor, P. (1962) The chipped stone industry of Çatal Hüyük. *Anatolian Studies* 12: 67–110.

Binder, D. (ed.) (1991) *Une économie de chasse au Néolithique ancien. La Grotte Lombard à Saint-Vallier-de-Thiey (Alpes-Maritimes),* Centre National de la Recherche Scientifique, Paris (Monographies du CRA 5).

Binford, L. R. (1968) Post-Pleistocene adaptations. In S. R. Binford and L. R. Binford (eds.), *New Perspectives in Archaeology,* Aldine, Chicago, pp. 313–41.

Bintliff, J. (1976a) The plain of western Macedonia and the neolithic site of Nea Nikomedeia. *Proceedings of the Prehistoric Society* 42: 241–62.

Bintliff, J. (1976b) Sediments and settlement in southern Greece. In D. A. Davidson and M. L. Shackley (eds.), *Geoarchaeology. Earth Science and the Past,* Duckworth, London, pp. 266–75.

Bintliff, J. (1977) *Natural Environment and Human Settlement in Prehistoric Greece, Based on Original Fieldwork,* British Archaeological Reports, 28, Oxford, 2 vols.

Bintliff, J. (1989) Cemetery populations, carrying capacity and the individual in history. In A. R. Hands and D. R. Walker (eds.), *Burial Archaeology: Current Research, Methods and Developments,* British Archaeological Reports, 211, Oxford, pp. 85–103.

Bintliff, J. (1994a) The history of the Greek countryside: as the wave breaks, prospects for future research. In P. N. Doukellis and L. G. Mendoni (eds.), *Structures rurales et sociétés antiques,* Annales Littéraires de l'Université de Besançon 508, Centre de Recherches d'Histoire Ancienne, Paris, vol. 126, pp. 7–15.

Bintliff, J. (1994b) Territorial behaviour and the natural history of the Greek Polis.

In *Stuttgarter Kolloquium zur historischen Geographie des Altertums 4, 1990*, Verlag Adolf M. Hakkert, Amsterdam, pp. 207–49.

Bintliff, J. and Snodgrass, A. M. (1985) The Boeotia Survey, a preliminary report: the first four years. *Journal of Field Archaeology* 12: 126–61.

Bisel, S. G. and Angel, J. L. (1985) Health and nutrition in Mycenean Greece. In N. C. Wilkie and W. D. E. Coulson (eds.), *Contributions to Aegean Archaeology. Studies in Honor of William A. McDonald*, Center for Ancient Studies, University of Minnesota, Minneapolis, pp. 197–210.

Björk, Cl. (1995) *Early Pottery in Greece: a Technological and Functional Analysis of the Evidence from Neolithic Achilleion, Thessaly*, Paul Aströms Förlag, Jonsered (SIMA 115).

Blegen, C. W. (1937) *Prosymna, the Helladic Settlement Preceding the Argive Heraeum*, Cambridge University Press, Cambridge, 2 vols.

Blegen, C. W. (1975) Neolithic remains at Nemea. *Hesperia* 44: 224–7.

Bloedow, E. F. (1991) The 'Aceramic' Neolithic phase in Greece reconsidered. *Mediterranean Archaeology* 4: 1–43.

Bloedow, E. F. (1992/3) The date of the earliest phase at Argissa Magoula in Thessaly and other Neolithic sites in Greece. *Mediterranean Archaeology* 5/6: 49–57.

Bocquet, A. with the collaboration of Berretrot, F. (1989) Le travail des fibres textiles au Néolithique récent à Charavines (Isère). In *Tissage, corderie, vannerie. Actes des IXèmes rencontres internationales d'archéologie et d'histoire d'Antibes*, Editions APDCA, Juan-les-Pins, pp. 113–28.

Boessneck, J. (1962) Die Tierreste aus der Argissa-Magula vom präkeramischen Neolithikum bis zur mittlere Bronzezeit. In V. Milojčić, J. Boessneck and M. Hopf, *Die deutschen Ausgrabungen auf der Argissa-Magula in Thessalien, I. Das präkeramische Neolithikum sowie die Tier- und Pflanzenreste*, Beiträge zur ur- und frühgeschichtlichen Archäologie des Mittelmeer-Kulturraumes 2, Rudolf Habelt, Bonn, pp. 27–99.

Boessneck, J. (1985) Die Domestikation und ihre Folgen. *Tierärztliche Praxis* 13: 479–97.

Bogucki, P. I. (1984) Ceramic sieves of the Linear Pottery culture and their economic implications. *Oxford Journal of Archaeology* 3(1): 15–30.

Bogucki, P. I. (1988) *Forest Farmers and Stockherders: Early Agriculture and its Consequences in North-Central Europe*, Cambridge University Press, Cambridge.

Bohannan, P. and Dalton, G. (1962) Introduction. In P. Bohannan and G. Dalton (eds.), *Markets in Africa*, Northwestern University Press, Chicago, pp. 1–26.

Bökönyi, S. (1973) Stock breeding. In D. Theocharis, *Neolithic Greece*, National Bank of Greece, Athens, pp. 165–78.

Bökönyi, S. (1974) *History of Domestic Mammals in Central and Eastern Europe*, Akademiai Kiado, Budapest.

Bökönyi, S. (1986) Faunal remains. In C. Renfrew, M. Gimbutas and E. Elster (eds.), *Excavations at Sitagroi. A Prehistoric Village in Northeast Greece*, Institute of Archaeology, Monumenta Archaeologica 13, University of California, Los Angeles, vol. I, pp. 63–96.

Bökönyi, S. (1989) Animal remains. In M. Gimbutas, Sh. Winn and D. Shimabuku (eds.), *Achilleion, a Neolithic Settlement in Thessaly, Greece, 6400–5600 B.C.*, Institute of Archaeology, Monumenta Archaeologica 14, University of California, Los Angeles, pp. 315–32.

Bolger, D. (1996) Figurines, fertility and the emergence of complex society in Prehistoric Cyprus. *Current Anthropology* 37(2): 365–73.

Bordaz, J. (1968) The Suberde excavations, southwestern Turkey. An interim report. *Türk Arkeoloji Dergisi* 17(2): 43–71.

Bostyn, F. and Lanchon, Y. (1992) *Jablines le Haut Château (Seine-et-Marne). Une minière de silex au Néolithique*, Editions de la Maison des Sciences de l'Homme, Paris (Documents d'Archéologie Française 35).

Bottema, S. (1974) Late Quaternary vegetation history of northwestern Greece, Ph. D. thesis, Biologisch-Archaeologisch Institute, Groningen.

Bottema, S. (1979) Pollen analytical investigations in Thessaly (Greece). *Palaeohistoria* 21: 19–40.

Bottema, S. (1982) Palynological investigations in Greece with special reference to pollen as an indicator of human activity. *Palaeohistoria* 24: 257–89.

Bottema, S. (1990) Holocene environment of the southern Argolid: a pollen core from Kiladha Bay. In T. J. Wilkinson and S. Duhon, *Franchthi Paralia, the Sediments, Stratigraphy, and Offshore Investigations*, Excavations at Franchthi Cave, Greece, fasc. 6, Indiana University Press, Bloomington and Indianapolis, pp. 117–38.

Bottema, S. (1991) Développement de la végétation et du climat dans le bassin méditerranéen oriental à la fin du Pléistocène et pendant l'Holocène. *L'Anthropologie* 95(4): 695–728.

Bottema, S. (1994) The Prehistoric environment of Greece: a review of the palynological record. In P. N. Kardulias (ed.), *Beyond the Site. Regional Studies in the Aegean Area*, University Press of America, Lanham, pp. 45–68.

Bottema, S. and Woldring, H. (1990) Anthropogenic indicators in the pollen record of the Eastern Mediterranean. In S. Bottema, G. Entjes-Nieborg and W. van Zeist (eds.), *Man's Role in the Shaping of the Eastern Mediterranean Landscape*, Balkema, Rotterdam, pp. 231–64.

Bower, B. (1993) Site surrenders fabric of prehistoric life. *Science News* 144: 54.

Braidwood, R. J. (1960) The agricultural revolution. *Scientific American* 203: 130–41.

Braidwood, R. J., Çambel, H. Schirmer, W. *et al.* (1981) Beginnings of village-farming communities in Southeastern Turkey: Çayönü Tepesi, 1978 and 1979. *Journal of Field Archaeology* 8(3): 249–58.

Bridault, A. (1993) Les économies de chasse epipaléolithiques et mésolithiques dans le nord et l'est de la France, Thèse de doctorat, Université de Paris X, 3 vols.

Briois, F., Gratuze, B. and Guilaine, J. (1997) Obsidiennes du site néolithique précéramique de Shillourokambos (Chypre). *Paléorient* 23(1): 95–112.

Brochier, J. E. (1991) Environnement et culture: état de la question dans le sud-est de la France et principes d'étude autour du Chasséen de la moyenne vallée du Rhône. In A. Beeching, D. Binder, J.-Cl. Blanchet *et al.* (eds.), *Identité du Chasséen*, APRAIF, Nemours, pp. 315–326 (Mémoires du Musée de Préhistoire d'Ile de France 4).

Brochier, J. L. (1994) Etude de la sédimentation anthropique. La stratégie des ethnofaciès sédimentaires en milieu de constructions en terre. *Bulletin de Correspondance Hellénique* 118(2): 619–45.

Broodbank, C. (1992) The Neolithic labyrinth: social change at Knossos before the Bronze Age. *Journal of Mediterranean Archaeology* 5(1): 39–75.

Broodbank, C. and Strasser, Th. F. (1991) Migrant farmers and the Neolithic colonization of Crete. *Antiquity* 65: 233–45.

Cahen, D. and Jadin, I. (1996) Economie et société dans le Rubané récent de Belgique. *Bulletin de la Société Préhistorique Française* 93(1): 55–62.

Calley, S. (1985) Les nucléus de Çafer Höyük. *Cahiers de l'Euphrate* 4: 87–107.

Caputo, R. (1990) *Geological and Structural Study of the Recent and Active Brittle Deformation of the Neogene-Quaternary Basins of Thessaly (Central Greece)*, Scientific Annals, Aristotle University of Thessaloniki, Thessaloniki.

Caputo, R., Bravard, J.-P. and Helly, B. (1994) The Pliocene-Quaternary tecto-sedimentary evolution of the Larissa Plain (Eastern Thessaly, Greece). *Geodinamica Acta* 7(4): 219–31.

Carington Smith, J. (1975) Spinning, weaving and textile manufacture in prehistoric Greece, Ph. D. thesis, University of Tasmania, Hobart, 2 vols.

Caskey, J. L. (1956) Excavations at Lerna, 1955. *Hesperia* 25: 157–73.

Caskey, J. L. (1957) Excavations at Lerna, 1956. *Hesperia* 26: 142–62.

Caskey, J. L. (1958) Excavations at Lerna, 1957. *Hesperia* 27: 125–44.

Caskey, J. L. and Caskey, E. G. (1960) The earliest settlements at Eutresis: supplementary excavations, 1958. *Hesperia* 29: 126–67.

Cauvin, J. (1978) *Les premiers villages de Syrie-Palestine du IXème au VIIème millénaire avant J. C.*, Maison de l'Orient, Lyon.

Cauvin, J. (1985) Les cultures villageoises et civilisations préurbaines d'Asie antérieure. In J. Lichardus, M. Lichardus-Itten, G. Bailloud and J. Cauvin, *La protohistoire de l'Europe. Le Néolithique et le Chalcolithique entre la Méditerranée et la Mer Baltique*, Presses Universitaires de France, Paris, pp. 156–206 (Nouvelle Clio 1 bis).

Cauvin, J. (1989) La néolithisation au Levant et sa première diffusion. In O. Aurenche and J. Cauvin (eds.), *Néolithisations: Proche et Moyen Orient, Méditerranée Orientale, Nord de l'Afrique, Europe Méridionale, Chine, Amérique du Sud*, British Archaeological Reports, Int. series 516, Oxford, pp. 3–32.

Cauvin, J. (1994) *Naissance des divinités, naissance de l'agriculture. La révolution des symboles au Néolithique*, CNRS Editions, Paris.

Cauvin, J. (1997) *Naissance des divinités, naissance de l'agriculture. La révolution des symboles au Néolithique*, CNRS Editions, 2nd revised edn, Paris.

Cauvin, M.-C. and Balkan-Atli, N. (1996) Rapport sur les recherches sur l'obsidienne en Cappadoce, 1993–1995. *Anatolia Antiqua* 4: 249–71.

Cavanagh, W., Crouwel, J., Catling, R. W. V. and Shipley, G. (eds.) (1996) *Continuity and Change in a Greek Rural Landscape: the Laconia Survey*, vol. II, British School at Athens, London.

Cavanagh, W. and Mee, Ch. (1998) *A Private Place: Death in Prehistoric Greece*, Paul Aströms Förlag, Jonsered.

Chapman, J. (1988) Ceramic production and social differentiation: the Dalmatian Neolithic and the Western Mediterranean. *Journal of Mediterranean Archaeology* 1(2): 3–25.

Chapman, J. (1989) The early Balkan village. In S. Bökönyi (ed.), *Neolithic of Southeastern Europe and its Near Eastern Connections, International Conference 1987, Szolnok-Szeged, Hungary*, Varia Archaeologica Hungarica 2, Budapest, pp. 33–53.

Chapman, J. (1991) Els origens de l'agricultura al Sud-Est d'Europa. *Cota Zero* 7: 126–35.

Chapman, J. (1994a) The living, the dead and the ancestors: time, life cycles and the mortuary domain in the later European Prehistory. In J. Davies (ed.), *Ritual and Remembrance: Responses to Death in Human Societies*, Sheffield Academic Press, Sheffield, pp. 40–85.

Chapman, J. (1994b) The origins of farming in south east Europe. *Préhistoire Européenne* 6: 133–56.

Chapman, J. (1994c) Social power in the early farming communities of Eastern Hungary. Perspectives from the Upper Tisza region. *Jósa András Múseum Evkönyve* 36: 79–99.

Chavaillon, J., Chavaillon, N. and Hours, F. (1967) Industries paléolithiques de l'Elide. I – Région d'Amalias. *Bulletin de Correspondance Hellénique* 91: 151–201.

Chavaillon, J., Chavaillon, N. and Hours, F. (1969) Industries paléolithiques de l'Elide. II – Région du Kastron. *Bulletin de Correspondance Hellénique* 93: 97–151.

Cherry, J. F. (1979) Four problems in Cycladic prehistory. In J. Davis and J. F. Cherry (eds.), *Papers in Cycladic Prehistory*, Institute of Archaeology, Monograph 14, University of California, Los Angeles, pp. 22–47.

Cherry, J. F. (1981) Pattern and process in the earliest colonization of the Mediterranean islands. *Proceedings of the Prehistoric Society* 47: 41–68.

Cherry, J. F. (1988) Pastoralism and the role of animals in pre- and proto-historic economies of the Aegean. In C. R. Whittaker (ed.), *Pastoral Economies in Classical Antiquity*, Cambridge Philological Society, supplement volume 14, pp. 6–34.

Cherry, J. F. (1990) The first colonization of the Mediterranean islands: a review of recent research. *Journal of Mediterranean Archaeology* 3(2): 145–221.

Cherry, J. F. (1994) Regional survey in the Aegean: the 'New Wave' (and after). In P. N. Kardulias (ed.), *Beyond the Site. Regional Studies in the Aegean Area*, University Press of America, Lanham, pp. 91–112.

Cherry, J. F., Davis, J. L., Demitrack, A., Mantzourani, E., Strasser, Th. and Talalay, L. (1988) Archaeological survey in an artifact-rich landscape: a Middle Neolithic example from Nemea, Greece. *American Journal of Archaeology* 92: 159–76.

Chevalier, J. (ed.) (1969) *Dictionnaire des Symboles*, Robert Laffont, Paris.

Childe, V. G. (1934) *New Light on the Most Ancient East: the Oriental Prelude to European Prehistory*, Kegan Paul, London.

Childe, V. G. (1951a) *Man Makes Himself*, Mentor Books, New York.

Childe, V. G. (1951b) The significance of the sling for Greek Prehistory. In G. E. Mylonas (ed.), *Studies Presented to David Moore Robinson*, I, Washington University Press, Saint-Louis, pp. 1–5.

Childe, V. G. (1957) *The Dawn of European Civilization*. Chaucer Press, Bungay, Suffolk.

Childe, V. G. (1958) *The Prehistory of European Society*, Harmondsworth, Penguin.

Christopoulou, A. (1992) Ichni chrisis sta leiasmena lithina ergaleia tou Sesklou A. In *Diethnes Synedrio gia tin Archaia Thessalia sti Mnimi tou Dimitri P. Theochari*, Ekdosi Tameiou Archaeiologikôn Porôn kai Apallotrioseôn, Athens, pp. 64–70.

Chrysostomou, P. (1991 (1994)) Oi neolithikes erevnes stin poli kai tin eparchia Giannitson kata to 1991. *To Archaiologiko Ergo sti Makedonia kai Thraki* 5: 111–25.

Chrysostomou, P. (1993 (1997)) O neolithikos oikismos Giannitson B. Nea anaskafika dedomena (1992–1993). *To Archaiologiko Ergo sti Makedonia kai Thraki* 7: 135–46.

Chrysostomou, P. and Chrysostomou, P. (1990 (1993)) Neolithikes erevnes sta Giannitsa kai stin periohi tou. *To Archaiologiko Ergo sti Makedonia kai Thraki* 4: 169–86.

Clark, J. E. (1987) Politics, prismatic blades, and Mesoamerican civilization. In J. Johnson and C. A. Morro (eds.), *The Organization of Core Technology*, Westview Press, Boulder and London, pp. 259–84.

Clark, J. E. and Parry, W. J. (1990) Craft specialization and cultural complexity. *Research in Economic Anthropology* 12: 289–346.

Clark, P. J. and Evans, F. C., (1954) Distance to nearest neighbour as a measure of spatial relationships in populations. *Ecology* 35: 444–53.

Close, A. and Wendorf, F. (1992) The beginnings of food production in the Eastern Sahara. In A. D. Gebauer and T. D. Price (eds.), *Transitions to Agriculture in Prehistory*, Prehistory Press, Madison, pp. 63–77 (Monographs in World Archaeology 4).

Cocchi Genick, D. (1990) La pratica della transumanza dal Neolitico all'età del Bronzo nella Toscana settentrionale: evidence archeologiche. *Rivista di Studi Liguri* A 56 (1–4): 241–63.

Coleman, J. E. (1992) Greece, the Aegean and Cyprus. In R. W. Ehrich (ed.), *Chronologies in Old World Archaeology*, 3rd edn, Chicago University Press, Chicago, vol. I, pp. 247–88; vol. II, pp. 203–21, 222–29.

Costin, C. L. (1991) Craft specialization: issues in defining, documenting and explaining the organization of production. In M. B. Schiffer (ed.), *Archaeological Method and Theory*, 3, University of Arizona Press, Tucson, vol. III, pp. 1–56.

Costin, C. L. and Hagstrum, M. B. (1995) Complexity, hierarchy and scale: a controlled comparison between Chaco Canyon, New Mexico, and La Quemada, Zacatecas. *American Antiquity* 60(4): 619–39.

Coudart, A. (1990) Tradition, uniformity and variability of the architecture in the Danubian Neolithic. In I. Rulf (ed.), *Proceedings of the International Seminar on the Neolithic Site of Bylany, Liblice (April 1987)*, Czekoslovenska Akademie Z. Ved, Archeologicky, Prague, pp. 199–223.

Coudart, A. (1991) Social structure and social relationships in prehistoric small-scale sedentary societies: the Bandkeramik groups in Neolithic Europe. In S. Gregg (ed.), *Between Bands and States: Sedentism, Subsistence and Interaction in Small-Scale Societies*, Center for Archaeological Investigations, occasional paper 9, Southern Illinois University, Carbondale, pp. 395–420.

Coudart, A. (1993) De l'usage de l'architecture domestique et de l'anthropologie sociale dans l'approche des sociétés néolithiques: l'exemple du Néolithique danubien. In *Le Néolithique du nord-ouest de la France et des régions limitrophes. 13ème Colloque Interrégional sur le Néolithique, Paris, 1986*, Editions de la Maison des Sciences de l'Homme, Paris, pp. 114–35 (Documents d'Archéologie Française 41).

Coudart, A. (1994) Maisons néolithiques, maisons de Nouvelle-Guinée. L'ethnologie comparée sur choix social et technique. In B. Latour and P. Lemonnier (eds.), *De la préhistoire aux missiles balistiques. L'intelligence sociale des techniques*, La Découverte, Paris, pp. 228–52.

Coudart, A. (1998) *Architecture et société néolithique,* Editions de la Maison des Sciences de l'Homme, Paris (Documents d'Archéologie Française 67).

Courty, M.-A., Macphail, R. J. and Wattez, J. (1991) Soil micromorphological indicators of pastoralism. *Rivista di Studi Liguri* A 57(1–4): 127–50.

Cullen, T. (1995) Mesolithic mortuary ritual at Franchthi Cave, Greece. *Antiquity* 69(263): 270–89.

Cullen, T. (in press) *Human Remains from the Franchthi Cave.* Excavations at Franchthi Cave, Indiana University Press, Bloomington.

Dakaris, S. I., Higgs, E. S. and Hey, R. W. (1964) The climate, environment and industries of Stone Age Greece, part I. *Proceedings of the Prehistoric Society* 30: 199–246.

Dalton, G. (1977) Aboriginal economies in stateless societies. In T. K. Earle and J. Ericson (eds.), *Exchange Systems in Prehistory,* Academic Press, New York, pp. 191–212.

Dandrau, A. (1997) La construction en terre dans le monde égéen au Néolithique et à l'Age du Bronze: les matériaux et leurs propriétés, Thèse de doctorat, Université Paris I, 2 vols.

Darcque, P. and Treuil, R. (1997) Un 'bucrane' néolithique. *Dossiers d'Archéologie* 222: 26–7.

Davis, J. L. (1991) Contributions to a Mediterranean rural archaeology: historical case studies from the Ottoman Cyclades. *Journal of Mediterranean Archaeology* 4(2): 131–216.

Davis, J. L. (1992) Review of the Aegean Prehistory I: the islands of the Aegean. *American Journal of Archaeology* 96(4): 699–756.

Deïlaki, E. (1973/4 (1979)) Eforeia klassikon archaiotiton Navplion 1973–1974. *Archaiologikon Deltion* 29 (B'), chronika: 202.

Deith, M. R. and Shackleton, N. J. (1988) Oxygen isotope analysis of marine molluscs from Franchthi Cave. In J. C. Shackleton, *Marine Molluscan Remains from Franchthi Cave,* Excavations at Franchthi Cave, Greece, fasc. 4, Indiana University Press, Bloomington and Indianapolis, pp. 133–56.

Demitrack, A. (1986) The Late Quaternary geologic history of the Larissa Plain, Thessaly, Greece: tectonic, climatic and human impact on the landscape, Ph. D. thesis, Stanford University.

Demoule, J.-P. (1993) Anatolie et Balkans: la logique évolutive du néolithique égéen. In J. Roodenberg (ed.), Anatolia and the Balkans, *Anatolica* 19: 1–13.

Demoule, J.-P. and Lichardus-Itten, M. with the collaboration of I. Kulov and M. Grebska-Kulova (1994) Les fouilles franco-bulgares du site néolithique ancien de Kovačevo: rapport préliminaire (campagnes 1986–1993). *Bulletin de Correspondance Hellénique* 118(2): 561–616.

Demoule, J.-P. and Perlès, C. (1993) The Greek Neolithic: a new review. *Journal of World Prehistory* 7(4): 355–416.

Dennell, R. (1974) Botanical evidence for prehistoric crop processing activities. *Journal of Archaeological Science* 1(3): 275–84.

Dennell, R. (1976) The economic importance of plant resources represented on archaeological sites. *Journal of Archaeological Science* 3(3): 229–47.

Dennell, R. (1983) *European Economic Prehistory: a New Approach,* Academic Press, London.

Dennell, R. (1984) The expansion of exogenous-based economies across Europe: the Balkans and central Europe. In S. P. De Atley and F. J. Findlow (eds.),

Exploring the Limits. Frontiers and Boundaries in Prehistory, British Archaeological Reports, Int. series 223, Oxford, pp. 93–115.

Dennell, R. (1985) The hunter-gatherer/agricultural frontier in prehistoric temperate Europe. In S. W. Green and S. J. Perlman (eds.), *The Archaeology of Frontiers and Boundaries,* Academic Press, New York, pp. 113–39.

Dennell, R. (1992) The origins of crop agriculture in Europe. In C. Wesley Cowan and P. J. Watson (eds.), *The Origins of Agriculture. An International Perspective,* Smithsonian Institution Press, Washington, DC, pp. 71–100.

Dianellos, St. (1994) Zoi 45.000 chronou. *Ta Nea* 3 September 1994: 24.

Dikaios, P. (1953) *Khirokitia,* Oxford University Press, Oxford.

Dōi, T. (1998) L'histoire et les formes de l'époque Jomon. In *Jomon, l'art du Japon des origines,* Maison de la Culture du Japon à Paris, Paris, pp. 20–9.

Dolukhanov, P. M. (1983) The Neolithic of SW Asia and of SE Europe as seen through the radiocarbon chronology. *14C and Archaeology, Symposium Held at Groningen, August 1981,* PACT 8, Strasbourg, pp. 469–90.

Driesch, A. von den (1987) Haus- und Jagdtiere im vorgeschichtlichen Thessalien. *Praehistorische Zeitschrift* 62: 1–21.

Dubin, L. S. (1987) *The History of Beads from 30,000 BC to the Present,* Thames and Hudson, London.

Efstratiou, N. (1985) *Agios Petros. A Neolithic Site in the Northern Sporades. Aegean Relationships During the Neolithic of the 5th Millennium,* British Archaeological Reports, Int. series 241, Oxford.

Efstratiou, N. (1992 [1995]) Proneolitika evrimata apo tin aigaiaki Thraki. *To Archaiologiko Ergo sti Makedonia kai Thraki* 6: 643–51.

Efstratiou, N. (1993) New prehistoric finds from western Thrace, Greece. In J. Roodenberg (ed.), Anatolia and the Balkans, *Anatolica* 19: 33–46.

Ehrenreich, R. M., Crumley, C. M., and Levy, J. E. (eds.) (1995) *Heterarchy and the Analysis of Complex Societies,* American Anthropological Association, Arlington, VA.

Elster, E. (1989) The chipped stone industries. In M. Gimbutas, Sh. Winn and D. Shimabuku (eds.), *Achilleion, a Neolithic Settlement in Thessaly, Greece, 6400–5600 B.C.,* Institute of Archaeology, Monumenta Archaeologica 14, University of California, Los Angeles, pp. 273–306.

Elster, E. (1997) Construction and use of the Early Bronze Age burnt house at Sitagroi: craft and technology. In R. Laffineur and Ph. P. Betancourt (eds.), *Techni. Craftsmen, Craftswomen and Craftsmanship in the Aegean Bronze Age,* Annales d'Archéologie Egéenne de l'Université de Liège and UT-PASP, Liège, Austin, pp. 20–35 (Aegaeum 16).

Evans, J. D. (1964) Excavations in the Neolithic settlement of Knossos 1957–1960, part I. *Annual of the British School at Athens* 59: 132–240.

Evans, J. D. (1968) Knossos Neolithic, part II: summary and conclusions. *Annual of the British School at Athens* 63: 267–76.

Evans, J. D. (1971) Neolithic Knossos, the growth of a settlement. *Proceedings of the Prehistoric Society* 37: 95–117.

Fagg, W. (1970) *Miniature Wood Carving of Africa,* Adams and Dart, Bath.

Farrugia, J.-P. (1992) *Les outils et les armes en pierre dans le rituel funéraire du Néolithique Danubien,* Tempus Reparatus, Oxford (BAR International Series 581).

Flannery, K. V. (1972) The origins of the village as a settlement type in Mesoamerica and the Near East: a comparative study. In P. J. Ucko, R.

Tringham and G. W. Dimbleby (eds.), *Man, Settlement and Urbanism,* Duckworth, London, pp. 23–53.

Forbes, H. (1989) Of grandfathers and grand theories: the hierarchised ordering of responses to hazard in a Greek rural community. In P. Halstead and J. O'Shea (eds.), *Bad Year Economics. Cultural Responses to Risk and Uncertainty,* Cambridge University Press, Cambridge, pp. 87–97.

Forest, J.-D. (1993) Çatal Höyük et son décor: pour le déchiffrement d'un code symbolique. *Anatolia Antiqua* 2: 1–42.

Fotiadis, M. (1985) Economy, ecology and settlement among subsistence farmers in the Serres Basin, northeastern Greece, 5000–1000 BC., Ph. D. thesis, Indiana University.

French, D. H. (1964) Prehistoric Pottery from Macedonia and Thrace. *Praehistorische Zeitschrift,* 42: 30–48.

French, D. H. (1970) Pottery distribution and the geographical regions of Macedonia. *Sbornik Narodnog Muzeja,* 6, Beograd, p. 5–19.

French, D. H. (s.d.) *A Survey of Prehistoric Sites in Thessaly,* manuscript on files.

Galili, E. *et al.* (1993) Atlit-Yam: a prehistoric site on the sea floor off the Israeli coast. *Journal of Field Archaeology* 20(2): 133–57.

Gallis, K. (1975) Kafseis necron apo tin archaioteran neolithikin epohin eis tin Thessalian. *Athens Annals of Archaeology* 8(2): 241–58.

Gallis, K. (1982) *Kafseis Nekron apo tin Neolithiki Epochi sti Thessalia,* Ekdosi Tameiou archaeiologikôn porôn kai apallotrioseôn, Athens.

Gallis, K. (1985) A Late Neolithic foundation offering from Thessaly. *Antiquity* 59: 20–4.

Gallis, K. (1989) Atlas proïstorikon oikismon tis anatolikis thessalikis pediadas. *Thessaliko Imerologio* 16: 6–144.

Gallis, K. (1992) *Atlas Proïstorikon Oikismon tis Anatolikis Thessalikis Pediadas,* Ephoria of Antiquities, Larisa.

Gallis, K. (1994) Results of recent excavations and topographical work in Neolithic Thessaly. In *La Thessalie. Quinze années de recherches archéologiques, 1975–1990,* vol. I, *Bilans et perspectives,* Ministère de la Culture, Editions Kapon, Athens, pp. 57–60.

Gallis, K. (1996a) Burial customs. In G. A. Papathanassopoulos (ed.), *Neolithic Culture in Greece,* Nicholas P. Goulandris Foundation, Museum of Cycladic Art, Athens, pp. 171–4.

Gallis, K. (1996b) Die Grabungen von Platia Magula Zarkou, Souphli Magula und Makrychori 2. In E. Alram-Stern. *Die ägäische Frühzeit. 2 Serie. Forschungsbericht 1975–1993,* vol. I, 1. Band. *Das Neolithikum in Griechenland.* Verlag der Österreichischen Akademie der Wissenchaften, Wien, pp. 521–62.

Gallis, K. and Orphanidis, L. (1996) *Figurines of Neolithic Thessaly,* vol. I. Academy of Athens, Research Center for Antiquity, Athens (Monograph 3).

Gamble, Cl. (1982) Animal husbandry, population and urbanisation. In C. Renfrew and J. M. Wagstaff (eds.), *An Island Polity. The Archaeology of Exploitation in Melos,* Cambridge University Press, Cambridge, pp. 161–71.

Gardner, E. J. (1978) The pottery technology of the Neolithic period in southeastern Europe, Ph. D. thesis, University of California, Los Angeles.

Gassin, B. (1993) Approche fonctionnelle des industries lithiques du Néolithique Provençal. L'exemple du site chasséen de la Grotte de l'eglise supérieure, Thèse de doctorat, Université de Paris X, 2 vols.

Gauthier, J.-G. (1989) Aspects socio-culturels du tissage et de ses productions dans les cultures anciennes et les sociétés traditionnelles d'Afrique noire. In *Tissage, corderie, vannerie. Actes des IXèmes rencontres internationales d'archéologie et d'histoire d'Antibes*, Editions APDCA, Juan-les-Pins, pp. 95–112.

Gautier, A. (1990) *La domestication. Et l'homme créa l'animal*, Editions Errance, Paris.

Gebauer, A. B. (1995) Pottery production and the introduction of agriculture in Southern Scandinavia. In W. K. Barnett and J. H. Hoopes (eds.), *The Emergence of Pottery. Technology and Innovation in Ancient Societies*, Smithsonian Institution Press, Washington, DC, pp. 99–112.

Gebauer, A. B. and Price, T. D. (eds.) (1992) *Transitions to Agriculture in Prehistory*, Prehistory Press, Madison (Monographs in World Prehistory 4).

Geijer, A. (1979) *A History of Textile Art*, Pasold Research Fund, Stockholm.

Gevjall, N.-G. (1969) *Lerna. A Preclassical Site in the Argolid. Results of Excavations Conducted by the American School of Classical Studies at Athens*, vol. I, *The Fauna*, American School of Classical Studies at Athens, Princeton.

Giere, R. N. (1988) *Explaining Science. A Cognitive Approach*, University of Chicago Press, Chicago.

Gifford, J. A. (1990) Analysis of submarine sediments off Paralia. In T. J. Wilkinson and S. Duhon, *Franchthi Paralia, the Sediments, Stratigraphy, and Offshore Investigations*, Excavations at Franchthi Cave, Greece, fasc. 6, Indiana University Press, Bloomington and Indianapolis, pp. 85–116.

Gimbutas, M. (1974) Achilleion: a neolithic mound in Thessaly. Preliminary report on the 1973/1974 excavation. *Journal of Field Archaeology* 1: 277–303.

Gimbutas, M. (1982) *The Goddesses and Gods of Old Europe, 6000–3500 BC. Myths and Cult Images*, Thames and Hudson, London.

Gimbutas, M. (1989a) Figurines and cult equipment: their role in the reconstruction of Neolithic religion. In M. Gimbutas, Sh. Winn and D. Shimabuku (eds.), *Achilleion, a Neolithic Settlement in Thessaly, Greece, 6400–5600 BC*, Institute of Archaeology, Monumenta Archaeologica 14, University of California, Los Angeles, pp. 171–250.

Gimbutas, M. (1989b) Ornaments and miscellaneous objects. In M. Gimbutas, Sh. Winn and D. Shimabuku (eds.), *Achilleion, a Neolithic Settlement in Thessaly, Greece, 6400–5600 BC*, Institute of Archaeology, Monumenta Archaeologica 14, University of California, Los Angeles, pp. 251–8.

Gimbutas, M. (1991) *The Civilization of the Goddess*, Harper San Francisco, San Francisco.

Gimbutas M., Winn Sh. and Shimabuku D. (eds.) (1989) *Achilleion, a Neolithic Settlement in Thessaly, Greece, 6400–5600 BC*, Institute of Archaeology, Monumenta Archaeologica 14, University of California, Los Angeles.

Gopher, A. and Gophna, R. (1993) Cultures of the eighth and seventh millennia BP in the Southern Levant: a review for the 1990s. *Journal of World Archaeology* 7(3): 297–353.

Gosselain, O. (1992) Bonfire of the enquiries. Pottery firing temperatures in archaeology: what for? *Journal of Archaeological Science* 19: 243–59.

Gosselain, O. (1995) Identités techniques. Le travail de la poterie au Cameroun Méridional, Thèse de doctorat, Université Libre de Bruxelles, 2 vols.

Gosselain, O. (1998) Social and technical identity in a clay crystal ball. In M. T. Stark (ed.), *The Archaeology of Social Boundaries*, Smithsonian Institution Press, Washington, DC, pp. 79–106.

Grammenos, D. (1991) *Neolithikes Erevnes stin Kentriki kai Anatoliki Makedonia*, Bibliothiki tis en Athinais Archaiologikis Etaireias 117, Athens.

Grammenos, D. (1997) *Neolithiki Makedonia*, Yporgeio politismou Tameiou Archaiologikon Poron kai Apallotrioseon, Athens.

Graves, M. W. (1991) Pottery production and distribution among the Kalinga: a study of household and regional organization and differentiation. In W. A. Longacre (ed.), *Ceramic Ethnoarchaeology*, University of Arizona Press, Tucson, pp. 112–43.

Greenfield, H. J. (1988) The origins of milk and wool production in the Old World: a zooarchaeological perspective from the Central Balkans. *Current Anthropology* 29: 573–93.

Greig, J. R. A. and Turner, J. (1974) Some pollen diagrams from Greece and their archaeological significance. *Journal of Archaeological Science* 1: 177–94.

Gronenborn, D. (1990) Mesolithic-Neolithic interactions. The lithic industry of the earliest Bandkeramik culture site at Friedberg-Bruchenbrücken, Wetteraukreis (West Germany). In P. Vermeersch and P. Van Peer (eds.), *Contributions to the Mesolithic in Europe*, Leuven University Press, Leuven, pp. 173–82.

Gropengiesser, H. (1986) Siphnos, Kap Agios Sostis: Keramische prähistorische Zeugnisse aus dem Gruben- und Hüttenrevier. *Athenische Mitteilungen* 101: 1–39.

Grundmann, K. (1937) Magula Hadzimissiotiki. Eine steinzeitlichen Siedlung im Karla-See. *Athenische Mitteilungen* 62: 56–62.

Guest-Papamanoli, A. (1978) L'emploi de la brique crue dans le domaine égéen à l'époque néolithique et à l'âge du bronze. *Bulletin de Correspondance Hellénique* 102: 3–24.

Guilaine, J. (1976) *Premiers bergers et paysans de l'Occident Méditerranéen*, Mouton, Paris.

Guilaine, J., Coularou, J., Briois, F., Carrère, I. and Philibert, S. (1993) Travaux de l'Ecole française à Amathonte en 1992. 6 – Fouille néolithique. *Bulletin de Correspondance Hellénique* 117(2): 716–17.

Guilaine, J., Coularou, J., Briois, F., Carrère, I. and Philibert, S. (1994) Travaux de l'Ecole française à Amathonte en 1993. 5 – Fouille préhistorique de Shillourokambos. *Bulletin de Correspondance Hellénique* 118(2): 499–501.

Guilaine, J., Coularou, J., Briois, F., Carrère, I. (1995) Le site néolithique de Shillourokambos (Chypre). *Bulletin de Correspondance Hellénique* 119: 737–41.

Guilaine, J., Coularou, J., Briois, F., Philibert, S., and Vigne, J.–D. (1997/8) Les débuts du Néolithique à Chypre. *L'Archéologue* 33: 35–40.

Haggett, P. (1973) *L'analyse spatiale en géographie humaine*, Paris, Armand Colin.

Halstead, P. (1977) Prehistoric Thessaly: the submergence of civilisation. In J. L. Bintliff (ed.), *Mycenaean Geography*, British Association for Mycenean Studies, Cambridge, pp. 23–9.

Halstead, P. (1981a) Counting sheep in Neolithic and Bronze Age Greece. In I. Hodder, G. Isaac and N. Hammond (eds.), *Patterns of the Past: Studies in Honor of David Clarke*, Cambridge University Press, Cambridge, pp. 307–39.

Halstead, P. (1981b) From determinism to uncertainty: social storage and the rise of the Minoan palace. In A. Sheridan and G. Bailey (eds.), *Economic Archaeology. Towards an Integration of Ecological and Social Approaches*, British Archaeological Reports, Int. series 96, Oxford, pp. 187–213.

Halstead, P. (1984) Strategies for survival: an ecological approach to social and economic change in early farming communities of Thessaly, N. Greece, Ph.D. thesis, University of Cambridge, Department of Archaeology.

Halstead, P. (1987) Man and other animals in later Greek prehistory. *Annual of the British School at Athens* 82: 71–83.

Halstead, P. (1989a) The economy has a normal surplus: economic stability and social change among early farming communities of Thessaly, Greece. In P. Halstead and J. O'Shea (eds.), *Bad Year Economics. Cultural Responses to Risk and Uncertainty*, Cambridge University Press, Cambridge, pp. 68–80.

Halstead, P. (1989b) Like rising damp? An ecological approach to the spread of farming in south-east and central Europe. In A. Milles, D. Williams and N. Gardner (eds.), *The Beginnings of Agriculture*, British Archaeological Reports, Int. series 496, Oxford, pp. 23–53.

Halstead, P. (1990a) Present to past in the Pindhos: diversification and specialisation in mountain economies. *Rivista di Studi Liguri* A 56(1–4): 61–80.

Halstead, P. (1990b) Waste not, want not: traditional responses to crop failure in Greece. *Rural History* 1(2): 147–64.

Halstead, P. (1992) From reciprocity to redistribution: modelling the exchange of livestock in Neolithic Greece. *Anthropozoologica* 16: 19–30.

Halstead, P. (1993) Banking on livestock: indirect storage in Greek agriculture. *Bulletin of Sumerian Agriculture* 7: 63–75.

Halstead, P. (1994) The North–South divide: regional paths to complexity in prehistoric Greece. In C. Mathers and S. Stoddart (eds.), *Development and Decline in the Mediterranean Bronze Age*, J. R. Collis Publications, Sheffield, pp. 195–219 (Sheffield Archaeological Monographs).

Halstead, P. (1995) From sharing to hoarding: the Neolithic foundations of Aegean Bronze Age society? In Laffineur, R. and Niemeier, W.-D. (eds.), *Politeia. Society and State in the Aegean Bronze Age. Proceedings of the 5th Aegean Conference*, Université de Liège, Liège, pp. 11–21 (Aegaeum 12).

Halstead, P. (ed.) (1999) *Neolithic Society in Greece*, Sheffield Academic Press, Sheffield.

Halstead, P. and Jones, Gl. (1980) Early Neolithic economy in Thessaly: some evidence from excavations at Prodromos. *Anthropologika* 1: 93–117.

Halstead, P. and Jones, Gl. (1989) Agrarian ecology in the Greek islands: time stress, scale and risk. *Journal of Hellenic Studies* 109: 41–55.

Halstead, P. and O'Shea, J. (1982) A friend in need is a friend indeed: social storage and the origins of social ranking. In C. Renfrew and S. Shennan (eds.), *Ranking, Resources and Exchange*, Cambridge University Press, Cambridge, pp. 92–9.

Hansen, J. M. (1978) The earliest seed remains from Greece: Paleolithic through Neolithic at Franchthi Cave. *Bericht der deutschen botanisches Gesellschaft* 91: 39–46.

Hansen, J. M. (1980) The palaeoethnobotany of Franchthi Cave, Greece, Ph. D. thesis, University of Minnesota.

Hansen, J. M. (1985) Palaeoethnobotany in Greece. Past, present and future. In N. C. Wilkie and W. D. E. Coulson (eds.), *Contributions to Aegean Archaeology. Studies in Honor of William A. McDonald*, Center for Ancient Studies, University of Minnesota, Minneapolis, pp. 171–81.

Hansen, J. M. (1988) Agriculture in the Prehistoric Aegean: data versus speculation. *American Journal of Archaeology* 92: 39–52.

Hansen, J. M. (1991) *The Palaeoethnobotany of Franchthi Cave*, Excavations at Franchthi Cave, Greece, fasc. 7, Indiana University Press, Bloomington and Indianapolis.

Hansen, J. M. (1992) Franchthi cave and the beginnings of agriculture in Greece and the Aegean. In P. C. Anderson-Gerfaud (ed.), *Préhistoire de l'agriculture. Nouvelles approches expérimentales et ethnographiques*, CNRS, Paris, pp. 231–47 (Monographie du CRA no. 6).

Hansen, J. M. and Renfrew, J. M. (1978) Paleolithic-Neolithic seed remains at Franchthi Cave, Greece. *Nature* 271: 349–52.

Harlan, J. R. (1989) Wild grass seed harvesting in the Sahara and Sub-Sahara of Africa. In H. D. Harris and G. C. Hillman (eds.), *Foraging and Farming. The Evolution of Plant Exploitation*, Unwin Hyman, London, pp. 79–98 (One World Archaeology).

Hather, G. (1994) A morphological classification of roots and tubers and its bearing on the origins of agriculture in Southwest Asia and Europe. *Journal of Archaeological Science* 21(6): 719–24.

Hauptmann, H. (1971) Forschungsbericht zur ägäischen Frühzeit: das Festland und die Kleineren Inseln. *Archäologischer Anzeiger* 86: 348–87.

Hauptmann, H. (1993) Eine Kultgebäude in Nevali Çori. In N. Frangipane, H. Hauptmann, M. Liverani, P. Matthiae and M. Millink (eds.), *Between the Rivers and Over the Mountains. Archaeologica Anatolica et Mesopotamica Alba Palmieri Dedicata*, Dipt. di Scienze Storiche, Università di Roma 'La Sapienza', Rome, pp. 37–69.

Hayden, B. (1992) Contrasting expectations in theories of domestication. In A. B. Gebauer and T. D. Price (eds.), *Transitions to Agriculture in Prehistory*, Prehistory Press, Madison, pp. 11–20 (Monographs in World Prehistory 4).

Hedges, R., Housley, R., Bronk, R. and van Klinken, G. J. (1990) Radiocarbon dates from the Oxford AMS system. Archaeometry datelist 11. *Archaeometry* 32(2): 211–37.

Heikel, R. (1985) *Mediterranean Cruising Handbook*, Imray Laurie Norie and Wilson, Huntingdon.

Helbaeck, H. (1963) Textiles from Çatal Hüyük. *Archaeology* 67: 39–46.

Helly, B., Bravard, J.-P., Caputo, R. (1994) La plaine orientale de Thessalie (Grèce): mobilité des paysages historiques et évolution texto-sédimentaire. *Rapport PACT*, manuscript on files, 97 pages.

Helly, B. *et al.* (1996) *Programme 'paysage: évolution et dynamique'. Evolution comparée des écosystèmes et des systèmes sociaux en Thessalie (Grèce): temps préhistoriques et antiquité. Rapport intermédiaire (1995)*, manuscript on files, 32 pages.

Helmer, D. (1992) *La domestication des animaux par les hommes préhistoriques*, Masson, Paris.

Helms, M. W. (1988) *Ulysses' Sail. An Ethnographic Odyssey of Power, Knowledge, and Geographical Distance*, Princeton University Press, Princeton.

Herz, N. (1992) Provenance determination of Neolithic to Classical Mediterranean marbles by stable isotopes. *Archaeometry* 43(2): 185–94.

Heurtley, W. A. (1939) *Prehistoric Macedonia. An Archaeological Reconnaissance of Greek Macedonia (West of the Struma) in the Neolithic, Bronze and Early Iron Ages*, Cambridge University Press, Cambridge.

Higgins, M. D. and Higgins, R. (1996) *A Geological Companion to Greece and the Aegean*, Duckworth, London.

Higgs, E. S., Clegg, I. M. and Kinnes, I. A. (1968) Appendix VII. Saliagos animal bones. In J. D. Evans and C. Renfrew, *Excavations at Saliagos near Antiparos*, British School at Athens, supplementary volume 5, Thames and Hudson, London, pp. 114–17.

Higgs, E. S. and Jarman, M. R. (1969) The origins of agriculture: a reconsideration. *Antiquity* 43 (169): 31–41.

Higgs, E. S. and Jarman, M. R. (1972) The origin of animal and plant husbandry. In E. S. Higgs and M. R. Jarman (eds.), *Papers in Economic Prehistory*, Cambridge University Press, Cambridge, pp. 3–13.

Higgs, E. S. and Vita-Finzi, C. (1966) The climate, environment and industries of Stone Age Greece, part II. *Proceedings of the Prehistoric Society* 32: 1–29.

Higgs, E. S., Vita-Finzi, C., Harris, D. R. and Fagg, A. E. (1967) The climate, environment and industries of Stone Age Greece, part 2. *Proceedings of the Prehistoric Society* 33: 1–29.

Hillman, G. C. (1981) Reconstructing crop husbandry practices from charred remains of crops. In R. Mercer (ed.), *Farming Practices in British Prehistory*, Edinburgh University Press, Edinburgh, pp. 123–62.

Hillman, G. C. and Davies, M. S. (1990) Measured domestication rates in wild wheats and barley under primitive cultivation, and their archaeological implications. *Journal of World Prehistory* 4(2): 157–222.

Hodder, I. (1990) *The Domestication of Europe. Structure and Contingency in Neolithic Societies*, Basil Blackwell, Oxford.

Hoffman, M. (1974) *The Warp-Weighted Loom. Studies in the History and Technology of an Ancient Implement*, Tromsö, Oslo and Bergen.

Holl, A. (1990) Unité de production et unité de consommation dans le Néolithique du Dhar Tichitt (Mauritanie). *L'Anthropologie* 94(3): 535–58.

Honea, K. (1975) Prehistoric remains on the island of Kythnos. *American Journal of Archaeology* 79: 277–9.

Hopf, M. (1962) Bericht über die Untersuchugen von Samen und Holzkohlenreste von der Argissa-Magula aus den präkeramischen bis mittlebronzezeitlichen Schichten. In V. Milojčić, J. Boessneck and M. Hopf, *Die deutschen Ausgrabungen auf der Argissa-Magula in Thessalien, I. Das präkeramische Neolithikum sowie die Tier- und Pflanzenreste*, Beiträge zur ur- und frühgeschichtlichen Archäologie des Mittelmeer-Kulturraumes 2, Rudolf Habelt, Bonn, pp. 101–10.

Hourmouziadis, G. (1969a) Magoula Koskina. *Athens Annals of Archaeology* 2(1): 93–5.

Hourmouziadis, G. (1969b) Eidiseis ek Thessalias. *Athens Annals of Archaeology* 2(2): 167–72.

Hourmouziadis, G. (1971a (1972)) I diakekozmimeni kerameiki tis archaioteras neolithikis periodou eis tin Thessalian. *Archaiologiki Efimerides 1971*: 165–87.

Hourmouziadis, G. (1971b) Dio neai egkatastaseis tis archaioteras Neolithikis eis tin dytikin Thessalian. *Athens Annals of Archaeology* 4(2): 164–75.

Hourmouziadis, G. (1972) Anaskafai is ton Prodromon Karditsis. *Archaiologikon Deltion* 27(B'), Chronika: 394–6.

Hourmouziadis, G. (1973a) *I Anthropomorphi Eidoloplastiki tis Neolithikis Thessalias*, Etaireia Thessalikon Erevnon, Volos.

Hourmouziadis, G. (1973b) Burial customs. In D. Theocharis, *Neolithic Greece*, National Bank of Greece, Athens, pp. 201–12.

Hours, F. and Copeland, L. (1982) Les rapports entre l'Anatolie et la Syrie du Nord
à l'époque des premières communautés villageoises de bergers et paysans. In
T. C. Young, Ph. E. L. Smith and P. Mortensen (eds.), *The Hilly Flanks. Essays
on the Prehistory of Southwestern Asia Presented to R. J. Braidwood*,
Oriental Institute of the University of Chicago, Chicago, pp. 75–90 (Studies
in Ancient Oriental Civilization 36).

Hubbard, R. N. (1975) Assessing the botanical component of human
palaeoeconomies. *Bulletin of the Institute of Archaeology* 12: 197–205.

Hubbard, R. N. (1976) Crops and climate in prehistoric Europe. *World
Archaeology* 8(2): 159–68.

Huntley, B. and Prentice, I. C. (1988) July temperatures in Europe from pollen
data, 6000 years Before Present. *Science* 241: 687–90.

Huot, J.-L. (1994) *Les premiers villageois de Mésopotamie: du village à la ville*,
Armand Colin, Paris.

Jacobsen, T. W. (1969) Excavations at Porto Cheli and vicinity, preliminary report,
II: the Franchthi Cave. *Hesperia* 38: 343–81.

Jacobscn, T. W. (1976) 17,000 years of Greek Prehistory. *Scientific American*
234(6): 76–88.

Jacobsen, T. W. (1981) Franchthi Cave and the beginning of settled village life in
Greece. *Hesperia* 50(4): 303–19.

Jacobsen, T. W. (1993) Maritime mobility in the Prehistoric Aegean. Paper
Presented at the XXth Meeting on Maritime Archaeology, Nafplion, 23
pages.

Jacobsen, T. W. and Cullen, T. (1981) A consideration of mortuary practices in
Neolithic Greece: burials from Franchthi Cave. In S. C. Humphreys and H.
King (eds.), *Mortality and Immortality: the Anthropology and Archaeology
of Death*, Academic Press, London, pp. 79–101.

Jacobsen, T. W. and Farrand, W. R. (1987) *Franchthi Cave and Paralia. Maps,
Plans and Sections*, Excavations at Franchthi Cave, fasc. 1, Indiana
University Press, Bloomington and Indianapolis.

Jacobshagen, V. (1986) *Geologie von Griechenland*, Gebrüde Borntraeger, Berlin,
Stuttgart.

Jahns, S. (1990) Preliminary notes on human influence and the history of
vegetation in S. Dalmatia and S. Greece. In S. Bottema, G. Entjes-Nieborg and
W. van Zeist (eds.), *Man's Role in the Shaping of the Eastern Mediterranean
Landscape*, Balkema, Rotterdam, pp. 333–40.

Jameson, M. H., Runnels, C. and van Andel, Tj. H. (1994) *A Greek Countryside:
the Southern Argolid from Prehistory to Present Day*, Stanford University
Press, Stanford.

Johnson, G. A. (1978) Information sources and the development of decision-
making organizations. In C. L. Redman *et al.* (eds.), *Social Archaeology:
Beyond Subsistence and Dating*, Academic Press, New York, pp. 87–112.

Johnson, G. A. (1982) Organization structure and scalar stress. In C. Renfrew, M.
J. Rowlands and B. A. Segraves (eds.), *Theory and Explanation in
Archaeology*, Academic Press, New York, pp. 389–421.

Johnson, M. (1996a) The Berbati-Limnes archaeological survey. The Neolithic
period. In B. Wells (ed.), *The Berbati-Limnes Archaeological Survey
1988–1990*, Acta Instituti Atheniensis Regni Sueciae, series in 4, 44,
Stockholm, pp. 37–73.

Johnson, M. (1996b) Water, animals and agricultural technology: a study of settlement patterns and economic change in Neolithic Southern Greece. *Oxford Journal of Archaeology* 15(3): 267–95.

Jones, G. (1987) A statistical approach to the archaeological identification of crop processing. *Journal of Archaeological Science* 14: 311–23.

Jones, G. (1992) Weed phytosociology and crop husbandry: identifying a contrast between ancient and modern practices. *Review of Palaeobotany and Palynology* 73: 133–43.

Jones, G. and Halstead, P. (1995) Maslins, mixtures and monocrops: on the interpretation of archaeobotanical crop samples of heterogeneous composition. *Journal of Archaeological Science* 22(1): 103–14.

Jones, R. E. (1986) *Greek and Cypriot Pottery. A Review of Scientific Studies*, British School at Athens, Fitch Laboratory occasional paper 1, Athens.

Kaiser, T. and Voytek, B. (1983) Sedentism and economic change in the Balkan Neolithic. *Journal of Anthropological Archaeology* 2(4): 323–53.

Kanafani-Zahar, A. (1994) *Mūne. La conservation alimentaire traditionelle au Liban*, Editions de la Maison des Sciences de l'Homme, Paris.

Keeley, L. H. (1992) The introduction of agriculture to the Western North European plain. In A. B. Gebauer and T. D. Price (eds.), *Transitions to Agriculture in Prehistory*, Prehistory Press, Madison, pp. 81–95 (Monographs in World Prehistory 4).

Keeley, L. H. (1996) *War Before Civilization*, Oxford University Press, New York and Oxford.

Keller, D. and Cullen, T. (1992) Prehistoric occupation of the Paximadhi Peninsula, Southern Euboea. *American Journal of Archaeology* 96: 341.

Kenyon, K. (1957) Excavations at Jericho 1957. *Palestine Exploration Quaterly* 89: 101–7.

Kirsten, E. (1950) Beiträge zur historischen Landeskunde von Thessalien. In A. Philippson, *Die Griechische Landschaften* 1.1: *Thessalien und die Spercheios-Senke*, Vittorio Klostermann, Frankfurt, pp. 259–308.

Kosmopoulos, L. M. (1948) *The Prehistoric Inhabitation of Corinth*, vol. I, Bisher F. Bruckmann, Munich.

Kotjabopoulou, E., Panagopoulou, E. and Adam, E. (1999) The Boila Rockshelter: further evidence of human activity in the Voidomatis gorge. In G. N. Bailey *et al.* (eds.), *The Palaeolithic Archaeology of Greece and Adjacent Areas: Proceedings of the ICOPAG Conference, Ioannina, September 1994*, British School at Athens Studies 3, London.

Kotsakis, K. (1983) *Kerameiki Technologia kai Kerameiki Diaforopoiisi. Provlimata tis Graptis Kerameikis tis Mesis Epohis tou Sesklou*, Didaktoriki Diatrivi, Thessaloniki.

Kotsakis, K. (1986) Aspects of technology and distribution of MN Pottery of Sesklo. In R. E. Jones and H. W. Catling (eds.), *Science in Archaeology. Proceedings of a Meeting Held at the British School at Athens, January 1985*, British School at Athens, Fitch Laboratory occasional paper 2, pp. 1–2.

Kotsakis, K. (1992) O neolithikos tropos paragogis. Ithagenis i apoikos. In *Diethnes Synedrio gia tin Archaia Thessalia sti Mnimi tou Dimitri P. Theochari*, Ekdosi Tameiou Archaeiologikôn Porôn kai Apallotrioseôn, Athens, pp. 120–35.

Kourtessi-Phillipakis, G. (1986) *Le Paléolithique de la Grèce continentale. Etat de la question et perspectives de recherche*, Publications de la Sorbonne, Paris.

Kourtessi-Phillipakis, G. (1992) I anthropini parousia sti Makedonia prin apo ti Neolithiki epochi. In I. Aslanis (ed.), *I Proïstoria tis Makedonias. I. I Neolithiki Epochi*, Ekdoseis Kardamitsa, Athens, pp. 39–47.

Kozłowski, J. K., Kaczanowska, M., and Pawlikowski, M. (1996) Chipped-stone industries from Neolithic levels at Lerna. *Hesperia* 65: 295–372.

Kraft, J. C. *et al.* (1985) Geological studies of coastal change applied to archaeological settings. In G. Rapp and J. A. Gifford (eds.), *Archaeological Geology*, Yale University Press, New Haven, pp. 57–84.

Kroll, H. (1981) Thessalische Kulturpflanzen. *Zeitschrift für Archäologie* 15(1): 97–103.

Kroll, H. (1983) *Kastanas, Ausgrabungen in einem Siedlungshügel der Bronze und Eisenzeit Makedoniens 1975–1979. Die Pflanzenfunde*, Volker Spiess, Berlin.

Kroll, H. (1991) Südosteuropa. In W. Van Zeist, K. Wasylikowa and K. H. Behre (eds.), *Progress in Old World Palaeoethnobotany*, Balkema, Rotterdam, pp. 161–77.

Kuijt, I. (1994) Pre-Pottery Ncolithic A settlement variability: evidence for sociopolitical developments in the Southern Levant. *Journal of Mediterranean Archaeology* 7(2): 165–92.

Kyparissi-Apostolika, N. (1992) Kozmimata tis neolithikis Thessalias. In *Diethnes Synedrio gia tin Archaia Thessalia sti Mnimi tou Dimitri P. Theochari*, Ekdosi Tameiou Archaeiologikôn Porôn kai Apallotrioseôn, Athens, pp. 185–90.

Kyparissi-Apostolika, N. (1999) The Palaeolithic deposits of Theopetra Cave. In G. N. Bailey *et al.* (eds.), *The Palaeolithic Archaeology of Greece and Adjacent Areas: Proceedings of the ICOPAG Conference, Ioannina, September 1994*, British School at Athens Studies 3, London.

L'Helgouach, J. (1997/8) L'art et la religion. *L'Archéologue* 33: 27–34.

Ladizinsky, G. (1989) Origin and domestication of the southwest Asian grain legumes. In D. R. Harris and G. C. Hillman (eds.), *Foraging and Farming. The Evolution of Plant Exploitation*, Unwin Hyman, London, pp. 374–89 (One World Archaeology).

Lambeck, K. (1996) Sea-level change and shoreline evolution in Aegean Greece since Upper Palaeolithic time. *Antiquity* 70: 588–611.

Laporte, L., Desse-Berset, N. Gruet, Y. and Tresset, A. (1998) Un lieu de fabrication de parure au Néolithique final et son économie de subsistance. Le site de Ponthezières à Saint-Georges-d'Oléron (Charente-Maritime). In X. Gutherz and R. Joussaume (eds.), *Le Néolithique du centre-ouest de la France, Actes du XXIe colloque inter-régional sur le Néolithique, Poitiers, 14–16 oct. 1994*, A. P. D., Chauvigny, pp. 237–55.

Larje, R. (1987) Animal bones. In P. Hellström (ed.), *Paradeisos. A Late Neolithic Settlement in Aegean Thrace*, Medelhavsmuseet, Memoir 7, Stockholm, pp. 89–118.

Launay, R. (1988) Warriors and traders. The political organization of a West African chiefdom. *Cahiers d'Etudes Africaines* 111–112, 28(3–4): 355–73.

Launay, R. (1982) *Traders Without Trade. Responses to Change in two Dyula Communities*. Cambridge University Press, Cambridge.

Le Brun, A. (1981) *Un site Néolithique en Chypre: Cap Andreas Kastros*, Editions ADPF, Paris.

Le Brun, A. (1989) Le traitement des morts et les représentations des vivants à

Khirokitia. In E. Peltenburg (ed.), *Early Society in Cyprus*, Edinburgh University Press, Edinburgh, pp. 71–81.

Le Brun, A. (ed.) (1984) *Fouilles récentes à Khirokitia (Chypre), 1977–1981*, Editions Recherche sur les Civilisations, Paris, 2 vols. (Mémoire 41).

Le Brun, A. (ed.) (1989) *Fouilles récentes à Khirokitia (Chypre), 1983–1986*, Editions Recherche sur les Civilisations, Paris (Mémoire 81).

Le Brun, A. (ed.) (1994) *Fouilles récentes à Khirokitia (Chypre), 1988–1991*, Editions Recherche sur les Civilisations, Paris.

Lebeuf, J.-P. (1962) *Archéologie tchadienne*, Hermann, Paris.

Leclerc, J. (1997) Analyse spatiale des sites funéraires néolithiques. In *Espaces physiques, espaces sociaux dans l'analyse interne des sites du Néolithique à l'Age du Fer, 119ème Congrès CTH, Amiens, 1994*, Editions du CTHS, Paris, pp. 397–405.

Le Mière, M. and Picon, M. (1998). Les débuts de la céramique au Proche-Orient. *Paléorient* 24(2): 5–26.

Lemonnier, P. (1990) *Guerres et festins, paix, échanges et compétitions dans les Highlands de la Nouvelle-Guinée*, Editions de la Maison des Sciences de l'Homme, Paris.

Levy, T. E. and Holl, A. (1987) Theory and practice in household archaeology: a case study from the Chalcolithic village at Shiqmim. In T. E. Levy (ed.), *Shiqmim I*, British Archaeological Reports, Int. series 356, Oxford, pp. 373–410 and 690–730.

Lewthwaite, J. (1986) The transition to food production: a Mediterranean perspective. In M. Zvelebil (ed.), *Hunters in Transition: Mesolithic Societies of Temperate Eurasia and their Transition to Farming*, Cambridge University Press, Cambridge, pp. 53–66.

Lichardus, J. and Lichardus-Itten, M. (1985) Diffusion de la civilisation néolithique en Europe et évolution historico-culturelle jusqu'à la fin du Néolithique: In J. Lichardus, M. Lichardus-Itten, G. Bailloud and J. Cauvin, *La protohistoire de l'Europe. Le Néolithique et le Chalcolithique entre la Méditerranée et la Mer Baltique*. Presses Universitaires de France, Paris, pp. 207–515 (Nouvelle Clio 1bis).

Lichardus, J., Lichardus-Itten, M., Bailloud, G. and Cauvin, J. (1985) *La protohistoire de l'Europe. Le Néolithique et le Chalcolithique entre la Méditerranée et la Mer Baltique*, Presses Universitaires de France, Paris (Nouvelle Clio 1bis).

Lichardus-Itten, M. (1993) Zum Beginn des Neolithikums im Tal der Struma (Südwest-Bulgarien). In J. Roodenberg (ed.), Anatolia and the Balkans, *Anatolica* 19: 99–116.

Liolios, D. (1992) *Approche des relations techno-économiques entre le lithique et l'os dans l'Aurignacien d'Aquitaine*, Mémoire de maîtrise, Université Paris X.

Maggi, R., Nisbet, R. and Barker, G. (eds.) (1991) *Atti della Tavola Rotonda Internazionale: Archeologia della Pastorizia nell' Europa Meridionale, I*, Estratto dalla Rivista di Studi Liguri, A. 56 (1990), Instituto Internazionale di Studi Liguri.

Maggi, R., Nisbet, R. and Barker, G. (eds.) (1992) *Atti della Tavola Rotonda Internazionale: Archeologia della Pastorizia nell' Europa Meridionale, II*, Estratto dalla Rivista di Studi Liguri, A. 57 (1991), Instituto Internazionale di Studi Liguri.

Maigrot, Y. (1997) Tracéologie des outils tranchants en os des Vème et IVème millénaires av. J. C. en Bassin Parisien. Essai méthodologique et application. *Bulletin de la Société Préhistorique Française* 94(2): 198–216.

Makkay, J. (1984) *Early Stamp Seals in South-East Europe*, Akademiai Kiado, Budapest.

Maniatis, Y. and Perdikatsis, V. (1983) Technologiki kai proelevsiaki meleti tis kerameikis tou Sesklou. In K. Kotsakis, *Kerameiki Technologia kai Kerameiki Diaforopoiisi. Provlimata tis Graptis Kerameikis tis Mesis Epohis tou Sesklou*, Didaktoriki Diatrivi, Thessaloniki, pp. 483–92.

Maniatis, Y., Perdikatsis, V. and Kotsakis, K. (1988) Assessment of in-site variability of pottery from Sesklo, Thessaly. *Archaeometry* 30(2): 264–74.

Maniatis, Y. and Tite, M. S. (1981) Technological examination of Neolithic-Bronze Age pottery from Central and Southeast Europe and from the Near-East. *Journal of Archaeological Science* 8: 59–76.

Manson, J. L. (1995) Starčevo pottery and Neolithic development in the central Balkans. In W. K. Barnett and J. H. Hoopes (eds.), *The Emergence of Pottery. Technology and Innovation in Ancient Societies*, Smithsonian Institution Press, Washington, DC, pp. 65–77.

Marangou, Ch. (1986) Problèmes d'interprétation des objets miniatures de Dikili Tash (Néolithique récent). In A. Bonanno (ed.), *Archaeology and Fertility Cult in the Ancient Mediterranean*, University of Malta, Malta, pp. 55–61.

Marangou, Ch. (1992) *Eidolia. Figurines et miniatures du Néolithique récent et du Bronze Ancien en Grèce*, British Archaeological Reports, Int. series 576, Oxford.

Marangou, L. (1985) Anaskafi Minoas Amorgou. *Praktika tis en Athinais Archaiologiki Etairias 1985*: 30.

Maréchal, Cl. (1989) Vannerie et tissage du site néolithique d'El Kown (Syrie, VIème millénaire). In D. Stordeur (ed.), *Tissage, corderie, vannerie. Actes des IXèmes rencontres internationales d'archéologie et d'histoire d'Antibes*, Editions APDCA, Juan-les-Pins, pp. 53–67.

Markovits, A. (1928) Peri ton mechri semeron erevnon epi tes lithikis periodou tis Ellados. *Praktika tis Ellinikis Anthropologikis Etairias 1928*: 114–34.

Markovits, A. (1932–3) Die Zaïmis-Höhle (Kaki-Skala, Megaris, Griechenland). *Speläologisches Jahrbuch* 13–14: 133–46.

Martini, F. (ed.) (1993) *Grotta della Serratura a Marina di Camerota. Culture e Ambienti dei Complessi Olocenici*, Garlatti and Razzai Editori, s.l.

Masset, Cl. (1971) Erreurs systématiques dans la détermination de l'âge par les sutures crâniennes. *Bulletins et Mémoires de la Société d'Anthropologie de Paris* 7(12): 85–105.

Mauss, M. (1960) Essai sur le don, forme et raison de l'échange dans les sociétés archaïques. In *Sociologie et Anthropologie*, Presses Universitaires de France, Paris, 2nd edn, pp. 145–279.

Mayor, A. (1994) Durée de vie des céramiques africaines: facteurs responsables et implications archéologiques. In *Terre cuite et société. la céramique, document technique, économique et culturel. Actes des XIVèmes rencontres internationales d'Archéologie et d'Histoire d'Antibes*, Editions APDCA, Juan-les-Pins, pp. 179–98.

McDonald, W. A. and Rapp, G. R. (1972) *The Minnesota Messenia Expedition: Reconstructing a Bronze Age Regional Environment*, University of Minnesota Press, Minneapolis.

McGeehan-Liritzis, V. (1983) The relationships between metalwork, copper sources and the evidence for settlement in the Greek Late Neolithic and Early Bronze Age. *Oxford Journal of Archaeology* 2(2): 147–80.

Mellaart, J. (1964) Excavations at Çatal Hüyük, 1963. Third preliminary report. *Anatolian Studies* 14: 39–119.

Mellaart, J. (1965) *Earliest Civilizations of the Near East*, McGraw-Hill, New York.

Mellaart, J. (1967) *Çatal Hüyük: a Neolithic Town in Anatolia*, Thames and Hudson, London.

Mellaart, J. (1971) *Çatal Hüyük, une des premières cités du monde*, Jardin des Arts/Taillandier, Paris.

Mellaart, J. (1975) *The Neolithic of the Near East*, Thames and Hudson, London.

Miller, M. A. (1996) The manufacture of cockle shell beads at Early Neolithic Franchthi Cave, Greece: a case of craft specialization? *Journal of Mediterranean Archaeology* 9(1): 7–37.

Milojčić, V. (1950/51) Zur Chronologie der jüngeren Steinzeit Griechenlands. *Jarhbuch des deutschen Archäologischen Instituts* 65–6: 1–90.

Milojčić, V. (1952) Die frühesten Ackerbauern in Mitteleuropa. *Germania* 30: 313–18.

Milojčić, V. (1955) Vorbericht über die Ausgrabungen auf den Magulen von Otzaki, Arapi und Gremnos bei Larisa 1955. *Archäologischer Anzeiger* 70: 182–231.

Milojčić, V. (1956) Bericht über die Ausgrabungen auf der Gremnos-Magula bei Larisa 1956. *Archäologischer Anzeiger* 71: 141–83.

Milojčić, V. (1959a) Bericht über die Ausgrabungen in Thessalien 1958, I: Die Ausgrabungen im Gebiet der Gremnos- Otzaki- und Soufli-Magula bei Larissa. *Archäologischer Anzeiger* 74: 35–56.

Milojčić, V. (1959b) Ergebnisse der deutschen Ausgrabungen in Thessalien 1953–1958. *Jarhbuch des Römisch-Germanischen Zentralmuseums* 6: 1–56.

Milojčić, V. (1960) Präkeramisches Neolithikum auf der Balkanhalbinsel. *Germania* 38: 320–55.

Milojčić, V. (1962) Die präkeramische neolithische Siedlung von Argissa in Thessalien. In V. Milojčić, J. Boessneck, and M. Hopf, *Die deutschen Ausgrabungen auf der Argissa-Magula in Thessalien*, vol. I, *Das präkeramische Neolithikum sowie die Tier- und Pflanzenreste*, Beiträge zur ur- und frühgeschichtlichen Archäologie des Mittelmeer-Kulturraumes 2, Rudolf Habelt, Bonn, pp. 1–24.

Milojčić, V. (1973) Zur Frage eines präkeramischen Neolithikums in Mitteleuropa. *Actes du VIIIème Congrès International des Sciences Préhistoriques et Protohistoriques, Belgrade 1971*, vol. II, Belgrade, pp. 248–51.

Milojčić, V., Boessneck, J. and Hopf, M. (1962) *Die deutschen Ausgrabungen auf der Argissa-Magula in Thessalien*, vol. I, *Das präkeramische Neolithikum sowie die Tier- und Pflanzenreste*, Beiträge zur ur- und frühgeschichtlichen Archäologie des Mittelmeer-Kulturraumes 2, Rudolf Habelt, Bonn.

Milojčić-von Zumbusch, J. and Milojčić, V. (1971) *Die deutschen Ausgrabungen auf der Otzaki-Magula in Thessalien*, vol. I, *Das Frühe Neolithikum*, Beiträge zur ur- und frühgeschichtlichen Archäologie des Mittelmeer-Kulturraumes 10–11, Rudolf Habelt, Bonn, 2 vols.

Modderman, P. J. R. (1982) Eléments non rubanés du Néolithique ancien entre les vallées du Rhin inférieur et de la Seine. VII. Conclusion générale. *Helinium* 22: 272–3.

Modderman, P. J. R. (1988) The Linear Pottery culture: diversity in uniformity. *Berichten van der Rijksdienst voor het Oudheidkundig Bodemonderzoek* [ROB], 38: 63–139.

Moffett, L., Robinson, M. A., Straker, V. (1989) Cereals, fruit and nuts: charred plant remains from Neolithic sites in England and Wales and the Neolithic economy. In A. Milles, D. Williams and N. Gardner (eds.), *The Beginnings of Agriculture*, British Archaeological Reports, Int. series 496, Oxford, pp. 243–61.

Molist, M. (1986) Les structures de combustion au Proche-Orient néolithique (10.000–3.700 B.C.), Thèse de doctorat, Université de Lyon II, 3 vols.

Molist Montaña, M. (1996) *Tell Halula (Siria). Un yacimiento neolítico del Valle Medio del Eufrates. Campañas de 1991 y 1992.* Ministerio de Educacion y cultura, Madrid.

Monnier, J.-L, Pétrequin, P., Richard, A., Pétrequin A.-M., and Gentizon, A.-L., (1991) *Construire une maison 3000 ans avant J.C. Le Lac de Chalain au Néolithique*, Editions Errance, Paris.

Morris, D. (1985) *The Art of Ancient Cyprus*, Phaidon Press, Oxford.

Morris, I. (1992) *Death-Ritual and Social Structure in Classical Antiquity*, Cambridge University Press, Cambridge.

Morrison, I. A. (1968) Appendix I. Relative sea-level change in the Saliagos area since Neolithic times. In J. D. Evans and C. Renfrew, *Excavations at Saliagos near Antiparos*, British School at Athens, supplementary volume 5, Thames and Hudson, London, pp. 92–8.

Mottier, Y. (1981) *Die deutschen Ausgrabungen auf der Otzaki-Magula in Thessalien*, vol. II, *Das mittlere Neolithikum*, Beiträge zur ur- und frühgeschichtlichen Archäologie des Mittelmeer-Kulturraumes 22, Rudolf Habelt, Bonn.

Moundrea, H. A. (1975) *Le site néolithique ancien de Prodromos (Grèce): outillage lithique et osseux. Position dans le contexte Thessalien*, Mémoire de maîtrise, Université Paris X.

Moundrea-Agrafioti, H. A. (1980) Palaioethnologika simperasmata apo ti meleti ton lithinou kai osteïnon ergaleion tou neolithikou oikismou Prodromou Karditsas. *Thessalika Chronika* 13: 489–97.

Moundrea-Agrafioti, H. A. (1981) La Thessalie du Sud-Est au néolithique: outillage lithique et osseux, Thèse de 3ème cycle, Dept. d'Ethnologie, Université Paris X, 2 vols.

Moundrea-Agrafioti, H. A. (1987) Problèmes d'emmanchement dans le Néolithique grec: les gaines et manches en bois de cervidé. In D. Stordeur (ed.), *La Main et l'outil. Manches et emmanchements préhistoriques*, Maison de l'Orient, Lyon, pp. 247–56.

Moundrea-Agrafioti, H. A. (1996) Tools. In G. A. Papathanassopoulos (ed.), *Neolithic Culture in Greece*, Nicholas P. Goulandris Foundation, Museum of Cycladic Art, Athens, pp. 103–6.

Moundrea-Agrafioti, H. A. and Gnardellis, Ch. (1991) Outils tranchants thessaliens en pierre polie: un réexamen de la typologie de Christos Tsountas. *Les cahiers de l'analyse des données* 16(2): 161–78.

Moundrea-Agrafioti, H. A. and Gnardellis, Ch. (1994) Classification des outils tranchants thessaliens en pierre polie par les méthodes multidimensionnelles. In *La Thessalie. Quinze années de recherches archéologiques, 1975–1990. Bilans et perspectives,* Ministère de la Culture, Editions Kapon, Athens, vol. I, pp. 189–200.

Muhly, J. D. (1989) Çayönü Tepesi and the beginnings of metallurgy in the Old World. In A. Hauptman, E. Pernicka and G. A. Wagner (eds.), *Old World Archaeometallurgy,* Selbstverlag des Deutschen Bergbau-Museums, Bochum, pp. 1–11 (Der Anschnitt, Beiheft 7).

Mylonas, G. (1929) *Excavations at Olynthus,* vol. I, *the Neolithic Settlement.* Johns Hopkins University Press, Baltimore.

Nandris, J. (1970) The development and relationships of the earlier Greek Neolithic. *Man* 5(2): 192–213.

Nandris, J. (1971a (1972)) Bos primigenius and the Bone Spoon. *Bulletin of the Institute of Archaeology* 10: 63–82.

Nandris, J. (1971b (1972)) Relations between the Mesolithic, the First Temperate Neolithic, and the Bandkeramik: the nature of the problem. *Alba Regia, Annales Musei Stephani Regis* 12: 61–70.

Nandris, J. (1977a) The perspective of long-term change in south-east Europe. In F. Carter (ed.), *An Historical Geography of the Balkans,* Academic Press, New York, pp. 25–57.

Nandris, J. (1977b) Review of *Migrations and Invasions in Greece and Adjacent Areas,* by N. G. L. Hammond (Noyes Press, N.J., 1976, 187 pages). *Journal of Archaeological Science* 4: 295–304.

Nandris, J. (1984) Man–animal relationships and validation of ethnoarchaeology in Highlands South-East Europe. In C. Grigson and J. Clutton-Brock (eds.), *Animals and Archaeology: 4. Husbandry in Europe,* British Archaeological Reports, Int. series 227, Oxford, pp. 13–21.

Nandris, J. (1990) Practical and theoretical considerations in Highland zone exploitation from ethnoarchaeological fieldwork in south-east Europe. In P. Biagi (ed.), *The Neolithisation of the Alpine Region,* Monografie di 'Natura Bresciana' 13, pp. 7–22.

Naroll, R. (1962) Floor area and settlement population. *American Antiquity* 27: 587–8.

Nielsen, A. E. (1991) Trampling the archaeological record: an experimental study. *American Antiquity* 56: 483–503.

Olszewski, D. I. (1993) Subsistence ecology in the Mediterranean forest: implications for the origin of cultivation in the Epipaleolithic southern Levant. *American Anthropologist* 95: 420–35.

Orphanidi, L. (1992) Ta neolithika zoomorpha eidolia tis Thessalias. In *Diethnes Synedrio gia tin Archaia Thessalia sti Mnimi tou Dimitri P. Theochari.* Ekdosi tou tameiou archaiologikon poron kai apallotrioseon, Athens, pp. 180–4.

Overweel, C. J. (1981) Appendix I. Petrographic thin section, and X-ray diffraction analysis of pottery from Sesklo and Achilleion. In M. Wijnen, *The Early Neolithic I Settlement at Sesklo: an Early Farming Community in Thessaly, Greece,* Universitaire Pers Leiden, Leiden, pp. 105–111.

Özdoğan, M. (1993) Vinca and Anatolia: a new look at a very old problem (or redefining Vinca culture from the perspective of Near Eastern tradition). In J. Roodenberg (ed.), Anatolia and the Balkans, *Anatolica* 19: 173–93.

Özdoğan M. and Özdoğan A. (1990) Çayönü. A conspectus of recent work. In O. Aurenche, M.-C. Cauvin and P. Sanlaville (eds.), *Préhistoire du Levant. Processus des Changements Culturels,* Editions du CNRS, Paris, pp. 387–96.

Pantelidou-Gkofa, M. (1991) *I Neolithiki Nea Makri. Ta Oikodomika*, Bibliothiki tis en Athinais archeologikis Etairias 119, Athens.

Papadopoulou, M. G. (1958) Magoulitsa, neolithikos synoikismos para tin Karditsan. *Thessalika* A': 39–49.

Papaefthymiou-Papanthimou, A. (1992) Ergaleia yfantikis apo to Sesklo. In *Diethnes Synedrio gia tin Archaia Thessalia sti Mnimi tou Dimitri P. Theochari*, Ekdosi Tameiou Archaeiologikôn Porôn kai Apallotrioseôn, Athens, pp. 78–82.

Papaefthymiou-Papanthimou, A. and Pilali-Papasteriou, A. (1997) *Odoiporiko Stin Proïstoriki Makedonia*, Paratiritis, Thessaloniki.

Papathanassopoulos, G. A. (1981) *Neolithic and Cycladic Civilization*, National Museum, Athens, Melissa Publishing House, Athens.

Papathanassopoulos, G. A. (ed.) (1996) *Neolithic Culture in Greece*, Nicholas P. Goulandris Foundation, Museum of Cycladic Art, Athens.

Pariente, A. (1993) Chronique des fouilles et découvertes archéologiques en Grèce en 1992. *Bulletin de Correspondance Hellénique* 117(2): 757–913.

Parlama, L. (1992) Oi proïstorikes egkatastaseis tis Skyrou. In *Diethnes Synedrio gia tin Archaia Thessalia sti Mnimi tou Dimitri P. Theochari*, Ekdosi Tameiou Archaeiologikôn Porôn kai Apallotrioseôn, Athens, pp. 257–66.

Payne, S. (1973) Kill-off patterns in sheep and goats: the mandibles from Asvan Kale. *Anatolian Studies* 23: 281–303.

Payne, S. (1975) Faunal change at the Franchthi Cave from 20.000 B.C. to 3.000 B.C. In A. T. Clason (ed.), *Archaeozoological Studies*, Elsevier, The Hague, pp. 120–31.

Payne, S. (1985) Zoo-archaeology in Greece: a readers' guide. In N. C. Wilkie and W. D. Coulson (eds.), *Contributions to Aegean Archaeology: Studies in Honor of William A. McDonald*, Center of Ancient Studies, University of Minessota, Minneapolis, pp. 211–43.

Pelegrin, J. (1984) Approche technologique expérimentale de la mise en forme de nucléus pour le débitage systématique par pression. In *Préhistoire de la pierre taillée*, 2, *Economie du débitage laminaire*, CREP, Paris, pp. 93–103.

Pelegrin, J. (1988) Débitage expérimental par pression: du plus petit au plus grand. In J. Tixier (ed.), *Technologie préhistorique*, Editions du CNRS, Valbonne, pp. 37–53 (Notes et Monographies techniques du CRA' 25).

Pelegrin, J. (in prep.) *Long Blades from the Chalcolithic: an Experimental Approach*, Lejre Research Centre, Lejre.

Perlès, C. (1979) Des navigateurs méditerranéens il y a 10 000 ans. *La Recherche* 96: 82–3.

Perlès, C. (1987) *Les industries lithiques taillées de Franchthi (Argolide, Grèce)*. vol. I, *Présentation générale et industries paléolithiques*, Excavations at Franchthi Cave, fasc. 3, Indiana University Press, Bloomington and Indianapolis.

Perlès, C. (1989a) La néolithisation de la Grèce. In O. Aurenche and J. Cauvin (eds.), *Néolithisations: Proche et Moyen Orient, Méditerranée Orientale, Nord de l'Afrique, Europe Méridionale, Chine, Amérique du Sud*, British Archaeological Reports, Int. series 516, Oxford, pp. 109–27.

Perlès, C. (1989b) From stone procurement to Neolithic society in Greece, David Skomp Distinguished Lectures in Anthropology, Indiana University, 29 pages.

Perlès, C. (1990a) *Les industries lithiques taillées de Franchthi (Argolide, Grèce)*, vol. II, *Les industries du Mésolithique et du Néolithique initial*, Excavations at Franchthi Cave, fasc. 5, Indiana University Press, Bloomington and Indianapolis.

Perlès, C. (1990b) L'outillage de pierre taillée néolithique en Grèce: approvisionnement et exploitation des matières premières. *Bulletin de Correspondance Hellénique* 114(1): 1–42.

Perlès, C. (1992) Systems of exchange and organization of production in Neolithic Greece. *Journal of Mediterranean Archaeology* 5(2): 115–64.

Perlès, C. (1995) La transition Pleistocène/Holocène et le problème du Mésolithique en Grèce. In V. Villaverde-Bonilla (ed.), *Los Ultimos Cazadores. Transformaciones Culturales y Económicas Durante el Tardiglaciar y el Inicio del Holoceno en al Ambito Mediterraneo*, Instituto Juan Gil-Alvert, Alicante, pp. 179–209.

Perlès, C. and Vaughan, P. (1983) Pièces lustrées, travail des plantes et moissons à Franchthi (Xème–IVème millennium B.C.). In M.-C. Cauvin (ed.), *Traces d'utilisations sur les outils néolithiques du Proche-Orient*, Maison de l'Orient, Lyon, pp. 209–29.

Perlès, C. and Vitelli, K. D. (1994) Technologie et fonction des premières productions céramiques de Grèce. In *Terre cuite et société. La céramique, document technique, économique et culturel. Actes des XIVèmes rencontres internationales d'archéologie et d'histoire d'Antibes*, Editions ADPCA, Juan-les-Pins, pp. 225–42.

Perlès, C. and Vitelli, K. D. (1999) Craft specialization in the Greek Neolithic. In P. Halstead (ed.), *Neolithic Society in Greece*, Sheffield Academic Press, Sheffield, pp. 96–107.

Pétrequin, A.-M. and Pétrequin, P. (1988) *Le Néolithique des lacs. Préhistoire des lacs de Chalain et de Clairvaux (4000–2000 av. J.-C.)*, Errance, Paris.

Pétrequin, P., Jeudy, F. and Jeunesse, Ch. (1993) Neolithic quarries, the exchange of axes and social control in the southern Vosges. In C. Scarre and F. Healy (eds.), *Trade and Exchange in Prehistoric Europe*, Oxbow Books, Oxford, pp. 45–67 (Oxbow Monograph 33).

Pétrequin, P. and Jeunesse, Ch. (1995) *La hache de pierre. Carrières vosgiennes et échanges de lames polies pendant le Néolithique (5400–2100 av. J.-C.)*, Errance, Paris.

Pétrequin, P. and Pétrequin, A.-M. (1993) *Ecologie d'un outil: la hache de pierre en Irian Jaya (Indonésie)*, CNRS Editions, Paris (Monographies du CRA' 12).

Phelps, W. W. (1975) The Neolithic pottery sequence in southern Greece, Ph. D. thesis, Institute of Archaeology, University of London.

Phelps, W. W. (1981–2) Three Peloponnesian Neolithic problems. In *Praktika B' Diethnous Synedriou Peloponnisiakon Spoudon*, Athens, pp. 363–72.

Phelps, W. W. (1987) Prehistoric figurines from Corinth. *Hesperia* 56: 235–53.

Pilali-Papasteriou, A. (1992) Oi sfragides apo to Sesklo kai ta problimata tis thessalikis neolithikis sfragidoglydias. In *Diethnes Synedrio gia tin Archaia Thessalia sti Mnimi tou Dimitri P. Theochari*, Ekdosi Tameiou Archaeiologikôn Porôn kai Apallotrioseôn, Athens, pp. 83–90.

Plog, S. (1995) Equality and hierarchy: holistic approaches to understanding social dynamics in the Pueblo southwest. In T. D. Price and G. M. Feinman (eds.), *Foundations of Social Inequality*, Plenum Press, New York, pp. 189–206.

Polunin, O. (1987) *Flowers of Greece and the Balkans. A Field Guide*, Oxford University Press, Oxford.

Pope, K. O. and van Andel, Tj. (1984) Late Quaternary alluviation and soil formation in the Southern Argolid: its history, causes and archaeological implications. *Journal of Archaeological Science* 11(4): 281–306.

Poplin, F., Poulain, Th., Méniel, P., Vigne, J.-D., Geddes, D. and Helmer, D. (1986) Les débuts de l'élevage en France. In J.-P. Demoule and J. Guilaine (eds.), *Le Néolithique de la France*, Picard, Paris, pp. 37–51.

Powell, J. (1996) *Fishing in the Prehistoric Aegean*, Paul Aströms Förlag, Jonsered (Studies in Mediterranean Archaeology and Literature, Pocket Book 137).

Prendi, F. (1990) Le Néolithique ancien en Albanie. *Germania* 68(2): 399–426.

Prévost, S. (1993) *Les fours et les foyers domestiques en Egée au Néolithique et à l'Age du Bronze*, Mémoire de DEA, Université de Paris I, 3 vols.

Price, T. D. and Brown, J. A. (eds.) (1985) *Prehistoric Hunter-Gatherers: the Emergence of Cultural Complexity*, Academic Press, London.

Price, T. D. and Feinman, G. M. (eds.) (1995) *Foundations of Social Inequality*, Plenum Press, New York.

Protonotariou-Deïlaki, E. (1992) Paratiriseis stin prokerameiki (apo ti Thessalia sta Dendra tis Argolidos). In *Diethnes Synedrio gia tin Archaia Thessalia sti Mnimi tou Dimitri P. Theochari*, Ekdosi Tameiou Archaeiologikôn Porôn kai Apallotrioseôn, Athens, pp. 97–111.

Protsch, R. and Berger, R. (1973) Earliest radiocarbon dates for domesticated animals. *Science* 179: 235–9.

Psychoyos, O. (1988) *Déplacements de la ligne de rivage et sites archéologiques dans les régions côtières de la Mer Egée, au Néolithique et à l'âge du Bronze*, Paul Aströms Förlag, Jonsered.

Pyke, G. and Yiouni, P. (1996) *The Excavation and the Ceramic Assemblage*, British School at Athens, Athens (Nea Nikomedeia I. The excavation of an Early Neolithic village in northern Greece 1981–1964, R. J. Rodden K. A. and Wardle (eds.)) (BSA, Supplementary vol. 25).

Rackham, O. (1982) Land-use and the native vegetation of Greece. In M. Bell and S. Limbrey (eds.), *Archaeological Aspects of Woodland Ecology*, British Archaeological Reports, Int. series 146, Oxford, pp. 177–98.

Rackham, O. (1983) Observations on the historical ecology of Boeotia. *Annual of the British School at Athens* 78: 291–351.

Rackham, O. (1990) Observations on the historical ecology of Santorini. In D. A. Hardy *et al.* (eds.), *Thera and the Aegean World*, vol. III, 2, *Earth Sciences*, Thera Foundation, London, pp. 384–91.

Redman, C. L. (1982) The Çayönü chipped stone industry: the 1968 and 1970 excavation seasons. In L. S. Braidwood and R. J. Braidwood (eds.), *Prehistoric Village Archaeology in South-Eastern Turkey. The Eighth Millennium B.C. Site at Çayönü: its Chipped and Ground Stones Industries and Faunal Remains*, British Archaeological Reports, Int. series 138, Oxford, pp. 17–71.

Renard, J. (1989) *Le site néolithique et helladique ancien de Kouphovouno (Laconie). Fouilles de O.-W. von Vacano (1941)*, Université de Liège, Liège (Aegaeum 4).

Renfrew, C. (1972) *The Emergence of Civilization: the Cyclades and the Aegean in the Third Millennium B.C.*, Methuen, London.

Renfrew, C. (1984) Trade as action at a distance. In C. Renfrew, *Approaches to Social Archaeology*, Harvard University Press, Cambridge, Mass., pp. 86–134.

Renfrew, C. (1986) Sitagroi in European Prehistory. In C. Renfrew, M. Gimbutas and E. Elster (eds.), *Excavations at Sitagroi. A Prehistoric Village in Northeast Greece*, vol.I, Institute of Archaeology University of California, Los Angeles, pp. 477–485 (Monumenta Archaeologica 13).

Renfrew, C. and Aspinall, A. (1990) Aegean obsidian and Franchthi Cave. In C. Perlès, *Les industries lithiques taillées de Franchthi (Argolide, Grèce)*, vol. II, *Les industries du mésolithique et du néolithique initial*, Excavations at Franchthi Cave, fasc. 5, Indiana University Press, Bloomington and Indianapolis, pp. 257–70.

Renfrew, C., Cann, J. R. and Dixon, J. E. (1965) Obsidian in the Aegean. *Annual of the British School at Athens* 60: 225–47.

Renfrew, J. (1966) A report on recent finds of carbonized cereal grains and seeds from prehistoric Thessaly. *Thessalika* 4: 21–36.

Renfrew, J. (1973) *Palaeoethnobotany. The Prehistoric Food Plants of the Near East and Europe*, Methuen, London.

Renfrew, J. (1979) The first farmers in south-east Europe. In U. Körber-Grohne (ed.), Festschrift Maria Hopf. *Archaeo-Physika* 8: 243–65.

Renfrew, J. (1989) Carbonized grain and seeds. In M. Gimbutas, Sh. Winn and D. Shimabuku (eds.), *Achilleion, a Neolithic Settlement in Thessaly, Greece, 6400–5600 B.C.*, Institute of Archaeology, University of California, Los Angeles, pp. 307–310 (Monumenta Archaeologica 14).

Renfrew, J. (1995) Palaeoethnobotanical finds of *Vitis* from Greece. In P. E. McGovern, S. J. Fleming and S. H. Katz (eds.), *The Origins and Ancient History of Wine*, Gordon and Breach, Philadelphia, pp. 255–67 (Food and Nutrition in History and Anthropology, 11).

Reynolds, R. G. (1984) A computational model of hierarchical decision systems. *Journal of Anthropological Archaeology* 3: 159–89.

Ricq-de Bouard, M. (1996) *Pétrographie et sociétés néolithiques en France Méditeranénne. L'outillage en pierre polie*, Editions du CNRS, Paris (Monographies du CRA 16).

Rodden, R. J. (1962) Excavations at the Early Neolithic site at Nea Nikomedeia, Greek Macedonia (1961 season). *Proceedings of the Prehistoric Society* 28: 267–88.

Rodden, R. J. (1964a) Early Neolithic frog figurines from Nea Nikomedeia. *Antiquity* 38(152): 294–5.

Rodden, R. J. (1964b) Recent discoveries from prehistoric Macedonia. An interim report. *Balkan Studies* 5: 109–24.

Rodden, R. J. (1965) An Early Neolithic village in Greece. *Scientific American* 212(4): 82–8.

Rodden, R. J. and Rodden, J. M. (1964a) A European link with Chatal Huyuk: uncovering a seventh millennium settlement in Macedonia. Part I. Site and pottery. *Illustrated London News* 11 April 1964: 564–7.

Rodden, R. J. and Rodden, J. M. (1964b) A European link with Chatal Huyuk: uncovering a seventh millennium settlement in Macedonia. Part II. Burials and the shrine. *Illustrated London News* 18 April 1964: 604–7.

Rolland, N. (1980) Le projet de l'Institut canadien d'archéologie à Athènes sur l'Age de la Pierre en Grèce centrale: campagne préliminaire 1980. *Teiresias (Archaeologica)* 3: 3–29.

Rolland, N. (1985) Exploitation du milieu et subsistance au cours de la préhistoire ancienne de la Grèce. *Culture* 5(1): 43–61.

Rolland, N. (1988) Palaeolithic Greece: subsistence and socio-economic formations. In B. V. Kennedy and G. LeMoine (eds.), *Diet and Subsistence: Current Archaeological Perspectives*, Chacmool, Archaeological Association of the University of Calgary, pp. 43–53.

Rollefson, G. O. and Simmons, A. (1986) The neolithic village of Ain Ghazal, Jordan: preliminary report on the 1984 season. *Bulletin of the American School for Oriental Research* supplement 24: 145–64.

Roodenberg, J. (1993) Ilıpınar X to VI: links and chronology. *Anatolica* 19: 251–67.

Rose, M. (in prep) *Fish Remains from Franchthi Cave.*

Roux, V. (1990) *Le Tour du potier. Spécialisation artisanale et compétences techniques*, Editions du CNRS, Paris (Monographies du CRA 4).

Rowley-Conwy, P. (1995) Making the first farmers younger: the West European evidence. *Current Anthropology* 36: 346–53.

Runnels, C. (1981) A diachronic study and economic analysis of millstones from the Argolid, Greece. Ph. D. thesis, University of Indiana, Bloomington.

Runnels, C. (1985) Trade and demand for millstones in Southern Greece in the Neolithic and the Early Bronze Age. In A. B. Knapp and T. Stech (eds.), *Prehistoric Production and Exchange. The Aegean and Eastern Mediterranean*, Institute of Archaeology, University of California, Los Angeles, pp. 30–43 (Monograph 25).

Runnels, C. (1988) A Prehistoric survey of Thessaly: new light on the Greek Middle Palaeolithic. *Journal of Field Archaeology* 15: 277–90.

Runnels, C. (1994) A Palaeolithic survey of Thessaly. In *La Thessalie. Quinze années de recherches archéologiques, 1975–1990. Bilans et perspectives*, Ministère de la Culture, Athènes, vol. I, pp. 55–6.

Runnels, C. (1995) Review of Aegean Prehistory IV: the Stone Age of Greece from the Palaeolithic to the advent of the Neolithic. *American Journal of Archaeology* 99: 699–728.

Runnels, C. and van Andel, Tj. (1988) Trade and the origins of agriculture in the Eastern Mediterranean. *Journal of Mediterranean Archaeology* 1(1): 83–109.

Runnels, C. and van Andel, Tj. (1993) The Lower and Middle Paleolithic of Thessaly, Greece. *Journal of Field Archaeology* 20(3): 299–317.

Runnels, C. *et al.* (1999) Human settlement and landscape in the Preveza region, Epirus, in the Pleistocene and Early Holocene. In G. N. Bailey *et al.* (eds.), *The Palaeolithic Archaeology of Greece and Adjacent Areas: Proceedings of the ICOPAG Conference, Ioannina, September 1994*, British School at Athens studies 3, London.

Runnels, C., Pullen, D. J., Langdon, S. H. (1995) *Artifacts and Assemblages: Finds from a Regional Survey of the Southern Argolid*, vol. I, *The Prehistoric and Early Iron Age Pottery and the Lithic Artifacts*. Stanford University Press, Stanford.

Ryder, M. L. (1965) Report of textiles from Çatal Hüyük. *Anatolian Studies* 15: 175–6.

Ryder, M. L. (1969) Changes in the fleece of sheep following domestication (with a note on the coat of cattle). In P. J. Ucko and G. W. Dimbleby (eds.), *The Domestication and Exploitation of Plants and Animals*, Duckworth, London, pp. 495–521.

Ryder, M. L. (1984) Sheep representations, written records and wool measurements. In J. Clutton-Brock and C. Grigson, C., *Animals and Archaeology*, vol. III, *Early Herders and their Flocks*, British Archaeological Reports, Int. series 202, Oxford, pp. 69–82.

Sahlins, M. (1974) *Stone Age Economics*, Tavistock Publications, London.

Saidel, B. A. (1993) Round house or square? Architectural form and socio-economic organization in the PPNB. *Journal of Mediterranean Archaeology* 6(1): 65–108.

Sampson, A. (1980) *I Neolithiki kai i Protoelladiki I stin Euboia*, Etaireia Euboïkon Spoudon, Athens (Archeion Euboïkon Meleton, supplement to vol. XXIV).

Sampson, A. (1996a) Excavation at the Cave of Cyclops on Youra, Alonnessos. In E. Alram-Stern, *Die ägäische Frühzeit. 2 Serie. Forschungsbericht 1975–1993*, vol. I, *Das Neolithikum in Griechenland*, Verlag der Österreichischen Akademie der Wissenchaften, Wien, pp. 507–20.

Sampson, A. (1996b) The Cyclops cave at Youra Alonnissos. In G. A. Papathanassopoulos (ed.), *Neolithic Culture in Greece*, Nicholas P. Goulandris Foundation, Museum of Cycladic Art, Athens, pp. 58–9.

Sampson, A. and Sugaya, C. (1988/9) The ground stone axes of Euboea. *Anthropologika kai Archaiologika Chronica* 3: 11–45.

Schick, T. (1989) Early Neolithic twined basketry and fabrics from the Nahal Hemar Cave, Israel. In *Tissage, corderie, vannerie. Actes des IXèmes rencontres internationales d'archéologie et d'histoire d'Antibes*, Editions APDCA, Juan-les-Pins, pp. 41–52.

Schirmer, W. (1990) Some aspects of building at the 'aceramic-neolithic' settlement of Çayönü Tepesi. *World Archaeology* 21(3): 363–87.

Schneider, G., Knoll, H., Gallis, K. and Demoule, J.-P. (1991) Transition entre les cultures néolithiques de Sesklo et de Dimini: recherches minéralogiques, chimiques et technologiques sur les céramiques et les argiles. *Bulletin de Correspondance Hellénique* 115(1): 1–64.

Schneider, G., Knoll, H., Gallis, K. and Demoule, J.-P. (1994) Production and circulation of Neolithic Thessalian pottery: chemical and mineralogical analyses. In *La Thessalie. Quinze années de Recherches Archéologiques, 1975–1990. Bilans et Perspectives*, Ministère de la Culture, Editions Kapon, Athens, vol. I, pp. 61–70.

Schneider, H. E. (1968) *Zur quartärgeologischen Entwicklungsgeschichte Thessaliens (Griechenland)*, Beiträge zur ur- und frühgeschichtlichen Archäologie des Mittelmeer-Kulturraumes 6, Rudolf Habelt, Bonn.

Schoumacker, A. (1993) Apports de la technologie et de la pétrographie pour la caractérisation des meules. In P. C. Anderson, S. Beyries, M. Otte and H. Plisson (eds.), *Traces et fonction. Les gestes retrouvés. Colloque international de Liège*, CRA et Université de Liège, Liège, pp. 165–76 (ERAUL 50).

Sénépart, I. (1991) Industrie osseuse et traitement thermique. Compte rendu de quelques expérimentations. In *Archéologie expérimentale*, vol. II, *La terre, l'os et la pierre, la maison et les champs*, Errance, Paris, pp. 49–55.

Sénépart, I. (1992) Les industries en matières dures animales de l'épipaléolithique au néolithique final dans le sud-est de la France, Thèse de doctorat, Université de Paris X, 3 vols.

Shackleton, J. C. (1988) *Marine Molluscan Remains from Franchthi Cave*, Excavations at Franchthi Cave, fasc. 4, Indiana University Press, Bloomington and Indianapolis.

Shennan, S., (1992) Population, prestige and production: some aspects of the development of copper and bronze metallurgy in Prehistoric Europe. *Universitätforschungen zur prähistorischen Archäologie aus dem Institut für Ur- und Frühgeschichte der Universität Innsbruck* 8: 535–42.

Sherratt, A. (1981) Plough and pastoralism: aspects of the secondary products revolution. In N. Hammond, I. Hodder and G. Isaac (eds.), *Pattern of the Past: Studies in Honor of David Clarke*, Cambridge University Press, Cambridge, pp. 261–305.

Sherratt, A. (1982) Mobile resources: settlement and exchange in early agricultural Europe. In C. Renfrew and S. Shennan (eds.), *Ranking, Resources and Exchange*, Cambridge University Press, Cambridge, pp. 13–26.

Sherratt, A. (1990) The genesis of megaliths: monumentality, ethnicity and social complexity in Neolithic north-west Europe. *World Archaeology* 22: 147–67.

Sherratt, A. (1995) Instruments of conversion? The role of megaliths in the Mesolithic/Neolithic transition in north-west Europe. *Oxford Journal of Archaeology* 14(3): 245–60.

Sidéra, I. (1993) Les assemblages osseux en Bassins Parisien et Rhénan du VIème au IVème millénaire B.C. Histoire, techno-économie et culture. Thèse de doctorat, Université de Paris I, 3 vols.

Sidéra, I. (1998) Nouveaux éléments d'origine proche-orientale dans le Néolithique ancien balkanique: analyse de l'industrie osseuse. In *Préhistoire d'Anatolie. Genèse de deux mondes*. Université de Liège, Liège, pp. 215–39.

Silistreli, U. (1989) Kösk Höyük'te bulunan kabartma insan ve hayvan figürleriyle bezeli vazolar. *Belleten* 3: 361–74.

Sivignon, M. (1975) *La Thessalie. Analyse géographique d'une province grecque*, Institut des Etudes Rhodaniennes des Universités de Lyon, Lyon (Mémoires et Documents 17).

Soffer, O., Adovasio, J. M., Hyland, D. C., (1998) Perishable industries from Upper Paleolithic Moravia: new insights into the origin and nature of the Gravettian. Paper presented at the Institute of Archaeology, AS CR, Prague and Masaryk University, Brno, June 1998, 39 pages.

Sordinas, A. (1967) Radiocarbon dates from Corfu, Greece. *Antiquity* 41: 64.

Sordinas, A. (1969) Investigations of the prehistory of Corfu during 1964–1966. *Balkan Studies* 10(2): 393–424.

Sordinas, A. (1970) *Stone Implements from Northwestern Corfu, Greece*, Anthropological Research Center, Memphis State University, Memphis.

Soudsky, B. (1969) Etude de la maison néolithique. *Slovenska Archeologia* 17: 5–96.

Spyropoulos, Th. (1973 (1977)) Archaiotites kai mnimeia Boiotias-Phtiotidos. Spilia Sarakinou Kopaïdos. *Archaiologikon Deltion* 28(B' 1), chronika: 263–4.

Stahl, A. B. (1989) Plant-food processing: implications for dietary quality. In D. R. Harris and G. C. Hillman (eds.), *Foraging and Farming. The Evolution of Plant Exploitation*, Unwin Hyman, London, pp. 171–94 (One World Archaeology).

Stanley Price, N. P. (1979) *Early Prehistoric Settlement in Cyprus 6500–3000 B.C.*, British Archaeological Reports, Int. series 65, Oxford.

Stekelis, M. (1972) *The Yarmukian Culture of the Neolithic Period*, Magnes Press, Hebrew University, Jerusalem.

Stiros, S. and Papageorgiou, S. (1994) Post Mesolithic evolution of the Thessalian landscape. In *La Thessalie. Quinze années de recherches archéologiques, 1975–1990. Bilans et perspectives*, Ministère de la Culture, Editions Kapon, Athens, vol. I, pp. 29–36.

Stordeur, D. (1988a) L'industrie osseuse de Çafer dans son contexte anatolien et Proche-Oriental. Note préliminaire. *Anatolica* 15: 203–13.

Stordeur, D. (1988b) *Outils et armes en os du gisement natoufien de Mallaha (Eynan) Israël*, Association Paléorient, Paris (Mémoires et Travaux du Centre de Recherche Français de Jerusalem 6).

Stordeur, D. (1989) Vannerie et tissage au Proche-Orient néolithique: IXème–Vème millénaire. In *Tissage, corderie, vannerie. Actes des IXèmes rencontres internationales d'archéologie et d'histoire d'Antibes*, Editions APDCA, Juan-les-Pins, pp. 19–39.

Stordeur, D. (ed.) (1987) *La Main et l'outil. Manches et emmanchements préhistoriques*, G. I. S. Maison de l'Orient, Diffusion de Boccard, Paris (Travaux de la Maison de l'Orient 15).

Stratouli, G. (1996) Die Fischerei in der Ägäis wärhend des Neolithikums. Zur Technik und zum potentiellen Ertrag. *Praehistoriche Zeitschrift* 71(1): 1–27.

Stroulia, A. (in prep.) *Flexible Stones: Ground Stone Tools from Franchthi*, Excavations at Franchthi Cave, fasc. 15, Indiana University Press, Bloomington and Indianapolis.

Struiver, M. and Reimer, P. J. (1993) Isotope laboratory radiocarbon calibration program revised 3.0. *Radiocarbon* 35: 211–30.

Sugaya, C. (1992) The function of the Neolithic stone axe. In *Diethnes Synedrio gia tin Archaia Thessalia sti Mnimi tou Dimitri P. Theochari*, Ekdosi Tameiou Archaeiologikôn Porôn kai Apallotrioseôn, Athens, pp. 71–7.

Sugaya, C. (1993) The stone axes of Tharrounia. In A. Sampson (ed.), *Skoteini Tharrounion*. Privately published, Athens, pp. 442–7.

Talalay, L. E. (1987) Rethinking the function of clay figurine legs from Neolithic Greece: an argument by analogy. *American Journal of Archaeology* 91: 161–9.

Talalay, L. E. (1993) *Deities, Dolls, and Devices. Neolithic Figurines from Franchthi Cave, Greece*, Excavations at Franchthi Cave, Greece, fasc. 9, Indiana University Press, Bloomington and Indianapolis.

Tellenbach, M. (1983) Materialien zum Präkeramischen Neolithikum in Süd-Ost-Europa. Typologisch-stratigraphische Untersuchungen zu litischen Gerätschaften, *Bericht der Römisch-Germanischen Kommission* 64: 21–138.

Theocharis, D. R. (1954) Anaskafi neolithikou sinoikismou en Nea Makri (Attikis). *Pratika tis en Athinais Archaiologikis Etairias 1954*: 114–22.

Theocharis, D. R. (1956) Nea Makri. Eine grosse neolithische Siedlung in der Nähe von Marathon. *Mitteilungen der Deutschen Archäologischen Instituts* 71: 1–29.

Theocharis, D. R. (1957) Ai archai tou politismou en Sesklo. *Praktika Akademia Athinon* 32: 151–9.

Theocharis, D. R. (1958) Ek tis prokeramikis Thessalias. *Thessalika* 1: 70–86.

Theocharis, D. R. (1959) Pyrasos. *Thessalika* 2: 29–68.

Theocharis, D. R. (1961/2) Archaiotites kai mnimeia Thessalias. *Archaiologikon Deltion* 17(B), chronika: 170–9.

Theocharis, D. R. (1962a (1966)) Anaskafai en Sesklo. *Praktika tis en Athinais Archaiologikis Etaireias 1962*: 24–35.

Theocharis, D. R. (1962b) Apo to neolithiki Thessalia I. *Thessalika* 4: 63–83.

Theocharis, D. R. (1962c [1963]) Sesklon. *To Ergon tis Archaiologikis Etairias 1962*: 39–48.

Theocharis, D. R. (1963a) Anaskafai en Sesklo. *Praktika tis en Athinais Archaiologikis Etaireias 1963*: 40–44.

Theocharis, D. R. (1963b (1964)) Sesklo. *To Ergon tis Archaiologikis Etairias 1963*: 27–35.

Theocharis, D. R. (1965 (1967)) Anaskafai en Sesklo. *Praktika tis en Athinais Archaiologikis Etaireias 1965*: 5–9.

Theocharis, D. R. (1966a (1968)) Anaskafai en Sesklo. *Praktika tis en Athinais Archaiologikis Etaireias 1966*: 5–7.

Theocharis, D. R. (1966b (1967)) Sesklo. *To Ergon tis Archaiologikis Etairias 1966*: 12–17.

Theocharis, D. R. (1967) *I Avgi tis Thessalikis Proïstorias. Archi kai Proïmi Exelidi tis Neolithikis*, Thessalika meletimata 1, Volos.

Theocharis, D. R. (1968a) Anaskafai en Sesklo. *Praktika tis en Athinais Arhaiologikis Etairias 1968*: 24–30.

Theocharis, D. R. (1968b (1969)) Sesklo. *To Ergon tis Archaiologikis Etairias 1968*: 27–34.

Theocharis, D. R. (1971 (1973)) Anaskafai en Sesklo. *Praktika tis en Athinais Archaiologikis Etairias 1971*: 15–19.

Theocharis, D. R. (1972a (1974)) Anaskafai en Sesklo. *Praktika tis en Athinais Archaiologikis Etairias 1972*: 8–11.

Theocharis, D. R. (1972b (1973)) Sesklo. Akropolis. *To Ergon tis Archaiologikis Etairias 1972*: 7–12.

Theocharis, D. R. (1973a (1975)) Anaskafai en Sesklo. *Praktika tis en Athinais Archaiologikis Etairias 1973*: 22–5.

Theocharis, D. R. (1973b) *Neolithic Greece*, National Bank of Greece, Athens.

Theocharis, D. R. (1973c (1974)) Sesklon. *To Ergon tis Archaiologikis Etairias 1973*: 14–20.

Theocharis, D. R. (1976a (1979)) Anaskafi Sesklou. *Praktika tis en Athinais Archaiologikis Etairias 1976*: 153–62.

Theocharis, D. R. (1976b (1977)) Sesklo. *To Ergon tis Archaiologikis Etairias 1976*: 88–99.

Theocharis, D. R. (1977 (1978)) Sesklo. *To Ergon tis Archaiologikis Etairias 1977*: 88–93.

Thomas, J. (1991) *Rethinking the Neolithic*, Cambridge University Press, Cambridge.

Tinè, S. (1983) *Passo di Corvo e la Civiltà Neolitica del Tavoliere*, Sagep Editrice, Genoa.

Torrence, R. (1986) *Production and Exchange of Stone Tools. Prehistoric Obsidian in the Aegean*, Cambridge University Press, Cambridge.

Touchais, G. (1978) Chronique des fouilles et découvertes archéologiques en Grèce en 1977. *Bulletin de Correspondance Hellénique* 102(2): 641–770.

Touchais, G. (1989) Chronique des fouilles et découvertes archéologiques en Grèce en 1988. *Bulletin de Correspondance Hellénique* 113(2): 581–700.

Toufexis, G. (1994) Neolithic animal figurines from Thessaly. In J.-C. Decourt, B. Helly and K. Gallis (eds.), *La Thessalie. Quinze années de recherches archéologiques, 1975–1990. Bilans et perspectives*, Ministère de la Culture, Editions Kapon, Athens, pp. 163–8.

Trantalidou, C. (1990) Animals and human diet in the prehistoric Aegean. In D. A. Hardy (ed.), *Thera and the Aegean World*, vol. III 2, *Earth Sciences*, Thera Foundation, London, pp. 392–405.

Tresset, A. (1996) Le rôle des relations homme/animal dans l'évolution économique et culturelle des sociétés des Vème-IVème millénaires av. J.-C. en Bassin Parisien. Thèse de doctorat, Université Paris I.

Treuil, R. (1983) *Le Néolithique et le Bronze ancien Egéens. Les problèmes stratigraphiques et chronologiques, les techniques, les hommes,* Ecole Française d'Athènes, diffusion de Boccard, Paris (Bibliothèque des Ecoles françaises d'Athènes et de Rome, 248).

Treuil, R. (1992a) Les figurines néolithiques: idoles ou jouets? In *Le Grand Atlas de l'Archéologie,* Encyclopaedia Universalis, Paris, pp. 66–7.

Treuil, R. (1992b) L'outillage. VI. La terre cuite. In Treuil, R. (ed.) *Dikili Tash. Village préhistorique de Macédoine orientale. I. Fouilles de Jean Deshayes (1961–1975).* De Boccard, Paris, pp. 120–144 (24th supplement of the Bulletin de Correspondance hellénique).

Tringham, R. (1968) A preliminary study of the Early Neolithic and latest Mesolithic blade industries in Southeast and Central Europe. In J. Coles and D. Simpson (eds.), *Studies in Ancient Europe,* Leicester University Press, Leicester, pp. 45–70.

Tringham, R. (1971) *Hunters, Fishers and Farmers of Eastern Europe 6000–3000 BC,* Hutchinson University Library, London.

Tsountas, Ch. (1908) *Ai Proïstorikai Akropoleis Diminiou kai Sesklou,* Sakellariou, Athens.

Turner, J. (1978) The vegetation of Greece during prehistoric times: the palynological evidence. In *Thera and the Aegean World,* vol. I, Thera Foundation, London, pp. 765–73.

Turner, J. and Greig J. R. A. (1975) Some Holocene pollen diagrams from Greece. *Review of Palaeobotany and Palynology* 20: 171–204.

Tzalas, H. (1995) On the obsidian trail. With a papyrus craft in the Cyclades, In *Tropis III. 3rd International Symposium on Ship Construction in Antiquity, Athens 1989,* Hellenic Institute for the Preservation of Nautical Traditions, Athens, pp. 441–69.

Tzedakis, P. C. (1993) Long-term tree population in northwest Greece through multiple Quaternary climatic cycles. *Nature* 364: 437–40.

Ucko, P. J. (1968) *Anthropomorphic Figurines of Predynastic Egypt and Neolithic Crete with Comparative Material from the Prehistoric Near East and Mainland Greece,* Andrew Szmidla, London (Royal Anthropological Institute occasional paper 24).

Upton, G. J. G. and Fingleton, B. (1985) *Spatial Data Analysis by Example. 1. Point Pattern and Quantitative Data,* John Wiley and Sons, Chichester.

Valamoti, S. (1992 (1995)) Georgika proïonta apo to neolitiko oikismo Giannitsa B: prokatartiki proseggisi meso ton archaiobotanikon dedomenon. *To Archaiologiko Ergo sti Makedonia kai Thraki* 6: 177–84.

Valmin, N. (1938) *The Swedish Messenia Expedition,* Skrifter utgivna av Kungl. Humanistika Vetenskapssamfundet i Lund 26, Lund.

Van Andel, Tj. (1987) Part I, The landscape. In Tj. van Andel and S. B. Sutton, *Landscape and People of the Franchthi Region,* Excavations at Franchthi Cave, Greece, fasc. 2, Indiana University Press, Bloomington and Indianapolis, pp. 3–62.

Van Andel, Tj., Gallis, K. and Toufexis, G. (1995) Early neolithic farming in a Thessalian river landscape, Greece. In J. Lewin, M. G. Macklin and J. C. Woodward (eds.), *Mediterranean Quaternary River Environments,* Balkema, Rotterdam, pp. 131–43.

Van Andel, Tj. and Lianos, N. (1983) Prehistoric and historic shorelines of the southern Argolid Peninsula: a subbottom profile study. *International Journal of Nautical Archaeology and Underwater Exploration* 12(4): 303–24.

Van Andel, Tj. and Lianos, N. (1984) High-resolution seismic reflection profiles for the reconstruction of Postglacial transgressive shorelines: an example from Greece. *Quaternary Research* 22: 31–45.

Van Andel, Tj. and Runnels, C. (1987) *Beyond the Acropolis. A Rural Greek Past*, Stanford University Press, Stanford.

Van Andel, Tj. and Runnels, C. (1995) The earliest farmers in Europe. *Antiquity* 69(264): 481–500.

Van Andel, Tj. and Shackleton, J. C. (1982) Late Palaeolithic and Mesolithic coastlines of Greece and the Aegean. *Journal of Field Archaeology* 9: 445–54.

Van Andel, Tj. and Sutton, S. B. (1987) *Landscape and People of the Franchthi region*, Excavations at Franchthi Cave, fasc. 2, Indiana University Press, Bloomington.

Van Andel, Tj. and Zangger, E. (1990) Landscape stability and destabilization in the prehistory of Greece. In S. Bottema, G. Entjes-Nieborg and W. van Zeist (eds.), *Man's Role in the Shaping of the Eastern Mediterranean Landscape*, Balkema, Rotterdam, pp. 139–57.

Van Andel, Tj., Zangger, E. and Demitrack, A. (1990) Land use and soil erosion in prehistoric and historical Greece. *Journal of Field Archaeology* 17: 379–96.

Van Berg, P.-L. (1990) La céramique néolithique ancienne non rubanée dans le Nord-Ouest de l'Europe. *Bulletin de la Société Préhistorique Luxembourgeoise* 12: 107–24.

Van Zeist, W. (1980) Aperçu sur la diffusion des végétaux cultivés dans la région Méditerranéenne. In *La Mise en place, l'évolution et la caractérisation de la flore et de la végétation circumméditerranéenne. Colloque de la Fondation L. Emberger, Montpellier 9–10 avril 1980.* Montpellier, pp. 129–45 (Naturalia Monspeliensa).

Van Zeist, W. and Bottema, S. (1971) Plant husbandry in Early Neolithic Nea Nikomedia, Greece. *Acta Botanica Neerlandica* 20: 524–38.

Vandiver, P. B., Soffer, O., Klima, B. and Svoboda, J. (1989) The origins of ceramic technology at Dolni Věstonice, Czechoslovaquia. *Science* 246: 1002–8.

Vandiver, P. B., Soffer, O., Klima, B. and Svoboda, J. (1990) Venuses and wolverines: the origins of ceramic technology, *c.* 26,000 B.P. In W. D. Kingery (ed.), *The Changing Roles of Ceramics in Society: 26,000 B.P. to the Present*, American Ceramic Society, Westerville, pp. 13–81 (Ceramics and Civilization 5).

Vaquer, J. (1990) *Le Néolithique en Languedoc occidental*, Editions du CNRS, Paris.

Vaughan, P. C. (1990) Use-wear analysis of Mesolithic chipped-stone artifacts from Franchthi Cave. In C. Perlès, *Les industries lithiques taillées de Franchthi (Argolide, Grèce)*, vol. II, *Les industries du Mésolithique et du Néolithique initial*, Excavations at Franchthi Cave, fasc. 5, Indiana University Press, Bloomington and Indianapolis, pp. 239–53.

Vaughan, P. C. (in prep.) Use-wear analysis of Neolithic chipped-stone artifacts from Franchthi Cave. In C. Perlès, *Les industries lithiques taillées de Franchthi (Argolide, Grèce)*, vol. III, *Les industries néolithiques*, Excavations at Franchthi Cave, fasc. 5, Indiana University Press, Bloomington and Indianapolis.

Vigne, J.-D. (1991) The meat and offal weight (MOW) method and the relative proportion of ovicaprines in some ancient meat diets of the north-western Mediterranean. *Rivista di Studi Liguri* A 57 (1–4): 21–47.

Vigne, J.-D. (1993) Domestication ou appropriation pour la chasse: histoire d'un choix culturel depuis le Néolithique. L'exemple des cerfs (*Cervus*). In *Exploitation des animaux sauvages à travers le temps. XIIIèmes rencontres internationales d'Archéologie et d'Histoire d'Antibes*, Editions ADPF, Juan-les-Pins, pp. 203–20.

Vigne, J.-D. (1994) Les transferts anciens de mammifères en Europe occidentale: histoires, mécanismes et implications dans les sciences de l'homme et les sciences de la vie. In L. Bodson (ed.), *Des animaux introduits par l'homme dans la faune d'Europe*, Université de Liège, Liège, pp. 15–38 (Colloques d'Histoire des Connaissances Zoologiques 5).

Villa, P. and Courtin, J. (1980) The interpretation of stratified sites: a view from the underground. *Journal of Archaeological Science* 10: 267–81.

Vita-Finzi, C. (1978) *Archaeological Sites in their Setting*, Thames and Hudson, London.

Vitelli, K. D. (1974) The Greek Neolithic patterned Urfinis ware from the Franchthi Cave and Lerna. Ph. D. Thesis, University of Pennsylvania.

Vitelli, K. D. (1984a) Greek Neolithic pottery by experiment. In P. M. Rice (ed.), *Pots and Potters. Current Approaches in Ceramic Archaeology*, Institute of Archaeology, Monograph 24, University of California, Los Angeles, pp. 113–31.

Vitelli, K. D. (1984b) Social implications of the EN pottery assemblage at Franchthi Cave. Paper presented at the Kleb and Vino Conference, Los Angeles, 1984, 12 pages.

Vitelli, K. D. (1988) From ceramic technique to social behavior. Paper presented at the Symposium on Ceramic Replication. SAA meeting, Phoenix, April 29, 1988, 12 pages.

Vitelli, K. D. (1989) Were pots first made for foods? Doubts from Franchthi. *World Archaeology* 21(1): 17–29.

Vitelli, K. D. (1991) The possible uses of plant extracts by prehistoric potters. Paper presented at the 1991 SAA Meeting, New Orleans, 7 pages.

Vitelli, K. D. (1993) *Franchthi Neolithic Pottery*, vol. I, *Classification and Ceramic Phases 1 and 2*, Excavations at Franchthi Cave, fasc. 8, Indiana University Press, Bloomington and Indianapolis.

Vitelli, K. D. (1995) Pots, potters and the shaping of Greek Neolithic society. In W. K. Barnett and J. W. Hoopes (eds.), *The Emergence of Pottery: Technology and Innovation in Ancient Societies*, Smithsonian Institution Press, Washington, DC, pp. 55–63.

Voutiropoulos, N. (1996) To oplo tou David. *Archaiologia* 59: 64–8.

Wace, A. J. and Thompson, M. S. (1912) *Prehistoric Thessaly*, AMS Press, New York.

Waterbolk, H. T. (1983) Ten guidelines for the archaeological interpretation of radiocarbon dates. In *14C and Archaeology, Symposium Held at Groningen, August 1981*, PACT 8, Strasbourg, pp. 57–70.

Waterbolk, H. T. (1987) Working with radiocarbon dates in southwestern Asia. In O. Aurenche, J. Evin and F. Hours (eds.), *Chronologies in the Near East. Relative Chronologies and Absolute Chronology 16,000–4,000 BP*, British Archaeological Reports, Int. series 379, Oxford, pp. 39–59.

Weinberg, S. (1937) Remains from prehistoric Corinth. *Hesperia* 6: 487–524.

Weinberg, S. (1947) Aegean chronology: Neolithic period and Early Bronze Age. *American Journal of Archaeology* 51(2): 165–82.

Weinberg, S. (1962) Excavations at prehistoric Elateia, 1959. *Hesperia* 31(2): 158–209.

Weinberg, S. (1970) The Stone Age in the Aegean. *Cambridge Ancient History I*, Part 1, Cambridge University Press, Cambridge, revised edn, pp. 557–618, 664–72.

Weinberg, S. (1974) KTL from Corinth. *Hesperia* 43(4): 522–34.

Wells, B. (ed.), with the collaboration of Runnels, C. (1996) *The Berbati-Limnes Archaeological Survey 1988–1990*, Acta Instituti Atheniensis Regni Sueciae, series in 4, 44, Stockholm.

White, J. C. and Pigott, V. C. (1996) From community craft specialization to regional specialization: intensification of copper production in pre-state Thailand. In B. Wailes (ed.), *Craft Specialization and Social Evolution: in Memory of V. Gordon Childe*, University Museum of Archaeology and Anthropology, University of Pennsylvania, Philadelphia, pp. 151–75.

Whitelaw, T. M. (1991) The ethnoarchaeology of recent rural settlement and land use in northwest Keos. In J. F. Cherry, J. L. Davis and E. Mantzourani, *Landscape Archaeology as Long-Term History. Northern Keos in the Cycladic Islands from Earliest Settlement to Modern Time*, Institute of Archaeology, University of California, Los Angeles, pp. 403–54 (Monumenta Archaeologica 16).

Wickens, J. (1986) The archaeology and history of cave use in Attica, Greece, from Prehistoric through Late Roman Times. Ph. D. Thesis, Program in Classical Archaeology, Indiana University.

Wijnen, M. (1981) *The Early Neolithic I Settlement at Sesklo: an Early Farming Community in Thessaly, Greece*, Universitaire Pers Leiden, Leiden.

Wijnen, M. (1992) Building remains of the Early Neolithic period at Sesklo. In *Diethnes Synedrio gia tin Archaia Thessalia sti Mnimi tou Dimitri P. Theochari*, Ekdosi Tameiou Archaeiologikôn Porôn kai Apallotrioseôn, Athens, pp. 55–63.

Wijnen, M. (1993) Early ceramics: local manufacture versus widespread distribution. In J. Roodenberg (ed.), Anatolia and the Balkans, *Anatolica* 19: 319–31.

Wijnen, M. (1994) Neolithic pottery from Sesklo – Technological aspects. In J.-C. Decourt, B. Helly and K. Gallis (eds.), *La Thessalie. Quinze années de recherches archéologiques, 1975–1990. Bilans et perspectives*, Ministère de la Culture, Editions Kapon, Athens, pp. 149–54.

Wilkie, N. C. and Savina, M. E. (1997) The earliest farmers in Macedonia. *Antiquity* 71: 201–7.

Wilkinson, T. J. (1992) Soil development and early land use in the Jazira region, Upper Mesopotamia. *World Archaeology* 22(1): 87–103.

Wilkinson, T. J. and Duhon, S. (1990) *Franchthi Paralia, the Sediments, Stratigraphy, and Offshore Investigations*, Excavations at Franchthi Cave, Greece, fasc. 6, Indiana University Press, Bloomington.

Willis, K. J. (1992a) The late Quaternary vegetational history of northwest Greece. I. Lake Gramousti. *New Phytologist* 121: 101–17.

Willis, K. J. (1992b) The late Quaternary vegetational history of northwest Greece. II. Rezina marsh. *New Phytologist* 121: 119–38.

Willis, K. J. (1992c) The late Quaternary vegetational history of northwest Greece. III. A comparative study of two contrasting sites. *New Phytologist* 121: 139–55.

Wilson, K. (1979) *A History of Textiles*, Westview Press, Boulder.

Winiger, J. (1995) Die Bekleidung des Eismannes und die Anfänge der Weberei nördlich der Alpen. In K. Spindler, E. Rastbichler-Zissernig, H. Wilfing, D. zur Nedden and H. Nothdurfter (eds.), *Der Mann im Eis. Neue Funde und Ergebnisse*, Springer Verlag, Wien, pp. 119–87.

Winn, Sh. and Shimabuku, D. (1989a) Architecture and sequence of building remains. In M. Gimbutas, Sh. Winn and D. Shimabuku (eds.), *Achilleion, a Neolithic Settlement in Thessaly, Greece, 6400–5600 B.C.*, Institute of Archaeology, University of California, Los Angeles, pp. 32–68 (Monumenta Archaeologica 14).

Winn, Sh. and Shimabuku, D. (1989b) Bone and ground stone tools. In M. Gimbutas, Sh. Winn and D. Shimabuku (eds.), *Achilleion, a Neolithic Settlement in Thessaly, Greece, 6400–5600 B.C.*, Institute of Archaeology, University of California, Los Angeles, pp. 259–72 (Monumenta Archaeologica 14).

Winn, Sh. and Shimabuku, D. (1989c) Pottery. In M. Gimbutas, Sh. Winn and D. Shimabuku (eds.), *Achilleion, a Neolithic Settlement in Thessaly, Greece, 6400–5600 B.C.*, Institute of Archaeology, University of California, Los Angeles, pp. 75–164 (Monumenta Archaeologica 14).

Wright, K. (1992) A classification system for ground stone tools from the Prehistoric Levant. *Paléorient* 18(2): 53–81.

Wuetrich, B. (1994) Domesticated cattle show their breeding. *New Scientist*, May 1994: 16–17.

Zangger, E. (1991) Prehistoric coastal environments in Greece: the vanished landscapes of Dimini Bay and Lake Lerna. *Journal of Field Archaeology* 18(1): 1–16.

Zilhão, J. (1993) The spread of agro-pastoral economies across Mediterranean Europe: a view from the far west. *Journal of Mediterranean Archaeology* 6(1): 5–63.

Zohary, D. (1969) The progenitors of wheat and barley in relation to domestication and agricultural dispersal in the Old World. In P. J. Ucko and G. W. Dimbleby (eds.), *The Domestication and Exploitation of Plants and Animals*, Duckworth, London, pp. 47–66.

Zohary, D. (1989) Domestication of the Southwest Asian Neolithic crop assemblages of cereals, pulses, and flax: the evidence from the living plants. In D. R. Harris and G. C. Hillman (eds.), *Foraging and Farming. The Evolution of Plant Exploitation*, Unwin Hyman, London, pp. 358–73 (One World Archaeology).

Zohary, D. and Hopf, M. (1993) *Domestication of Plants in the Old World. The Origin and Spread of Cultivated Plants in West Asia, Europe and the Nile Valley*, Clarendon Press, Oxford, 2nd edn.

Zvelebil, M. (1994) Plant use in the Mesolithic and its role in the transition to farming. *Proceedings of the Prehistoric Society* 60: 35–74.

Zvelebil, M. (1995) Indo-Europeans origins and the agricultural transition in Europe. In M. Kuna and N. Venclova (eds.), *Whither Archaeology? Papers in Honour of Evzen Neustupny*, Institute of Archaeology, Praha, pp. 173–203.

Zvelebil, M. (ed.) (1986) *Hunters in Transition: Mesolithic Societies of Temperate Eurasia and their Transition to Farming*, Cambridge University Press, Cambridge.

Zvelebil, M. and Dolukhanov, P. M. (1991) The transition to farming in eastern and northern Europe. *Journal of World Prehistory* 5(3): 233–78.

INDEX